Julian Henneberg
Subjects of Substance

**Julian Henneberg**, born in 1981, earned his doctorate from the Graduate School of North American Studies at Freie Universität Berlin. He lives and works in Berlin.

Julian Henneberg

# Subjects of Substance

Recent American Literature and the Materiality of Mind

[transcript]

This work has been published with financial assistance by the Ernst-Reuter-Gesellschaft of Freie Universität Berlin.

**Bibliographic information published by the Deutsche Nationalbibliothek**
The Deutsche Nationalbibliothek lists this publication in the Deutsche National-bibliografie; detailed bibliographic data are available in the Internet at http://dnb.d-nb.de

© 2020 transcript Verlag, Bielefeld

Cover layout: Maria Arndt, Bielefeld
Cover illustration: Ramón y Cajal "Plan fundamental de la retina de los insectos", 1915, Boletín de la Sociedad Española de Biología, 4, 105-115.
Typeset by Mark-Sebastian Schneider, Bielefeld

Print-ISBN 978-3-8376-4929-1
PDF-ISBN 978-3-8394-4929-5
https://doi.org/10.14361/9783839449295

# Contents

# Acknowledgments

I would like to thank my supervisors, Winfried Fluck, Frank Kelleter, and Ulla Haselstein, for their continued encouragement, guidance, and support through all phases of the present study, from the development and formulation of the research project to the writing and editing of the manuscript.

Furthermore, I would like to thank David Bosold and Gabi Bodmeier of the GSNAS, who have been of invaluable assistance over the years, as well as the staff at the JFKI library, whose competence and care are second to none.

For their companionship and advice both on and off campus, thanks are also due to friends and colleagues, at the graduate school and elsewhere. Writing a dissertation is by necessity a solitary endeavor, but thanks to you, it has never been a lonely one. Unable to list all your names here, I rest assured that you know who you are.

Finally and most importantly, my deepest gratitude goes to my parents, Elisabeth and Thomas Henneberg, for their unwavering and unconditional support, as well as to my wonderful girlfriend, Juli Sonnhütter, who has accompanied this project since the beginning and stuck with me through thick and thin. I could not have done it without you, and neither would I have wanted to.

# 1. Introduction: Materialist Minds

> The essence of dignity is the power to order; it is the will. Hence, the attention given to setting out the boundaries between those movements that are simply animal (involuntary) and those expressly human, the fruit of will or reason.
>
> *Georges Canguilhem, La formation du concept du réflexe* [1]

> The human body is the best picture of the human soul.
>
> *Ludwig Wittgenstein, Philosophical Investigations*

## Minding Matter

In 1641, René Descartes introduced the concept of *res cogitans*—a "thinking thing" or "thinking substance"—into Western philosophy. [2] In his Second Meditation, he defined mind in opposition to body or corporeal substance (*res extensa*), identifying the self with immaterial, first-person consciousness: "the human mind, when turned in on itself, does not perceive itself to be anything other than a thinking thing" (51). [3] Roughly 350 years later, Nobel laureate Francis Crick, famous for his co-discovery of the structure of the DNA molecule, radically revised this conception of consciousness. In his 1994 book *The Astonishing Hypothesis*, he proposed that the self could be described in terms of material entities and processes that could be

---

1  Canguilhem's work on the formation of the reflex concept has yet to be published in English. The translated quotation appears in Ehrenberg, *Weariness* 7.

2  For the 1647 publication of the *Meditations* in French, Descartes translated the Latin term as "thinking substance" (*substance intelligente*). However, the medieval philosophers from whom Descartes inherited the term "substance" conventionally used it in the sense of "thing" or "object" (Rowlands 10).

3  Richard Rorty argues that with this definition, Descartes effectively "invented" the modern concept of the mind (*Philosophy* 17-69).

observed from an empirical, third-person perspective: "'You,' your joys and your sorrows, your memories and your ambitions, your sense of personal identity and free will, are in fact no more than the behavior of a vast assembly of nerve cells and their associated molecules" (3). After three and a half centuries, Descartes's *res cogitans* was apparently on the way of becoming, quite literally, a *thinking thing*: it was now being equated with the material entity that is the human brain. Prioritizing matter over mind, this reversion of the original Cartesian emphasis abolishes mind-body dualism and treats consciousness as a secondary phenomenon, thus bringing psychic life within the purview of empirical inquiry. In this new materialist paradigm, philosophy finally gives way to science.[4] Or so it would seem.

Descartes, at any rate, is still frequently cited in current debates—and with good reason: the neuropsychologist Paul Broks writes that the philosopher "released a pack of troublesome dichotomies into the Western way of thinking: mind versus matter; subjective versus objective; observer versus observed," so that for good or ill, his ideas about mind and body "set the terms of all subsequent debate about the relationship" (137).[5] However, this is not to say that the terms cannot be reversed. In their 1999 book *Memory: From Mind to Molecules*, cognitive psychologist Larry R. Squire and renowned neuropsychiatrist Eric Kandel[6] begin their account by inverting the most famous dictum of Cartesian ontology: "It would be more correct to rephrase Descartes' statement by reversing it to read 'I am, therefore I think,'" the authors propose, since "all the activities of the mind arise from a specialized part of our body: our brain" (ix). As Liah Greenfeld observes, this proposition is expressive of a "fundamentally materialistic view of reality," which is taken to encompass subjective, mental experience as well as "objective," physical structures (162). In this view, which regards "all the activities

---

4  Cromby et al. point out that those considering neuroscience newly relevant to human self-understanding "frequently proclaim a new 'hard science', 'objective' or 'real' understanding of ourselves" (218). This process of naturalization is often cast as a benchmark in the forward march of scientific progress. "If science can invade everything," Bruno Latour suggests cheekily, "it surely can put an end to Descartes' long lasting fallacy and make the mind a wiggling and squiggling part of nature" ("Reality" 9).

5  "If Descartes did not exist we would have had to invent him, for how else could we explain mind's pernicious representation of itself as an isolated substance," Claire Colebrook remarks (*Deleuze* 31), and Antonio Damasio suggests that his discussion of the relation between "mind, brain, and body" needs to take place "under the Sign of Descartes, since there was no way of approaching such themes without evoking the emblematic figure who shaped the most commonly held account of their relationship" (*Error* xix; original capitalization). Damasio, in turn, is singled out by Martensen as representative of the current tendency to invoke Descartes as a "bogeyman for something alleged to be lacking in biomedicine's emotional and/or cultural dimensions" (210).

6  Kandel received the 2000 Nobel Prize in Physiology/Medicine for his research on the physiological basis of memory storage in neurons and is the author of several much noted publications on neuroscience and its relation to neighboring fields like biology, psychiatry, and psychoanalysis.

of the mind" as describable in the materialist terms of modern science (and thus amenable, in principle, to scientific inquiry and intervention), Crick's *Astonishing Hypothesis* becomes the basis for a new anthropology, personified in the figure of "Neuronal Man" (Changeux).[7]

Of course this figure only appears radically new when placed in opposition to an earlier, ostensibly less materialist situation. What made his hypothesis astonishing, Crick believed, was that despite the advance of the scientific method and its attendant worldview, most people remained Cartesian dualists at heart, identifying themselves with their mental faculties rather than their material constitution.[8] In common parlance, the self is generally described as coterminous with *interiority*—a realm composed of thoughts, feelings, and memories, to which the body stands in a more or less incidental relation. Hence, Gilbert Ryle's famous critique of the "official doctrine" of Cartesianism as the "dogma of the Ghost in the Machine" (5; original capitalization). However, if you "are" your mind, which in turn "arises" from your brain, as Squire and Kandel put it, such dualistic differentiation loses its legitimacy. "No matter how immaterial you understand your thoughts to be," Bill Brown points out, they are the "outcome" of electrochemical impulses or the "effect" of synaptic activity within a neural network, so that one has to conclude that "the process of thinking has a materiality of its own" (49).[9] Following this line of thought, soma and psyche become integrated, but not equal. The new materialism of the mind also entails a new hierarchization: subjectivity is usurped by materiality; *mind* becomes a function of *matter*.[10]

## A New Naturalism?

As has often been observed, literature has throughout history fed on, probed into, or implicitly contained philosophies of subjectivity. According to the *OED*, our modern use of the term as "the condition of viewing things through the medium of one's own mind or individuality," which is "dominated by personal feelings, thoughts, concerns" derives from Coleridge's reception of Kant—and thereby

---

7  See also Alain Ehrenberg's observation that "the project of the cognitive neurosciences [...] is essentially anthropological, in the sense that it seeks to account for the totality of the human: thinking, feeling, acting" ("Se définir" 70; my translation).

8  Crick proposes that his hypothesis of the neural, molecular self "is so alien to the ideas of most people today that it can truly be called astonishing" (3).

9  While Brown's use of the terms "outcome" and "effect" implies a rather uncomplicated one-way causality, there is no lack of accounts that view the relation between consciousness and its material substrate (i.e., brain and body) not in unidirectional but in circular terms, such as a feedback loops or Möbius strips. See, for instance, Grosz, *Volatile* xii and Humphrey 184-87.

10  The technical philosophical term for this would be materialistic monism (Greenfeld 163).

attests to the entanglement of philosophical and literary accounts of subjectivity (qtd. in A. Rorty 35). Literary narrative appears intrinsically beholden to the mechanisms and dynamics of identity formation and the forms of social interaction in which they take effect. In a wide range of novels, "existence—and by extension identity—have been predominantly defined in terms of social construction" (Burn, "Mind" 193), while literary authors have continually relied on existing discourses and models of mind for their ideas about psychic life.

As Jonathan Lethem observes, the emergence of "new vocabularies for human perceptual life creates fresh textures in fiction, both particular and universal" (xiv). Therefore, it comes as no surprise that the emergence of a new materialist anthropology should also leave its marks in literature. What is more, there is historical precedent for this dynamic:[11] Justine Murison has demonstrated that following the 1840s, the United States saw not only an "unprecedented explosion of interest" in neurology and "the workings and meanings of the nervous system" but also an attendant transformation of conceptions of the self in various popular literatures (30), all of which can be read as aspects of a larger "neurological modernity" (Bentley 247-48). Likewise, at the turn of the nineteenth century, literary naturalism famously codified the findings of its own era's psychology, evolutionary biology, and social science into narratives of "brute nature," in which the individual mind struggled against the forces of natural and social history. In this earlier incarnation, naturalism adopts the "somatic style" of nineteenth-century psychology,[12] which sought to link mental processes to the workings of the nervous system. The result is commonly described as inherently deterministic:[13] "A like determinism," Émile Zola ventured, "will govern the stones of the roadway and the brain of man" (17).

Today, we are confronted with similar prospects. By "tracing behavior back to the architecture of the human brain or the chemistry of neurotransmitters, instead of to remembered epiphanies or hard lessons learned in love affairs," our contemporary sciences of the mind could well be seen as eliciting a return to determinism in literary writing, Stephen Burn proposes ("Mind" 194). But is determinism—the

---

11   See Littlefield and Johnson's observation that the neuroscientific turn "is historical" and that its adoption by multiple disciplines and discourses, including literature, "is not a novel phenomenon but one with a distinct history" (17).

12   For the concept of "somatic style," see N. Hale 47.

13   "American literary naturalists, who embraced the Darwinian belief that human beings are products of heredity and environment, were naturally led to descriptions of mind congenial with that deterministic world view" Stephen Brennan remarks in a representative assessment (182). Yet this is not to argue that all naturalist narratives had a narrowly deterministic bent: as Brennan notes, the aim rather was to present an accurate portrayal of the psychic conflict and "struggle for dignity" taking place in human consciousness, a portrayal that was informed by the psychological theories of the day (183).

notion that biology explains human experience, that nature trumps nurture—the only conceivable outcome when the self is understood in terms of physiology and biology? Do we indeed stand on the cusp of a new literary naturalism that deals in neurochemistry rather than heredity and necessarily produces a "medicalization of human experience" (Burn, "Mind" 194)?[14] And are we even justified in assuming that scientific and medical discourses inform literary writing in a unidirectional dynamic that runs "from the lab to literature"?[15]

Some signs do indeed point to this possibility. In Jeffrey Eugenides's 2011 novel *The Marriage Plot*, for instance, free indirect discourse expands from its traditional province, the representation of a character's consciousness, to include explications of the underlying operations of the nervous system. When the novel's distraught protagonist, a "lovelorn English major," notices the restorative powers of nature, this mental movement is conveyed in a biomedical rather than a Romantic register: "In a thin little park she'd never noticed before, Madeleine sat on a bench. Natural opiates were flooding her system and, after a few minutes, she started to feel a bit better" (104). Here, what Patricia Waugh calls the novelist's "molecular gaze" reveals that neural processes precede and produce the effects of his heroine's subjective experience. Waugh has suggested that "a new fiction, armed with the insights of the brain sciences, may proceed beyond a talking cure that offers only hermeneutic access to mind," and if passages like the above are any indication, neurochemical explanations have demonstrably arrived in U.S. literature ("Thinking" 79). What is more, they are being integrated into the form of the novel, which has traditionally been associated less with external and empirical observation of the workings of the body than with the interiority and subjectivity of literary characters—a realm crucially informed by, and often understood in, the terms and concepts of dynamic psychology.[16] But are these two modes of description truly at odds with each other? Does a medicalized view of body and brain invalidate the report of psychologically or spiritually "profound" subjective experience?

---

14 Here and in subsequent cases, British spellings in quotations are changed to conform to U.S. spelling.

15 Here I am adapting Rose and Abi-Rached's concept of the "translational imperative": en route to their social and cultural effects, scientific ideas partake in a "move from the lab to the social world," a conceptual migration that necessarily entails significant processes of translation and modification (229).

16 To be sure, this description is a better fit for the traditional realist novel than its experimental, avant-garde manifestations, but even the latter have not been immune to the influence of culturally dominant psychological models: "The explosion of psychotherapeutic metaphors into the narrative arts in the twentieth century is so complete and pervasive that it would be hard to overstate" (Lethem xiv). On the influence of therapeutic discourse on twentieth-century and contemporary culture, see Illouz.

This question, too, was already being asked at the beginning of the twentieth century. In "Religion and Neurology," the first lecture in *The Varieties of Religious Experience*, William James coined the phrase "medical materialism" to describe the dismissal of religious emotions as organically conditioned.[17] James rejected this mode of explanation, since in his view, "we know that, whatever our organism's peculiarities, our mental states have their substantive value as revelations of the living truth; and we wish that all this medical materialism could be made to hold its tongue" ("Religion" 24). Recently, James's wish has been reiterated by literary critic Marco Roth, who put forth a strongly worded polemic against a new naturalism in literature with his tellingly titled article "The Rise of the Neuronovel."[18] Roth's essay provides a fitting introduction to the concerns of my project, since it opens up a line of argument that I would like to question and complicate.

## Marco Roth's "The Rise of the Neuronovel"

In "The Rise of the Neuronovel," Roth claims that in recent years, "the novel of consciousness or the psychological or confessional novel—the novel, at any rate, about the workings of a mind—has transformed itself into the neurological novel, wherein the mind becomes the brain" (n. pag.). Listing as evidence a number of Anglophone novels ostensibly "about" neurological disorders, Roth looks for the reasons behind this paradigm shift. These he identifies in the exhaustion of the linguistic turn and the declining prestige of Freudian psychoanalysis as well as in the concomitant strengthening of biologistic, materialist, and reductionist explanatory models.[19] Since the nineties—the decade by which psychotropic drugs had indisputably "arrived" in psychiatric practice as well as mainstream culture—Americans could consider themselves in the presence of a "new reduc-

---

17  James's view that medical materialism leads to *reductio ad absurdum*, that it "finishes up Saint Paul by calling his vision on the road to Damascus a discharging lesion of the occipital cortex" ("Religion" 24), has a precursor in Hegel's rejection, in the *Phenomenology of Mind*, of the scientific "formalism" of *Naturphilosophie*, which "takes the shape of teaching that understanding is electricity, animals are nitrogen [...] and so on" (31).

18  The title of Roth's essay alludes to Ian Watt's classic study *The Rise of the Novel*, which also relates the emergence of a new literary form to a change in the intellectual and social milieu of its time. Thus Roth's title implies that a similar epistemic shift might be at hand today.

19  Roth is certainly not alone in linking the waning allure of "relativistic" poststructuralist and postmodern modes of criticism to the rise of methods modeled on the "hard sciences." See for instance Claire Colebrook's description of "a series of turns to 'affect,' 'life,' 'matter' or 'the brain'— all of which would be *after* theory or after the linguistic turn" ("Vitalism" 31; original emphasis), or Patricia Waugh's caustic comment that "the obituaries for postmodernism had hardly been written when the arrival of cognitive neuroscience was loudly proclaimed" (20).

tionism," identifiable by two main properties: "it explained proximate causes of mental function in terms of neurochemistry, and ultimate causes in terms of evolution and heredity" (n. pag.).[20]

This "new reductionism" now haunts contemporary literary production as the imperialism of psychoanalytic language once haunted Western culture, Roth suggests,[21] and though it might appear like a limited phenomenon, its rise bodes ill for literary culture as a whole. In a devil's bargain, novelists are surrendering what should be their core competence—the intricate rendering of the complexities of human psychology—in exchange for often poorly understood scientific theories, in the hopes of borrowing from science the status and credibility they themselves are shedding rapidly in today's digital age ("a world of giant publishing conglomerates and falling reading rates," Roth helpfully explains). In the process, literature is robbed of its defining characteristics. Novelists have "ceded their ground to science," in this reading, for fear of cultural irrelevance: "the neuronovel tends to become a variety of meta-novel, allegorizing the novelist's fear of his isolation and meaninglessness, and the alleged capacity of science to explain him better than he can explain himself" (Roth, n. pag.).

Books about brain science thus become the heralds of a culture in which "morality, society, and selfhood"—a triad presented by Roth as the rightful domain of literature—no longer fall within the unifying purview of the novel. Instead, they are fragmenting into "the property of specialists writing in the idioms of their disciplines" (n. pag.). But the neuronovel is not only a symptom of cultural change; it is also a cultural force in its own right, promoting a climate of desemanticization (because in contrast to a psychological symptom, a neurological symptom

---

20  Despite my disagreement with his argument, my study largely adopts Roth's periodization. "More may have been learned about the brain and the mind in the 1990s [...] than during the entire previous history of psychology and neuroscience," Antonio Damasio suggests ("Brain" 4). For support of the notion that the advent of current materialist paradigms of the psyche can be dated to the nineties (or, as some would argue, the late eighties) and coincides with the mass-marketing of psychiatric drugs, see Angell, "Epidemic" and "Illusion." See also Ehrenberg, who suggests that the "neurochemical practices of self-fabrication" surrounding psychopharmaceuticals, drugs, and doping prepared the ground for the contemporary figure of the "cerebral subject" ("Le sujet" 147; my translation), as well as Rose and Abi-Rached, who date the inception of neuroscience as a research program to the sixties but also note that that the field truly begins to consolidate itself in the nineties, when "the history of neuroscience becomes a kind of subdiscipline in its own right" (29).

21  The essay's subtitle reads, "A specter is haunting the contemporary novel," by which Roth references an earlier critique of reductionism: in 1949, Lionel Trilling wrote that "[a] specter haunts our culture—it is that people will eventually be unable to say, 'They fell in love and married,' let alone understand the language of *Romeo and Juliet*, but will as a matter of course say 'Their libidinal impulses being reciprocal, they activated their individual erotic drives and integrated them within the same frame of reference'" (285).

is presumed to be essentially devoid of meaning) and depoliticization (because individual and social dysfunction become objects of medical rather than political intervention). "By turning so aggressively inward, to an almost cellular level, this kind of novel bypasses the self, let alone society, or history, to arrive at neurology," Roth argues (n. pag.). To sum up: in training their sights on the organic and the (literally) cerebral, contemporary authors administer their own abolition as cultural arbiters, and trivialize literature in the process.

## A Critique of Roth's Critique

Even if one is sympathetically disposed to critiques of vulgar bio-materialism as a heuristic for literary and cultural history (after all, resisting or subverting "biologistic" explanatory approaches has long been one of the central tenets of the humanities), one cannot but note that Roth's analysis leaves something to be desired.[22] In what follows, I will draw attention to some of the problems of Roth's argument and outline how to avoid or correct them in my own readings.

To begin with, it is far from settled that psychological and neurological descriptions necessarily have to be at odds with each other. Not only is it conceivable that the former could coexist with the latter in a given literary text; it is also likely that instead of the wholesale displacement of dynamic, or "depth" psychology by neo-naturalist paradigms, we might be witnessing the emergence of a complementary rather than a competing method of accounting for the subjective experience and objective behavior of human beings.[23] In other words, it is not at all plausible that there should exist something like a "pure" neurological novel; nor is there reason to conceive of the literary sphere as a zero-sum game in which a new development can occur only at the cost of other, i.e., older forms.

Going further, one might also question the conceptual distinction between psychological and neurological descriptions itself, which effectively perpetuates mind-body dualism by neatly assigning ideational characteristics to the former and materialist characteristics to the latter, as if one excluded the other. But even psychoanalysis—Roth's prime example for the kind of discourse of deep interiority he deems at risk of being displaced—cannot unproblematically be placed on

---

22  On the anti-biologistic bias of the humanities, see Elizabeth Wilson, who, with a view toward feminist scholarship, laments "a theoretical scene that is bent instinctively toward correcting, reversing, or resisting the forces of biological reductionism"—a comment that also applies to the wider realm of cultural studies (*Psychosomatic* 3).

23  See Ortega, who notes that the "psy complex,"—the entirety of discourses that operate with the assumption of a "deep" interior psychological space—has not been replaced altogether: "rather, it coexists more or less harmoniously with new ways of acting, thinking and speaking about ourselves as corporeal, somatic selves" (*Corporeality* 81).

the "immaterial" side of the mind-body divide. For Roth's claim that the novel as an art form "makes most sense not from a neurological standpoint, but under the lens of an old-fashioned Freudian interpretation," this "old-fashioned" hermeneutical tradition would have to be categorically separated from neurology (n. pag.).

This, however, seems impossible. After all, from Freud's early neuroanatomical studies and his *Project for a Scientific Psychology* to his admission that some forms of actual neurosis [*Aktualneurose*], like neurasthenia, might be due to "direct *somatic* consequences of sexual disturbances" rather than symbolically codified mental experiences, Freudian psychoanalysis has never been solely concerned with the exclusively psychological—if such a thing even exists (*Project* 388; original emphasis). In fact, some of the most fundamental assumptions of psychoanalytical theory, like its attention to excitatory and inhibitory impulses or psychosomatic symptoms, suggest that Freud's theory should be understood not merely in terms of psychogenic phenomena but also as the product of a materialist (and yes: neurological) imaginary.[24] This much, at any rate, has been suggested by Robert Solomon, who insists on Freud's "materialist moorings," ("Neurological" 25), by Thomas Nagel, who unambiguously asserts that Freud "was a materialist" ("Anthropomorphism" 11), and by Elizabeth Wilson, who contends that glimpses of Freud's materialist imaginary should not be dismissed as regressive remnants of an abandoned physicalist approach, since "these moments of biological reduction often produce Freud's most acute formulations about the nature of the body and the character of the psyche" (*Psychosomatic* 3).

This observation can be extended to other areas of investigation: by itself, the mere inclusion of discourses that attend to neurological embodiment and the material substrates of human consciousness does not automatically render a given text epistemologically short-sighted or aesthetically inferior.[25] Fear of

---

24  In an essay on Freud's materialist allegiances, William Gass notes that for the early Freud, "[p]sychic processes had to be regarded as quantitatively determined states of specifiable material particles," and suggests that this commitment might have been more durable than commonly supposed: "As his work went on Freud found it increasingly difficult to retain his quantitative materialism in undiluted form, but [...] although he weaseled and he waffled, although dualisms bent him and mentalisms encouraged another language, at least every other heartbeat was for the work he set aside and never published, the 'Project for a Scientific Psychology,' and that his later romance with destruction and death is a disguised return to the old and drier flame" (221-22).

25  As Paul Giles observes, "it is by no means the case that an emphasis on the body in itself indicates the rejection of any kind of theoretical compass ("Afterword" 210). Neither should materialist accounts of the mind be regarded as inherently irreconcilable with the tenets of critical theory: Victoria Pitts-Taylor notes that scholars like Catherine Malabou, Elizabeth Wilson, and Andy Clark view the "new biology" of neuroscience as a potential "material grounding for views of the self that are politically progressive—postmodern, plural, queer, unfixed, open to change, always unfolding, and even potentially libratory" ("Social Brains" 173).

reductionism looms large in Roth's rhetoric, but before setting out to combat or dispel reductionist ideas, one may want to make sure that there is good reason to do so. While it may be true that by incorporating biomedical research, contemporary authors run the risk of foregoing the play of signification and interpretation in favor of clear-cut diagnosis, such claims would still have to be evaluated on a case-by-case basis. Alleging that any and all literary texts interested in materialist explanations are a priori complicit with a pernicious reductionism that precludes linguistic meaning and experimentation alike would not seem like a promising method of determining how neo-naturalist tropes actually function within these texts.

Furthermore, one can take issue with the rhetorical sleight of hand by which Roth equates the "the novel of consciousness or the psychological or confessional novel" with the novelistic form per se. When Roth writes that the neuronovel attests to "the defeat of the metaphoric impulse" and that "mere biological contingency has a way of repelling meaning," the implication is clear: medical materialism is bad for literature, because literature is (or, in a normative prescription, *should be*) the domain in which social, political, and personal phenomena are represented in an allegorical operation that yields "the pleasure of finding the general in the particular" (n. pag.). One hardly needs to point out that this is an extraordinarily narrow understanding of the novel, albeit one that possesses a long and eminent tradition and continues to exert considerable influence, not least via its implementation in modern-day creative-writing programs and workshops.[26]

To consider, as Roth does, literary texts' investment or interest in the materiality of mental life as inimical to "the informal psychological explorations of novelists" is to posit two untenable assumptions at once: first, that psychology is irreconcilable with materialism; second, that the novel is primarily characterized by psychological realism. Since I would like to discuss different genres and modes of writing and look beyond the already much-discussed rift between the material and the mental to possible syntheses between the two, my analysis will attempt to avoid such conceptual presuppositions. After all, it may well be the case, as one commentator on Roth has proposed, that the turn to neuroscience "indicates with equal measure that the novel remains a record of human experience and society—and [that] neuroscience, in recent decades, has developed a set of compelling accounts of what human experience might consist of" (McAuley, n. pag.).

Finally, by classifying a plurality of texts under the (ultimately derogatory) rubric of the neuronovel, Roth produces homogeneity where one could also find

---

26  For a classic account placing psychological, realist fiction at the beginning of the novelistic tradition, see Watt; for a survey of the history and influence of modern MFA programs, see McGurl, *Program*.

diversity. To be sure, the texts chosen by Roth share certain formal features.[27] For one thing, they all produce what one might call a stable fictional world, in which the diegetic reality of the text remains largely undisturbed by metafictional operations, a world that largely conforms to the demands of conventional novelistic presentation. However, chances are that their grouping owes more to Roth's Platonic ideal of The Novel than to genuine family resemblances. A highly experimental text like Infinite Jest for instance, which is undeniably shaped by the "modernist impulse" whose absence Roth laments, certainly has to be counted among the contemporary works that engage with materialist paradigms of the mind. What is more, Roth does unto his textual examples what he wishes they had not done unto the psychological novel. "Neuronovels" allegedly flatten out psychological depth into superficial symptomatology and reduce the complexities of the social world to the terminology of biomedical diagnosis, yet their denunciation by Roth follows the same logic: analysis is foreshortened and (aesthetic, intentional, and contextual) complexity sacrificed in favor of unambiguous classification.

If I am reading an apologist for symptomatic reading symptomatically here myself, I am doing so in the hopes of drawing attention to the impossibility of maintaining cut-and-dried categories and neat characterization in the realm of literature. While I am wholly sympathetic to the claim that terms like "neuronovel," "new materialism," "new vitalism," "neo-naturalism," "biomedicalization," or "neurochemical selves"[28] fulfill important functions in that they enable us to pinpoint a quality of contemporary discourse that might otherwise elude us, I also believe that in the transposition of cultural analysis to literary study, it is imperative not to lose sight of the singularity of the aesthetic object and its specific modes of functioning. In what follows I will therefore attempt to keep these two aspects—the macro level of scientific, institutional, cultural, and epistemological contexts and the micro level of aesthetic, textual, thematic, and formal characteristics—in view simultaneously. Like Roth, I will trace out the permutations of literary writing under the sign of materialist models of mind, but unlike him, I do not assume that we can already comfortably agree on what these models consist in, what functions they serve, or what consequences they entail. Rather, my analysis will operate under the assumption that new materialist discourses can be put to use in ways that are absolutely contingent on their respective contexts, and that

---

27  The texts Roth cites are Ian McEwan's Enduring Love and Saturday, Jonathan Lethem's Motherless Brooklyn, Mark Haddon's Curious Incident of the Dog in the Night-Time, Richard Powers's The Echo Maker, Rivka Galchen's Atmospheric Disturbances, and John Wray's Lowboy, a list that through Roth's "quite influential" article has acquired the status of a "micro-canon" for scholars of "brain-based literary studies" (Burn, "Neuroscience" 213, 211).

28  See, in that order, Roth, A. Johnston, Colebrook ("Vitalism"), Kelleter, Clarke et al., and Rose ("Becoming"; "Neurochemical"; "Anomalies").

each literary text that invokes them needs to be encountered and examined on its own terms.

## Materialist Minds in Literature: Other Accounts

This is not to say that singularity rules supreme and we have to surrender all hope of finding an analytical scope capable of uniting a group of literary texts for the purpose of scholarly research and description. In fact, even though Roth overshoots the mark in constructing the neuronovel as a unified phenomenon with homogenous functions and effects, his general observation holds true: one can indeed observe a distinct tendency in recent American literature to address what Roth calls the "new medical-materialist world" and come to terms with the research programs of neuroscience, evolutionary psychology, cognitive science, and pharmaceutical psychiatry, which strive toward a redescription of human psychic life in terms of material processes and physically observable entities (n. pag.).

In recent years there have been a number of attempts to grasp this phenomenon analytically, resulting in publications that discuss the "neurological novel," "neuronarrative," "cognitive fictions," the "syndrome novel," the "naturalistic turn" in literature, or the displacement of agency from human persons to "sentient things."[29] As Stephen Burn has argued, literary authors draw on scientific research "in part to incorporate neuroscience's ability to address questions at an explanatory level—of the species, or of human history—that postmodern epistemological critiques had denied to other discursive forms" ("Mapping" 47). Consequently, the "neuroscientific turn" (Littlefield and Johnson) would have to be contextualized as part of the still only incompletely theorized "intimations of a new order" that is succeeding postmodernism (Hoberek 241). Yet there exists no unproblematic relation between post-postmodernism and a new materialism of the mind, not least since "those who reject postmodernism often blame cognitive science and neo-Darwinianism for the decline of a humanist conception of interiority" (Waugh, "Turn" 20). Furthermore, this newfound interest in the biological and physical side of subjectivity is not restricted to academic scholars. Literary authors—even those formerly identified as postmodernist—also appear increasingly aware of this shift toward a "somaticization of the subject" (Groves 264). This is evidenced by publications like Paul Auster's recent *Winter Journal*, a memoir dedicated to an examination of "what it has felt like to live inside this body," which Auster bills as a "catalogue of sensory data" and a *"phenomenology of breathing"* (1; original emphasis).

---

29  See, in that order, Thrailkill, G. Johnson, Tabbi (*Cognitive*), Burn ("Mapping"), Waugh ("Turn"), and Chodat.

On the academic side, one can identify the scholars who have provided the most substantial examinations of this phenomenon. T. J. Lustig and James Peacock's 2013 collection *Diseases and Disorders in Contemporary Fiction: The Syndrome Syndrome* gathers contributions from literary critics as well as researchers in psychiatry and neuroscience to discuss literary writing that betrays a "preoccupation with neurological conditions" and attests to a view of the self as "bound up in any number of complex systems, [...] largely determined not by its choices or its past, but by the very cells with which it becomes aware (or ceases to be) or by its own conditioning," as the editors phrase it in their introduction (1, 10). The volume goes a long way toward a systematic examination of what Roth's polemic dismisses rather glibly, providing in-depth analyses of individual texts like Richard Powers's *The Echo Maker*, overviews of postmodern fiction's engagement with neurological themes (Burn, "Mapping") and speculations about the turn to neo-naturalist discourses (Waugh, "Turn") as well as annotated bibliographies of primary and secondary materials.

Stephen Burn, one of the contributors to this anthology, can be singled out as perhaps the most active analyst of recent American fiction's materialist tendencies. Apart from his article in *Diseases and Disorders*, Burn has published extensively on the role that "science of mind" plays in contemporary fiction.[30] Like Lustig and Peacock's collection, Burn's work can function as a corrective to Roth's editorializing, as it suggests that materialist scientific discourses do not automatically force authors down a path of determinism and reductionism. Instead, Burn points out, such discourses should be viewed as a rich resource that provides writers with resonant tropes and ideas that fuel rather than impoverish the literary imagination—a critical stance with which it becomes possible, for instance, to delineate how in *Great Jones Street*, DeLillo's interest in neurophysiological structures "subtly underwrites the book's psychological investigations, literary strategies, and overall architecture" (Burn, "DeLillo" 350).

While the publications by Lustig/Peacock and Burn are commendable for their attempts to discuss literature's engagement with scientific and medical accounts of mental life in a more nuanced fashion, they by no means exhaust the subject. Focusing exclusively on the titular "diseases and disorders" of neurology and psychiatry, Lustig and Peacock investigate a crucial aspect of the new materialist paradigm. However, in limiting their approach to pathological phenomena, they exclusively follow what Rose and Abi-Rached call "the path through madness," which is but one way to arrive at the "new style of thought" identified by these

---

30  Since Burn also discusses Don DeLillo, David Foster Wallace and Richard Powers, his publications are of great interest for my purposes and will be frequently referenced throughout the present study.

authors as the molecular-materialist approach (31, 30).[31] In other words, neuroscience and psychiatry are not the only fields operating with and feeding back into a contemporary materialist imaginary. To this list can be added other discourses and disciplines like genetics, evolutionary biology and psychology, sociobiology, behaviorism, cognitive science, some strands of the philosophy of mind, as well as a number of monist and vitalist philosophies and their contemporary appropriations. As we will see, one should also mention the increasingly vocal proponents of alternative "materialisms," based on phenomenological and pragmatic traditions and systems theoretical approaches, which shift the emphasis from the strictly cognitive and cerebral to more holistic notions of embodied and embedded interaction.

If Lustig and Peacock's collection thus only manages to illuminate a partial aspect of the broader phenomenon I am concerned with here, the books and articles by Stephen Burn remain limited for other reasons. In his attempts to trace out a "cognitive revolution" in American literature ("Mapping" 43), Burn does manage to cover a variety of materialist "sciences of mind," from the proto-behaviorist philosophy of Gilbert Ryle to neuroscientist David MacLean's model of the triune brain, but in the end this project remains fragmentary due to its distribution over several discrete investigations.[32] Having examined Jonathan Franzen's critique of "materialist explanation of selfhood" (*Franzen* 26) or the function of optical theory in Don DeLillo ("Mind" 195-200), and announced but not yet published a monograph on the American novel in the age of neuroscience, Burn still has to provide a comprehensive account of the role of new materialist ideas in literary fiction that expands the scope beyond its individual manifestations.

## Research Assumptions and Questions

The present study represents an attempt to fill these lacunae and examine not merely the occurrences and sources but, more centrally, the *forms and functions* of materialist tropes and theories of the mind (including, but not limited to the realm of neuroscience) in recent American writing (including, but not limited to the realm of the novel). If, as Julian Murphet suggests, a materialist view of the mind arguably "represents the greatest challenge to representations of the subject, the self, since Freud," then we may wonder whether its influence on literature

---

31  Rose and Abi-Rached specify that one can also write the history of neuroscience by taking either "the path through the nerves" or "the path through the brain" (31).

32  For Burn's analysis of the deployment of MacLean's model in literary fiction, see "DeLillo," "Mapping," and his interview with Richard Powers; for his account of the influence of Gilbert Ryle on *Infinite Jest*, see his *Reader's Guide*. The term "sciences of mind" is Burn's.

might prove similarly transformative, and "what artistic representation is going to make of the figures of subjectivity fashioned by neuroscience" (189, 193). Accordingly, the analytical focus of this project will be on the question of how "materialist minds" modify literary conceptions and productions of subjectivity. Throughout my study, I use the term "materialist minds" to refer simultaneously to the reconceptualization of the mind in biological, material terms and to the theorists whose materialist ideas are fueling this effort. Denoting both materialist philosophies and materialist philosophers, its double meaning encompasses fictional characters who personify subjecthood recast in materialist terms as well as historical persons—scientists, doctors, theorists, authors—who subscribe to, or engage with, a materialist reconfiguration of the self.

That *some* kind of reconfiguration of a "traditional" understanding of the human subject might occur in these texts is to be expected. As Patricia Waugh argues, "the liberal self is challenged in all its shibboleths by the molecular revolution" ("Thinking" 80), and there is widespread agreement that recently developed materialist accounts of the mind have a direct bearing on the constitutive components of the category of the human, such as agency and free will.[33] As Lustig and Peacock point out, there is a great deal at stake in this question, "not least whether we still believe in an autonomous subjecthood and a liberal understanding of individual responsibility" (10). In her ethnographic study of the training of American psychiatrists, the psychological anthropologist Tanya Luhrmann writes: "biodynamical and psychodynamic approaches nurture two very different moral instincts." Ultimately, she argues, it matters a great deal whether a society views mental illness as an organic or a psychogenic phenomenon, because each perspective "affects our moral instincts about what it is to be human" (*Minds* 23, 266). Wary of assigning ontological reality to either the psychodynamic/humanistic or the biomedical view, Luhrmann describes these different approaches to the psyche as "lenses" that not only represent but also construct the objects they disclose: "Lenses are important; they enable us to see. But when we use this metaphor to describe how we come to understand one another, we must remember that lenses, while necessary, are a distortion, for humans always slip away from the clarity we impose on them" (*Minds* 23-24).

We might do well to heed this reminder and think of the materiality of mind not as a newly proven fact but, employing a visual metaphor, as a perspective; or, employing a linguistic one, as a narrative or trope. Accordingly, in their work on the "cerebral subject," Ortega and Vidal emphasize that they wish the term to be

---

33  "In the past two decades, the brain has become a space where people look to answer a huge range of questions, and even to shape the kinds of questions we ask, about ourselves," Victoria Pitts Taylor observes in a typical assessment, adding: "The stakes are high: at issue is our understanding of what it is to be human" ("Social" 172).

understood as referring to an "*anthropological figure* that embodies the idea that the human being is essentially reducible to his or her brain" ("Mapping" 255; my emphasis). In the following, I, too, will treat the claims that are being made by, or on behalf of, "materialist minds" not as facts, but as *ideas* about being human— ideas that acquire meaning through their expression in language.[34] As Ian Hacking suggests, "[i]t is inept to talk of 'mind' and 'matter' in the first place, when we are talking about people, but if we do, mind and matter are *different ways of describing* our experience" ("Cartesian" 158; my emphasis).[35]

Even if one grants the supposition that the medical-materialist perspective is supplanting the psychodynamic-humanistic view, there is still disagreement over the consequences of this shift. Depending on their source, contemporary accounts of the materiality of the mental can take on different valences, from cautious optimism to dystopian alarmism. For every voice that welcomes the chance to enrich existing discourses and debates, a warning is sounded about the dangers of reductionism or determinism.[36] In the former view, the influx of new materialist ideas does not allow for foregone conclusions; in the latter, their increasing influence announces a full-blown crisis of the human subject. Little wonder that hard-line positions like eliminative materialism, which endorses the idea that "our commonsense conception of psychological phenomena constitutes a radically false theory [...] that will eventually be displaced [...] by completed neuroscience" (P. Churchland 67) provoke equally uncompromising rebuttals denying the possibility that materialist inquiries might prove successful or questioning the very legitimacy of their methodological assumptions. Thus a number of researchers in the humanities and the sciences have called for a "reality check" of the claims made by or on behalf of materialist models of mind, thereby ushering in the study of "critical neuroscience" (Choudhury and Slaby 6). In terms of complexity, science journalist John Horgan notes, "particle physics is a child's game [...] compared to neuroscience," so that "[w]hen it comes to the human brain, there may *be* no unifying insight that transforms chaos into order" (261; original emphasis). Horgan is

---

34  On this point, my position is aligned with Davi Johnson Thornton's conception of the "rhetorical brain," a term Thornton uses to describe "the unique ways we conceptualize the brain in contemporary culture" and to emphasize that the brain is not a stable concept but rather "contingent on numerous social, political, and scientific factors (3, 27).

35  This view is shared by Roger Scruton, who draws our attention to the seemingly unbridgeable gap between "two distinct ontologies of the human condition, one about brains and bodily behavior, the other about people and their acts" ("Neurononsense" 347).

36  Often, these conflicting voices can even be heard within the same article. See Cromby et al., who, shortly after mentioning "the *potentials*" that the neurosciences harbor for studies of subjectivity, qualify that they "can still unleash the interdependent problems of essentialism, determinism, decontextualism and reductionism" (219-20; original emphasis). Typical criticisms of neuroscientific perspectives as reductionist can be found in Ehrenberg, Martin, and Pitts-Taylor.

joined by a host of fellow "neuroskeptics,"[37] the most prominent of which is physician and philosopher Raymond Tallis, whose 2012 book *Aping Mankind* diagnoses
large parts of the scientific community with "Darwinitis" and "neuromania" and
summarily dismisses attempts at materialist reduction of behavior and experience.

While the high stakes and heated exchanges of this debate make for fascinating reading material (and, ideological blinders aside, one can find intriguing positions and ideas on both sides), it is apparent by the sheer vigor of the participants
that the fundamental point of contention is a question that has been at the center of literature and humanistic inquiry—and indeed of American literature and
American Studies—for a long time: the question of the abilities and limitations of
the subject.[38] Manfred Frank suggests that since the subject has been pronounced
dead in the wake of Heidegger, Wittgenstein, and structuralism, brain research
"has, in its own way, taken up this topic again" ("Mensch" 52; my translation).
This is confirmed by even a cursory survey of recent publications, which ponder
the question whether brains can double as subjects (Krüger), ask, "How did we
become neurochemical selves?" (N. Rose, "Neurochemical" 46), discuss "self-making and the brain" (Martin), or attempt to map the "cerebral subject" (Ehrenberg;
Ortega and Vidal).[39]

Clearly, the proposed materialist transformations of subjectivity spark a
search for answers, and as soon as we shift the focus to literature, more questions
appear. How, and why, we might ask, do these ideas enter literary production, and
how do literature and "materialist minds" mutually transform each other? What
happens to terms like personality and character, which arguably are central to
humanist inquiry as well as traditional literary study, when the self is understood
as a mere epiphenomenon of materiality, and how does the literary representation
of consciousness change when it is reconsidered as a biological phenomenon? Do
texts that engage with the new materialism of the mind share certain assumptions about the nature of the self, in the same way that earlier traditions did?[40]
After all, literary history has traditionally established strong correlations between
philosophy and psychology and literary form. If modernism drew on psychoanal-

---

37  See, for instance, Nagel; Choudhury and Slaby; Legrenzi and Umilta; Satel and Lilienfeld.

38  "Social scientists and interpretive theorists of culture have struggled with the 'mind-body problem' since the inception of the human sciences," William Connolly reminds us (67).

39  For German contributions to the debate surrounding neurological subjectivity see Krüger as
well as Beckermann.

40  By way of example, I am thinking here of the ways in which (generally speaking), realism dra-
matized the divide between the private and the public self, modernism emphasized the phenomenological subjectivity of experience, and postmodernism deconstructed and dispersed
the unified subject.

ysis,[41] and postmodernism on poststructuralism and deconstruction,[42] do we now see a new kind of writing that corresponds to a newly dominant medical materialism? If so, what affordances does the new paradigm provide for authors, and what effects does it have on literary forms and aesthetics?

## Thesis

In what follows, my study will advance the thesis that recent American writing has increasingly been producing its own configurations of the simultaneously problematic and productive tensions between subjectivity and materiality. If U.S. literature is "reacting to" what some consider a new materialism, it does not do so in a manner that should be understood in terms of a simplistic model of pre-existing cultural reality and subsequent literary response, but rather through mechanisms of incorporation, transformation, and performance. I argue that the texts under consideration do not simply reiterate scientific and medical theories of subjectivity (though they are certainly aware of them); instead they develop their own, often alternative, conceptions of "materialist minds," and—a crucial qualification—they do so by means of aesthetic processes. By producing literary versions of the biological, neurological, or otherwise materially embodied subject, these texts put epistemological theories in the service of aesthetic efficacy, and vice versa. The issue of the biological basis of self thus figures not only as a theme but is also translated into a poetological problem. In making this claim, I am therefore not carrying over philosophical and ethical questions into the disinterested realm of the aesthetic but rather pursuing a question already inherent in my objects of study: as a general rule, the texts I discuss signal their curiosity about the place of the self in a biomedical-materialist imaginary in thematic as well as in formal terms.

41  See, for instance, Maud Ellmann's disentanglement of the strands of technology, literature and psychoanalysis in modernist "nets of meaning" (9), or Steven Frosh's assessment of psychoanalysis as an "emblematic modernist discipline" (116).

42  The three movements are seen as intimately interrelated to such a degree that there has been some conceptual confusion, as Hans Bertens notes: "For a good many, mainly American critics, French poststructuralism and its American deconstructionist offshoot are practically identical with postmodernism" (16).

## Structure and Method

My study will trace the emergence of "materialist minds" in U.S. literary production across generic boundaries and through its temporal development. Since it is predicated on a number of ambiguous terms and concepts, most importantly the relation between mind and matter, the analytical part of the dissertation is prefaced by a discussion of central terminological questions. Here I preview a number of concerns that will be of interest throughout the subsequent readings and explain how I intend to use or not to use certain key terms and concepts.

The textual analyses begin with a discussion of "neuro-memoirs," i.e., autobiographical texts focusing on the relation between subjectivity and the nervous system in the context of medical, or medicalized, conditions. This chapter introduces the relation between the new medical materialism, conceptions of subjectivity, and narrative forms.[43] Since terms like the "cerebral subject" or the "neurochemical self" figure prominently throughout my study, this section also serves to highlight the existential dimensions of these rather abstract concepts, giving voice to those most directly affected by the epistemic and ethical transformations that a new biomedical paradigm produces.

Shifting the focus from non-fiction to fiction, the subsequent three chapters follow the implementations and transformations of the "materialist minds" motif chronologically through novels by Don DeLillo, David Foster Wallace, and Richard Powers. This body of texts has been selected for thematic coherence and continuity: not only have these authors produced the most interesting and intensive treatments of "materialist minds" in recent U.S. fiction; they are also linked in an aesthetic tradition that sees both Wallace and Powers building upon the work of DeLillo. The three chapters, each of which is dedicated to one of the three authors, examine the cultural contexts and scientific sources of their work, analyze how the underlying discourses shape the texts in question, and discuss what functions they serve.

---

43 Considering what he, following Marco Roth, calls "neuronovels," i.e., texts that address "the confounding gap between what we're learning about the physiology of the brain and the various forms of immaterial experience that emerge from it," Jason Tougaw has suggested that "the 'brain memoir'—or autobiographical account of neurological difference, disease, injury, or experience—is the genre's closest living relative" ("Touching" 337, 339).

## 2. Key Terms and Concepts

### Minds, Selves, and Subjects

Faced with what Brook Miller calls "the notorious slipperiness of concepts like consciousness and self, and the intractability of the mind-body problem," some reflections on terminology may be in order (5). After all, none of the central terms of this study are unambiguous or uncontroversial. To begin with, what kinds of "things" can we take minds or selves to be?[1] Clifford Geertz calls the mind "the specter that is haunting the study of man," noting that the word has often served "to communicate—and sometimes to exploit—a fear rather than to define a process, a fear of subjectivism on the one hand and of mechanism on the other." Historically, the term has "not functioned as a scientific concept at all but as a rhetorical device," Geertz notes, and been employed to support multiple, often opposing, positions (56-57). If any consensus currently exists, it might be that the localization of mind, agency, or will in an individual subject is a problematic, perhaps an obsolete notion.[2]

Objectifying nouns like "the mind" or "the self" may be misleading, since they create the impression of a stable and discrete *thing*, "an empirical entity, a substance with tangible form and describable content" (Kelleter 173), when the phenomena in question are perhaps better described as processual rather than substantive, dispersed rather than unified.[3] Thus, Rose and Abi-Rached submit that

---

1  Lalvitie notes that "the most fundamental obstacle encountered in the study of the mind and the mental is that there is no consensus on what the words mean and to which entities they refer" (18), and Jerrold Seigel observes in his historical study of the concept that "[f]ew ideas are both as weighty and as slippery as the notion of the self" (*Idea* 3). See also A. Rorty.

2  Nigel Thrift polemically remarks that "pretty well everyone seems to subscribe to the idea that [a localized, centered] kind of identity is an invented Western tradition that has had its day" (84). See also Heehs, who states that "at the beginning of the twenty-first century, the consensus of opinion among philosophers, social scientists, cultural theorists, and neuroscientists is that the self is not a substance but a construct, not an entity in its own right but the product of corporeal and social operations that will cease when its physical support dissolves" (227).

3  Charles Taylor would disagree: he believes that the use of the reflexive pronoun hints at the deep-seated cultural belief that inwardness, self-reflection, and self-control ("the essential pow-

"cognitive capacities, affective flows, and the powers of volition and the will are not individual, but distributed" and that all these aspects of what we habitually call mind, consciousness, or the self need to be regarded as "enabled by a supra-in-dividual, material, symbolic, and cultural matrix" (223). In accordance with this assessment, some scholars understand mind as socially and materially embodied and "extended" rather than "brainbound" (Clark xxvii), or propose to replace the nounal "self" with the verbal "selfing" (Franks 620).[4] Finally, what we believe the mind to be depends on what level of analysis we bring to bear on the phenomenon: as Robert Burton observes, the term mind is "a placeholder for *descriptions of different levels of phenomena* arising from quite different types of mechanisms without obvious causal links" (93; my emphasis).

I am mentioning these ideas here as a caveat to my "traditional" use of terms like mind, self, subject, and consciousness in the introduction. Though I am aware that they might best be understood as complex processes rather than simple substances, I will nonetheless adhere to the communicative convention of using these terms in their singular forms—partly because the transformation of their established meanings is itself a main interest of my study, partly in the interest of conciseness. To a degree, I will also use some of these concepts interchangeably, since they are inherently related.[5] As I use the term, the self denotes the reflective sense of being a conscious, thinking, or "mindful" subject: "an individual, therefore, that also knows itself to be," as Kerby phrases it (4).[6] This is by no means meant to signal a bias toward "psychism." If selves are "heterogeneous entities, more or less stable compounds of elements that derive from biology, social relations, and their own psychic and mental activity," as Seigel, suggests, it is nonetheless imperative to insist on the primacy of a conception of self *as* mind. Seigel believes it is "possible to conceive the self as formed out of a single one of these elements," but to

---

ers of human agency") are what characterizes the self in the modern, secular West ("Inwardness" 94; 101).

4  John Protevi has coined the shorthand "4EA" for a new conception of the mind that eschews the narrowly mentalistic and cerebrally located model for one that is embodied, embedded, enacted, extended, and affective (4). For the idea of the distributed self, see also Turk et al.

5  Colin McGinn notes that the "subject of consciousness" can variously be described as self, subject, person, or ego (*Mysterious* 156).

6  See Kihlstrom and Klein for a definition of the self as a representation (composed of concepts, narratives, images, and associations) of what we know about ourselves. For a comprehensive study that describes the genealogy of modern subjectivity as a process of increasing self-objectification and –reflection, see Zwilgmeyer. See also Grawe et al.: "In the course of this process of reflective distancing human beings formed an increasingly clear consciousness of themselves as autonomous individuals who confronted their environment through reflection and action" (6; my translation).

*qualify as* a self, it clearly would require some variant of what we habitually call mind ("Problematizing" 284).[7]

Throughout the text, I use subjectivity as largely coterminous with the self, simultaneously denoting the quality of subjecthood and the first-person perspective of subjective experience, a conjunction of *Selbstbewusstsein* and *Selbstgefühl*. Crucially linked with embodiment, materiality and cultural context, the term is both general and particular, referring to the universal givenness of the first person as well as its emergence in a specific social situation.[8] Subjectivity thus refers to an "ensemble of modes of perception, affect, thought, desire, fear, and so forth that animate acting subjects" (Ortner 31).[9] It may be possible to imagine a state of "disembodied" subjectivity—dreams are one example—but the notion of a self that is completely devoid of any kind of mental activity (perception, consciousness etc.) or interiority (emotions, thoughts etc.) appears nonsensical. Marcel Mauss contends "that there has never existed a human being who has not been aware, not only of his body, but also at the same time of his individuality, both spiritual and physical" (3), and Paul Smith proposes that for good or bad, "[n]one of us lives without a reference to an imaginary singularity which we call our 'self'" (6). Charles Taylor argues the case by inviting us to imagine a Paleolithic hunter faced with a charging mammoth: if he is spared and his fellow hunter trampled instead, he is likely to feel both relieved for having survived and saddened for the loss of his friend, but both emotional states are rooted in an awareness of personal identity. "We can probably be confident," Taylor concludes, "that on one level human beings of all times and places have shared a very similar sense of 'me' and 'mine'" (112). It appears warranted, then, to continue to understand the self as a conscious, thinking, or mindful/mental subject. This initial theoretical assumption already implies attentiveness to language, since, as Benveniste argues, "there is no other objective testimony to the identity of the subject except that which he himself thus gives about himself" (226).[10] In the absence of such testimony, we can only speculate about the subjectivity of prehistoric hunters.

The concept of the subject, one needs to add at this point, has three important senses. First, it invokes the notion of agency and accountability: the subject is a conscientious social actor in control of his or her own actions who can thus be

---

7  Seigel refers to such one-sided presentations of the self, which prioritize one elements to the exclusion of the others as "abstract selfhood" ("Problematizing" 299).

8  "What is called 'subjectivity', understood as the lived and imaginary experience of the subject, is itself derived from the material rituals by which subjects are constituted" (Butler, "Psychic" 122).

9  See also Luhrmann's definition of subjectivity as "inner life of the subject, […] the way subjects feel, respond, experience" ("Subjectivity" 345).

10  Even Seigel, who emphasizes the diversity of the "three ways of self-existence" enumerated above, contends that the self is "most emphatically present when it takes itself for an object, constituting itself in reflection" ("Problematizing" 285; 287).

held responsible for them (this is the cornerstone of Enlightenment ethics and the liberal tradition).[11] Second, the subject denotes the faculty of the cogito, mind, or consciousness: the subject is a thinking, perceiving, and experiencing agent that stands in a non-identical relation to the world it encounters (this is the foundation of the subject-object or subject-world distinction bestowed upon modern philosophy by Descartes and later elaborated by Kant). Third, the subject can also be understood as a social, cultural, or linguistic construction, *subjected* to external/ social as well as internal/psychological power:[12] in this view, the subject is a subject of knowledge, laws, or discourses, possibly to the degree of being constituted by them and becoming a mere function of their operations (this is the sense of the term famously emphasized by Foucault and other theorists of social, cultural or linguistic construction).[13]

These different ways of conceptualizing the subject share the common quality of being in some crucial sense "immaterial." Following Freud's dictum that the ego "is first and foremost a body ego" (*Ego* 21)[14] we might add a fourth sense, in which the subject is both connected to, and distinguished from, others and the world through the boundaries of the body.[15] As William James writes, the body is "the storm center, the origin of coordinates, the constant place of stress in all that experience-train. Everything circles round it, and is felt from its point of view." In this view, the bodily self serves first and foremost a deictic function: "The word 'I,' then, is primarily a noun of position, just like 'this' and 'here'" (*Essays* xxxvii). However, there have been very few attempts to think subjectivity as completely

---

11  See Nida-Rümelin for a discussion of this conception as the "natural view" in Western societies. Frow calls it "the contractual or promissory dimension of selfhood that is most fully formulated in the market economies of early capitalism" (81). In *On Liberty*, Mill opposes this view to a materialist, mechanistic conception of the self: "A person whose desires and impulses are his own—are the expression of his own nature, as it has been developed and modified by his own culture—is said to have a character. One whose desires and impulses are not his own, has no character, no more than a steam-engine has a character" (67).

12  See Paul Smith, who notes that apart from its other meanings (coterminous with "individual" or "self") the subject "might be understood as the specifically subjected *object* of social and historical forces and determinations" (xxvii).

13  In this context, Foucault speaks of *assujetissement* (subjection), a term that evokes both the constitution of subjects and their subjection to power—two processes that are seen as ultimately inseparable. "A power *exerted* on a subject, subjection is nevertheless a power *assumed* by the subject, an assumption that constitutes the instrument of that subject's becoming," Judith Butler writes, adroitly emphasizing the dialectical dynamic of this process (*Psychic* 11; original emphases).

14  Freud's meaning here is that the ego is produced through representations of the body's internal and external sensory apparatuses: it is the only partly conscious "projection of a surface" (*Ego* 21).

15  See Gagnier 8 for a list that includes corporeal distinctness in the characteristics of the subject.

identical with, or indistinguishable from, corporeality.[16] Although there can be no subject without a body (or a brain), and although the means of its *asujetissement* may be thoroughly material, working upon and through the body, the subject is usually understood as something other, or more, than his or her body.[17] Therefore, materialist theories of the mind that shift attention to the physical entities of body and brain run the risk of dispensing with subjectivity altogether. The Sciences of the mind aspire to objectivity, but, as Oliver Sacks has observed, "a living creature, and especially a human being, is first and last *active*—a subject, not an object" (*Leg* 177; original emphasis). Yet neuroscience and related philosophical approaches, like Daniel Dennett's "heterophenomenology," are characterized precisely by their attempts to take a third-person approach to the study of consciousness and other mental phenomena.[18] In disciplines like neurology, Sacks suggests, "[i]t is precisely the subject, the living 'I,' which is being excluded" (*Leg* 177). As a consequence, reality, now reduced to the impersonal perspective of physics (which Thomas Nagel famously dubbed the "view from nowhere"), is "thoroughly dehumanized" (L. R. Baker, *Naturalism* 26). This is a source of great controversy and perhaps the defining problem of materialist models of mind, so it should come as no surprise that in the following, we encounter this problem repeatedly in the literary texts I examine.

It bears mentioning that the terminological reconfigurations discussed above, from "selfing" to the "extended mind," are of a kind with the revisions that the concept of the subject has undergone in the twentieth century, which, broadly speaking, have shifted the emphasis from identity, stability, autonomy, rationality, and agency to tropes of dispersal, multiplicity, (cultural and social) conditioning, fluidity, affect, and the unconscious. There is not space enough here to rehearse the history of the self and the subject, nor is there need to, given the number of publications on the topic.[19] Suffice it to note that contemporary materialist perspectives on the self in many ways continue the "*decentering* of that formerly

---

16  Apart from current neurobiological theories, attempts in this direction have mainly been undertaken by phenomenology and feminist philosophy: see Merleau-Ponty and Grosz as examples.

17  One early and important source of the view that subjectivity is contingent upon bodily life is Spinoza, who notes that people "know by experience, that it is in the mind's power alone both to speak and to be silent, and to do many other things which they therefore believe depend on the mind's decision," but then adds, "does not experience also teach that if, on the other hand, the body is inactive, the mind is at the same time incapable of thinking?" (72).

18  "Dennett, whose ontology is wholly at the level of physics, is an eliminativist about the intentional stance," Lynne Rudder Baker writes (*Naturalism* 25). See Dennett, "Heterophenomenology Explained" and "Heterophenomenology Reconsidered" as well as chapter four of his *Consciousness Explained*.

19  On the history of the modern subject, see Cascardi as well as Solomon; on the genealogy of the concept of the self, see Martin and Barresi as well as Taylor.

centered subject or psyche" that characterizes so much of twentieth-century culture and thought (Jameson, *Postmodernism* 15; original emphasis). As Claire Colebrook remarks, the "turn away from Cartesianism" that we find in neurological or new materialist paradigms is characterized by a decentering, "a rejection of any center, model or privileged term from which relations would follow" (*Deleuze* 32). In making the body, the nervous system, or the brain the central term of analysis, such paradigms do not, in fact, focus their inquiry on one physiological part but actually disperse it into a multitude of physical stimuli: "The bounded organism, the embodied mind, or the active and 'synaptic' self [...] do not exist in order to relate to the world, for the organism *is its ongoing relations*" (Colebrook, *Deleuze* 29; original emphasis). Just as the psyche was fragmented into linguistic operations and cultural signifiers by psychoanalytic and poststructuralist criticism, brain and self are fragmented into environmental and neural interactions by the new materialism of the mind.[20] Little wonder, then, that in a recent book on the history of the self, the penultimate chapter, which addresses "The Death of the Subject," ends with a section that discusses postmodern philosophy alongside contemporary neuroscience (Heehs 224-26). In their implications for the ontological status of the subject, it turns out, the two are not altogether unalike.

## The Unconscious

In what ways, then, can the new materialism of the mind be regarded as complicit in the decentering of the subject? For one thing, neuroscientific research has largely confirmed the centrality of the subliminal, automatic, and autonomous cognitive processes that Freud postulated in his theory of the unconscious. However, one cannot say the same about its specific (libidinal) dynamics,[21] so that "[n]euroscientists are on the whole much happier with the adjectival version of unconscious" than with the substantive psychic structure posited by Freud (Pugh 47). Tellingly, in those rare cases where the term retains its substantival form, it is in need of being modified. Thus, in their recent *Philosophy in the Flesh*, Lakoff and Johnson speak of a "cognitive unconscious"—a phrase that, in stark contrast to their earlier work on metaphor, entails the claim that conceptual structures are

---

20  "The meaning or sense of the world would not be a specifically human nor even mind-based quality; minds only experience sense and meaning because they, like all living systems, are bounded by the possible responses, encounters, stimuli and selections of their own milieu" (Colebrook 29).

21  See Kandel's assertion that the neural unconscious "bears no resemblance to Freud's unconscious. It is not related to instinctual strivings or to sexual conflicts, and the information never enters consciousness" ("Framework" 468).

not only based on but actually coterminous with "neural structures in the brain," i.e., that they are "embodied in this strong sense" (20). As Alan Richardson notes, there may be "more opposition than common ground" between the Freudian and the cognitive unconscious: the former is "hot, seething, a 'boiling pot,'" while the latter "seems efficient, logical, cool as a computer" (63).[22] Still, theories that emphasize the materiality of mind tend to foreground the comparative power-lessness and lack of control of the cogito in the face of automatic and unconscious mechanisms, and this disenfranchisement of the conscious "I" constitutes an undeniable and evocative analogy to the original Freudian dictum, "*The ego is not master in its own house*" ("Difficulty" 143; original emphasis). What is more, much recent neuroscience has vowed to integrate the "emotive, instinctive and irra-tional into its picture of unconscious mental life, often with a respectful nod to Freud" (Richardson 63).[23]

Surely the key difference between today's materialist or neural unconscious and the turn-of-the-century dynamic unconscious has to be that in contrast to the latter, the former is localized within the structures of the body itself. To be sure, the dynamic unconscious also has its basis in the development of the body and its capabilities, but ultimately, it is described as obeying an intrapsychic logic that owes more to biography and socialization than to physiological events. In contrast, physiology stands squarely at the center of what is variously called the "new unconscious" (Mlodinow; Hassin et al.) or the "adaptive unconscious" (T. Wil-son)—a phrase that emphasizes the deep roots of unconscious or automatic evalu-ation and action in evolutionary selection.[24]

---

22  In the realm of literary study, the discrepancy between the dynamic and the cognitive uncon-scious also translates into different modes of reading and interpreting, as Stephen Best and Sharon Marcus note: "For Jameson, the unconscious is a function of repression, but for [...] a cog-nitive reader, the unconscious consists simply of mental activities too rapid and too complex to be perceived" (6).

23  Psychoanalysis remains a valuable resource for neuroscientists like Gerald Edelman, Joseph LeDoux, and Eric Kandel, who contends that "psychoanalysis still represents the most coher-ent and intellectually satisfying view of the mind" ("Biology" 505). There have also been first attempts to merge the two discourses into the new discipline of neuropsychoanalysis, whose theorists see it as taking the first steps toward fulfilling Freud's hope that his psychological ideas would "one day be based on an organic substructure" ("Narcissism" 2). See Northoff as well as Solms and Turnbull for work in this new field; see Bezerra for an account of the debates within psychoanalysis over the adoption of neuroscientific paradigms.

24  We can also add Daniel Kahneman, winner of the Nobel Prize in Economics, to this list of pro-ponents of a "new" unconscious. What unites these accounts is a view of the unconscious as a collection of modular brain processes (T. Wilson 7) or systems (Kahneman 20). For an overview of the new paradigm, see James Uleman's introduction in Hassin et al. as well as chapter 4 of Franks, *Neurosociology*.

## Habit and Plasticity

Through its focus on processes of physiological and neurological automatism as well as affective, behavioral, and cognitive conditioning, this contemporary, materialist unconscious is intimately connected to the concept of habit, which has been a subject of interest for thinkers ranging from Aristotle and Montaigne to William James, Maurice Merleau-Ponty, and Pierre Bourdieu.[25] Here *habitus*, with its medieval roots, meets neuroplasticity, the structural and functional malleability of the brain understood in medical terms.[26] As William James notes, acts of will (e.g., "attention and effort") can be classified as material rather than as "pure acts of the spirit" because they are "subject to the law of habit, which is a material law" ("Habit" 126). It had long been assumed that after reaching a certain age, the organization and structure of the brain would remain stable, from when on its cell count could only diminish. Yet recent research has led to a modified understanding of the brain as a highly adaptable and generative organ that never ceases to change the number and nature of its connections and is capable of generating new brain cells over the course of the lifespan. Neurogenesis and neuroplasticity depend heavily on environmental factors as well as individual mental activity.[27] For instance, the biologist Gerald Edelman has advanced a theory—neuronal group selection, also known as Neural Darwinism—according to which human brain development occurs in a manner analogous to the production of an immunological identity.[28] Like the immune system, the brain develops in response to the environment, strengthening connections that are used frequently while pruning those that are not. Since this is a process that is contingent upon intellectual and physical experience, a mutual reciprocity between mental and material domains has to be assumed, so that the plastic brain is viewed as "simultaneously consti-

---

25  See Sparrow and Hutchinson.

26  The idea of plasticity "can be traced back to the Anglo-American nineteenth century. It is there in Darwin, Pierce, and James" (Sparrow and Hutchinson, Introduction 12). In fact, William James coined the term "plasticity" in 1890 in the first volume of *The Principles of Psychology*. In his chapter on habit, James suggests that nervous tissue is characterized by "an extraordinary degree of plasticity" and proposes that "phenomena of habit in living beings are due to the plasticity of the organic materials of which their bodies are composed" (105).

27  For an overview of research on neuroplasticity, see Shaw and McEachern; for its philosophical implications, see Malabou, *What Should We Do* and *Plasticity*. Important research on adult neurogenesis has been conducted in the sixties by American biologist Joseph Altman and in the eighties by Michael Kaplan at the University of New Mexico; its breakthrough came in the nineties with researchers like neuroendocrinologist Robert Sapolsky at Stanford and Princeton psychologist Elizabeth Gould. See also Lehrer; Wall; Gould.

28  For the theory of neuronal group selection, see Edelman, *Neural*; for its inclusion into a comprehensive biological theory of consciousness, see Edelman, *Remembered*.

tuting (i.e., it shapes the mental life arising from its) and [...] constituted (i.e., it is shaped by the mental life arising from it)" (Johnston, *Prologomena* 102).

The concept of plasticity marks a qualitative difference between older forms of materialism and its contemporary manifestations: whereas nineteenth-century naturalists regarded individuals as determined by a physiological constitution fixed by the mechanisms of inheritance, contemporary materialist discourses are acutely interested in the mutability of physiology and neurology, a feature that is often cited as a safeguard against the deterministic and mechanistic tendencies of past materialisms. "The nervous systems adapts, is tailored, evolves," Oliver Sacks observes, emphatically stressing that the continual revision of perception and memory and the concomitant material transformations of the brain "cannot be caught in any mechanical model" ("Neurology" 49). For Adrian Johnston neural plasticity holds the key to an overhaul of outdated dualisms like the nature/nurture distinction, while simultaneously spelling "the invalidation of reductively mechanistic/eliminative materialisms" as well as "the debunking of vulgar genetic determinism in relation to human beings." To Johnston's mind, "[t]hese consequences make possible *a new materialism* and correlative conception of subjectivity" (*Prologomena* 102; my emphasis).

## New Materialism

It is in this sense that I would like to use the term "new materialism" in the present study: as an indicator of texts and theories that emphasize the material, i.e., bodily or biological substrates and modalities (including, but not restricted to the brain) of mental processes, and ultimately of subjectivity as such. My use of the term "new materialism" thus always refers to a materialism that is directed toward the mind and wholly distinct from the "new materialisms" of contemporary object-oriented ontology (OOO) and related approaches.[29] What is new about this materialism of the mind is its preoccupation with the terminological and conceptual universe produced by recent scientific and medical discourse, from neurotransmitters and neuroplasticity to addiction and depression. This new materialism gains traction through a "move from the lab to the social world," which is crucially facilitated by cultural artifacts such as fictional narratives, popular science books, television programs, and the science pages of newspapers (Rose & Abi-Rached 229).[30] Yet, as we will see, the realm of culture and literature is not merely a pathway or a receptacle for new materialist thought; it is also a constantly running engine of transla-

---

29  For overviews, see Coole and Frost as well as Dolphijn and van der Tuin.

30  For an in-depth study of such a move, see Dumit, who traces how the images of the brain produced by PET scanners migrate from medical into legal and popular discourses.

tion, resignification, and imaginative reinvention, whose function transcends the mere storage or dissemination of readymade material.

Like Adrian Johnston, Victoria Pitts-Taylor distinguishes the "new biology" of the brain from an earlier "brute reductionism," noting that "[r]ecent developments in neuroscience give the brain not only a history (a story of its past on an evolutionary level) but also a historicity (a character of historical situatedness, on both an individual and cultural level)" ("Social Brains" 173). This historical situatedness of the new materialism links it to another brute force: capitalism. Since current accounts of the constitutive role of brain and body in mental life overwhelmingly emphasize flexibility, adaptability, and learning—characteristics and capabilities commonly associated with neoliberal forms of production—Pitts-Taylor and other commentators have suggested a connection to neoliberalism as the economic and political order under whose sign these theories are being developed.[31] As Kélina Gotman argues, "the particular quality of the 'neural metaphor' offers a seductive portrait of society and human life: networked, changeable, full of flows of information and capital and goods, conveniently biological as well as subject to a form of free will" (72). It remains yet to be seen if the "new spirit of capitalism" (Boltanski and Chiapello) is indeed "the ideological avatar" of neuroplasticity, as Catherine Malabou suspects (*What Should We Do* 12). It may be the case, after all, that we are merely witnessing a "superficial correspondence in some formulations," like adaptability or the decentralized network (Slaby, "Brain" 240), rather than a genuine complicity of a new materialist anthropology and the new world order of neoliberalism, a communion some critics already proclaim as "neurocapitalism" (Hess and Jokeit). Given the fact that we can observe something like a historical co-emergence of neoliberal management practices and neuroscientific research programs (both are initiated in the wake of the sixties and begin to gather speed in the late eighties and early nineties),[32] it does not appear far-fetched to hypothe-

---

31  See Pitts-Taylor, who holds that "[p]opular uses of neuroscientific theories of brain plasticity are saturated with a neoliberal vision of the subject" (635) and Thornton, who sees "the rhetoric of plasticity" as supporting "a conception of humans as adaptable, malleable creatures that can willfully change themselves" as required by neoliberal economics (62). Noting that "brain training" and "cerebral self-help" are not novel phenomena, Ortega provides an important qualification to these arguments, tracing practices of "neuroascesis" back to the 19th century ("Genealogy" 31-32).

32  Discussing the history of psychiatry and neurology, Alain Ehrenberg describes the 1980s as a period when "the atmosphere changes completely: the 'subject,' the self, and 'consciousness' now occupy a central place in the research agenda of the cognitive neurosciences"—a development that continues to this day, fueling intra- and interdisciplinary debate ("Se définir" 69; my translation). Likewise, in his study of the shift to neoliberal economic policies in Anglo-American democracies, Jonathan Swarts observes that "the 1980s heralded long-term shifts in each country's political-economic imaginary," and that "one of the most significant effects of neoliberalism in the 1980s was to lay the philosophical basis for governments to follow in the 1990s and

size a connection between the two, especially when the "plastic brain" is described as "a site of choice, prudence, and responsibility for each individual" (Rose & Abi-Rached 52).

## Agency, Autonomy, and Automaticity

Seen this way, the new materialism promoted by the sciences of the mind may yet fail to abolish Cartesian dualism. As Bruno Latour's counterintuitive catchphrase goes, "objects too have agency," and the physical object that is the brain is often awarded astoundingly high degrees of agency and autonomy in recent materialist discourses (*Reassembling* 63). Thus, we read about brains that feel, act, plan, and perceive *in lieu* of their human owners. "Somehow, this 1.5 kg lump of tissue inside our skull can contemplate the vastness of interstellar space, appreciate Van Gogh and enjoy Beethoven," developmental psychologist Bruce Hood marvels in a characteristic passage, concluding that since the brain "is primarily responsible for coordinating these activities," the self that *experiences* them needs to be debunked as an "illusion" produced by lower-level neural processes (x-xi).[33] Maxwell Bennett and Peter Hacker, who have submitted the most influential and incisive critique of the unexamined philosophical assumptions of much recent neuroscience, call this the "mereological fallacy." They hold that equating the brain with the whole person by making it into an agent in its own right perpetuates a "mutant form of Cartesianism" in which the agency of the cogito is merely displaced from the level of the individual to that of brain function (*Foundations* 73).[34]

However, the occurrence of residual or "mutant" forms of Cartesianism can be traced back even further, for what contemporary accounts of the autonomy and agency of the brain—or its neural circuits and evolutionary "modules"—often imply is the imperative need for *us* (and not our brains) to face up to these newly discovered facts, and to adjust our individual outlook and behavior as well as our social compacts and institutions accordingly. Depending on the account, the experiencing subject changes from being in charge of its brain to being con-

---

beyond" (114). David Harvey also dates the beginnings of the "neoliberal turn" to the eighties (9), as do Duménil and Lévy (38).

33  An oft-quoted book on this idea is *Making Up the Mind: How the Brain Creates our Mental World* by the psychologist and cognitive neuroscientist Chris Frith, who writes: "We experience ourselves as agents with minds of our own. This is the final illusion created by our brains" (184).

34  "The Cartesian self lives on in inverted shape as the mind is reduced to the brain and the brain to an extension of a body running off the molecular script" (Waugh, "Thinking" 80). As one would expect, this conception has elicited critical responses, like Manfred Frank's assertion that "[a] C-fiber in the brain cannot suffer a 'crisis of meaning,' for the simple reason that only subjects can recognize something like a meaning" ("Subjectivity" 180).

structed by it, and shifts back and forth between powerlessness and responsibility. As soon as the physical and biological constituents of the self—and the remarkable degree to which they are capable of autonomous action and amenable to material manipulation—are taken into account, the picture of the sovereign human agent that underlies the modern, liberal worldview begins to show some cracks.[35] After all, as Hilary and Steven Rose ask, "[i]f the neurosciences had shown that minds were no more than the epiphenomenal product of brain processes, what becomes of the concept of free will and autonomy?" (247). The possible ramifications of this question can be glimpsed in book titles like *Did My Neurons Make Me Do It?* or in the emerging field of neurolaw, which studies the implications of neuroscientific findings for judicial matters.[36]

This problem returns us to the question of habit, for it is precisely the capability of the biological body to function in a non-conscious, automatic manner that underwrites the idea that our feeling of being in control of our actions deceives us. Thus, in an effort to demonstrate "how the brain creates our mental world," accounts that cast the psychological self as a construct of the material brain routinely cite experiments that reveal the tendency of visual perception to produce gestalts, to compensate for missing information, and to rely on previous interpretations of sensory data (Frith, Mlodinow). Extrapolating from such observations, larger questions like agency and free will are assumed to be similarly dependent upon unconscious, lower-level biological processes and thus inaccessible to conscious reflection, whose role is consequentially restricted to after-the-fact interpretation and self-justification (Gazzaniga, *Charge*; Harris; Wegner).[37]

Whether conceptualized in psychological, biological, or neurological terms, the automatic function of habit obviously plays a key role in ensuring the survival of the human organism in a constantly changing natural and social environment. "For beings subject to change, habit is the law of being," Catherine Malabou observes. "Without a general and permanent disposition, [...] the finite being cannot endure, would not have time to live" ("Addiction" vii). Consciousness, one has to acknowledge, can never be total, for this would prove paralyzing. Nowhere has this insight, and its implications for a philosophy of the subject, been recorded

---

35   This notion even makes its way into the paratexts of popular science books: the back cover of my 1994 paperback edition of Peter Kramer's 1993 bestseller *Listening to Prozac* invites the prospective reader to entertain the idea that "if personality can be shaped by chemicals, then serious questions must be asked about the nature of the self."

36   On neurolaw and neuroethics see Eagleman, "Trial," Rosen, and chapter 6 of Gazzaniga, *Ethical*.

37   See also Gazzaniga, "Cerebral," for the concept of the "left-hemisphere interpreter," and Dennett, *Consciousness* for the "multiple drafts model." Both authors assume that the subject is not given a priori but laboriously constructed "after the fact," so that the distributed and diverse information processed by the human organism is interpreted (Gazzaniga) or edited (Dennett) retrospectively, creating the unitary sense of self in the process.

more memorably than in Maurice Merleau Ponty's reflections on proprioception and motor intentionality, the "knowledge in our hands" that allows us to grasp objects and position our bodies in space without having to consciously reflect on each and every movement to calculate its effects (*Phenomenology* 145).

Automatic operations free us to engage in the deliberations of higher consciousness. While our habitual, preconscious bodies expertly maneuver and manipulate the natural world, "we," i.e., our minds, are at liberty to attend to what our brains have adapted to master: interacting with the social world.[38] Yet it would be a mistake to understand habit in purely physical terms. It is a "liminal concept," as Sparrow and Hutchinson point out, and as such it "tends to mingle oppositional concepts like freedom/determination, natural/artificial, active/passive, cause/effect, spontaneity/instinct, and agent/patient." Most importantly, habit merges mind with body. While Sparrow and Hutchinson initially appear to neglect this fundamental binary, they later mention that "the philosophy of habit encourages us to conceive [thought, passion, behavior, and action] as occurring *between* mind and body, spirit and matter" (3-4; original emphasis).

In the context of my study, this would appear to be the crucial point: habit provides us with a prime example of an "unruly" phenomenon that cannot be squarely located on either side of the mind-matter divide. In this, it resembles medical terms like addiction and compulsion that likewise hint at the intimate connection between pathology and subjectivity. This connection will figure prominently in the chapters to come. For now, suffice it to note that in nearly all of its philosophical and scientific manifestations the concept of habit, which Sparrow and Hutchinson describe as "indispensable for constructing a nondualist metaphysics along with new accounts of subjectivity," can function as a paradigmatic case of mind-body liminality: a phenomenon that highlights the utter entanglement of mind and matter (4).

## Matter/Materiality

But what, in fact, constitutes materiality? According to Raymond Williams, materialism refers to a "very long, difficult and varying set of arguments which propose matter as the primary substance of all living and non-living things, including human beings," which give rise to a "related or consequent but again highly various set of explanations and judgments of mental, moral and social activities" (*Keywords* 197). However, if we discuss matter as the "primary substance" of human beings, we quickly run into terminological trouble, since "material" here gains its

---

38  As Frith puts it, because the brain saves us from the "tedious chores" of perception and corporeal self-control, we are free to "concentrate on the important things in life" (Preface, n. pag.).

meaning largely in opposition to terms like "mental" or "immaterial," which thus appear aligned in some essential way.[39] Such an antonymic relation also underlies the nature/culture distinction and its attendant problems. Agency and free will, for instance, are intimately connected to discussions of dualism as problems predicated on a distinction between subjects and objects, between culture and nature, between human beings, who *determine themselves* through autonomous volition, and the material world, which *is determined by* natural laws.[40]

Upon closer inspection, it is precisely this opposition between nature and culture, or material world and immaterial self, that casts freely willed thought and action as problems: once we accept this dichotomous arrangement, it becomes questionable whether the human subject can exist simultaneously under the purview of the natural sciences—as an object of study to be analyzed in parts rather than as a whole—and as a self-determined actor possessing volition and agency. One could say then that the deeper problem is not to which degree mind is constrained by matter but rather our inability to conceive the two terms in a non-dualistic and non-deterministic fashion. Thus John Searle describes materialism as a way of thinking that "begins by accepting the Cartesian categories" and therefore ends up producing "the finest flower of dualism" (*Rediscovery* 26).[41] Searle believes we should simultaneously grant two suppositions that are often presented as mutually exclusive, namely that "the world is made up entirely of physical particles in fields of force" and that "we are all conscious and that our conscious states have quite specific *irreducible* phenomenological properties" (*Rediscovery* 28; original emphasis). Our mistake is to regard these assumptions as irreconcilable, a mistake that results from accepting the "traditional vocabulary" of mind-body dualism.

Renouncing dualism, however, is easier said than done. It has proven frustratingly difficult to abandon the traditional vocabulary and the conceptual baggage that comes with it.[42] Not only is the aptly named "hard problem" of consciousness—

---

39   Talvitie discusses the origin of the words "mind" and "consciousness" and notes that "the terms 'mental' and 'mind' are based on the distinction between *mind and matter*" (21; original emphasis).

40   Latour describes this as "a division between the realm of necessity and the realm of liberty" that creates "two domains, *one that is inanimate and has no agency, and one which is animated and concentrates all the agencies*" ("Agency" 14; original emphasis).

41   See also Galen Strawson's remark about the "wonderful irony" of materialists who, "even as they doubt or deflate or deny the existence of experience, and revile Descartes, their favorite target, [...] are themselves in the grip of a fundamentally Cartesian conviction: the conviction that experience can't possibly be physical, that matter can't possibly be conscious" ("Naturalism" n. pag.).

42   As Frank Kelleter remarks, "we have seen a long row of isms come and go. Social Darwinism, positivism, behaviorism, structuralism, etc., all had their day, promising that the final frontier is just within reach and that some 'third' alternative is available at last to eliminate the binary

the question how observable, quantifiable physical structures can give rise to the famously unquantifiable phenomena of subjective experience, or "qualia"—based on a conceptual distinction between materiality and mind; attempts to unravel the mind-body problem (of which the hard problem is a subset) also appear to be doomed to perpetuate the language that, by all accounts, constitutes a major part of its difficulty.[43] Thus even the most sophisticated attempts to develop a solution, like Donald Davidson's "Anomalous Monism," continue to refer, albeit heuristically, to mental events and physical events as separate entities.[44]

In the framework of Searle's "traditional vocabulary," the material is generally understood to fall under the purview of the sciences, whereas the mental remains the domain of psychology and literature, but such clear-cut divisions are increasingly being called into question. In 1994, the fourth edition of the *Diagnostic Statistical Manual for Mental Disorders*, the "psychiatric bible" published by the American Psychiatric Association (APA), introduced a crucial qualification: "the term mental disorder," the *DSM-IV* editors conceded, "unfortunately implies a distinction between 'mental' disorders and 'physical' disorders that is *a reductionistic anachronism* of mind-body dualism" (XXI; my emphasis).[45] General discontent with the linguistic and conceptual constraints of a dualism that sunders mind from matter, presented as the problematic inheritance of Cartesian ontology, thus coincides with an inability to transcend them in either theory or practice.[46] It appears that philosophically, we have become too sophisticated to believe in dualism, while pragmatically, we cannot do without it.

---

opposition of fact and meaning. What has remained is exactly this opposition and the desire to eliminate it" (154).

43  On the "hard problem" of consciousness in the philosophy of mind, see Chalmers, *Conscious* and *Puzzle*, as well as Blackmore, *Consciousness*.

44  Davidson develops his theory of Anomalous Monism (which proposes that while strict psychophysical laws may not exist and mental events can not be reduced to physical events, every mental event is also a physical event, so that causation can work both ways) in three interrelated essays: see Davidson, "Mental," "Psychology," and "Material." For an explication of Davidson's theory, see Fitz and Gumm; for a critique, see Fodor as well as Kim.

45  The subsequent edition, the *DSM-V*, published in 2013, no longer contains the sentence but continues to adhere to a notion of dualism as inherently unscientific: a section entitled "Somatic Symptom and Related Disorders" notes that "[t]he reliability of determining that a somatic symptom is medically unexplained is limited, and grounding a diagnosis on the absence of an explanation is problematic and reinforces mind-body dualism" (309).

46  The introduction to the *DSM-IV* illustrates this point in almost comical clarity. After helpfully noting that "there is much 'physical' in 'mental' disorders and much 'mental' in 'physical' disorders," the editors end their discussion of the dualism problematic by excusing themselves: "The problem raised by the term 'mental' disorders has been much clearer than its solution, and, unfortunately, the term persists in the title of *DSM-IV* because we have not found an appropriate substitute" (xxi).

There may be plausible reasons, however, for the stubborn persistence of dualism in language and experience, as Paul Broks points out:

> According to Western intellectual tradition, which distinguishes between Nature and Culture, we have a curious, duplex kind of existence. We move in a natural realm of time, space, and matter and, concurrently, through a social-cultural dimension of people and ideas, a world saturated with customs and beliefs, rituals, traditions, laws, conventions, fashions, language, arts, and science. In the first world we are subject, ultimately, to the laws of physics and, in the second, to the influence of customs, beliefs, rituals, traditions, etc. (51)

We live in two worlds, then, a social as well as a physical world, and, as Broks writes, "the negotiation of our complex social environments requires the attribution of mental states (feelings, beliefs, desires, intentions) to ourselves and others, perhaps inevitably inclining us to believe that the world contains two sorts of stuff, material and immaterial." Dualism, he concludes, "may have deep evolutionary roots," which might explain why "there is no stronger intuition" (61, 107).[47]

To complicate matters even further, the tension between science, popularly understood as describing the *facts* of the "material world," and literature and philosophy, popularly understood as describing the human in all its lofty and "immaterial" *meanings*, represents an oppositional structure that can itself be questioned, and historicized. Alluding to Foucault's assertion that "man is an invention of recent date" (*Order* 387), Bruno Latour suggests that matter, too, is "not given but a recent historical creation" ("Collective" 207). What Latour means is that we mistakenly assume matter to be an unproblematic given—a palpable constant of reality that can be easily observed and described—despite the fact that it is a concept with a complex history.[48] Far from being a nomological fact, materiality is embedded in narrative and meaning.[49] Even where we encounter things that appear to possess an unambiguous material existence, there is always more to the story than meets the eye, as Latour illustrates via the example of a speed bump on a road: "The speed bump is ultimately *not* made of matter; it is full

---

47  This point has also famously been made by Bertrand Russell in *The Analysis of Mind*: "The dualism of mind and matter [...] cannot be allowed as metaphysically valid. Nevertheless, we seem to find a certain dualism, perhaps not ultimate, within the world as we observe it" (137).

48  In particular, Latour dates back our current conceptions of materiality to the 18th and 19th centuries, invoking "[t]his famous shapeless matter, celebrated so fervently throughout the eighteenth and nineteenth centuries, which is there for Man's—but rarely Woman's—ingenuity to mold and fashion" ("Collective" 206).

49  Matter, in this reading, is profoundly cultural and social, not least because the social itself is understood mechanically: "We take matter as mechanistic, forgetting that mechanism is one half of the modern definition of society" ("Collective" 206-07).

of engineers and chancellors and lawmakers, commingling their wills and their story lines with those of gravel, concrete, paint, and standard calculations" ("Collective" 190; original emphasis).

What is more, the complication of classical Newtonian physics by its modern successor theories, which deal with relativity and quantum events, have transformed our understanding of matter far beyond any meaning the term once held. As Marilynne Robinson points out, "'the material' itself is an artifact of the scale at which we observe," an artifact of questionable significance for us who "abide with quarks and constellations, in a reality unknowable by us," where "indeterminacy reigns" (*Absence* 126).[50] Coole and Frost's observation that "for postclassical physics matter has become considerably more elusive (one might even say more immaterial)" is apt here (12). In the contemporary world, we take it, designating something as *material* may raise more questions than it answers.

Yet Coole and Frost's particular brand of "new materialism," a term whose primary function appears to be to corral and promote the work of such philosophers and critical theorists as Jane Bennett, William Connolly, and Manuel DeLanda, is not coterminous with the kind of materialism we find in contemporary theories that attempt to explain the mind in terms of material processes.[51] While the former emphasizes "active processes of materialization of which embodied humans are an integral part, rather than the monotonous repetitions of dead matter from which human subjects are apart" and aims to produce an "account of emergent, generative material being" (Coole and Frost 8), the latter often operate in accordance with less avant-garde and vitalistic conceptions of materiality. A typical assumption is that as a physical organ, the brain is subject to the same causal determination as the rest of nature. Gerald Edelman, in formulating his "global brain theory," cautions that "principles of physics must be strictly obeyed and that the world defined by physics is causally closed. No spooky forces that contravene

---

50  This new, indeterminate complexity of the physical universe also bears implications for the study of the brain, the methods of which might well be not up to the task: "If, as some have suggested, quantum phenomena govern the brain, evidence for the fact is not likely to be found in scrutiny of lobes or glands or by means of any primitive understanding of the brain's materiality" (Robinson, *Absence* 113).

51  At this point, some of the recent attempts at dialogue between the natural and the human sciences deserve mention, such as *What Makes Us Think*, Paul Ricoeur's extended conversation with the neuroscientist Jean-Pierre Changeux. In recent years, the novelist and essayist Siri Hustvedt has engaged in similar dialogues with neurobiologist Antonio Damasio. Likewise, historian Liah Greenfeld has completed her trilogy on nationalism with a volume titled *Mind, Modernity, Madness*, and issued an "Invitation to Dialogue" between the study of the brain and the study of culture. We also see steps in this direction in the work of scholars like Alva Noë, who is trained in philosophy as well as neuroscience, and aims to shift the focus from purely cerebral localization to analyses of the embodied organism in interaction with its social and cultural environment.

thermodynamics can be included" (*Sky* 114). For some, this means free will has to be replaced by a neural determinism (Singer, "Selbsterfahrung").

The notion of determinism inevitably evokes echoes of earlier materialisms. It is only a small step from Coole and Frost's observation that "[w]e are ourselves composed of matter" to the position that mental life should, in principle, be explainable as a physical process (1). "Holding that only material things (and, perhaps, forces and forcefields) exist, materialists deny independent status to the mind," Eugene Kelly writes, adding that such assumptions often lead to epiphenomenalism: "Matter alone exists; the mind is simply what the brain does" (87).[52] To be sure, this is not an altogether novel notion. Carl Zimmer dates the beginning of the "Neurocentric Age"[53] to the first stirrings of a medical-mechanistic imaginary in mid-seventeenth-century England, where Thomas Willis coined the term *neurologie* for his new "doctrine of the nerves" (6-7). For a robustly materialist system of thought that emerges after the completion of the scientific revolution, seeking to describe and explain a wide array of phenomena, including psychic life, by recourse to physical "laws," we need look no further than the nineteenth century.[54]

Materialism thrived particularly in the second half of the century, not only thanks to Marx and Comte, but also because under the sign of modern science, "[e]xperimental physiology and practical medicine greatly encouraged physical conceptions of human existence," which reverberated through the era's philosophy and psychology much as they do now (Smith 14). William James's 1879 essay "Are We Automata?" poses a question that remains relevant today, and the speculations made by James's contemporary Thomas Huxley about human beings as conscious automata can be read as prefiguring current neuro-materialist ideas: then as now, we are presented with the notion that consciousness "would appear to be related to the mechanism of [the] body simply as a collateral product of its working, and to be as completely without any power of modifying that working as

---

52  Thomas Nagel calls this view physicalism: "mental states are states of the body; mental events are physical events" ("Bat" 446).

53  Zimmer defines the Neurocentric Age, which continues into the present day, as the era "in which the brain is central not only to the body but to our conceptions of ourselves" (7).

54  Which is not to say that we could not look further back to earlier materialist accounts, like those provided by Thomas Hobbes and Pierre Gassendi in the seventeenth century, or by d'Holbach (*The System of Nature*) and de La Mettrie (*L'homme machine*) in the eighteenth, under the influence of Cartesian mechanistic philosophy. For an account that traces the origins of the materialist worldview into antiquity, see Vitzthum, who begins his study with a survey of the classical materialism of ancient Greek and Roman thought, noting, however, that subsequently Greco-Roman materialism "disappeared from European civilization" for a millennium and a half, "driven underground by Christianity" until its reemergence in England and France in the seventeenth century (13).

the steam-whistle which accompanies the work of a locomotive engine is without influence upon its machinery" (Huxley 575). Such epiphenomenalism is making a comeback these days, for instance in the notion that volition might be a belated byproduct of unconscious neurological processes (Libet; Singer).

Interest in automatism famously fuelled turn-of-the-century techniques and theories like mesmerism, hypnosis, and dynamic psychology, which emphasized the autonomy of the mental, but it also continues to resonate in twentieth- and twenty-first-century accounts that regard mind as a function of matter. The observation that "[c]onsciousness and its relation to the body became a topic of acute interest in the nineteenth century as physiology and neurology revealed increasingly detailed connections between brain processes and conscious experience" could apply just as well to the present (Anger 50), and few critical surveys of neuroscience fail to discuss nineteenth-century phrenology as a precursor of contemporary attempts to localize the functions of the mind in specific regions of the brain (Uttal; Rose & Abi-Rached 61-62). Given this apparent indebtedness of the new materialism to its historical precursors, Paul Giles deems the "cognitive turn" a misnomer: "what we see in this historical process is a cognitive turn and turn about," since "we have for the most part been here before" ("Afterword" 208).

We certainly find echoes of earlier, more strictly Newtonian notions of mechanistic materialism in contemporary psychological theories, for instance when Daniel Wegner, in his book *The Illusion of Conscious Will*,[55] postulates that "[w]e can't possibly know (let alone keep track of) the tremendous number of mechanical influences on our behavior because we inhabit an extraordinarily complicated machine" (27). As the difference between the monistic idea of "being matter" and the Cartesian notion of "inhabiting machines" suggests, materialist tropes are being deployed in different ways by various intellectual projects against the ever-present background of the mind-body problem.[56] Therefore a central objective of my study is to draw attention to the plurality of functions that "materialist minds" perform in recent American writing. As we will see, it is not only that the role of material substances and processes in mental life is being described differently by different theories, but also that these descriptions are being received, rejected, adopted, and adapted by literary authors in highly heterogeneous ways.

---

55  Fittingly, the cover of the first edition of Wegner's book features a design drawing of a human figure whose joints are diagrammed and numbered to resemble the moving parts of a mechanical machine.

56  Generally, the problem of materialism is understood in relation to idealism and dualism (E. Kelly 87). Today, the latter is widely understood as the oppositional term: "You have a choice between dualism and materialism" (Searle, *Consciousness* 47). See also David Chalmers's insistence that "those who want to come to grips with the phenomenon [of consciousness] must embrace a form of dualism," since "[y]ou can't have your materialist cake and eat your consciousness too" (*Conscious* 168).

## Neo-Naturalism

Its fidelity to the natural sciences aligns the new materialism of the mind with another updated "ism" that has been making the rounds lately. Why, one might ask, have I chosen to speak of "new materialism" and not "neo-naturalism," and what would be the difference? In his survey of neo-naturalism in the humanities, Frank Kelleter distinguishes between cognitive and evolutionary variants, i.e., those that focus on the operations of the human mind and those that focus on the brain as the natural organ supporting these operations (155). Both share "the recognition that human culture depends, in ways still to be clarified, on the prior existence of human bodies with basic biological needs and capacities" and the conviction that the natural or "hard" sciences provide a privileged mode of inquiry with which to study these natural (one might also say, universal) propensities (Kelleter 157). Though he is primarily interested in the use of naturalist methodologies in literary and cultural study, Kelleter's observations translate well to other areas, precisely because neo-naturalism aspires to the status of a master discourse capable of explaining all areas of human life—an "intellectual imperialism" couched in a "rhetoric of fundamental grounding" (Kelleter 182, 157). That neo-naturalist theories profess their loyalty to the scientific method "almost instinctively" (Kelleter 155) points us toward their central conceptual allegiance: like its earlier forms, this latest manifestation of naturalism supposes that only natural (i.e., physical) phenomena exist. These are described (or delimited) by science, so that at any given moment, science determines what counts as physical or natural.[57] It is for this reason that Lynne Rudder Baker calls naturalism the "philosophical companion" of science (*Naturalism* 3).

Naturalism, through notoriously difficult to define in its theoretical rather than its aesthetic commitments, can thus be broadly understood as an outlook that has its roots in the "new science" of Bacon and Descartes and the Enlightenment[58] and that privileges the scientific method over philosophical investigation, the physical over the metaphysical, matter over mind. Or, as Arthur Danto writes:

Naturalism, in recent usage, is a species of philosophical monism according to which whatever exists or happens is natural in the sense of being susceptible to

---

57  With characteristic (and comical) precision, Galen Strawson remarks, "we may be very wrong about the physical. We can't be sure we know the nature and limits of the physical. So we can't be sure we know the nature and limits of the natural: we can't be sure we know the nature and limits of the natural even if we're right [...] that the natural is the physical. This is putting it mildly, because physics and cosmology are in turmoil. It's not just that we don't definitely know the nature and limits of the physical. We definitely don't know the nature or limits of the physical" ("Naturalism," n. pag.).

58  For a comprehensive account of the ways in which Enlightenment naturalism transformed the view of the relation between mind and body, see Porter, *Flesh*.

explanation through methods which, although paradigmatically exemplified in the natural sciences, are continuous from domain to domain of objects and events. Hence, naturalism is polemically defined as repudiating the view that there exists or could exist any entities which lie, in principle, beyond the scope of scientific explanation. (448)

Obviously, then, naturalist and materialist views can be regarded as mutually sympathetic physicalist doctrines. Acceptance of scientific inquiry as a privileged route to insights about "human nature" and acquiescence to the claim that "any mental and biological causes must themselves be physically constituted, if they are to produce physical effects" represent particularly important areas of overlap (Papineau; n. pag.). Attention to the role of evolutionary processes in materialist explanation is another. Here we can recall Marco Roth's criticism of the reductionist tendency to explain "proximate causes of mental function in terms of neurochemistry, and ultimate causes in terms of evolution and heredity" (n. pag.). This is in fact an apt description of the "neuromolecular style of thought" identified by Rose and Abi-Rached, one of whose "key structuring principles" consists in the notion that "many basic neural processes and structures have been conserved by evolution" (43).[59]

Even though new materialist and neo-naturalist approaches thus seem inherently related, I have opted to speak of "new materialism" or "materialist minds" rather than "neo-naturalism," since the former terms allow for an analytical purview that is simultaneously broader and more specifically directed. The main interest of this project consists in the ways in which materialist conceptions of subjectivity figure in literary production, and while such conceptions are often tied to scientific modes of inquiry, they are often the result of loose philosophical or psychological ideas that do not spring directly from narrow naturalist commitments. Just as often, materialist views of the mind emerge in the framework of psychiatric or neurological discourse, a discursive realm that the Jamesian term "medical materialism" captures more accurately than "neo-naturalism" ("Religion" 24). For the purposes of my study, I therefore propose to view neo-naturalism as one among many manifestations of larger new materialist trends—a manifestation that may at times overlap with my concerns, but will only be addressed when it is of immediate relevance to the subject at hand.

---

59  See also Abi-Rached and Rose, "Birth."

# 3. "My wayward brain": Cerebral Subjectivity and Narrative Identity in the Neuro-Memoir

> Men ought to know that from the brain, and from the brain only, arise our pleasures, joy, laughter and jests, as well as our sorrows, pains, griefs, and tears. Through it, in particular, we think, see, hear, and distinguish the ugly from the beautiful, the bad from the good, the pleasant from the unpleasant.
> *Hippocrates, "On the Sacred Disease"*

> And who are you, said he?
> Don't puzzle me, said I.
> *Laurence Sterne, Tristram Shandy*

## What (or When) is the Neuro-Memoir?

Psychology and psychiatry have long been important "sources of the self," to use Charles Taylor's term, so that changing views and concepts in these disciplines are also sure to generate new discourses of subjectivity. Historically, the relation between mind and madness and the question of self-control have had a direct bearing on conceptions of soul or self, just as the philosophy of the subject—in its affirmative as well as its critical strands—has at all times entertained intimate links to the "sciences of the mind."[1] We need only look to Nietzsche, wishing to be known as a psychologist rather than a philosopher; or to Foucault, tracing Enlightenment reason as the silhouette cast by madness; or to the ways in which Freudian and Lacanian psychoanalysis have been appropriated in philosophical attempts to develop a critical model of subjecthood, based on the lack rather than the pos-

---

1 Needless to say, the idea of self-control as a *value* has a history that links it to the concept of rationality. Emily Martin argues that modern Western culture posits "a rational mental apparatus located inside the brain" as a "battleground on which the mind's rationality and will fought to control the 'uncivilized' animal impulses of the body" (*Bipolar* 66). See also Illouz 117 and MacIntyre.

session of control. Psychological pathology and psychic conflict have often been described both as a philosophical puzzle and as a pragmatic problem, with reflections on universal principles deriving from the quandaries of individual conduct. "How is Weakness of the Will Possible?" asks a seminal essay by Donald Davidson, but the question is at least as old as Augustine's *Confessions*, where *incontinentia*, the phenomenon of acting contrary to one's better judgment, poses a theological as well as a personal problem for the ancient autobiographer.[2]

The suspicion that in modernity, medical and psychological concepts might come to characterize the very fabric of the self has found a famous expression in Philip Rieff's *The Triumph of the Therapeutic*. Here Freudian psychoanalysis is envisioned as the master discourse of "psychological man," the dominant moral type in a thoroughly secularized world less concerned with salvation or final causes than with regulating the affects and drives to avoid displeasure—a dynamic Rieff calls "the predicate of impulse release" (17). Yet it would appear that as psychology changes, "psychological man" changes, too. With the rise of new discourses of mental (dys)function, new registers of self-understanding become available. The title of one of Lacan's English publications famously declared psychoanalysis *The Language of the Self*, but it is not the only such language: autobiographical writing, that practice of externalized interiority exemplified by Augustine, is another.[3] Yet it appears that neither is immune to change. Unlike Augustine, the majority of today's autobiographers no longer frame their reports of inner turmoil in theological terms; unlike Rieff, they may no longer invoke psychoanalytic concepts. Does this mean that the dominant language of self-understanding in the twentieth century is headed for a similar fate as religion? Is psychoanalysis—or even dynamic psychology in general—in the process of being displaced not only in mental health care[4] but also in autobiographical writing, with an increasingly materialist and biomedical language taking its place?

Some signs seem to point in this direction. The last three decades have seen the publication of a number of memoirs that revolve around psychiatric diagnoses. There have been, among others, first-person accounts of depression, manic depression, schizophrenia, addiction, anxiety, phobia, stroke, obsessive-compul-

---

2 Going back further, we find *akrasia*, the Greek antecedent of Augustine's Latin *incontinentia*, in Plato's *Protagoras* and Aristotle's *Nichomachean Ethics*.

3 I would suggest that it is no coincidence that Foucault, who at the end of his career described his project as one of creating "a history of the different modes by which, in our culture, human beings are made subjects" ("Subject" 777), looked toward psychology and the autobiographical techniques of confession (*Sexuality* 56) and life writing, in the form of the Greek *hypomnemata* ("Self Writing" 209) as ways to approach this topic.

4 See Angell and Luhrmann for analyses of the transformation of psychiatry.

sive disorder, and somatoform disorder.[5] Obviously, such narratives only become possible once the experience in question has become "knowable" as a clinical picture with a proper name, as well as "speakable" as a distinct set of symptoms that can be separated from the afflicted person.[6] Furthermore, the emergence of illness narratives in memoirs and novels can be interpreted as a reaction to the "elimination of the patient's perspective from medical science" that occurred in twentieth-century medicine (Draaisma 430). But I would also like to suggest that insofar as they treat psychopathology (partly or primarily) as organic disturbance, these accounts share important features with the "materialist minds" I have been invoking. In fact, it is a defining feature of these recent medical memoirs that in some form or other, they need to come to terms with the medical materialism that one finds in biological psychiatry and neuroscience. However, "coming to terms" does not necessarily mean wholesale acceptance or adoption; rather, these texts consider, discuss, and often find fault with, medical-materialist thought.

If autobiography is "nothing if not a referential art, and the self or subject is its principal referent," as Paul John Eakin claims, then in such texts we see memoirists grapple with this referent in novel ways (*Touching* 3). In this chapter, I propose "neuro-memoir" as a name for this phenomenon. By this term I understand recent[7] autobiographical writing that is interested (and personally invested) in the relation between subjectivity and the nervous system, and that uses medical (or medicalized) conditions as an occasion to examine this relation. Analyzing select examples, I ask what roles psychodynamic and materialist explanatory models play in these texts, how the two are related to each other, and what happens to the psychological, philosophical, and literary notion of the self when subjectivity is re-conceptualized in materialist terms.

Autobiographical writing promises to answer this question in an immediate and personal manner, recording as it does the impressions and reflections of someone who has "lived to tell the tale": personal experience with neurological,

---

5  In addition, we have memoirs written by practicing clinicians or the friends and family members of those suffering from psychiatric or neurological disorders, which maintain the first-person form while providing an third-person perspective of the afflicted person.

6  This is not to say that diagnoses are made in a vacuum, or that they simply appear in the course of the natural progression of history. The problem of diagnosis can figure in a number of ways in cultural analysis. Thus Emily Martin focuses on the role of bipolar disorder in U.S. socioeconomic life, (*Bipolar*), Alain Ehrenberg views depression as a signature illness of "individualized" societies (*Weariness*), Louis Sass examines the relation between schizophrenia and modernity ("Negative"), while Eve Sedgwick considers addiction a byproduct of consumer capitalism ("Epidemics"), and all of these stories can be integrated into the even larger narrative about the *medicalization* of society (Conrad) or everyday life (Szasz). See also Bell and Figert for a collection of perspectives from medical sociology.

7  I am considering publications from the 1990s onwards.

psychiatric, or psychological disorders tends to make "philosophical or abstract questions about the connections between body, mind, self, and world physically and experientially concrete," as Jason Tougaw observes in his review of recent "brain memoirs" (172). However, I do not intend to read these texts naively, as only thinly mediated records of personal experience. Two points in particular advise against such an approach. First, neuro-memoirs are not transparent testimony to some extratextual reality but personal, rhetorical constructs bearing the stamp of particular views and ideas. This is not to argue that the authors write in bad faith, but to emphasize that here as elsewhere, materialist tropes are being discussed for specific purposes and deployed to create specific effects. One author might invoke neurological concepts to argue for the importance of biology to human subjectivity, while the next might do so to establish the explanatory inferiority of brain research vis-à-vis psychoanalytic knowledge.

Second, as much scholarship on memoirs, or "life writing"[8] has shown, such texts need to be understood as products of deliberate composition and rhetorical artifice, even when they appear most immediate: "the distinction between fiction and autobiography is not an either/or polarity," Paul de Man writes; "it is unde-cidable" (921). Supplanting an earlier understanding of autobiographical writing as the expression of an authentic, essential, and given self, the construction of identity through literary techniques, which the memoir shares with the novel, is now viewed in most circles as "intimately interwoven with the autobiographical process itself, a process that appears to be essentially narrative in nature" (Brock-meier 456). Like other forms of literary writing, the autobiographical text is no longer seen as representing a pre-existing reality; rather, it becomes a site "where concepts of subject, self, and author collapse into the act of producing a text" (Sprinker 342). First-person narratives, the critical consensus has it, do not simply reproduce personality but actively generate "identity constructions" (Kehily) or "allegories of self" (Herman).

As its etymology implies, the most important constructions effected by auto-biography are the *autos* (self) and the *bios* (life) of its author, but whereas the lat-ter is merely mediated, the former, it could be said, is *nothing but* mediation. In Eakin's words, an autobiographer "constructs a self that would not otherwise exist," one that is "necessarily a fictive structure" (*Fictions* 26, 3). Biographical data can be checked, verified, or disproved, but the self that emerges in the process of reading is considerably less tangible: in Steinian parlance, there is no there there. Even when we have no reason to doubt the veracity of a given account, we can

---

8  Life writing is generally used as a larger category that includes biography, autobiography, mem-oir, and countless other historical and classificatory distinctions. For an overview, see Winslow or Jolly.

never be sure to what degree the character jointly constructed by author, text, and reader resembles a person beyond the page.

If in reading fictional characters, we are faced with the task of "holding together in a single frame at once the ontological discontinuity which allows us to distinguish a representational act from other acts, and the ontological continuity that binds them to each other," as John Frow writes, this task becomes only more pressing when decoding the "I-characters" of autobiographical texts (70). There exists a definite relation between the subjectivity the text constructs and the historical person who authored it—we may even assume the narrative in question to have been written in good faith, with the aim of producing a representational act that does justice to its "original"—but a person is not a text,[9] so we need to be acutely aware that the processes of selection, compression, and temporal ordering that characterize memoirs are liable to produce a "textual self" with specific (and perhaps strategic) characteristics rather than an exhaustive, immediate account of the author's interiority. To invert Whitman: Camerado, this is no man, Who touches this touches a book.[10]

And still: in its insistence that "something happened to *me*," which Carolyn Barros regards as the fundamental impulse of autobiographical narrative, authorial and textual selves contract into one rhetorical amalgamation (vii; original emphasis). Like fictional characters and real persons, they are "at once ontologically discontinuous [...] and logically interdependent" (Frow vii). In its conflation of a linguistic-textual "I" and an actual (living or historical) person, autobiographical writing brings to a head debates about the reality of the self and its relation to language.[11] This much, of course, has been true for as long as autobiography has been recognized as a distinct literary genre (Anderson 2-3), and perhaps one could say it was truer still in the heyday of structuralist and poststructuralist methodologies, some of which looked to linguistic relations to account for the structure of the psyche itself.[12] It will be worthwhile to ask, therefore, what new configurations of subjectivity emerge under a paradigm that deems materiality (in the extratextual realm) *as well as* language (in the intratextual realm) the crucial determinants

---

9  For a list of works that address this impossibility, see Barros (20).

10  This is not, upon reversion, to consider "actual," historical persons as simply, unproblematically given. As Frow notes, social persons, too, may be regarded as "constructs, which are in part made out of the same materials as fictional characters," so that social personhood "works as a kind of fiction" (vii).

11  Linda Anderson calls autobiography "an important testing ground for critical controversies about a range of ideas including authorship, selfhood, representation, and the division between fact and fiction" (1). What is also conflated here is "the pronoun system and the system of social nomenclature," which Frow regards as crucial to the construction of persons as well as characters, literary or otherwise (ix).

12  Claude Lévi-Strauss and Jacques Lacan are the most prominent representatives of this view.

of the self. For this, I submit, is what is at the heart of the burgeoning genre of the neuro-memoir: readers are treated to first-person accounts of the ways in which mental life depends on biological materiality, but the "I" that simultaneously indexes author, narrator, and character[13] is nevertheless invoked—and performed—in and through the "immaterial," symbolic system of language.

If the *production of self* takes center stage in neuro-memoirs, it is not only because they, like all autobiographical writing, generate the "I" that authors them, but also because they discuss phenomena that affect the very fabric of subjectivity and self-understanding. Paul Broks writes that "neurological disease sometimes goes straight to the core and distorts the person in essence," that it "can penetrate the substructures of the self" (188-89). Accordingly, psychiatric or neurological dysfunction often entails what have been called "perturbations of the self" (Feinberg, "Interesting" 129), "self-disorders," (Zahavi and Parnas 699) or "altered egos" (Feinberg, *Altered* 1). Mania, depression, and schizophrenia, for instance, transform perception, emotion, cognition, and behavior to such a degree that it should come as no surprise that those who record the effects of these afflictions often resort to descriptions in which several types of "me" compete for supremacy: the "sick me," the "real me," the "old me," the "new me."[14] Since they involve constant shifts in, and revaluations of, feeling and experience, these are, as Alain Ehrenberg observes, profoundly "moral" illnesses—not in the sense that they stem from weakness of the will as a moral failing, but in the sense that their symptoms are experienced as charged with deeply personal, meaningful qualities.[15] These qualities are aligned in what Charles Taylor calls a "moral space," which constitutes a primordial, often preconscious framework for assigning value to embodied emotion and thus provides an intimate link between subjectivity and pathology.[16]

The development of personality has traditionally been viewed as a central interest of autobiography (Lejeune 4). Neuro-memoirs retain this interest and examine how material or medical factors can constitute as well as disintegrate

---

13  See Lejeune.

14  "One of the most frequently voiced questions is whether the 'illness' is some kind of foreign body or in fact an intrinsic part of the self," Darian Leader observes of manic-depression, a question that he links to the problem of accountability: "Not knowing whether the manias and depressions belong to us or not reflects the difficulty of not knowing whether the responsibility is ours or someone else's" (*Bipolar* 55).

15  Ehrenberg mentions the feelings of shame and guilt associated with depression as an example ("Le sujet" 150).

16  Taylor postulates an "essential link between identity and a kind of orientation," which he understands by way of a spatial metaphor: "To know who you are is to be oriented in moral space, a space in which questions arise about what is good or bad, what is worth doing and what not, what has meaning and importance for you and what is trivial or secondary" (*Sources* 28). Needless to say, such moral valuations are radically altered in depression and related disorders.

the self. "Where many traditional memoirs take selfhood for granted," Tougaw proposes, "brain memoirs investigate how mind, brain, body, and culture interact to create or perform selfhood, and that investigation has social, scientific, and philosophical implications" ("Memoirs" 174). I would like to follow up on this claim and ask what specific—and possibly new—forms and models of subjectivity these texts produce, and how they reconcile the material (molecular, pharmaceutical, neurological) aspects of the self with the reflective, linguistic subject authoring these accounts and writing itself into existence in the process. We will be dealing, then, with two different (and possibly conflicting) kinds of subjects, a somatic or cerebral one and a textual or narrative one. Therefore it will be helpful to dedicate some space to these concepts before moving on to the texts themselves.

## The Cerebral Subject

In their introduction to the collection *Neurocultures*, editors Francisco Ortega and Fernando Vidal discuss a number of ways in which we can understand the idea of the "cerebral subject." To begin with, the term can refer to the brain itself. In many recent neuro-materialist accounts, agency and cognition are ascribed to the brain, so that it is the brain itself that acts and knows, and the organ becomes "personified and equated with the person" (Ortega and Vidal 15). I began my introduction with this notion, which we might now qualify: if "you are your brain," as not only Francis Crick but also present-day neuroscientists like Michael Gazzaniga and Eric Kandel have proposed, the justification usually given for this substitution is that your brain produces the "I" you believe you are.[17] To make the claim that the brain *creates* the self (Feinberg, *Altered Egos*) or the mind (Frith) or that "[t] the mind is what the brain does" (Pinker, *Mind* 21) is qualitatively different from merely stating the obvious fact that without brains, we would not have minds, and that consequently, our feelings, perceptions, and ideas—in short, our *selves*—are dependent upon the physiology of the brain (or that, in Donald Davidson's terminology, the former are *supervenient* on the latter). It is to perform a reduction that transposes agency from the human subject to a part of the human anatomy and assigns the thinking, feeling "I" the status of a secondary phenomenon resulting from, and reducible to, physical processes.

Ortega and Vidal's conception of the cerebral subject is shared by French sociologist Alain Ehrenberg, who sees the "return of the subject" (Giddens; Touraine) occurring once more, only this time in a "biological version" that ascribes to the brain characteristics previously attributed to the individual. This is neither the brain of the old-fashioned Taylorist worker nor that of classical neurology, Ehren-

---

17  See Gazzaniga, *Ethical*, and Kandel, *Memory*.

berg writes, but rather one which, "thanks to an endogenous system of self-acti-vation, triggers itself in a dynamic, proactive manner, which takes the initiative, and, by testing assumptions or simulating the minds of others, makes decisions in order to adjust its behavior"—a brain, in other words, that acts on behalf or in stead of its "owner" ("Se définir" 72; my translation). However, Ehrenberg points out, such redescriptions need to be understood in their social contexts: not only does neuroscientific rhetoric draw on well-established cultural tropes of the adaptable, resilient, and mobile subject produced by modern societies ("Se définir" 70-71); it is also strategically deployed by social actors as a means of navigating the psychological and social demands of these societies ("Le sujet" 150-52). This is why, while he sees many proponents of neuroscientific ideas equating brain with mind or self, Ehrenberg is not willing to subscribe to this equation himself. Rather, he directs our attention to the purposes that "defining oneself as one's brain" might serve, as well as to the social and psychological moves it enables. In his account, then, brain and self remain analytically separable, with the latter able to make "good use" of the former.

Ortega and Vidal also develop a similar understanding of the cerebral subject, in which the term comes to describe not the brain-as-subject but rather a person who understands him- or herself (perhaps only partly or temporarily) in terms of neurological structures and functions, or who is being described in this way. In this reading, cerebral subjects "shape themselves and are shaped through technol-ogies of the self which are partly sustained by expert knowledge and its transmis-sion in popular culture" (16).[18] This notion is especially suitable in instances where biomedical categories meld with those indexing identity. As "an understanding of subjectivity that derives from a scientific, third-person perspective," Ortega and Vidal note, medical diagnoses and neurological concepts become "a way to be a person" (17).[19] The neurodiversity movement, seeking to establish autism as a bio-identity rather than a disease, is one example; the ongoing "A.D.H.D. epi-demic" is another.[20]

---

18  The Foucauldian phrase "technologies of the self" is employed here for a reason: Ortega and Vidal's main sources are Ian Hacking and Nikolas Rose, two scholars whose work has been sub-stantially influenced by Foucault.

19  Here we recognize the authors' debt to Hacking, who famously put forth the notion idea that new ways of description produce new subjectivities: "a new scientific classification may bring into being a new kind of person, conceived and experienced as a way to be a person" ("Kinds" 285) See also Hacking, "Making."

20  See Ortega, "Cerebral" on the biodiversity movement and cerebral subjectivity; on the A.D.H.D. "epidemic," see, for instance, the editorial "An Epidemic of Attention Deficit Disorder" in the 18 December 2013 edition of the New York Times: www.nytimes.com/2013/12/19/opinion/an-epi-demic-of-attention-deficit-disorder.html

## The Cerebral Subject and the Neurochemical Self

The concept of the cerebral subject bears some resemblance to Nikolas Rose's term "the neurochemical self," which he introduces and develops in three interrelated articles.[21] At a very general level, Rose observes, "we in the West, most especially in the United States, have come to understand our minds and selves in terms of our brains and bodies," so that as a consequence, the meaning of psychological and cultural phenomena is increasingly being described in biomedical terms. Sadness and worry, for instance, are partly redefined as depression and anxiety ("Neurochemical" 46).[22] To explain this new medical materialism, Rose invokes the economic and structural power of the pharmaceutical industry, which has a vested interest in such redescriptions, as well as the efforts undertaken by drug companies, psychiatrists, and campaigning groups to transform mental illness into an organic disease ("Neurochemical" 53). However, Rose also notes that while he emphasizes the shift toward neurochemistry, one could focus equally well on brain imaging, or on genomics ("Neurochemical" 46). The implication is that the new materialism of the "neurochemical self" is a multifaceted phenomenon that can be approached via multiple "paths" (Rose and Abi-Rached 31).[23]

Though he points out that he finds the "global cultural account" put forth by Alain Ehrenberg "unconvincing," Rose's work nonetheless bears some resemblance to that of the French sociologist. For one thing, both authors suggest a correlation between the rise in depression diagnoses and the post-WWII ideal of individual autonomy and responsibility.[24] Depression, Rose argues, "can only be understood in relation to contemporary conceptions of the self that involve the obligation of freedom: responsibility, choice and active self-fulfillment" ("Neurochemical" 53-54). Taken together, it is implied, the salience of health to the aspirations of modern Westerners, the redescription of life problems as pathologies to be treated by materialist medicine, and the influence of big pharma and the managed-care regime amount to a "profound transformation in personhood." Increasingly, the psychological sense of self, based on interiority and biography, is being supplanted by a sense of "somatic individuality," a term by which Rose means "the tendency to define key aspects of one's individuality in bodily terms, that is to say to think of oneself as 'embodied,' and to understand that body in the language of contemporary biomedicine" ("Neurochemical" 54). One example is addiction, which has long been viewed as primarily psychogenic and relatively

---

21  See Rose, "Becoming," "Neurochemical," and "Anomalies."

22  See also Horwitz and Wakefield, who put forward a similar hypothesis.

23  Thus, in "The Neurochemical Self and its Anomalies," Rose defines the neurochemical and the genetic self as sub-categories of the somatic self (408).

24  See Ehrenberg's study *The Weariness of the Self* for this thesis.

difficult to treat pharmaceutically, but is now being recast as "at least in part, not a disease of the person, or of the will, but a disease of the brain." The same holds true for depression or schizophrenia: all these are being rewritten as *diseases* that can afflict the "susceptible neurochemical and genetic self" ("Anomalies" 432).

Crucially, somatic individuality is not understood to be displacing subjectivity altogether. In fact, individuals are not relieved of their responsibilities; they are being tasked with additional ones.[25] "An ethics is engineered into the molecular make up of these drugs, and the drugs themselves embody and incite particular forms of life in which the 'real me' is both 'natural' and to be produced," Rose writes, thus presenting neurochemical subjectivity as something of a cultural and economical imperative.[26]

## The Cerebral Subject and the Sufficiently Separate Self

Lest all this sound too much like an epochal shift, both Ortega/Vidal and Rose add caveats and qualifications to their models of materialist subjectivity. Ortega and Vidal concede that "life is overdetermined," so that no single mode of description or lens of analysis can claim exclusive explanatory power, not even the new materialism with its recourse to the "hard" or natural sciences ("Approaching" 7). Just because phenomena of human life can be examined not only at the sociological, political, and cultural level but also at the biological, anatomical, biochemical, and molecular level, "matter at its most minimal" does not necessarily have to become the most legitimate object of study. Some "new materialists" may certainly propose such a shift (Johnston, *Adventures* 170), but the sheer number of available explanatory models, from naturalist to culturalist narratives, means that human subjects are free to view themselves in a variety of ways, and to mix and match existing interpretations. Despite the seemingly inescapable dynamics of an increasingly materialist culture, we are for all intents and purposes faced with a "coexistence of ontologies, both in society and in the individual," as Ortega and Vidal observe. While the authors consider the term "cerebral subject" useful as a historical and cultural datum, they also speak of a "cohabitation of self-concepts, from the psychoanalytical to the cerebral, from the spiritualist to the neu-

---

25  Accordingly, the shift to somatic individuality need not necessarily be understood as a "rebirth of essentialism, reductionism, geneticism," Rose points out; rather, "plenty of scope remains for autonomy, choice, individuality, and responsibility" ("Anomalies" 408-09).

26  In an age of increasing personal responsibility, the new materialism of the mind "obliges the individual to engage in constant risk management, and to act continually on him or herself to minimize risks by reshaping diet, lifestyle and now, by means of pharmaceuticals, the body itself" ("Neurochemical" 58-59).

rochemical, which people may invoke when talking about themselves and going about their lives" ("Approaching" 17). Likewise, in their 2013 book *Neuro*, Rose and his collaborator Abi-Rached make sure to include a note stating that Rose's concept of the neurochemical self—developed roughly a decade earlier—was "meant to imply, not a wholesale mutation in personhood, but the *availability* of a neurochemical register within which individuals could describe, judge, and seek to modulate their mental states and ailments (272 n3; my emphasis).

The most striking "coexistence of ontologies"—and the one that bears the greatest relevance to this chapter—is the contentious relation between physical and psychological truth claims. As already mentioned, biochemical or neural conceptions of subjectivity differ from the generally accepted notion of the correlation of mental and brain states, even as they build upon it. We can probably all agree, Robert Burton suggests, that "mental states, no matter how seemingly psychological in origin, ultimately arise out of brain states." Notwithstanding this truism, we still experience a personal self that is *"sufficiently separate* from these states to have an understanding of this proposition" (Burton 15; my emphasis). In other words, even if one subscribes to a materialist notion of mind, one does so as an experiential self with subjective states and impressions.[27] Galen Strawson suggests that this should be regarded as the most basic definition of the term "self": an internal mental presence, a subject of experience ("Phenomenology" 39). If this notion of perceptive interiority is one key component of the selves produced by and in autobiographical writing, another can be found among the more "specialized" variants of self that Strawson lists in his essay,[28] namely the narrative or autobiographical self.[29]

---

27  What is more, our attachments to value judgments deriving from the "folk psychology" of interpersonal, everyday life—especially regarding the question of personal responsibility—are exceedingly persistent and impervious to change, as Peter Strawson has demonstrated in his landmark essay "Freedom and Resentment."

28  In his article, Strawson mentions an almost comically diverse array that includes "the cognitive self, the conceptual self, the contextualized self, the core self, the dialogic self, the ecological self, the embodied self, the emergent self, the empirical self, the existential self, the extended self, the fictional self, the full-grown self, the interpersonal self, the material self, the narrative self, the philosophical self, the physical self, the private self, the representational self, the rock bottom essential self, the semiotic self, the social self, the transparent self, and the verbal self" ("Phenomenology" 39).

29  In what follows, I will be using these terms interchangeably, since developmental psychologists, from whose work these terms derive, tend to do so as well, as noted by Amy Allen (167).

## The Narrative or Autobiographical Self

Starting from Strawson's minimal definition of the self as the internal, mental subject of experience, a narrative understanding of the self appears cogent, if only for the simple reason that in order for experience to achieve any kind of reality, its contents need to be processed, ordered, stored and/or communicated in some way. While it may not be accurate to say that we experience the world in the form of a story on a moment-to-moment basis, *some* narrative modality would seem to have to be in place for experience and memory to merge into self-understanding. That in the seventeenth century philosophical treatments of personal identity, like John Locke's *Essay Concerning Personal Understanding*, emerge synchronously with the practice of recording one's life in written form over an extended period of time also points toward a historical correlation between narrativity and the self (Brockmeier 455).[30] In the same vein, research in developmental psychology has shown that children acquire narrative techniques from their parents: "Almost from the start of language, self-report is framed by stylistic conventions and by rules of genre," a dynamic that by all accounts persists throughout adult life (Bruner and Weisser 129). Clearly, autobiographical techniques and subjectivity need to be seen, at the very least, as intimately related phenomena.

Accordingly, theorists from a number of fields have commented on this correlation. Long a staple of philosophy and philology, the notion of a narrative or autobiographical self gained prominence in the human sciences and cultural theory in the late seventies; as a "traveling concept," it had begun migrating to other disciplines by the 1990s (Hatavara et al.). Here we find psychologists like Jerome Bruner or Kenneth and Mary Gergen and sociologists like Margaret Somers among the first adopters.[31] By now, we can identify veritable subdisciplines like narrative psychology and trace the influence of narratological concepts on fields

---

30  Surely one can find even earlier examples of the correlation between first-person speech and the self. Thus, Jerome Bruner notes that the French historian Georges Gusdorf "sees the birth of literary autobiography as issuing from the mixed and unstable marriage between Christian and classical thought in the Middle Ages, further inflamed by the doubts kindled in the Copernican revolution," adding that "[d]oubtless the Reformation also added fuel to the passion for written self-revelation" ("Life" 695). We might also consider the letters of Roman philosophers, or Augustine's *Confessions*, which Girard considers "the first great literary autobiography in a sense that the ancient world did not really know" (272). However, as Peter Heehs notes, the latter was followed by "a gap of more than a thousand years before people in Europe began to write personal histories again" Heehs, too, views the seventeenth century as the crucial point, when "the memoir flourished" (7).

31  See Bruner, "Autobiographical" and "Narrative" and Gergen & Gergen, "Narratives" and "Scanning," as well as Somers, "Narrativity" and "Narrative." In the larger context of the migration of narratological concepts to other disciplines, we may also want to mention Hayden White, whose work was pathbreaking in the eighties. See White, *Metahistory* and *Content*.

like history and anthropology (Brockmeier & Carbaugh 9-10). Even in economics, the psychological role of narrative has become a focus of attention.[32]

In theories of narrative identity, the temporal and semantic ordering mechanisms of autobiographical texts are detached from the act of writing and adopted as anthropological constants, central to the activity of the psyche. This is what Galen Strawson, in his critique of the narrativity paradigm, calls the "psychological Narrativity thesis," which holds that narrative is integral to human nature ("Against" 428). Paul John Eakin, for instance, proposes to view narrative as "a mode of experience rather than merely a literary form" (*Fictions* 130) and as an "existential imperative" (*Living* 86), while Calvin Schrag calls narrative "an ontological structure of human experience" (43). The universalist bent of these arguments is readily apparent. As Jerome Bruner remarks, "the self-told life narrative is, by all accounts, ancient and universal ("Life" 695). Here Bruner clearly echoes Barthes, who saw narrative "present at all times, in all places, in all societies" ("Structural" 237) as well as Hayden White, who considers narrative "a metacode, a human universal" ("Value" 6). Narrativity, in this view, is deemed geographically and temporally universal; what varies are the forms of its expression.[33]

Such theories of the narrative or autobiographical self are often characterized by an attempt to give equal weight to the deterministic forces of linguistic and cultural construction (or, in a Focauldian register, subjection through power) and the creative dynamics of developing and expressing the self in social and symbolic systems. In Jerome Bruner's words, "we *become* the autobiographical narratives by which we 'tell about' our lives," but since these narratives have to draw on a pre-existing storehouse of cultural symbols, patterns, and meanings, we also become "variants of the culture's canonical forms" rather than bona fide individuals ("Life" 694; original emphasis). If this sounds not too far removed from Roland Barthes's "quotations drawn from the innumerable centers of culture" ("Death" 145), the reason might be that historically, theories of narrative identity develop in synchrony with, and in response to, structuralist and poststructuralist theories of the linguistic-cultural subject.[34] Yet the crucial word term in Bruner's thesis is "variants," a term that provides a loophole out of the unwelcome scenario of total

---

32  In particular, the work of Nobel laureate Robert J. Shiller has drawn attention to the ways in which emotional dynamics, codified and circulated in narrative form, influence global markets: "stock markets are driven by popular narratives, which don't need basis in solid fact" ("Contagious"). See also Shiller, *Animal Spirits*, as well as Fluck and Lindner, who make a similar point.

33  See Jens Brockmeier's suggestion that "it is through the many forms of discourse that we order our experiences, memories, desires, and concerns in an autobiographical perspective," using the cultural models available to us (456).

34  Sometimes, this genealogy is also explicitly avowed: in "Life as Narrative," Bruner names the Russian formalists as well as Roman Jakobson as formative influences for his theory of narrative, in which "it is form rather than content that matters" (696).

and irrevocable cultural determination. If "eventually the culturally shaped cognitive and linguistic processes that guide the self-telling of life narratives achieve
the power to structure perceptual experience, to organize memory, to segment
and purpose-build the very 'events' of a life" (Bruner, "Life" 694), then this process,
which we need to imagine as taking place continually over the course of one's life,
will to some degree have to be a personalized affair, tailored to the subject's needs,
desires, hopes, fears, and the like. But who is to do the tailoring? Switching the
sartorial metaphor for a literary one, Paul Ricoeur suggests that "we never cease to
reinterpret the narrative identity that constitutes us, in the light of the narratives
proposed to us by our culture" and thereby "learn to become the *narrator* and the
hero *of our own story* without actually becoming the *author of our own life*" ("Life" 32;
original emphases). Ricoeur's statement is diligently phrased to balance out freedom and constraint, and it gets the job done: once more it is "we" who are doing
the interpreting and learning, we who read culture rather than being written by
it.[35] A quantum of agency (even if it is only the freedom to accept certain cultural
"proposals" and reject others) is wrested from the ominous, impersonal forces of
subjection and restored to the self.

Despite its apparent indebtedness to poststructuralist theories about the discursive nature of the subject, the idea of the narrative or autobiographical self
should therefore be contextualized as an effort to overcome poststructuralisms's
emphasis on subjectivity as "being spoken" by language, and to secure a more
active and productive role for the self. The latter may be a provisional construct,
but from the standpoint of narrative psychology, it still commands interest *as a
fiction*—and a highly useful one—in the realms of both literature and life.[36] This is
why a large share of theories about narrative identity should indeed be understood
as an attempt to "replace in neo-Romantic fashion the unself-conscious illusion
of autobiographical selfhood with the self-conscious quest for self-present selfhood through the autobiographical-cum-fictional act," as Louis Renza phrases it
in somewhat convoluted fashion in his review of Eakin's *Fictions in Autobiography*
(273).[37]

---

35 Critical-minded readers might find fault with the way in which Ricoeur interpellates his readers into a collective "we" that exudes the distinct aroma of the much-dreaded normative (and
   normalizing) "universalist" subject position, but for now, let "us" agree that the presumption of
   innocence applies here.

36 In a characteristic passage, Eakin writes: "Let us grant the very concept of the self as a fiction, let
   us speak in the French way of textuality of the self. After such knowledge, why do authors still
   indulge in, and readers consent to, a fiction of this kind" (*Fictions* 27).

37 See also Schrag, who attempts to salvage *The Self after Postmodernity* without rejecting poststructuralism outright by arguing that "discourse provides its own resources for self-unification
   and self-identity, and it does so specifically in the form and dynamics of narrative" (19).

## The Narrative Self in Paul Ricoeur

This reconciliation of the linguistic and the lived aspects of subjectivity has been a central project of Paul Ricoeur's, who has been singularly influential in promoting a view of the self as both fictional and indispensable. After completing his transition from existential to hermeneutic phenomenology, Ricoeur held that "there is no self-understanding that is not mediated by signs, symbols, and texts" and that "it is *language* that is the primary condition of all human experience" ("On Interpretation" 15; original emphasis). While we clearly see him attempting to accommodate structuralist and poststructuralist philosophies of language in passages like these, Ricoeur's work has always been dedicated to developing a philosophical anthropology that would yield an accurate picture of the capabilities, liabilities, and vulnerabilities of the self.[38] To this end, Ricoeur advances a theory of the self as embodied (and thus produced in part by biological and cultural factors), discursively produced, *and* individually responsible. "Who is 'I,' when the subject says that he or she is nothing," Ricoeur asks in his important essay "Narrative Identity," countering postmodern *Subjektkritik* with an appeal to the ineluctable individual responsibility to answer existential questions: "What cannot be abolished is the question, 'who am I'?" (79-80). In "Life in Quest of Narrative," which functions as something of a companion piece to "Narrative Identity," Ricoeur proposes that a "narrative understanding of ourselves" needs to be regarded as "the only kind that escapes the apparent choice between sheer change and absolute identity. Between the two lies narrative identity" (33).

Sheer change and absolute identity: we can read the first term as referring to the elusive, ephemeral play of signifiers and identities invoked in postmodern and poststructuralist critiques of transcendental, unified subjectivity, while the second term calls up what Ricoeur calls the "reductionist" view of personal identity, exemplified in the work of Derek Parfit, which understands life in biological terms. ("Narrative Identity" 76).[39] The latter, Ricoeur argues, is in need of or narrative in

---

38  Regarding Ricoeur's relation to the philosophy of the subject, Slaby and Bernhardt note: "All his life, Ricoeur resists the temptation of joining in the swan song of the subject that is emanating so forcefully, and with astounding consonance, from a choir of structuralists, semioticians, and discourse theorists. At all times, a commitment to a core substance of the personal can be sensed in Ricoeur, an alignment toward an entity that, throughout all the ruptures and mediations, is capable of making promises, and thus to remain morally and ethically responsible" ("Der verblassende Glanz" 3; my translation).

39  We can also read this binary as marking the distance between the position of Descartes (stable, unitary identity) on the on side and Nietzsche and Hume (the "bundle" theory of discontinuous, temporary selves) on the other, as Ricoeur describes it in *Time and Narrative, Vol.3* (246). That being said, given the indebtedness of much postmodern and poststructuralist thought on Nietzschean ideas, I still consider this a valid reading.

order to become a properly "human life" ("Life" 20).[40] In contrast, the biological or reductionist view sacrifices the plurality of narrative meaning for an "impersonal understanding of identity" that takes the physical brain, or the biological body, as "the substitutable equivalent of the human person" ("Narrative Identity" 79).

Certainly, we should distinguish the question of the narrative self from the problem of personal identity, which, as Marya Schechtman has argued, is really a set of two problems, namely that of reidentification, i.e., accounting for the consistence of the identity of a person over time, and that of characterization, i.e., determining the psychological features that make a person who he or she is (1-2). In fact, Schechtman's reidentification-characterization distinction is inscribed into Ricoeur's theory as the difference between *ipse* and *idem*, or "identity as sameness" and "identity as self" ("Narrative Identity" 73). The self, Ricoeur suggests, is not a thing but an "emplotment" ("Life" 21), a narrative gestalt that, while certainly constructed, is being actively produced by the human subject in conjunction with its (cultural, social, and material) environment.

It should come as no surprise that this notion has since attained considerable popularity,[41] for it restores to the subject a measure of the agency that, in the eyes of many, its poststructuralist critics had ruled out.[42] Thus we find Ricoeur's notion of the *pre-narrative quality of human experience*," of "life as a story in its nascent state" ("Life" 29; original emphasis) in Eakin, who transcribes it as the suggestion that "experience itself [...] is already autobiography in the making" and deploys it to create a way out of the freedom-determinism conundrum: "While our narrative self-fashioning is certainly constrained [...] I conclude nonetheless that *we* perform it according to our lights; we get the good of saying and writing who we are" (*Living* 170, 89). Eakin appears here as a paradigmatic example of those theorists of

---

40  See Ricoeur's assertion, later in the same essay, that "[a] life is no more than a biological phenomenon as long as it has not been interpreted" (27). Here we see Ricoeur subscribing to what Galen Strawson calls the "ethical Narrativity thesis," which states that "experiencing or conceiving one's life as a narrative is a good thing; a richly Narrative outlook is essential to a well-lived life, to true or full personhood" ("Against" 428).

41  In his critique of the narrative identity paradigm, Dan Zahavi calls the notion that the self arises out of discursive practices "a popular view" ("Self" 179). Galen Strawson likewise attests to its popularity by observing that the idea that we create or invent the self by narrating it "has come to dominate vast regions of the humanities and human sciences—in psychology, anthropology, philosophy, sociology, political theory, literary studies, religious studies and psychotherapy" ("Tales," n. pag.)

42  On this point, it matters little whether the charge is an accurate representation of the majority of poststructuralist thinkers, which could easily be contested—see, for instance, Foucault's assertion that "it is not power but the subject which is the general theme of my research" ("Subject" 778), or his focus on the "care of oneself" late in his career (*Hermeneutics* 2). What matters is the widespread *impression* that poststructuralism sought to do away with agency, which lead to a plurality of "rescue attempts."

the narrative self who, following in the Ricoeurian mould, try to chart a third way between linguistic construction on the one side and the fundamental *givenness* of subjectivity on the other.[43]

But we also find Ricoeur's influence elsewhere: it can be identified not only in philologically-minded philosophers such as Anthony Paul Kerby, who explicitly states that his *Narrative and the Self* was inspired "by a reading of works by Paul Ricoeur" (1), and Adriana Cavarero, who is "trying to have a dialogue" with the Ricoeurian position regarding the unity of the *"narratable self"* (41; original emphasis), but also in philosophers of mind such as Shaun Gallagher, who works in cognitive science and draws on Ricoeur for "a concept of the self that can account for the findings of the cognitive neurosciences, as well as our own experience of what it is to be a continuous self, discoverable in phenomenological reflection" (20).[44] In such statements, it becomes apparent that narrative and neurological models need not be mutually exclusive. In fact, the idea of the autobiographical self has been widely adopted by the cognitive and neural sciences. We find evidence of this in the work of Daniel Dennett and Antonio Damasio, to name only two of the most frequently cited examples.[45]

## The Narrative Self in Materialist Theories of Consciousness

Working in the philosophy of mind, Daniel Dennett sees no reason why cognitive science should not in principle be able to account for the workings of consciousness in physical terms—a view he bases in large part on an understanding of the self as a narrative construction.[46] Dennett views "narrative selfhood" as a product of the manifold distributed process of information collected by the biological body and processed by the brain. The self, for Dennett, is a not an entity possessing any ontological reality but a *"center of narrative gravity,"* a construct produced by the brain for the evolutionary purposes of coordination and survival (*Consciousness*

---

43  "I tried to steer a middle course," Eakin writes, "between the position that self is an effect of language and a more traditional belief that self is some sort of innate, transcendental endowment, something we are born with, something we just 'have'" (*Living* 65). On the notion of *givenness*, see Zahavi's characterization of the narrative account of the self: "Who I am is not something given, but something evolving, something that is realized through my projects" ("Self" 179).

44  We may add Jerome Bruner here, who in two important works sets forth the significance of narrative models of self- and worldmaking for cognitive science. See Bruner, *Actual* and *Acts*.

45  In the following, I will concentrate more on Damasio, who has been more readily appropriated by theorists of narrative identity.

46  I discuss Dennett in greater detail in my chapter on Richard Powers, who has been influenced by these theories; this outline is merely meant to call attention to Dennett's reliance on narrative models.

418; original emphasis). In this "multiple drafts model," narrative dynamics are of central importance, but it is not the human subject who actively and consciously constructs stories; rather, the sense of subjectivity is itself produced by the "editorial revision" of neural processes. In Dennett's view, while we may be storytelling animals, we are also ourselves stories told by our brains (*Consciousness* 111).[47]

The neurobiologist Antonio Damasio presents a similar picture of a "materialist" self that is principally explainable in terms of biological functions dictated by evolutionary utility. Like Dennett, he delivers an account of the narrative self that makes subjectivity itself the result of "somatic storytelling." The latter occurs in hierarchical stages so that different levels of self can be distinguished and assigned to specific biological functions. "The deep roots for the self, including the elaborate self which encompasses identity and personhood," Damasio writes, "are to be found in the ensemble of brain devices which continuously and nonconsciously maintain the body state within the narrow range and relative stability required for survival. These devices continually represent, nonconsciously, the state of the living body, along its many dimensions" (*Feeling* 22). This is the first and fundamental level, on which the need for homeostasis (maintaining "the body state within the narrow range and relative stability required for survival") leads to the evolutionary development of an apparatus for the self-monitoring and self-control of the organism.[48] Damasio calls this the "proto-self," an unconscious mechanism of neural representation that humans share with all other life forms who need to monitor their internal states and external environment in this way.[49] It is "the connection that guarantees that proper attention is paid to the matters of individual life by creating a *concern*" (*Feeling* 304; original emphasis).

Building on this rudimentary mechanism, the next level is that of the "core self" or core consciousness, the non- or preverbal subject of conscious experience that humans possibly share with reptiles, likely with birds, and certainly with other mammals (*Self* 27). The core self, "a transient entity, ceaselessly re-created for each and every object with which the brain interacts," is the result of a process by which the organism comes to recognize the primordial feelings associated with the fluctuations in its internal bodily states as its own (*Feeling* 17). "The first basis

---

47  Dennett compares the neural spinning of stories to other "natural" productions occurring in the animal kingdom, like the weaving of spiders' nets or the building of beavers' dams (*Consciousness* 414-16).

48  Homeostasis also serves Damasio as an evolutionary explanation for the utility of consciousness, which is "valuable because it introduces a new means of achieving homeostasis. [...] Creatures with consciousness have some advantages over those that do not have consciousness" (*Feeling* 303).

49  Damasio holds that "the conscious mind emerges within the history of life regulation" that can already be attributed to single-cell organisms, which could thus be said to possess proto-selves as well (*Self* 27).

for the conscious you is a feeling which arises in the re-representation of the non-conscious proto-self," Damasio submits, adding that it is this feeling of owner-ship which generates the first *conscious* level of self, already expressed in narrative terms: "The first trick behind consciousness is *the creation of this account*, and its first result is the feeling of knowing" (*Feeling* 172; my emphasis).

It is here that narrative enters the model, for Damasio explains the genera-tion of core consciousness via tropes of narrativity. Assuming the viewpoint of the organism, he writes: "You know you exist because the narrative exhibits you as protagonist in the act of knowing. [...] You know it is *you* seeing because the story depicts a character—you—doing the seeing" (*Feeling* 172; original emphasis). Damasio is at pains to emphasize that these processes are nonlinguistic and that his use of terms like "story" is figural rather than literal.[50] "Better to think of film" than language, he muses at one point, maintaining the underlying notion of nar-rative but shedding its associations with orality and writing (*Feeling* 185). Instead, we are encouraged to think of the storytelling mechanisms of consciousness para-doxically as a "nonverbal narrative of knowing," or "wordless storytelling" (*Feeling* 186, 188). Yet it seems that Damasio cannot do without literary models altogether. In order to distinguish his theory of consciousness from others that require a cen-tral "observer" in the brain, he qualifies his idea about the self-as-story: "The story contained in the images of core consciousness is not told by some clever homuncu-lus. Nor is the story really told by *you* as a self because the core *you* is only born as the story is told, *within the story itself*. You exist as a mental being when primordial stories are being told, and only then." To convey this perplexing idea of the self as an entity coinciding with its observations, Damasio invokes T.S. Eliot: "You are the music while the music lasts" (*Feeling* 191; original emphases).

While tropes of narrativity thus provide Damasio with a suitable model for explicating the proto-self and the core self, it is with the final layer, the "autobi-ographical self," that narrative acquires significance as a conscious rather than an unconscious or preconscious production. Taken together, the proto-self and the core self constitute what Damasio calls the "material me"; the autobiographical self, on the other hand, makes up the "social me" and the "spiritual me" (*Self* 24). Building on the previous two levels, the autobiographical self, or extended con-sciousness, comprises "the organized record of the main aspects of an organism's biography" and is tied to temporality and memory (*Feeling* 18). In organisms with extensive memory capacities, the instances of self-experience that Damasio calls core self accrue and are assigned emotional valence in a process of sedimentation that produces an autobiographical self aware of its past and its possible future

---

50 "I do not mean narrative or story in the sense of putting together words or signs in phrases and sentences. I do mean telling a narrative or story in the sense of creating a nonlanguaged map of logically related events," Damasio explains (*Feeling* 184-85).

(*Feeling* 172-73). However, even at this level, Damasio presents a model of self that is not necessarily linguistic, as evidenced by his speculation that it might not be humans alone who possess both core and autobiographical self.[51]

## Materialist Theories of Consciousness in Theories of the Narrative Self

Damasio thus explicitly positions his model in opposition to theories that regard language as the primary factor for the development of human consciousness and subjectivity. "Language may not be the source of the self," Damasio suggests, "but it certainly is the source of the 'I'" (*Error* 243).[52] In his three-level system, consciousness is still conceived as some form of intentionality, but as the case of the proto-self suggests, this intentionality is pre-conscious; in the case of the core self, it is pre-linguistic. This is a dramatic reconceptualization of subjectivity, a term we usually associate with conscious awareness and linguistic self-consciousness. Eakin is right to note that in performing this reconceptualization, Damasio "radically expands the meaning of *self*, suggesting its deep implication in the life of the organism at every level" (*Living* 67; original emphasis).

It may give us pause that a scholar of autobiography with a vested interest in a conception of the self as a conscious, narrative production would cite Damasio's materialist model, which focuses on the unconscious, somatic constituents of a self understood in neurobiological terms. But Eakin, whose previous studies focused on the socio-cultural foundations of narrative identity, in fact finds a place for Damasio's theory in his latest book, *Living Autobiographically*.[53] Here, and "in the light of research in developmental psychology and neurobiology," he now sees "good reason to pursue the origins of the self before and beneath language"

---

51   "A number of mammals are likely to have both as well, namely wolves, our ape cousins, marine mammals and elephants, cats, and, of course, that off-the-scale species called the domestic dog" (Damasio, *Self* 25).

52   "To be sure," Damasio writes, "memory, intelligent inferences, and language are critical to the generation of what I call the autobiographical self and the process of extended consciousness. Some interpretation of the events that take place in an organism can surely arise after the process of autobiographical self and extended consciousness are in place. But I do not believe consciousness began that way, at that high a level in the hierarchy of cognitive processes and that late in the history of life and of each of us. I propose that the earliest forms of consciousness precede inferences and interpretations—they are part of the biological transition that eventually enables inferences and interpretations" (*Feeling* 18).

53   Eakin had already demonstrated an interest in neurological models of the self in *How Our Lives Become Stories*, but neuroscience has a much more pronounced theoretical function in the later work.

(*Living* 66). One wonders: would such a project not be fundamentally opposed to theories of narrative identity, which, after all, emphasize the intelligibility, coherence, and meaningfulness of narrative self-constructions? That Eakin would answer in the negative illustrates the increasing cross-fertilization between cognitive neuroscience and theories of the narrative self.

Eakin's foray into neurological terrain is ultimately motivated by his belief that selfhood derives from the creation of identity in narrative. If the latter is true, then the status of those who are not (or no longer) able to perform this feat of narrative self-production becomes precarious indeed. What about those living with intellectual disability or mental illness, or, for that matter, those who suffer from brain injury or neurodegenerative disease?[54] Unnerved by the prospect that such biological contingencies might foreclose any possibility of producing and maintaining a self, so that certain groups of persons are deemed effectively "de-selved," Eakin feels obliged to consider "nonnarrative modes of selfhood" (*Living* 30). For this he turns to Damasio's *The Feeling of What Happens*, a book that presents a multi-layered model of psychophysical life in which narrative paradoxically provides the foundation for the pre-linguistic core self.

Narrative is understood here as "a sense-making structure that maps and monitors temporal events" while operating under the threshold of consciousness, a "wordless storytelling" occurring at the physiological level (Eakin, *Living* 76n7). The brain, Damasio says, "inherently represents the structures and states of the organism, and in the course of regulating the organism as it is mandated to do, the brain naturally weaves wordless stories about what happens to an organism immersed in an environment" (*Feeling* 189). As Eakin is right to point out, this global understanding of narrative is "not only wordless but *untold*," since the internal representations of the organism's internal states and its relations to its external environment constitute the very essence of the experience of self (*Living* 75; original emphasis). As outlined above in my presentation of Damasio's theory, in this model the self cannot be separated from the stream of (core) consciousness that produces it; the two are one and the same.[55] In Damasio, narrative once again assumes the status Barthes had awarded it thirty years prior: "Like life itself, it

---

54 "Brain injured individuals may lose their linguistic, mathematic, syllogistic, visuospatial, mnestic, or kinesthetic competencies and still be recognizably the same persons. Individuals who have lost the ability to construct narrative, however, have lost their selves," Young and Saver, proponents of an "inseparable connection between narrativity and personhood," propose in a telling passage (78).

55 Damasio uses the concept of the stream of consciousness with deliberate reference to William James, while also enlisting Locke, Brentano, Kant, and Freud as allies in his approach of treating consciousness as an "inner sense" with the following characteristics: "it is selective; it is continuous; it pertains to objects other than itself; it is personal" (*Feeling* 172).

is there, international, transhistorical, transcultural" ("Structural" 237). Only this time around, it has become biological, material.

If, as already discussed, narrative theories of the self betray a tendency to consider narrativity as a general and universal principle, Damasio's model might be the most extreme form of this argument: here, a biological form of storytelling constitutes the autobiographical self, which would not even exist were it not for the narrative, i.e., temporal ordering mechanisms of the brain. It should become clear by now what appeal neurobiological research holds for theorists of narrative identity. In making narrative even more fundamental than subjectivity itself, theories like Damasio's produce a compatibility of biological knowledge with literary criticism and linguistic conceptions of the self, a move that appears to solve both the question of autobiographical reference and the stubborn problem of first-person, ostensibly extralinguistic, experience. In this regard, Damasio's "wordless storytelling" presents the solution to the "face-off between experiential accounts of the 'I' [...] and deconstructive analyses of the 'I' as illusion" that Eakin described in his previous book (*Our Lives* 4). Suddenly two positions that seemed irreconcilable become congruent: yes, subjectivity is produced in and through language, and yes, subjectivity is a biological reality.

The benefits of this conflation are equally apparent. On the one hand, it spares proponents of the narrative self the inconvenience of denying "nonnarrative" individuals a sense of self. If the narrative impulse constituting the self is already present "in the neurobiological rhythms of consciousness," as Eakin puts it, then conscious expression ceases to be a shibboleth for claims to self-possession (*Living* 79). On the other hand, the discovery of narrative "*beneath* language" (Eakin, *Living* 67; original emphasis), a biological form of narrative coterminous with subjectivity, globalizes the occurrence of self in autobiographical writing as well: "If, in the counterintuitive syntax of consciousness, self inhabits both subject and predicate, narrative as well as character, then autobiography not only delivers metaphors of self; it *is* a metaphor of self" (Eakin, *Living* 78; original emphasis). It is no longer only the I-characters and I-narrators that instantiate subjectivity; instead, the whole of the text becomes a performance of self-production, in the act of writing as much as in the act of reading (Eakin, *Living* 84). For scholars of autobiographical writing this is a somewhat liberating notion, since it frees them from "looking for the real person" in the relevant texts, instead encouraging them to view the text as a whole—including its formal aspects—as expressive of conscious as well as unconscious forms of subjectivity.

Though one might not necessarily need neurobiological theories to arrive at this insight, one notable effect of considering such concepts in autobiographical scholarship is that the "textual" self undergoes an extension and is distributed throughout the text (rather than concentrated in those parts that explicitly name or address the authorial subject) so that it becomes its *function*, just as nerve cells are distributed throughout the brain that, at the same time, they also *constitute*. Another, inverse effect is that a similar extension occurs on the part of the "historical" self: as Eakin writes, "from a neuro-evolutionary perspective, the *bios* of autobiography [...] expands to include the life of the body and especially the nervous system" as it stretches out along the lifetime of the individual (*Lives* 18). A memoir thus no longer needs to be a record of purely "internal" or "mental" motions; it can become a "History of My Nerves," as Siri Hustvedt subtitles her book *The Shaking Woman*. The memoir, previously associated primarily with psychological reflection, thus becomes the neuro-memoir, which chronicles physical states and the acquisition of bodily experience.

Yet it would be mistaken to assume that somatic concerns eclipse interiority and psychology altogether. In fact, it is precisely the new attentiveness to the materiality of mind that gives rise to an imperative of psychological accountability. An expansion of the *bios* in somatic terms has consequences, among them a newfound awareness of the mutability and inconstancy of the self. From the perspective of neurobiology, Eakin notes, "it is fair to say that we are all becoming different persons all the time, we are not who we were; self and memory are emergent, in process, constantly evolving, and both are grounded in the body" ("Lives" 20). But to account for this processuality, it is necessary to record its fluctuations, to interpret them, and doing so requires the ordering and stabilizing powers of what Karl Ameriks calls the "ineliminable subject," with its "various higher kinds of recognitive, reflective, or interpretive intentionality" (226).

Body and *bios*; neurology and narrative: these pairs seem to be linked, and if they appear increasingly reconcilable these days, one reason might be that the implications of certain psychic pathologies point toward the internal continuity of "storytelling" and subjectivity. We can observe this dynamic at work in Eakin's method of invoking neurological theories and psychological case histories to underwrite the centrality of narrative for processes of self-construction: Helen Keller's autobiography demonstrates "the emergence of selfhood that occurs [...] at the moment when language is acquired" (*Fictions* 209-10), while Oliver Sacks's "Mr. Thompson," suffering from Korsakoff's syndrome and unable to make new long-term memories, illustrates how "the self is defined by and transacted in narrative process" (*Lives* 101). If developmental or neurological pathologies interfere with the process of subject-formation, it is implied, selfhood itself becomes tenuous. What is more, neurology points to an inherent tendency on the part of the patient to counteract deficiencies by developing additional, compensatory narratives, to "confabulate."[56] All the more reason, then, to insist on the importance

---

56  Sacks notes that "there is always a reaction, on the part of the affected organism or individual, to restore, to replace, to compensate for and preserve its identity" (quoted in Eakin, *Touching* 189). For the concept of confabulation, see Feinberg and Hirstein.

of narrating the self, Keller's autobiographical narrative of self-development and Sacks's conviction that it is the individual history of a patient where "the physical foundations of the *persona*, the self, are [...] revealed for our study" seem to suggest (*Man* 5).[57]

It seems, then, that somatic individuality and narrative identity are not necessarily at odds with each other; rather, one can bee seen as explicable in terms of the other, even though the question of which one is to serve as the master term is far from settled. The latter is illustrated nicely in an extended discussion between Paul Ricoeur and Jean-Pierre Changeux, published in English as *What Makes Us Think: A Neuroscientist and a Philosopher Argue about Ethics, Human Nature, and the Brain*. Here, Changeux proposes that the narrative self can be subsumed under the notion of consciousness as a biological phenomenon "involving distinct systems of neurons" (134), whereas Ricoeur insists that narrative needs to be understood as a primordial phenomenological process that precedes and in fact encompasses scientific concepts, to the effect that "the notion of the neuronal self is itself a mental construction" (44).

## A Hypothesis

With these two seemingly conflicting positions we have returned to the question of the cerebral subject, an "anthropological figure" elastic enough to incorporate both Changeux's view of the brain as producing the narrative out of which the self is assembled and Ricoeur's view that narrative self-understanding necessarily precedes scientific inquiry. In its double sense of brain-as-subject and subject-as-brain, the concept of the cerebral subject is able to contain both the neural and the narrative understanding of self. The same can be said of the neuro-memoir, which likewise combines a narrative mode of self-production with an inquiry into the biological and neural determinants of subjectivity. If this is the case, then we might view this burgeoning sub-genre of life writing not only as tied to textual subject-formation in the way of all other autobiographical narratives, but, given the neuro-memoir's focus on historically specific and newly emerged clinical pictures, moreover as indicative of "new," or "alternative," or "revised" modes of subjectivity that are characterized precisely by their integration of mental and material (or psychological and biological) aspects of psychic life.

---

57   In keeping with his investment in Damasio's notion of a pre-linguistic self-narrative, Eakin makes sure to qualify that forms of *dysnarrativia*, or narrative disorders, affect not all strata of subjectivity but only the "extended" or autobiographical self (*Lives* 125).

This, then, would be my preliminary thesis: in presenting personal narratives of embodied mental pathologies,[58] neuro-memoirs nonetheless go beyond the realm of individual "character."[59] Instead, by claiming previously underrepresented or misrecognized areas of human experience and subjectivity as legitimate subject positions, they aim to foster more inclusive, less severely policed conceptions of "rational," functional, or otherwise acceptable variants of self, producing new modes and models of subjectivity. My main interest in the following will lie in tracing the revisions of the human subject produced by these texts, in the rhetorical strategies employed to generate these revisions, as well as in the relation between cerebral subjectivities and narrative selves.

Having already coined a neologism to unify this chapter's object of study, I hesitate to further homogenize it by fitting all my textual examples into one discussion. Instead, I will employ a sub-differentiation that yields three pairs of two texts each. In a first step, I will examine two rather straightforward autobiographical accounts of severe, psychiatrically diagnosed mental illness (manic depression and schizophrenia). Next, I will turn my attention to two texts in which minor dysfunctions (shaking fits and phobias) are probed for their biological and psychological origins and investigated for clues about mental functioning as such. Finally, I will read two instructively dissimilar memoirs of drug addiction side by side to inquire into the diverging models of dependency that are available within the biomedical paradigm.[60]

---

58  I use the term "embodied mental pathologies" here to evoke an understanding of psychopathology that always already encompasses the bodily. I have in mind a position resembling Ricoeur's assertion that "the term *mental* is not equivalent to the term *immaterial* in the sense of something noncorporeal. Mental experience implies the corporeal, but in a sense that is irreducible to the objective bodies studied by the natural sciences" (Changeux and Ricoeur 14-15; original emphases).

59  It might be helpful here to think of "character" not in its modern sense as the individual nature of a single person, but rather in the ancient Greek sense of *kharakter*, a term that in Aeschylus' *Suppliants* denoted "the impression stamped on a coin" so that "the notion of the distinctive mark then generates a series of moral equivalents" (Frow 7). The neuro-memoir, I submit, traces a similar arc from individuality to universality.

60  This ordering, in which "conditions" or illnesses are grouped together, is not meant to replicate the sorting mechanisms of medical diagnostics, and thus to generate homogeneity, but on the contrary to direct attention to the diverse ways in which of cerebral subjectivity can be narrativized.

## Kay Redfield Jamison and Elyn R. Saks: Revising Subjectivity

In the early pages of her memoir of manic depression *An Unquiet Mind: A Memoir of Moods and Madness*, Kay Redfield Jamison recounts an educational trip she made at the age of fifteen, before the onset of her illness, before her diagnosis, before she went on to become famous as a "manic-depressive academic psychiatrist" (Porter, *Madness* 83).[61] While volunteering as a "candy striper," Jamison and her fellow nurse's aides are taken on a visit to the local psychiatric hospital. Jamison describes how, en route to their destination, she and the other girls were "giggling and making terribly insensitive schoolgirlish remarks" to mask the fact that they were, in fact, "afraid of the strangeness, of possible violence, and what it would be like to see someone completely out of control" (22). Once inside the wards, "the world of the mad," the following encounter takes place:

> Another patient, who at one time must have been quite beautiful, stood in the middle of the dayroom talking to herself and braiding and unbraiding her long reddish-hair. All the while, she was tracking, with her quick eyes, the movements of anyone who attempted to come anywhere near her. At first I was frightened by her, but I was also intrigued, somehow captivated. I slowly walked toward her. Finally, after standing several feet away from her for a few minutes, I gathered up my nerve to ask her why she was in the hospital. By this time I noticed out of the corner of my eye that all of the other candy stripers were huddled together, talking among themselves, at the far end of the room. I decided to stay put, however; my curiosity had made strong inroads on my fears.
>
> The patient, in the meantime, stared through me for a very long time. Then turning sideways so she would not see me directly, she explained why she was in St. Elizabeths. Her parents, she said, had put a pinball machine inside her head when she was five years old. The red balls told her when she should laugh, the blue ones when she should be silent and keep away from other people; the green balls told her that she should start multiplying by three. Every few days a silver ball would make its way through the pins of the machine. At this point her head turned and she stared at me; I assumed she was checking to see if I was still listening. I was, of course. How could one not? The whole thing was bizarre but riveting. I asked her, What does the silver ball mean? She looked at me intently, and then everything went dead in her eyes. She stared off into space, caught up in some internal world. I never found out what the silver ball meant. (24-25)

---

61  Roy Porter actually misidentifies Jamison here: she is a psychologist, not a psychiatrist. A common mistake, it turns out: Jamison had to correct the same assumption in a response to Oliver Sack's review of her work in the September 25, 2008 issue of the *New York Review of Books*.

Clearly this scene is more than a retelling of Jamison's first encounter with the "world of the mad"; it also contains implicit instructions on how we are to read her book. Written with hindsight by Kay Redfield Jamison, the renowned psychologist specializing in mood disorders, but focalized through the first-person perspective of her teenaged self, the latter serves as a stand-in for the readers of her memoir, who learn from this passage how the former hopes to be read.[62]

Like her 15-year old self, readers might approach a text about severe mental illness expecting strangeness and "someone completely out of control." It is no coincidence that this passage directly follows the retelling of an earlier outing: a trip to the zoo. As if she were standing in front of a yet another caged animal, Jamison remains at a distance, "several feet away" from the female patient, who is described in a way that divests her of humanity and agency. Jameson does not write that the patient "turns her head," as conventional language use would suggest. Instead she writes, "her head turned," as if the woman were an automaton rather than a human being, a mechanical contraption, like the pinball machine she believes to be lodged inside her skull.

Jamison recounts that she was bored at the zoo, but here she is "fascinated," "riveted"—a common reaction evoked by encounters with people suffering from curious and complex disorders.[63] But by itself, such curiosity is a cold, detached form of interest that designates mental illness as radically foreign or "other," a response that is exemplified here by Jamison's fellow candy stripers huddling together, as if to ward off the signs of madness that threaten to impinge upon their "normal" group. Jamison, the odd one out, risks the solitary encounter, thus enabling empathy, imaginary role-taking, and the replacement of a detached third-person perspective with the subjective view: she ends her description of the trip by remembering that faced with the plight of the patients, she "instinctively reached out, and in an odd way understood this pain, never imagining that

---

62 Following René Girard, we can call this narratorial stance, which characterizes all autobiographical writing, a *dual perspective*. Girard distinguishes between "the pre-conversion and the post-conversion perspective," so that texts operating in this mode are "written from both ends at the same time" (272). While Girard applies this notion primarily to the novel, it clearly translates well to autobiography—after all, Girard develops the concept out of his reading of the autobiographically inflected Proust cycle and notes Augustine's *Confessions* as a prime example. Alternatively, one might also make sense of the two temporally distinct "speaking positions" in the light of Benveniste's disjunction between the *sujet de l'énonciation*—the speaking subject— and the *sujet de l'énoncé*—the subject spoken of (223-30). See also Wright on the distinction between the "ontological" and the "rhetorical" self in the dual perspective of autobiography (46) as well as chapter 1 of Barros.

63 Case in point: a prominently placed *Entertainment Weekly* blurb on the cover of my paperback edition of Saks's book proclaims, "Her descriptions of her descents into psychosis are riveting."

I would someday look into the mirror and see their sadness and insanity in my own eyes" (25).

Obviously, this last statement expresses the author's hope that readers of her memoir might bring a similar degree of empathic interest to their efforts to understand her experience. The image of looking into the mirror and seeing "their sadness and insanity" in one's own eyes foreshadows Jamison's imminent struggle with manic depression, but it also functions as a trope for the process of reading a first-person account of mental illness. If Jamison the teenager doubles as the figure of the reader in this passage, Jamison the author presents a model of her implied ideal reader that culminates in a scene of specular recognition. Looking into the mirror of memoir, it is implied, her readers are to temporarily and imaginarily inhabit the subject position of the author. They are called on to empathize, to cease to be spectators of otherness, like the visitors at a zoo, and to enter instead into a foreign subjectivity, with the ultimate aim of learning and familiarization. For this is the crucial difference between Jamison at fifteen and her readers: the latter are given a chance to find out "what the silver ball means."

Revealing the "world of the mad" as a divergent yet acceptable variation of human subjectivity rather than a realm of chaotic and frightening otherness is one of Jamison's key objectives. "We are all [...] differently organized," she proposes; "We each move within the restraints of our temperament" (210). Elsewhere, she writes, "We all build internal sea walls to keep at bay the sadness of life and the often overwhelming forces within our minds" (214), or: "We all move uneasily within our restraints" (109). In these instances, Jamison uses the repeated invocation of the collective "we" or "we all" as a rhetorical device to emphasize a sense of continuity and commonality between "normal" and "pathological" subjectivities.[64] In the words of Elyn Saks, whose book *The Center Cannot Hold: My Journey through Madness* is noticeably influenced by Jamison's memoir, "it turns out that we all overlap with one another a little bit" (284).[65]

---

64  See also Martin, who voices her hope that in analogy to the reappropriation of the term *gay*, "the word 'crazy' could come to mark the way that everyone belongs in one way or another—even if only in their dreams—to the realm of the irrational" (*Bipolar* xix).

65  "It would be hard to exaggerate the impact of Jamison's work," Emily Martin observes, and Elyn Saks's memoir of living with schizophrenia is one example where its impact is clearly visible (*Bipolar* 23). There is not enough space here for a detailed account of Jamison's influence on Saks; suffice it to mention that both books invoke "madness" in their titles, and that Saks adopts both Jamison's chronological and dramatic structure (from childhood to adult illness to acceptance and recovery) and many of Jamison's rhetorical gestures, such as avowals of gratitude (to friends, family and doctors) and expressions of hope for the work's impact on those suffering from a similar diagnosis as well as those whose professional lives may be jeopardized by owning up their illness.

Such appeals to a shared humanity are not only meant to destabilize the duality of sick and healthy, but also to develop new, or alternative, models of subjectivity whose appeal goes beyond the pathological to the universal. I would argue that this is a common concern of all the neuro-memoirs I discuss here: by providing autobiographical accounts that combine first-person phenomenology with third-person descriptions that draw on medical and scientific knowledge, by calling into question the autonomy of the self, and by challenging the consensus on who counts as a rational person, they extend or redefine what we take a subject to be. Thus Saks's book, a record of her struggles with schizophrenia, is memorable for how it presents her illness as both an obstacle and an inspiration to her career as a law professor, so that her "madness" functions not as the opposite of rationality but as one of its driving forces.

It is no coincidence that these interventions occur within the genre of the memoir. Formally, autobiographical writing is particularly well suited to projects of self-understanding, self-production, and self-transformation, while historically, it has often been deployed to promote the recognition of the subjecthood of previously silent or silenced individuals.[66] One scholar of autobiography has remarked that a key function of contemplative first-person memoir is that it "opens the door from a private sensibility to a general psychology" (Buckley viii). This is an apt description of the neuro-memoir, which characteristically begins by investigating singular pathology, but ends by redefining subjectivity per se. This redefinition, I submit, is effected by strategically deploying the potential of the autobiographical form. That formal conventionality plays an important role in making the case for social acceptance in both Jamison and Saks—a point I argue in the following—suggests *control* as a crucial topos of the neuro-memoir.

## Jamison and Saks: Control

In her ethnographic study of the social and symbolic status of manic depression in U.S. culture, the anthropologist Emily Martin, herself diagnosed as bipolar, states that when she began to suffer from psychotic hallucinations during the writing of her previous book, she felt "trapped, frightened, and out of control" (*Bipolar* xv). I would like to focus on the last of these three terms and suggest *control* as a key term for the neuro-memoir.[67] All of the authors discussed in this chapter describe loss or lack of control as their fundamental pragmatic problem, which then gives

---

66  Here we need only think of the slave narrative, of "collaborative autobiographies" like *Black Elk Speaks*, or of the autobiography of Helen Keller.

67  Recall also Jamison's remark that what she and her fellow nurse's aides expected to see on their visit to the mental hospital was "someone completely out of control."

rise to reflections on the philosophical implications of this issue, and it is the regaining of self-control in some form or other that leads to the conclusion of their narratives. This should come as no surprise as under the new materialist paradigm, agency partly shifts from the ego to neural and somatic processes, with the subject left to confront and manage this partial loss of its responsibilities.[68] Thus Jamison reflects on how advances in brain scanning and imaging technologies might be helpful in "convincing some of my more literary and skeptical patients that (a) there is a brain, (b) their moods are related to their brains, and (c) there may be specific brain-damaging effects of going off their medications" (197), while Saks remarks, "My brain was the instrument of my success and my pride, but it also carried all the tools for my destruction" (245). There is a clear separation here between self and brain. Even when the organic basis for mental operations is pondered, the two are still viewed as "sufficiently separate," as suggested by Burton (15). One implication is that brain and self are linked in a relation of susceptibility and vulnerability, so that the burden of managing one's brain falls at the feet of the individual subject. Both Jamison and Saks note that a crucial first step toward managing their conditions was to acknowledge they suffered from a "disease" or illness that was ontologically distinct from their selves (Jamison 91; Saks 244).[69] Notably, in both accounts, this control of neurochemistry and control of behavior is also tied to *narrative control*.

Given that Jamison and Saks have to deal with the terrifying experience of psychosis, with "loss of one's self," (Jamison 40) and with the difficulty of producing a reliable, manageable, and socially shared reality while depending on an "unpredictable brain" (Saks 244), their memoirs adhere to a fairly conventional and surprisingly orderly pattern. Both accounts follow a roughly linear chronology and contain a clearly discernible narrative arc that leads from the onset of illness to the struggle with its effects and the efforts to understand them, onward to a moment when they become manageable. The authors, we take it, have attained a degree of stability and sanity that allows them to reflect on their problems and present them in a coherent narrative. In both books, this moment is figured as primarily characterized by *acceptance*. Ironically, it is precisely the volatile characteristics of cerebral subjectivity as these authors understand it that lead to these extremely well ordered and highly controlled narrative self-productions.

Neuro-memoirs ponder the possibility that the self, including our most heartfelt convictions and concerns, might be contingent on brain chemistry. When

---

68    As discussed in my introduction.

69    The adoption of the disease model of mental illness by Jamison and Saks is not unproblematic: "As references to it multiply [...] it becomes equated with an immutable biological entity," psychoanalyst Darian Leader cautions (87).

Jamison describes her manic episodes, she emphasizes the extent to which they appear to transform her very personality:

> My normal Brooks Brothers conservatism would go by the board; my hemlines would go up, my neckline down, and I would enjoy the sensuality of my youth. [...] I also would become immersed in a variety of political and social causes that included everything from campus antiwar activities to slightly more idiosyncratic zealotries, such as protesting cosmetic firms that killed turtles in order to manufacture and sell beauty products. (42)

While we might take umbrage at the suggestion that sensuality, political activism, and animal welfare are the province of the lunatic,[70] we understand what it is that Jamison implies here. If personality and behavior are dependent on brain states, then we would do well to reconceptualize subjectivity as contingent upon biology, as open to potentially radical change, and as amenable to material intervention and manipulation. The cerebral subjectivity we encounter in these texts can thus be characterized as susceptible, vulnerable, and mutable. These characteristics are described as resulting directly from the brain's biology: both Jamison and Saks leave no doubt that their conditions are best understood as diseases that are genetic in origin and organic in nature.[71] As has been widely noted, the disease model of mental illness exteriorizes the respective condition and decreases personal responsibility.[72] In accordance with this tendency, both Jamison and Saks describe how they had to learn to accept the exteriority of their conditions and the powerlessness and lack of control that came along with it—a process triggered, not insignificantly, by their experiences with psychotropic medication—before being able to regain a satisfactory degree of control over their lives.

Jamison believes her reluctance to manage her manic-depressive illness with lithium stemmed in part "from a fundamental denial that what I had was a real disease. [...] Moods are such an essential part of the substance of one's life, of one's notion of oneself, that even psychotic extremes [...] somehow can be seen as temporary, even understandable" (91). Likewise, Saks remembers wondering, "Who was I, at my core? Was I primarily a schizophrenic? Did that illness define me? Or

---

70  Leader points out that this "idiosyncratic zealotry" is in fact quite common in bipolar conditions, which are characterized by a distinctly altruistic grammar in the manic stages: "The arc in mania includes this aim to protect another person, which can then extend to charitable or benevolent acts and projects, such as animal welfare or environmental preservation" (45).

71  See, for instance, Saks's description of schizophrenia as "a brain disease which entails a profound loss of connection to reality" (168), or Jamison's insistence on "[t]he fact that manic-depressive illness is a genetic disease" (188).

72  For a cogent discussion of this issue, see Tanya Luhrmann's chapter on "Madness and Moral Responsibility" in Of Two Minds, her anthropological study of American psychiatry.

was it an 'accident' of being—and only peripheral to me rather than the 'essence' of me?" (255). Like Jamison, Saks struggles continuously to accept her need for medication, believing for a long time, "if I could figure it out, I could conquer it. My problem was not that I was crazy; it was that I was weak" (167). It takes an excruciating number of failed attempts for Saks to take antipsychotic medication continuously and to accept what her psychiatrist tells her: "You need to accept that you have an illness and need to take medicine to control it" (276). In these narratives, viewing pathology as integral rather than external to oneself is presented as a dangerous mistake that obstructs the way to recovery, whereas accepting the "accidental" nature, the contingency of mental illness becomes a crucial prerequisite to controlling it.

In a telling contrast to postmodern celebrations of mental illness, particularly schizophrenia, as liberation from ego-identity and the strictures of capitalist society,[73] Jamison and Saks figure the relation between self-control and the lack thereof as an opposition between authentic and inauthentic selves. Like William Styron before her, Jamison thinks of her illness as a "darkness," and observes, "however lodged within my mind and soul the darkness became, it almost seemed an outside force that was at war with my natural self" (15). And Saks writes, "More than anything, I wanted to be healthy and whole; I wanted to exist in the world as my authentic self" (245). Therein lies the problem, "because mental illness involves your mind and your core self as well," so that access to this nexus of personality is barred (Saks 255). Here, a concomitant effect of biomedicalization—viewing mental illness primarily as an organic disease—seems to be the naturalization of the "healthy" self, which is granted ontological priority over the "sick" self, while mental illness, in accordance with the disease model, is imagined as invading and eroding the very nucleus of one's authentic subjectivity. Where the former is characterized by agency and the ability to control its behavior, the latter is powerless, divested of conscious control. Saks even outlines three conflicting identities—"One me was Elyn, one me was Professor Saks, and the third me was 'the Lady of the Charts'–the person who was a mental patient"—and recounts thinking, "If I could just exert control over my wayward brain, my mission to dissolve the Lady of the Charts would not fail" (263, 275).

If regaining control over one's "wayward brain" involves psychotropic medication, it also, in Jamison's and Saks's accounts, involves narrative mastery. After all, both texts are presented as productions of the authors' "natural" or "authentic" selves, and their acquiescence to regimes of medication and treatment is presented as conditional on modes of narrative integration. "My temperament,

---

73  See Deleuze and Guattari's account of the "stroll of the schizo," in which "the self and the non-self, outside and inside, no longer have any meaning whatsoever" (2). See also Woods for an overview of the ways in which schizophrenia has been appropriated by cultural theory.

moods, and illness clearly, and deeply, affected the relationships I had with others and the fabric of my work," Jamison writes, "[b]ut my moods were themselves powerfully shaped by the same relationships and work" (88). Saks, for her part, credits the psychoanalytic process with enabling her to view her psychosis as more than a mere accident of neurological malfunctioning. Her analyst, she writes, "helps me to understand how I sometimes use my psychotic thoughts to avoid the ordinary bad feelings that everyone experiences—sadness, rage, garden-variety disappointments. [...] he tries to understand my psychotic thoughts as unconsciously motivated and meaningful (which of course they are)" (324-25). Both Jamison and Saks, then, transform contingency by imbuing it with narrative significance, and it is this process of assigning social and personal meaning to the accidents of biology that ultimately accounts for the production of subjectivity in their autobiographical texts.

This dialectical relation between biological contingency and narrative integration flies in the face of the widespread assumption that psychiatric symptoms become essentially meaningless once they are understood in biological or neurological terms. In a survey of critical accounts of the state of American psychiatry, Louis Menand finds little to recommend the disease model of mental illness, particularly because it gives short thrift to the question of meaning:

> A fever is not a disease; it's a symptom of disease, and the disease, not the symptom, is what medicine seeks to cure. Is depression—insomnia, irritability, lack of energy, loss of libido, and so on—like a fever or like a disease? Do patients complain of these symptoms because they have contracted the neurological equivalent of an infection? Or do the accompanying mental states (thoughts that my existence is pointless, nobody loves me, etc.) have real meaning? If people feel depressed because they have a disease in their brains, then there is no reason to pay much attention to their tales of woe, and medication is the most sensible way to cure them. ("Head Case," n. pag.)

Menand's dichotomous distinction between subjective mental states, which have "real meaning," and objectively diagnosable diseases, which do not, is one that neither Jamison nor Saks would subscribe to. Both understand themselves as suffering from a disease, and both credit this realization to their experiences with psychotropic drugs, which they see as an indispensable precondition for managing their conditions.[74] But contrary to Menand's assumption that a materialist view

---

74  Jamison makes sure to begin her narrative by acknowledging that lithium "saved my life and restored my sanity" (2), while Saks places the dramatic impact of the right medication at the end of her memoir: Placed on a new regime of Zyprexa, she writes, "The most profound effect of the new drug was to convince me, once and for all, that I actually had a real illness. For twenty

of psychopathology entails favoring pharmaceutical intervention at the expense of other avenues of therapy, both Jamison and Saks also speak highly of psychoanalytic practice: Jamison, who considers her training in dynamic psychotherapy "invaluable," states that she has "never been able to fathom the often unnecessarily arbitrary distinctions between 'biological' psychiatry, which emphasizes medical causes and treatments of mental illness, and the 'dynamic' psychologies, which focus more on early developmental issues, personality structure, conflict and motivation, and unconscious thought" (59-60). Like Jamison, Saks, too, places a premium on the combined benefits of the psychodynamic and the biomedical approaches: "While medication had kept me alive, it had been psychoanalysis that had helped me find a life worth living," she concludes (298).

As "an illness that is biological in its origins, yet one that feels psychological in the experience of it," severe psychiatric illness is more than an organic phenomenon that subsides when medicated correctly (Jamison 6). To quote Menand again:

> Mental disorders sit at the intersection of three distinct fields. They are biological conditions, since they correspond to changes in the body. They are also psychological conditions, since they are experienced cognitively and emotionally—they are part of our conscious life. And they have moral significance, since they involve us in matters such as personal agency and responsibility, social norms and values, and character, and these all vary as cultures vary. ("Head Case," n. pag.)

Like Menand's presentation of mental disorders as overdetermined phenomena that can appear in the frameworks of different "fields," Jamison's and Saks's neuro-memoirs reject a simple either/or structure, and emphasize the interplay between narrative and cerebral subjectivity. While the contingency of mental illness—which is understood here *initially* as an external force—needs to be accepted and treated with medication, it nonetheless also calls for narrative integration, modeled on psychoanalytic practice, to establish an internal, personal meaning of how the illness fits into the life story written by the "authentic" or "natural" self. In both texts, this is the final step that needs to be taken before the mature self that is simultaneously the end point and the author of the autobiographical narrative can emerge:[75] what has been perceived as either displacing the "true" self or as

---

years, I'd struggled with that acceptance, coming right up to it on some days, backing away from it on most others. The clarity that Zyprexa gave me knocked down my last remaining argument" (304).

75  "As a text of a life, autobiography presents the 'before' and 'after' of individual who have undergone transformations of some kind," Barros submits (1). The transformation that interests me most here is not the change from "sick" to "cured" but from character to author, a transformation in which the drama of subjectivization is performed in exemplary fashion: this is what had to happen to me for me to become who I am.

external to it needs to become internalized through the mechanisms of narrative. Toward the end of *An Unquiet Mind*, Jamison writes:

> I long ago abandoned the notion of a life without storms, or a world without dry and killing seasons. Life is too complicated, too constantly changing, to be anything but what it is. And I am, by nature, too mercurial to be anything but deeply wary of the grave unnaturalness involved in any attempt to exert too much control over essentially uncontrollable forces. There will always be propelling, disturbing elements, and they will be there until, as Lowell put it, the watch is taken from the wrist. (213-14)

For Jamison, in the end, controlling her condition means relinquishing control, and accepting, through narrative understanding, her "mercurial nature," the product of biological contingency. Saks paints a similar picture. "Ironically, the more I accepted I had a mental illness, the less the illness defined me" she states; and we find her echoing Jamison's rhetoric of resignation when she writes: "My life today is not without its troubles. I have a major mental illness. I will never fully recover from schizophrenia. I will always have good days and bad, and I still get sick. But the treatment I have received has allowed me a life I consider wonderfully worth living" (304, 334).

One way to describe the relation between the cerebral or somatic self and the autobiographical or narrative self in these texts would thus be to say that the latter is deployed in order to bring the former under control, to tame its excesses and integrate its destabilizing aspects into a stable, coherent production of subjectivity. Both narratives begin in childhood (the traditional setting of all manners of psychoanalytic *Urszenen*), then go on to present memorable depictions of the phenomenology of brain dysfunction, and finally culminate in the achievement of a new synthesis that could only be reached through the experience that preceded it. If "normality" is an awkward term for this new synthesis, which has come to include the pathological instead of displacing it altogether, it is perhaps more aptly described by adopting Ricoeur's notion of "felicitous function" (Changeux and Ricoeur 49).

Yet in their adherence to a highly conventional and formalized model of autobiography as a "narrative of transformation,"[76] and in their eventual attaining of a felicitous state that enables them to live, love, work, and write within "normal" or socially accepted boundaries, Jamison and Saks put forward texts—and subjectivities—that betray a curious amount of control in the face of that which cannot be controlled. The reason for this, I argue, is to be found less in the attempt to produce a portrait of pathology that is as "true to life" as possible than in a stra-

---

76 See Barros.

tegically deployed rhetoric of conventionality that aims at creating social acceptance for new subject positions.[77] Even though there is no need to doubt that they
were written with a sense of personal as well as political urgency, or to question
whether textual and historical subjects are as congruent as the "autobiographical
pact"[78] demands it, we should read these texts not only as personal testimonies,
but also as strategic rhetorical interventions into public discourse about mental
illness.

To an extent, the authors themselves suggest we do so. Jamison mentions
those who, "because of a lack of information, poor medical advice, stigma, or fear
of personal and professional reprisals" may fail to seek treatment, and describes
herself as "tired of hiding, tired of misspent and knotted energies, tired of the
hypocrisy, and tired of acting as if I have something to hide" (6-7). Saks likewise
voices a hope that her story might "help implode some myths held by many mental
health professionals as well as the general public" and that shedding light on her
experience might "lessen the social stigma by reducing fear and hostility" (347).
This language clearly is expressive of a quest for recognition, which needs to be
considered when trying to make sense of the formal characteristics of these texts.

As I have been suggesting, the unobtrusive conventionality of these narratives
serves a distinct purpose: it is a useful rhetorical form for memoirists of mental dysfunction who wish to be read not as case studies that arouse only medical
curiosity, but as competent chroniclers and communicators of their own experiences who can make claims on the behalf of previously misrecognized subjects.
This is particularly important for Jamison and Saks, who live with diagnoses that
threaten to call their mental competency into question,[79] a constant danger that,
as Mary Elene Wood suggests, memoirists of mental illness "must contend with
and *write against*" (1; my emphasis). By producing highly ordered, clearly written,
and formally conventional autobiographical texts, Jamison and Saks signal that
despite their illnesses, they are rational authors, and, more importantly, account-
able human subjects whose interiority does not diverge too dramatically from
that of their readers. Emily Martin argues that those living under the descrip-

---

77  This notion dovetails with Eakin's understanding of autobiographical writing as "not merely as
the passive, transparent record of an already completed self but rather as an integral and often
decisive phase of the drama of self-definition" (*Fictions* 226).

78  See Lejeune. See also chapter 1 of Eakin, *Living*, for a discussion of the "ethical implications of
narrative identity" (x).

79  "In the popular cultural view," Mary Elene Wood reminds us, "schizophrenia means madness
and madness invokes any number of images and associations, including raving lunacy, incoher-
ence, homelessness, violence, isolation, pitifulness, staring catatonia, out-of-control sexuality,
wild laughter, babbling speech, and just plain meaninglessness" (1). More succinctly, Emily Martin states, "Being known as a manic-depressive person throws one's rationality into question"
(*Bipolar* 5).

tion of mental illness are capable of *performing* their conditions in strategic ways, and that performance "provides a way, in actions as well as words, for people cast into the category of the irrational to comment *on* their putative 'irrationality.' In so doing, they demonstrate that they *are* rational" (*Bipolar* 59; original emphases). I propose that we should regard Jamison's and Saks's texts precisely as such performances of rationality, control, and self-formation. Their "journey into madness" (Saks) culminates in the production of the "present, 'normal' self" that has been narrating the journey (Jamison 92). In retrospect, the turmoil of psychopathology becomes "a necessary stage for development" the autobiographical subject needs to pass through to become a "full-fledged self" (Saks 282).

Mental illness, Martin claims, is "a threat to the conception of American personhood that has prevailed for centuries: a person with a central controlling principle based on the will, who is owner of himself and acts out of individual intention and desire toward rational ends" (*Bipolar* 269). In the hands of Jamison and Saks, the neuro-memoir is deployed to defuse this threat through a performance of narrative mastery signaling self-control. For them, as for their readers, the "ability to articulate an identity narrative [...] confirms the possession of a working identity" (Eakin, "Introduction" 6). In their memoirs, we see the striving for narrative integration and social acceptance winning out over a more immediate, experimental, or untidy representation of mental illness. For good reason, then, mental disorder never translates to narrative disorder in either account.

## Siri Hustvedt and Allen Shawn: Integrating Mind and Matter

In *An Unquiet Mind* and *The Center Cannot Hold*, occasioned by a lack or loss of control, biological contingency becomes controllable through narrative integration. We see the same dynamic at work in two other recent neuro-memoirs that also devise new forms of subjectivity capable of reconciling both psychodynamic and materialist models of self, but do so with a different approach. Whereas Jamison's and Saks's books are, to an extent, the products of expert knowledge,[80] Allen Shawn's *Wish I Could Be There: Notes from a Phobic Life* and Siri Hustvedt's *The Shaking Woman, or A History of My Nerves* represent laypersons' attempts to make sense of their embodied afflictions in the light of psychological and psychoanalytical as well as neurological and biological discourses. Both are artists—Hustvedt is an essayist and novelist; Shawn is a composer and writer—and both have ventured far into scholarly terrain for their memoirs, producing hybrid texts that combine

---

80  Jamison is a renowned specialist for mood disorders and co-author of a reference work on manic-depressive illness; Saks, specializing in mental health law, is the Orrin B. Evans Professor of Law, Psychology, and Psychiatry and the Behavioral Sciences at USC.

autobiographical reflection with excursions into scientific, medical, and philosophical knowledge.

The loss of control that triggers the autobiographical narrative occurs gradually in Shawn's case, and suddenly in Hustvedt's. *Wish I Could Be There* presents the
cumulative tally of an adult life spent grappling with agoraphobia. Allen Shawn,
the son of longtime *New Yorker* editor William Shawn, has produced a book that
is genealogical in a double sense: it traces both Shawn's family history as a possible source of his personal dispositions and the phylogenetic past of humankind
as an explanation of phobia as a biological phenomenon. Accordingly, Shawn
informs us that he has written "not a conventional memoir" but rather chroni-
cled "a search" into the nature of phobia, which occurs on two levels: "*internal*, into
my own personal past, and *external*, into regions of science and psychology" (ix-
x; my emphasis). Such parallel description of subjective and objective or internal
and external phenomena is a crucial characteristic of the neuro-memoir, which
attempts to integrate the "third-person" knowledge of science and medicine with
the first-person narration of subjective experience. We will encounter it again as a
major conceptual and structuring device in the next section.

In contrast to Lewis's genealogical approach, *The Shaking Woman* is the story of
a singular personal event. The book chronicles Hustvedt's attempts to understand
a mysterious shaking fit that seized her as she delivered a speech in memory of her
recently deceased father. She is able to finish her speech, since curiously enough,
the episode affects her whole body but spares her head: "From the chin up, I was
my familiar self. From the neck down, I was a shuddering stranger" (7).[81] Hustvedt
decides to go in search of the "shaking woman," as she calls this other, unfamiliar
part of herself. The book recounts what she learns about the mind/body problem
as she consults the relevant literature and the relevant specialists, covering areas
from the history of hysteria and psychiatry to current research in neuroscience.
As initial questions such as "what is psychic and what is somatic?" or "Is a psyche
different from a brain?" attest, Hustvedt simultaneously frames her search for the
shaking woman as a quest for the nature of the embodied self (15-16). This ambition to extract a general truth from personal reflection is something Hustvedt
shares with Shawn, who describes himself as "a layman trying to grasp the origins,
*both personal and universal*, of his own predicament" (x; my emphasis). Rather than
a personal memoir focusing on the subject of phobias, what his book is "actually

---

81  Hustvedt points out that after the initial event, the problem resurfaced at other speaking en-
    gagements as well. That she at no point had to cancel a performance would perhaps not exactly
    suffice to argue against David Harvey's claim that that under capitalism sickness is defined as
    the inability to work, but it does point toward the persistence of the notion of pathology as the
    disturbance of normal function. See Harvey, "Accumulation."

about," Shawn writes, is "a search for understanding the origins of [...] the flaws of being human" (x).

While this may sound like outlining the features of some universal *conditio humana*, I would argue that Hustvedt and Shawn's aim transcends the merely descriptive. Their neuro-memoirs do not only record or represent an ontology of the self; instead, they seek to develop alternative accounts, and in doing so, they issue appeals for epistemological and social transformation. Having summarized neurological research on autoscopic hallucinations, during which migraineurs or epileptics see their doubles as if they were separate persons, Hustvedt proposes that what "these stories indicate" is that "any conception of the self as unitary might be subject to revision"—a revision undertaken, to be sure, by herself, over the course of her memoir (49). Shawn makes this aspiration to reconceptualize subjectivity even more explicit: "I mean to challenge our assumptions about what a normal person is," he announces in his foreword (xi).

There are two things to point out here. First, as academically trained writers, Hustvedt and Shawn likely are aware that the imperative of revising the picture of a unitary, autonomous, fully conscious, responsible and active self as constituting baseline normality is not exactly news, at least in the humanities.[82] However, it is one thing to reiterate this truism by appealing to tried-and-tested patron saints of progressive *Subjektkritik*, like Nietzsche, Derrida, or Foucault, and another to base it on psychopathology and contemporary research in neuroscience, not least because the mechanisms of legitimation differ so dramatically.[83] This leads us to the second point, which is that in making their personal histories into a platform for generalized claims about subjectivity as such, Shawn and Hustvedt adopt the neurological method of deducing general function from its morbid distortion.[84] This is indicative of a larger tendency inherent in the neuro-memoirs I am consid-

---

82  Hustvedt holds a PhD. in English from Columbia University; Shawn is on the faculty of Bennington College and has published a scholarly study of Arnold Schönberg.

83  This difference notwithstanding, the parallels between the twentieth-century philosophy of the subject (and its critiques) and current-day debates about the implications of neuroscientific research for human freedom, already remarked upon in my introduction, remain of central interest to my study.

84  "By teasing apart the normal operations of the human brain, [...] neurological disease provides a unique entry into the fortified citadel of the human brain and mind" (Damasio, *Spinoza* 5). Famous examples include Roger Sperry and Michael Gazzaniga's experiments with split-brain patients, which yielded the paradigm of hemispheric specialization, and V.S. Ramachandran's work on phantom limbs, which demonstrated how lower level brain processes can "trump" conscious cognition. One might of course also point to the ways in which neurological pathology has inspired philosophical work, for instance in Merleau-Ponty's reflections on the Schneider case in *The Phenomenology of Perception*, which demonstrates for him the importance of the intentional arc and the body schema.

ering here, all of which extract universality from pathology in one way or another. This epistemic jump results partly from emphasizing the contiguity of health and sickness, and partly from the internal dynamic peculiar to a form of autobiographical writing that projects a stable, coherent self as endpoint and (prospective) author of its own (retrospective) medical history.

"At one time or another all of us go to pieces, and it isn't necessarily a bad thing," Hustvedt writes, emphasizing the generative power of "disunity" (80-81). How we break down individually and cease to function as an organic whole, it is implied, can tell us something about the psyche and its embodiment. Hustvedt begins with an incident in her life, an embodied event that is then examined from a number of different angles, but in the process she arrives at more universal insights: "Subjectivity is not the story of a stable, absolute 'I' that marches through life making one conscious decision after another. It is not a disembodied brain machine either, genetically preprogrammed to act in specified and predictable ways" (89). The trajectory runs from a pragmatic problem (loss of control) to a philosophical project (revision of subjectivity), and in the two views Hustvedt rejects here—the autonomous subject of liberalism on the one side and a mechanistic, computational model on the other—we can glimpse the middle ground she wants to stake out: a notion of the self as neither completely free nor wholly determined, and one that takes into account consciousness as well as corporeality.

Shawn advances a similar conception in his memoir. "To discuss phobias takes us both into the realm of physiology and into the realm of personal history," he announces, since "to describe the [phobic] reaction as simply a mental phenomenon is misleading." Instead, it needs to be understood as a "habitual response of both body and mind" (4-5). As far as the original impetus leading to the composition of these texts is concerned, this seems to be the crux of the matter: both Hustvedt and Shawn have come face to face with an embodied phenomenon that cannot be fully attributed to either end of the mind-body spectrum, which renders their experience not only problematic on a pragmatic level (how best to combat phobia—with medication or psychotherapy?) but also intellectually interesting (what is the relation between body and mind?).[85] Under the guise of the personal memoir, Hustvedt's and Shawn's books are, in fact, contemporary accounts of the mind-body problem.

What marks these accounts as *contemporary* is a pervasive sense that we need to account for physiology if we are to gain an accurate picture of the self, that materialist perspectives have a role to play in considerations of subjectivity, and

---

85  "In a sense it is a trivial problem," Shawn writes, "merely an inconvenient personality trait. [...] But as I have worked on the problem, I have found it more and more intriguing" (xvi). Likewise, Hustvedt observes that as she delved deeper into the topic, "[w]hat began with curiosity about the mystery of my own nervous system had developed into an overriding passion" (6).

that they might have been neglected in the recent past. "We need to remember that we are creatures," Shawn proposes, and it is the Darwinian notion that "at every moment our bodies and minds are perpetuating behaviors refined over millions of years" that leads him to review neuroscientific research on the emotions to better understand his condition (46-47). A Freudian analyst, Hustvedt writes, would understand her symptoms as signs of repression, and "he wouldn't spend much time worrying about my brain," but a psychiatrist she eventually sees considers her problem a form of panic disorder, and prescribes lorazepam, whose effectiveness she renders in prosaic terms: "I took the pill. I didn't shake" (31). Despite her sympathies for Freud—in fact *The Shaking Woman* is nothing if not an impassioned argument for the continual relevance of psychoanalytic thought and psychodynamic concepts—Hustvedt is also keenly aware that we ignore materiality and corporeality at our own peril. Noting the "recent fashion for social construction," she observes, "sometimes the intense focus on the social turns humans into floating busts." Questioning whether such a focus can account for the totality of embodied phenomena, Hustvedt notes that while it is "of course, socially constructed, [...] from another perspective, birth is a physical event that is always fundamentally the same" (183-84).

The key word here is *perspective*, for in making room in their texts for neurology and evolutionary biology, Shawn and Hustvedt do not simply flee the camp of the psychologists to join that of the new materialists. Rather, both authors are at pains to emphasize the need for complementary perspectives to make sense of inherently overdetermined phenomena. "A phobia is clearly a constellation of interconnected components: physiology, thoughts, feelings, behavior. These enmeshed elements are not easily untangled," Shawn cautions (92), so just as Hustvedt refuses to regard her shaking fit as nothing but repression, or nothing but a brain event, phobia becomes a complex condition that is best approached via multiple avenues. Here we see Ortega and Vidal's "coexistence of ontologies" at work. "Disciplinary lenses inevitably inform perception," and consequently, "a single paroxysmal event might be construed differently, depending on your field of expertise" (Hustvedt 28). No wonder Hustvedt believes that in order to understand the shaking woman, one "cannot be satisfied with looking at her through a single window" but has to "see her from every angle" (73), or that Shawn assumes "we are working our way toward a new definition of psychology" that would include materialist discourses like "behavior, genetics, neurology, physiology, and evolution" in a modernized understanding of the mind (250).

Acknowledging overdetermination means one can no longer acquiesce to reductionism. For Shawn, therefore, "knowing the mechanics of the brain doesn't preclude the continued need for theories of the 'mind'" (Shawn 173). Rather, what we see in Shawn's and Hustvedt's neuro-memoirs are attempts to think "mechanics of the brain" in conjunction with theories of mental function. In the process, what has often been criticized as Freudian psychologism is retroactively afforded a neurobiological support. Freud, described by the authors as "a materialist all his life" who was "fascinated by neurons" (Hustvedt 18, 20) and "never thought that psychology began and ended in exclusively mental activity" (Shawn 24), is thus brought in line with current-day brain research. Thus Shawn can claim that "Freud's view that the first five years are the crucial ones in determining personality [...] is compatible with our current understanding of brain development" (69), and Hustvedt can find it "striking how well Freud's distinction between the visuo-spatial and the audioverbal tallies with research gleaned from split-brain patients" (60). One wonders, though, whether the calls for a new psychology or an updated understanding of the self are adequately answered by holding fast to psychoanalysis and simply declaring the "new unconscious" of the brain sciences compatible with its older, Freudian version.[86]

One reason to question this overhaul is that the symbolic mechanisms of the Freudian unconscious cannot easily be reconciled with the physiological reactions implicated in the materialist unconscious posited by evolutionary psychology and neuroscience. "Associations and memories are so deeply, neurologically, physically encoded in us that they trigger physiological responses before the conscious mind is aware," Shawn suggests in an attempt to account for the difficulty of avoiding phobic reactions (61). But surely this is an altogether different dynamic than repressing Oedipal guilt or developing a hysterical symptom. Just because Freud "discovered" the unconscious (a problematic assumption in itself),[87] we are not justified in describing any and all unconscious processes as, in effect, anticipated by psychoanalysis. In fact, if one wishes to connect such automatic, physiological processes with symbolic significance, it may make more sense to invoke phenomenology, as Hustvedt does when she writes that we "respond to what is beyond our own bodies with feeling that is *prereflective, an embodied meaning*" (196; my emphasis).

If in Hustvedt and Shawn the unconscious becomes somatized, one of the more intriguing and persuasive aspects of this somatization is the abolition of a putative opposition between biographical meaning and neurobiological function. That one needs to choose between neurochemistry, which empties symptoms of meaning, and a consideration of the life story, which insists on the significance

---

86  In a typical phrase, Shawn writes, "As Freud predicted, the brain, and so consciousness, operates on many different levels simultaneously," thus making Freud into a precursor (and indeed visionary) of contemporary brain science (61). For the idea of the "new unconscious," see my introduction.

87  For a discussion of Freud's indebtedness to earlier formulations of the unconscious, see Ellenberger; for a presentation of the roots of the concept in nineteenth-century German thought, see Angus & Lebscher as well as Ffytche; for general histories of the concept, see F. Tallis.

and function of symptomatology, is a recurrent idea in discussions of biological psychiatry and other new materialist discourses.[88] In contrast to this rather
simplistic view, in which symptoms are either redolent with meaning or utterly
devoid of it, Shawn and Hustvedt consider the ways in which something can be
"all in your head" and entirely organic at the same time. Both the physical and
the mental, Shawn writes, "are registered in the same organ, the brain," but only
because the brain can be described in material terms, this does not mean we can
privilege one over the other. Our brains are "molded and formed by what occurs
to us and are changed by our histories, including the histories of our thoughts and
feelings," so that inside (subjectivity and feeling) and outside (actions and behaviors) can no longer be separated in a meaningful way (Shawn 24). This neurological
description of habituation and learning, is, of course, nothing else but the notion
of neuroplasticity, the ability of the brain to fashion new neural connections, and
to prune or modify already existing ones. Hustvedt also picks up on this, noting
that brains are "plastic and adaptive to changed circumstances" (54).

Viewing the brain not as a material object that causes mental functions but
as implicated in a "continuous loop" (Shawn 24) that is both productive of and
shaped by embodied experience unsettles the dichotomies of inside-outside and
mental-physical that Hustvedt and Shawn consider as an obstacle to understanding their overdetermined situations. As Oliver Sacks, whom both authors invoke,
phrases it, "the individual nervous system, as it reflects the life experience of each
individual human being [...] adapts, is tailored, evolves, so that experience, will,
sensibility, moral sense, and all that one would call personality or soul becomes
engraved" in it ("Neurology" 49). Such a view also entails personal responsibility. While the sheer complexity of the organism's cellular organization makes it
impossible at this stage of neurological knowledge to exert complete control over
one's "soul" (to use Sacks's term), the notion that experience, thought and feeling
become embodied in the nervous system assigns individuals a degree of agency
in shaping their selves. "Just as our faces, our hands, our skin, our hearts, and
our lungs reflect our habits, so do our brains," so that "what we do, feel, and live
through is what we become" (Shawn 70). Since, to varying degrees, we have a say
in the development of our habits of thought and action, the idea is that we can
modify them, thus changing those elusive beings we call our selves. The relation
of this notion to the responsibility and accountability implicit in the idea of the
cerebral subject should be readily apparent.

But until this process becomes less mystical (the term "soul" is a fitting one
in this context), the role one plays in fashioning this continuous loop of embodied, habitualized subjectivity is perhaps best expressed in Judith Butler's concept

---

88  See Luhrmann, as well as the contribution by Louis Menand quoted in the preceding section on
    Jamison and Saks.

of "giving an account of oneself," which simultaneously emphasizes the ethical imperative of reflecting on one's subjectivity and agency and the impossibility of achieving complete self-transparency while doing so.[89] This, at any rate, is what Shawn and Hustvedt imply. Both stress that we should not neglect the role of the body and the brain, but both also point out that matter cannot exhaustively explain mind, so that consequently, self-reflection and self-interpretation remain of vital importance. The materialist discourses mobilized in their neuro-memoirs help neither author to arrive at an conclusive, incontrovertible explanation of their conditions. While final causes thus remain elusive, both Hustvedt and Shawn manage in the end to reduce contingency and increase control by deploying the notion of embodiment and its concomitant destabilization of the inside-outside dichotomy toward the end of narrative integration.

Both texts begin with the problem of a somatic situation gone haywire, which results in a loss of control as well as the formulation of problematic dualistic descriptions: when Shawn says of the phobic reaction that "the mind races to pin a logical explanation on the body's panic" (3), does this not neglect the likeliness that "the mind" also had a role to play in triggering the reaction in the first place? The sequential model of temporal succession might be ill equipped to describe this embodied event. Temporality is also a problem in Hustvedt's observation that the shaking woman "felt like me and not like me at the same time," only here it is synchronicity, the coincidence of "familiar self" and "shuddering stranger" in the same body at the same time, that causes the confusion, bringing to mind the idea of possession by "some external power" (7-8). Mind and brain, inside and outside: in both cases a dualistic construction presents itself both as the only way to describe an experience and as a grossly insufficient way to do so. It is this unsatisfactory state of affairs as much as the actual experience of dysfunction that prompts the composition of these narratives, which become charged with the hope that they might afford a more suitable mode of description. Even if full recovery remains elusive, this hope is fulfilled in the end; it is precisely through the reintegration of previously irreconcilable elements that dualism can yield to holism and the auto-biographical self can accept its simultaneous existence as a "cerebral subject."

At several points throughout his book, Shawn encounters the impossibility of separating genetic, biological, developmental, social, and cultural factors in the description of phobia. In the end he comes to the conclusion that such a separation might not be necessary after all, but this conclusion is only made possible by invoking the neurological concept of plasticity. Realizing over the course of his memoir that a key biographical factor in the genesis of his agoraphobia was the experience of having an autistic sister, whom his parents sent off to an institution,

89  Butler claims that the "I," in reflecting upon its nature, "will find that his self is already implicated in a social temporality that exceeds its own capacities for narration" (*Account* 8).

Shawn draws on a neural metaphor to describe the ways this relation has left its mark on him. "Psychologists call the bonding of early relationships imprinting," Shawn tells us, a term he takes to mean that "[t]he formative people in your life are in your cells" (241). One feels reminded here of the notion of the subject as an effect of differential relations to others, which Chris Lundberg identifies as a key assumption of what he calls "'post' accounts of the subject" (330). And in fact Shawn performs a curious double movement that both decenters the subject theoretically and unifies it narratively. By adopting the notion of a nervous system indistinguishable from one's self, his memoir attests to the development of a revised vocabulary of subjectivity, in which the distinction between inside and outside, self and other, or brain and mind matters less than one's ability to integrate the two, in imagination and narrative. It is fitting, then, that the text ends with Shawn in the bathtub, noticing "my sense of being myself, a small creature in a tub of water," considering the sheer wonder of perception, of "consciousness of the world directly outside the window, and then the world beyond that, and the world beyond that, and the immensities, the dark immensities beyond all these worlds" (252). Here, for the first time, this thought appears not as a frightening prospect but as a promise for the integration of inside (consciousness) and outside (the world beyond).

Integration is no less important for Hustvedt. Her memoir also traces a gradually growing insight into the importance of incorporating what might only *seem* external. "It is a question of ownership, of me and mine," Hustvedt realizes, and "cutting the inside of a person (the neurological and the psychological) off from what is outside him (other people, language, the world) is artificial" (196, 186). She recounts that the key to managing her migraine has been understanding that "[t]he headache is me," and suspects, "Perhaps the trick will now be to integrate the shaking woman as well, and acknowledge that she, too, is part of myself" (174). This, however, cannot be achieved as a feat of pure ratiocination. Such an integration can only take the form of a "new configuration," one that "includes both knowing and feeling" (197). An act of embodiment, appropriation, incorporation has to take place, and Hustvedt suggests that this act is synonymous with the writing of her memoir. But how can the process of narration perform this function, if, as Hustvedt writes, "telling is not enough"? How do we get from intellectualization to incorporation?

For Hustvedt, the key lies in the characteristics of writing and memory. She invokes the Platonic view of writing as a "memory tool," but combines it with the neurological notion of memory as continuous invention rather than storage and retrieval (68).[90] Memory and imagination are related processes, which makes

---

90  By emphasizing its creative and constructive nature, recent research in cognitive neuroscience challenges the established model of memory as a triadic process involving encoding, storage,

autobiographical writing a form of self-production rather than self-representa-tion.[91] For Hustvedt, automatic writing, which bypasses conscious composition, demonstrates that this process of self-production is never wholly deliberate; rather it includes "semantic, procedural, and episodic memories" and can bring to light unconscious emotions (61). Commenting on Crick's "astonishing hypothesis" that "you [...] are, in fact, no more than the behavior of a vast assembly of nerve cells and their associated molecules," Hustvedt draws a telling comparison between the relation of media and meaning and the relation between brain and self:

> Would anyone deny that Tolstoy's "The Death of Ivan Ilyich" is paper and ink or that Giorgione's *The Tempest* is canvas and paint? And yet, how far does that get us in expressing what these works are? Am I wrong in feeling that 'a vast assembly of nerve cells' is an inadequate description of *me* or that those words fail to answer the question, What happened to me? (116-17; original emphasis)

Taken seriously, Hustvedt's analogy means that the subject "embodied" in the autobiographical text stands in the same relation to its material conditions of existence as the self to the brain. *Pace* Paul de Man, Hustvedt ascribes an ontologi-cal quality to the textual subject, so it should come as no surprise that in her mem-oir, it can also fulfill some of the functions of an "actual" subject. This is why what Hustvedt writes at the end of her book about an (imagined) veteran of the First World War recovering from a trauma also applies to herself, as both her memoir's textual subject and its author:

> he sees a change, a new configuration of his consciousness that includes both knowing and feeling. He retells the story, and in the retelling, which is also reinven-tion, he feels the undercurrents and rhythms of his body. He makes the wrenching loss his own in an act of creative memory; it becomes part of his narrative self. And there are neuronal changes in his brain accordingly, in the limbic emotional sys-tems and the prefrontal executive areas. (197-98)

As in Shawn's account, self and brain become integrated, only here it is a more overtly literary act of "creative memory." Mind and matter become one in an act of embodiment: the act of writing, of telling, which changes the neural as well as the

---

and retrieval. In this view, which supports ideas first advanced by Frederic Bartlett in the 1930s, memory is "not a literal reproduction of the past, but rather is a constructive process in which bits and pieces of information from various sources are pulled together" (Schacter and Addis 773).

91 Memories, Hustvedt paraphrases neuroscientific research on the topic (see above note), "are not only kept, *consolidated* in memory, they are re-kept, *reconsolidated*" (108; original emphases).

psychic configuration of the teller. Thus, cerebral subject and "narrative self" are reconciled, and Hustvedt's neuro-memoir can end with a final, integrative speech act. Referring back to the beginning of her book and thereby completing a "continuous loop" not only of mind and body but also of memory and (self-) invention, Hustvedt writes:

> In May of 2006, I stood outside under a cloudless blue sky and started to speak about my father, who had been dead for over two years. As soon as I opened my mouth, I began to shake violently. I shook that day and I shook again on other days. I am the shaking woman. (199)

With this avowal, what has seemed like "some external power" has been accepted, incorporated into a "new configuration," and, in a sense, tamed. In the best psychoanalytical tradition, Hustvedt's condition has become manageable, *livable* for her by virtue of having been addressed and worked through, but, as we have see, this process had a twist to it: it needed to include neuroscientific research as well as biographical narrative, and it needed to take seriously the prerogative of the body just as much as that of the psyche.

## Marc Lewis and Michael W. Clune: Addiction and Agency

In the last section of this chapter, I offer a reading of two recent memoirs of addiction, which has been transformed into a paradigmatic medical-materialist condition in the twentieth century.[92] Widely understood these days as a public health issue, if not an outright organic "disease," addiction effectively unsettles the binary mind-body relation by substantiating the view that material manipulation has drastic effects on human subjectivity, so that the self cannot be understood to exist in neat separation from its biological and chemical substrates. Furthermore, the embodied experience of addiction is often described as one of severe identity crisis, in which the all-encompassing, visceral craving for the substance or activity in question runs counter to the addict's vital interests as a person, giving rise to questions about agency, psychic conflict, the status of the "authentic" self, and the problem of weakness of the will. Yet even our small sample size of two texts

---

92  In the eighteenth and nineteenth centuries, addiction was overwhelmingly viewed as *akrasia*, or weakness of the will, and as a sign of immorality: Benjamin Rush still described alcoholism as a "palsy of the will" (qtd. in Valverde 2). In the twentieth century, this view has gradually been replaced by one that understands addiction as a biomedical (rather than a metaphysical or psychological) disease and entertains important cross-linkages with the aforementioned disease model of mental illness.

will reveal that autobiographical writing that deploys materialist discourses and ideas to convey the dynamics of addiction is by no means a homogenous field, and that the notion of substance abuse as a biochemical intervention into the body's nervous system can be made to underwrite very different projects whose aims are contingent upon the respective author's interests and persuasions. To bring out this illustrative difference, I will not discuss the two texts conjointly, as in the last sections, but successively, so that the second text, Michael Clune's *White Out*, can serve as something of a limit case for the neuro-memoir and, in its role as an outlier, shed some additional light on the characteristics of the texts discussed in this chapter.

## Marc Lewis: Learning, Inside and Out

But first, I would like to turn to Marc Lewis's *Memoirs of an Addicted Brain*,[93] in which, as the subtitle informs us, *A Neuroscientist Examines his Former Life on Drugs*. If *integration*—of body and mind, of inside and outside, of symptom and meaning—has emerged over the course of this chapter as a leitmotif of the neuro-memoir, then *Memoirs of an Addicted Brain* certainly adds to this impression. In the introduction, Lewis claims that as a "drug addict turned neuroscientist," he is uniquely qualified to provide an account of the problem of addiction "from inside out and outside in," by using his biography "as a springboard to the addicted brain" (1).[94] Neuroscience is to be regarded as the master discourse of addiction, Lewis implies, since drugs "talk to the brain in its own language—the language of dopamine and peptides, neuromodulators and receptors" (2). However, as a language of description, it "doesn't go all the way," Lewis adds, "because it ignores *the actual experiences*" of addiction (2; my emphasis). Lewis's neuro-memoir sets out to fill this gap: "This book brings the brain and human experience together, by telling the story of my descent into drug addiction, interspersed with lessons on the brain and its workings drawn from contemporary neuroscience" (2).

Right from the beginning, then, the author positions his text as work of synthesis, announcing an integration of objective scientific description and reported subjective experience. On the one side, the visible and experimentally testable anatomy and function of the nervous system; on the other, the rendering of, in Joan Didion's words, "*How it felt to me*," widely regarded as the linchpin of first-person writing (134; original emphasis). One way to read the book, then, is as a spir-

---

93  This is the second book in my corpus that bills itself as a memoir not of the author but of his or her physiology: as already noted above, Hustvedt subtitled her book *A History of My Nerves*.

94  We are reminded here of Shawn's attempt, cited in the previous section, to reconcile "internal" and "external" descriptions of phobia.

ited attempt to overcome the subject-object problem.[95] This is not to say that Lewis attempts to bridge the infamous "explanatory gap" between the materialist outlook of modern science and the problem of qualia (subjective, conscious perceptions and feelings); his aim remains limited to the neural mechanisms involved in substance abuse.[96] This restriction in scope entails a dissection of the mental into discrete sets of cerebral functions, processes, and parts, a process of differentiation that Lewis also adopts as a structuring principle for his memoir: "Each chapter introduces a new drug experience, or a new stage of drug addiction, as the central theme of an episode from my own life [...]. Each of these experiences is shown to emerge from a particular brain system, neurochemical flow, or synaptic process" (3). Modularity thus becomes the supreme organizing principle of both brain and book.

This strict imposition of correlation, in which biographical and brain events are made to correspond rather neatly, is both somewhat questionable, since multiple systems, flows and processes are likely to be involved in any given "drug experience" or "stage of addiction," and highly schematic, resulting in some repetitiveness. Each chapter reenacts a similar script, in which Lewis's experiences provide the occasion to recapitulate yet again the beholdenness of mind to brain, and of brain to experience. A substance is ingested, a neural process triggered, a behavior elicited, a scientific explanation delivered. In the process, Lewis's original project of accounting for drug addiction occasionally gives way to more global pronouncements. The proposition that "brain change" corresponds to "mood change," or that the frontal cortex acts "on our behalf" are, for obvious reasons, well suited to explain some of the central problems of addictive behavior, but they lead inevitably to the notion that the brain is the true site of our ontological occurrence: "This is home. Not the changing landscape of people and events around us. No, this electrical sea is where we really live" (21, 63, 23).

Readers may be excused, then, for seeing in Lewis first and foremost a reductionist who seeks to rid psychological experience of its cultural and social contexts by disassembling it into its cellular and molecular components and describing them exclusively in materialist terms. Such an impression is particularly warranted for the reason that Lewis does not limit his neurochemical explanations to

---

95  The subject-object problem is an age-old philosophical problem, as attested by Cassirer, who traces it back to Descartes and the transition from Renaissance to modern philosophy (123), but has seen a number of "updates" throughout the centuries, including the recent one in which subjectivity itself is brought into a relation with neural processes. The problem then becomes that "[e]pistemically, the mind is determined by mental states, which are accessible in First-Person Perspective. In contrast, the brain, as characterized by neuronal states, can be accessed in Third-Person Perspective" (Northoff 5).

96  For the concept of the explanatory gap, see Levine, who provided the initial account of the problem that later commentators like Dennett and Chalmers continue to reference.

addiction, but extends them beyond his purported subject to include an ever-increasing host of other phenomena. Thus it is not enough for him to develop a biological version of the problem of weakness of the will, in which the exhaustion of neurotransmitters in the dorsal anterior cingulated cortex (dACC) during acts of willed self-control and conscious choice accounts for the psychological problem of "ego fatigue," and explains why addicts "lose the mental muscle tone for self-direction, for resolve, for strength of character, and for decency itself" (246-47).[97] Enlarging the focus to include other activities involving reward systems and goal-oriented behavior (but sustaining the muscular metaphor), Lewis sees the "isometric tension of wanting" at work not only in drug abuse, but also in one's family relations, romantic attachments, and professional career (61).[98]

The central role afforded to neurotransmitters in this account can be traced back to its author's disciplinary specialization. As a developmental neuroscientist, Lewis has done extensive research on the neural mechanism underlying emotional regulation, an area in which neurochemistry is regarded as particularly relevant. This is representative of a general tendency of recent "brain books" that attempt to account for the self in materialist terms: the author's area of expertise is likely to be presented as the one that affords the best approach for understanding subjectivity. In Lewis's book, neurotransmitters are the crucial components of brain activity, determining what we call the self by regulating mood, emotion, and behavior; whereas in the work of a neurobiologist like Damasio, the significance of these chemical messengers is vastly subordinate to larger physiological dynamics involving every level of the organism.

Owing to the author's research background, then, brain chemicals are presented here as the very stuff of life. Lewis is particularly enamored with dopamine,[99] which he lauds as "both high-octane and renewable, so evolution decreed that almost everything to do with action requires dopamine," but opioids are granted almost equal significance as the molecules responsible for social attachment as well as the "relaxation and warmth" of inner contentment (64, 253). "Mother's milk contains opioids, which seems a kind of original sin when it comes to drug addiction," Lewis observes, and while there is no reason to object to the

---

97  Lewis describes the dACC as "in charge of choice, self-monitoring, and the resolution of conflicting goals. The dACC is where context and judgment come together to create the will, that beam of self-direction that makes it possible to choose consciously and act morally" (244).

98  In a section on how the brain manufactures "meaning" from "sense," Lewis notes, "We learn meaning from the earliest weeks and months of life—the goodness and safety of our mother's arms—until it starts to stabilize in adolescence and early adulthood, into that classic quest for love, admiration, and success" (35).

99  Lewis singles out dopamine for good reason, as addiction specialist Gabor Maté acknowledges: "To write about the biology of addiction one must write about dopamine, a key brain chemical 'messenger' that plays a central role in all forms of addiction" (151).

general suggestion that pleasurable substances have a role to play in the development of the human organism, which processes all such substances in similar ways, the more reductive and speculative claim that babies "love opioids, and presumably their mothers, because of the feeling of warmth and safety produced by these molecules" is sure to send up a red flag for many readers (133).

However, to dismiss his book as exemplary of the worst tendencies of "neuro-reductionism" (Martin, "Talking Back"), and to understand his rush to conflate mothers with molecules as an attempt to displace the former with the latter, would be to caricature rather than critique Lewis's neuro-memoir. His interest in the ontogenetic origins of embodied adult subjectivity actually point toward the central concept of his autobiographical-cum-scientific narrative, a concept that, when examined closely, puts the lie to the book's reductionist tendencies and opens what initially seems like a narrow neurological perspective up to social, cultural, and linguistic dimensions. The concept in question is *learning*, and if its internal linkages to related concepts like plasticity and habit are not already apparent by now, Lewis's memoir renders them explicit. "It makes evolutionary sense that anything that feels good should become the target of goal-seeking," he writes, and when "liking and wanting" become linked, neural and chemical pathways in the brain are altered, making it more likely that the associated patterns of thought and behavior are repeated in the future: a habit is formed (135).[100] The synaptic plasticity involved in this process "really just means the capacity to learn," Lewis notes (35), so that "the slippery slope, the repetition compulsion, that constitutes addiction" can be understood, quite simply, as "a form of learning gone bad" (135).

In this view, addiction constitutes a perversion of a fundamental process of human life. "If the brain did not form habits, if synapses didn't adjust to new events and *remain* adjusted, then we would have no memories, no skills, no biases, no knowledge," Lewis points out. In evolutionary terms, the "habit forming machine" of the brain is a necessary adaptation, but it harbors the inherent risk of excess (155; original emphasis). This is why Lewis also describes the counterproductive learning process of addiction as "a basic vulnerability of the nervous system," aligning his account with other voices that have recently presented a model of the self as inherently susceptible, vulnerable, and open to intervention (3).[101] Yet

---

100  Lewis emphasizes that while this process is at work in all manners of activities, such as playing the piano (155), in addiction, this "neural sculpting" is one of narrowing options: "more repetition, less flexibility; more habit, less choice" (227-28).

101  Here one would have to include critical sociologists like Nikolas Rose, who traces "the emergence of an idea of the susceptible somatic individual" ("Anomalies" 411) as well as theorists of subjectivity like Judith Butler, who submits that "the disposition of ourselves outside ourselves" follows "from the bodily life, from its vulnerability and its exposure" ("Violence" 25).

unlike Jamison and Saks, who link the organic aspect of psychopathology to the disease model of mental illness, Lewis argues that despite its implication in brain function, addiction is, emphatically, not a disease. Rather, it is a developmental process, a pattern of thought and behavior that has become habitualized but can also be unlearned.[102] Since this implies a shift from neural to social, embodied, and psychological learning, this idea represents the fulcrum on which Lewis can perform a turn from the biological to the narrative.

As a learned behavior, a mechanism for manipulating emotional states and fulfilling emotional needs, addiction is inextricably tied to the addict's cultural world and social relations. Thus, a key moment occurs when Lewis first gets drunk as a teenager, an experience that he recalls as yielding a crucial insight: "I had learned that my brain was accessible, mutable" (26). To be sure, drinking alcohol involves chemical changes in the brain, which are dutifully described by Lewis, but the learning that takes place here is as much psychological as neural. In accordance with his developmental view of addiction, Lewis presents his proneness to intoxication as a coping mechanism, generated in defiance toward societal and parental authority and in reaction to a scary, uncontrollable world.[103] The "secret of changing how you *feel*" comes to represent a "safety valve, en escape hatch, a way out" (21, 26; original emphasis). Paradoxically, the very mechanism that has Lewis spinning out of control and turning, against his better judgment, into an habitual liar and thief, has its origins in a search for control.

Here we have clearly entered the realm of psychological, narrative meaning, as exemplified by Lewis's avowal, phrased in the language of dynamic psychology, that one aspect of his drug habit was compensatory, that "self-destruction paid off some of my guilt" (269). That his *Memoirs of an Addicted Brain* operate with the assumptions of social psychology as much as with those of neuroscience becomes even more apparent when Lewis turns to the phenomenon of inner, or "imagined" voices. Far from an exclusively pathological condition only afflicting schizophrenics, the experience of hearing one or more internal voices has been said to constitute a central aspect of thinking and self-reflection,[104] and Lewis's description of the phenomenon revolves around its simultaneously neural and narrative character:

---

102  Lewis has announced a comprehensive presentation of this theory in his upcoming book *The Biology of Desire*.

103  Lewis recounts his experience of being sent to boarding school, where he is bullied, as one of extreme unmooring: "There was no safety in my world, no home, no peace" (17).

104  Daniel Dennett has notably argued that that much of our conscious thinking is "a variety of a particularly efficient and private talking to oneself" ("Everyone" 472). This view is also popular in cognitive science; Robert Cummins and Martin Roth trace it back to Plato (182).

So the critical, scolding voices we "hear" are interpretations formed by the OFC—recurring messages of rejection, betrayal, and isolation, based on associations nested in the amygdala and seasoned by a dozen different brain parts. It may not take very much—just a rendition of "oops, I did it again" to start the meaning machine, to get it up and running. And this meaning then recruits all kinds of specifics to bear on our wrongdoing. You *always* do this because you're *weak* or *bad* or *selfish*. That makes sense. That's a coherent story, quickly fleshed out in the prefrontal circuits with the help of more limbic input. But it doesn't come from any specific speaker. It's just an elaborate monologue activated by one or two associations. (276-77; original emphases)

Needless to say, these associations need to originate somewhere, as does the language of the interpretations formed by the OFC (orbitofrontal cortex). That this process of fashioning a "coherent story" is not exclusively cerebral but also inherently social is clarified by Lewis's comments in a newspaper article about his book:

When you're a kid and you're four or five years old, you feel shame when your parents shame you. It's pretty straightforward. When they say something like 'I told you nine times not to do that' or 'you're being selfish,' we feel shame, we hang our heads, we try not to do that thing. [...] Where does it come from, the shame, after you've grown up? No one is actually saying things to you any more, but I think you internalize the parent. (qtd. in Brown, n. pag.)

Internalization of social relations, we take it, is what accounts for all the "kinds of specifics" that ultimately provide the *content* of one's internal voices.[105] This amounts to another way of saying, as Shawn did, that "[t]he formative people in your life are in your cells," their voices in your brain. It seems that we are approximating here a neuroscientific reformulation of the Lacanian view of the subject as underwritten by the "discourse of the Other" and constituted by language.[106] But in Lewis, this socially generated and psychically internalized language is not exclusively an instrument of alienation; it can also provide an avenue into authenticity and recovery. As his "efforts to stop continued to diversify, through psychotherapy, journal writing, meditation, talking with friends"—all practices of a narrative, psychological, and social nature—Lewis reaches a point at which internal voices pronounce the end of his ordeal (291). "But something has shifted

---

105  In Lewis's example, the ubiquity of the guilt motif in the respective "content" reminds one of Richard Gloucester's soliloquy in Shakespeare's *Richard III*: "My conscience hath a thousand several tongues / And every tongue brings in a several tale / And every tale condemns me for a villain" (5.5.147-49).

106  "Man speaks therefore, but it is because the symbol has made him man" (Lacan 39).

momentarily," Lewis notes as he sits weeping at the kitchen table. "A voice—one of my voices—sounded like it was on my side." The voice tells him, "I deserve a chance to live," and it is validated, significantly, by an internal response ascribed to a significant other: "The words of a past therapist float up from underground: 'The strongest thing an existentialist can say is *no*'" (294; original emphasis). It is this internal dialogue that finally leads to Lewis's breakthrough and the epiphany that he can simply reject drugs "every hour of every day" (295).

Despite Lewis's avowal of a resolute materialism, then, his rejection of the disease model, his focus on learning (both in its neural and psychological aspects), and his portrayal of a plastic, susceptible self, developing its habits and its internal voices in response to and in conjunction with its social context, produce an account that proves significantly less "brain-centered" than its title suggests. Like Hustvedt's and Shawn's memoirs, Lewis's book is at its core an appeal for an integration of the meanings produced in embodied social existence and the empirically determinable facts about the functioning of the human nervous system.[107] Thus Lewis's claim that "the mind parallels the brain," that "the biological laws of synaptic sculpting and neurochemical enhancement [...] are what constrict the addict's mind, his behavior, his hopes, his dreams" (228) is effectively countered by his own closing remarks:

> The sculpting of synapses in my early twenties is irrevocable. The meaning of drugs, the imagined value they represent, is still inscribed on my orbitofrontal cortex; and a resonant flair of dopamine can still be ignited in my ventral striatum, at least to some degree. These are the conditions of my nervous system, and they are not reversible. As is well know in the addiction lore, there is no final cure, just recovery, abstention, and self-awareness. But there are happy endings. Mine is a happy ending. (300-301)

Abstention and self-awareness: in affirming the individual's responsibility for his susceptible nervous system, Lewis stumbles onto the "secret opening for mind to rise up over matter" that he assumed not to exist earlier in his memoir (228). If addiction is merely a perverted form of learning, and it can be escaped, as his memoir attests, by forming new habits, new or stronger social attachments, psychological insights, and new narratives, the degree to which an addict needs to be regarded as at the mercy of his "addicted brain" can never be total.

---

107  See also Lewis's remark that "you can think of that in terms of the gradual shaping of thought through experience, or you can think of it at the brain level, in terms of synaptic wiring, and the formation of stable synaptic networks in the brain. It's the same thing, really" (qtd. in Brown, n. pag.).

## Michael W. Clune: The Futility of Attempting to Forget the Self

Michael Clune prefaces his addiction memoir *White Out: The Secret Life of Heroin* with two epigraphs. One is attributed to renowned neuropsychiatrist Steven Hyman, formerly Director of the National Institute of Mental Health (NIMH) and Provost of Harvard University; the other to 13th-century Buddhist teacher Dogen, pioneer of Zen meditation in Japan. Hyman is quoted from one of his scholarly articles, in which he states that addiction "represents a pathological usurpation of the neural mechanisms of learning and memory." The Dogen quotation is taken from his fascicle "Genjōkōan," and reads, "To study the self is to forget the self." Taken together, the two epigraphs announce the similarities as well as the discontinuities between Clune's text and the other neuro-memoirs I have been discussing here.

After Allen Shawn's reflections on phobia as a psychological maladaptation and Marc Lewis's conception of "learning gone bad," Hyman's description of addiction as "a pathological usurpation of the neural mechanisms of learning and memory" strikes a familiar chord. As we will see, Clune, too, engages with the notion of addiction as a disease, though he largely divests the concept of its biomedical content, preferring instead to use it metaphorically and to emphasize the aspect of memory over that of learning. Likewise, the saying by Dogen introduces a concern with subjectivity before the memoir proper even begins; the mere fact of its inclusion implies that the phenomenon of addiction can provide insight into the nature of the self. However, the Humean notion[108] that self-study or introspection, which stands in an obvious relation to autobiographical writing, actually leads to the dissolution of the very entity it presupposes alerts us to the possibility that Clune's account might prove dissimilar from the previously discussed texts, which emphasized narrative integration and the production of a coherent, stable sense of self and authorship. As we will see, in *White Out* the modifications of the "neural mechanisms of learning and memory" in addiction and recovery give rise to deeply conflicting urges of affirming and rejecting the self.

In his twenties, Michael Clune, now an associate professor of English at Case Western and author of two scholarly monographs, was a graduate student and a heroin addict. In his memoir, he presents an account of drug addiction that can rightly be called phenomenological, for its interest in temporality and perception, as well as poetic, for its virtuosic use of motif and metaphor. Unlike Lewis, Clune

---

108  David Hume famously observed that when he turned his attention inward in search of his self, it was nowhere to be found: "I never can catch *myself* at any time without a perception, and never can observe any thing but the perception." He allowed that others might feel differently, but was assured of his own essential selflessness: "I am certain there is no such principle in me" (165; original emphasis).

spends no time positioning, framing, or introducing his recollections; instead his memoir begins in medias res, in a summer in Baltimore in the mid-nineties, with an avowal of morbidity: "My past is infected. I have a memory disease. It grips me through what I remember" (1). This statement is followed by the recollection of a visit to a local acquaintance and small-time drug dealer after a sobriety period of six-months. The OxyContin tablets Clune hoped to buy as a heroin substitute turn out to be unavailable; instead, he lays eyes on a half empty heroin vial with a white stopper, which, like Proust's madeleine, launches an involuntary memory cascade. It is the whiteness that does it: "You might think that the whiteness of the white tops isn't that important. [...] But the first stuff I ever did was in a vial with a white top, and its whiteness showed me the dope's magic secret." This secret, and the drug's power, Clune elaborates, "comes from the first time you do it," but it is altogether unlike nostalgia; it is not a yearning for something in the past (5). Rather, the issue is one of recurring presence:

> The addict's problem is that something that happened a long time ago never goes away. To me, the white tops are still as new and fresh as the first time. It is still the first time in the white of the white tops. There's a deep rip in my memory.
> Dope never gets old for addicts. It never looks old. It never looks like something I've seen before. It always looks like nothing I've ever seen. I kind of stare. I'm kind of shocked. (5)

In the pages that follow as well as in his scholarly book *Writing Against Time*, Clune develops this notion of eternal novelty into a full-fledged theory about the effects of aesthetic habitualization. Like Viktor Shklovsky in "Art as Technique," Clune detects in perception a mechanism of familiarization and automatization that renders the living world inert and divests objects of their vibrancy. An object encountered in this manner elicits no real recognition; instead, it is turned into a symbol, a silhouette of its former, fuller being. "We see the object as though it were enveloped in a sack," Shklovsky writes, so that "ultimately, even the essence of what it was is forgotten" (11). Clune adopts Shklovsky's notion, applying it to literary representation in *Writing Against Time*, which argues that writers have developed techniques for arresting or dispelling neurobiological time, and to the experience of addiction in *White Out*, where he presents the neural allure of drug use as a similar bulwark against temporal oblivion:

> Something that's always new, that's immune to habit, that never gets old. That's something worth having. Because habit is what destroys the world. Take a new car and put it in an air-controlled garage. Go look at it everyday. After one year all that

will remain of the car is a vague outline. Trees, stop signs, people, and books grow old, crumble and disappear inside our habits. (6)[109]

In a counterintuitive transvaluation, Clune understands addiction not as habitual compulsion, as it is conventionally described, but as a respite from habit. Addiction, he proposes, is "really an antihabit," because drug use appears exempt from the neural mechanisms of familiarization that affect all other realms of experience (233). The allure of addiction consists in its effects on memory and its ability to bypass what Shklovsky describes as the "over-automatization" of experience (12). In his gloss on Shklovsky's concept of *ostranenie*, Clune identifies the addict as standing apart from the rest of mortal humanity, the lone figure that has stumbled onto an escape from the dilemma of temporal progression and forgetting:

> People love whatever's new. Humans love the first time. The first time is life. Life is always fading. The work of art is to make things new. The work of advertising is to make things new. The work of religion, the work of science, the work of philosophy, the work of medicine, the work of car mechanics. Their tricks all work, for a little while, then they get old. The addict, alone among humans, is given something that is always new. (6-7)

What is novel, Clune makes sure to point out, is not the drug high itself, which swiftly loses its luster and reveals its malevolent flipside. Predictably, the addict resolves to quit and never relapse again. But:

> Then you see a white top. Or even imagine you're seeing one. And it's the first time you've ever seen it. Addiction is a memory disease. Memory keeps things in the past. Dope white is a memory disruption agent. The powder in the vial is a distribution technology. It carries the white down the tiny neural tunnels where the body manufactures time. Dope white turns up in my earliest memories. I remember Mom's white teeth. My future whites out. (7)

In this reflection on the temporality of addicted memory, we can identify a crucial modification of the disease model of addiction. For Clune, addiction is a metaphorical rather than an organic illness: it is a "memory disease," not a brain disease. Given that it appears to eschew a more narrowly materialist view of addiction as a biological problem, we might question whether *White Out* even qualifies as a neuro-memoir. On the one hand, as the above passage attests, the body is

---

109  This sentence can only be read as a deliberate nod to Shklovsky, who describes in "Art as Technique" how habitualization "devours work, clothes, furniture, one's wife, and the fear of war," fashioning a similarly eclectic list of "objects" that fall victim to overfamiliarity (12).

involved in Clune's account, as are the "neural tunnels" of the nervous system. On the other, the intricacies of the biochemical processes involved are by no means this book's main concern, as we realize when Clune describes his ingestion of ReVia, an opioid antagonist used in heroin withdrawal:

> When the drop touched my tongue, it seeped into my blood. When it hit my blood, it sped to my heart. My heart shot it into my brain. Once inside, the tiny ReVia molecules began covering up all my dope receptors. Putting chemical gags in the open dope holes. I'm not an expert on the science. (47)

Clune's laconic and dryly funny remark that he is "not an expert on the science" distinguishes him from his fellow neuro-memoirists, who either are experts in their respective fields (Jamison, Saks, Lewis) or have invested considerable time and energy in reading up on the scientific and medical literature on their conditions (Shawn, Hustvedt). Nonetheless I would argue that *White Out* is informed by a materialist sensibility and an intense interest in the relation between materiality and subjectivity that warrants including it in the corpus of neuro-memoirs I have been assembling. For evidence of this claim, let us return to the notion of addiction as a memory disease that generates the perennially new.

Could we not say that the imperative of aesthetic novelty outlined by Clune is itself implicated in a materialist sensibility preoccupied with bodily perception, affect, and visceral immediacy? Does it not betray a view that privileges an idealized form of some primeval, prereflective, bodily jouissance, which can only be rooted in a neural now, over intellectual reflection? Perhaps the true agent of corruption in Clune's model is not time itself but reflection, detachment, knowledge in its temporal dimension. Novelty can only be validated as a higher good at the cost of devaluing familiarity per se. In this view, however, no incremental accumulation of experience can lead to an increase in understanding. Nothing can be gained from extended exposure. Familiarity breeds contempt.

While such a critique might be overly harsh and is, at any rate, refuted by the text itself, which does eventually manage to find virtue in familiarity (about which more later), the suspicion that Clune's reworking of Shklovsky holds brain processes responsible for the "drop-off in vivacity" is confirmed by a closer examination of his argument in *Writing Against Time*. Here Clune cites neuroscientist David Eagleman to construct a picture of habitualization that draws heavily on neurological and biological discourses. "Once the brain has learned to recognize the image, it no longer requires the high 'metabolic costs' of intense sensory engagement," Clune states, adding that this progression to a "more efficient encoding," which Eagleman sees at the heart of perceptual dimming, possesses "clear evolutionary advantages" (3). Whereas Shklovsky deployed literary and mathematical analogies, comparing automatized perception to prose writing and the substitutive operations of algebra (24, 11), Clune invokes "the flow of neurobiological time, the tendency of the brain to reduce sensory engagement with repeated exposure" and speculates that a "link between dopamine and novelty suggests that the experience of the drug cue for the addict is a very particular kind of experience: the fascination of a novel object" (*Writing* 10, 79).

If, as Clune provocatively argues in *Writing Against Time*, addiction "lends salience to consciousness" and "makes experience matter," this claim resembles the familiar picture of the self as susceptible, mutable, and open to biochemical manipulation that has gradually emerged over the course of my analysis (86). The brain is responsible for perceptual dimming; substances can alter our experience of the world. While the latter notion stands at the center of *White Out*, the former merely hovers in its conceptual background, making Clune's book a less-than-prototypical neuro-memoir whose indirect, or circuitous approach to the relation of mind and matter should not prevent us from recognizing that this question is deeply relevant to its project.

If the signature effect of the "memory disease" consists in the titular "white out," which eradicates the past, a logical consequence to be assumed would be the "forgetting of the self" invoked in the book's epigraph. Clune's rendering of his first heroin experience seems to support this notion. Having done heroin at a friend's apartment one summer day in New York and subsequently made his way to the building's rooftop, Clune describes the drug's effects:

> A single cloud moved through the blue sky. I was on my back looking up. My eye was a glass box, and inside it there was no time. I kept the cloud inside it. I wish I could show it to you. I never imagined this could happen. A breath entering my nostrils coiled over the nerves, losing all dimension. This was the end of desire. The end of wanting. The end of fear. The end of desire. I had carefully preserved memories from my childhood. Those memories seemed to promise a great happiness at the end of things. I had taken them as signs from the invisible world, and made a private religion of them. Lying on my back on Chip's roof, all the memories of my childhood turned white one by one. (90)

As the quasi-Buddhist "end of wanting" and the whitening out of childhood memories suggest, this is a scene of progressive (and ecstatic) self-dissolution. But Clune also describes the transition from "sober" to addicted self as akin to metempsychosis, the transmigration of souls. "Dope gives me a new, dope body," Clune writes, a "white metal angel body," an "exoskeletal astro body" (138-39). Two bodies, then: a human body, containing childhood memories, and a dope body, containing only timeless white. Can the dope body produce a self in the absence of memory? Is not the very project of writing a memoir about the eradication of memory paradoxical? Clune addresses this problem at the beginning of the third chapter, in

a passage that problematizes the view of autobiographical writing as the representation of the experiences of a self that exists independently from the "I" of the
textual subject. Here the author remembers waiting in his car for a dealer, "The
sweat-soaked twenty clenched in the bones of my hand. The ghetto street scene
clenched in the bones of my face," before adding a crucial caveat:

> That moment never existed. I wasn't there.
> Well, I was there, kind of. It's hard to explain. If you've ever looked out at the sea on
> a clear day you know there is a line where the sea and sky meet. The line doesn't
> really exist. It's an optical illusion. I was there in the car on Edmondson Avenue the
> way that imaginary line is there between the sea and the sky.
> I hung there suspended between the first time I did dope and the next time.
> Between the original eternal white bliss of my first time, and the next eternal white
> hit. I was the imaginary line that kept those two halves from meeting. Those two
> heavens. The pressure of all that white bliss above and below, and I was between
> and thin and imaginary. (39)

The evocation of perceptual details (the sweat-soaked banknote, the urban environment), which are generally generated by and focalized through a central subject of experience, is undercut here by a disavowal of just such subjectivity. The
"eternal" hits of heroin abolish not only time and memory but also the self, which
becomes an imaginary effect, an "optical illusion." Yet as soon as the drug takes
effect, Clune writes, he "felt thicker" again. "After fixing, I watched myself getting fatter there in the car," until he can conclude, "So I was there in my car on
Edmondson Avenue after all" (39). If there is a dope self to go along with the dope
body, it would seem that it cannot subsist apart from engagement with the drug.
How, then, is recovery possible? Is it merely a question of switching bodies yet
again, prompting the self that goes with the body to return along with it? The
answer Clune gives to this question initially appears to distinguish his account
from the other neuro-memoirs I have discussed.

   While those texts framed the quest to come to terms with the contingency of
biology and the susceptibility of the body as one that largely depended on a feat of
narrative integration, of formulating a self-narrative capable of including pathological aspects rather than externalizing them, *White Out* advances the possibility
that rejection rather than assertion of self might the best recourse. "The only way
to recover from a memory disease is to forget yourself," Clune suggests. "You must
make forgetfulness into a habit. Like a waterwheel that continually pours forgetfulness over your life" (228, 233). Forgetting is an effect of the memory disease, but
it is also its cure, while inquiring after the narrative of the self becomes associated
with pathological compulsion: "I know no way of answering that question that
satisfies. The questioner is insatiable. A restless, reckless, endless desire drives

the questioning. Who am I? Who am I? But who am I *really*? It's best to just forget it" (234; original emphasis). But, just as it is hard to rid oneself of the "restless, reckless, endless desire" of addiction, it is also not so easy to do away with the compulsion to inquire into "this trouble with the self"—partly because memory and the body provide a stubborn mechanism of unification, partly because auto-biographical writing inevitably reinforces this unity (65). Paradoxically, it is habit, the mechanism of forgetfulness, which initiates the return of memory and the re-emergence of self.

The "antihabit" of addiction "isolates you from things, where a real habit marries you to things," Clune observes. "If I am a body, a habit is like a room containing my body and a bunch of other things. Outside things. A treadmill, a TV, books, snow, dayghosts, relatives, dinosaurs, mercury, an alligator, a toothbrush, a car" (233). In his final attempt at recovery, Clune successfully establishes such habits and keeps the question "who am I?" at bay. But once the process bears fruit, the self returns with a vengeance. "That spring, everything I'd lost found me," he recalls, and the final act of transmigration entails a reunion between subject and object, body and world, memories and the self. At the end of his memoir, Clune reflects on what he has written, and states:

> But that's just the history of my dope body. And in that first post-heroin spring, my ageless dope body was gone. I'd traded it for a body that was like an empty hive. In the spring the missing swarms flew back through the sunset to fill it up again. Age five, age eight, age thirteen, age twenty.
> "I'm part of you," each new memory said as it flew through my eyes. (240)

Human memory and body are returned to each other, in a reunion that effectively abolishes the problem of the self, but as a fact of embodied existence and not as an active act of volitional of forgetting: "The holy question 'who am I?' was hard to sustain. It was hard to pretend I was some great mystery when every puddle and every slant of light knew me" (241). If this grand return is achieved by virtue of cultivating bodily habits, it is writing that keeps calling attention to subjectivity: "For example, I'm writing this. I'm drinking some water. I do this and that. Now I'm happy and now I'm sad. But where do the different states of me stop and start?" (66). In passages like these, Clune approaches a poststructuralist, linguistic view of the subject, in which it is only the pronoun "I" that unites the different modalities of textual and historical subjectivity. But if the self is so insubstantial, if "[w]ho I am isn't the first thing I need to know to get better, it's maybe the last thing," then why keep posing the question? The answer, Clune writes, lies in the act of writing itself: "To be honest, it's this writing that brings it up. Here where there's nothing to hang on to, the question occurs" (235). Clune's text compulsively reiterates the Platonic notion of writing as an "aid to memory" (26, 39, 40, 211, 235), and in asserting that the act of writing effects a self-production he might be perceived as echoing his fellow neuro-memoirists, who, as we have seen, likewise fashion narratives that generate textual subjects that are presented as coterminous with their authors. Yet in Clune, this coevolution of grammatical subject and biographical self is figured and valued differently.

"Who am I? Writing is an aid. I prop myself up on this cane of ink and paper," Clune states, reinforcing the notion that speaking or writing of the self lends it an air of substantiality it might not otherwise possess (211). Foucault, who was similarly opposed to the notion that autobiographical writing can be seen as the mere representation of a pre-existing subject, argues in "Writing the Self" that memoiristic practice is generative rather than reflective; its end is "nothing less than the constitution of the self" (237). What, then, of the revision of subjectivity, which I have claimed as a key aim of the neuro-memoir? Does *White Out* leave us with a refusal of the self, with a view of the subject as little more than an effect of language and literary convention? For an answer to this question we can turn to the book's penultimate chapter, "Outside," whose title evokes the "outside things" included in the conjugal dynamic of habit (see above) as well as the relief of having escaped the "memory trap" of addiction (228). This is where Clune provides his final, if not definitive, answer to the problem of the self:

> Who am I? I am a being who is alive, fills up with time, and must die. In this human world, who I am has a simple answer. A first name and a last name. A body and a brain. Nothing more to me than what is in the mind of anyone who sees me passing and calls out my name.
> Pretending there's more to me than that is dangerous. Perhaps it conceals a secret longing for the dope body, the timeless body, the white eternity. Worse, this chasing after mystery is tasteless. It looks pretentious on a being who is born and then passes away. A being so full of dead time that it sinks when everything else rises. (242)

Here the link between the compulsion of addiction and the compulsion of inquiring after the nature of the self is bolstered one last time. The "holy question" and the "white eternity": both are rejected as equally metaphysical and equally unlivable. Instead, subjectivity is reduced to materiality ("A body and a brain"), to social appellation ("A first name and a last name"), and to mutual recognition ("what is in the mind of anyone who sees me passing and calls out my name"). We should take the latter aspect to also include recognition by the (implied, imagined) reader, as Foucault reminds us. Autobiographical writing implies an assumed, internalized gaze of the other; in Foucault's terms, it is "a matter of bringing into congruence the gaze of the other and that gaze which one aims at oneself" ("Self Writing" 221). There are then two sources of self to be found in *White Out*: habit (both in its positive and negative forms), and social life, of which writing is an aspect. The above description of an empty self, then, is a better fit for the addict than the recovered addict. The former could indeed be described by Clune in thoroughly materialist terms, as a "switchboard" for physical interactions:

> Blood circulates within the borders of the skin. But the addict's need for dope opens his mind-body system to the world. To the circulatory system of the world dope supply. The addict's veins and nerves spool out through prices on bags, fiber-optic cables where dealers voices peel away from their bodies, airplanes landing in empty fields. The dope body spreads out like an open fire hydrant.
> So when people stand looking at the addict face-to-face, they don't see much. […] An addict doesn't fully materialize in the present. When I looked in the mirror back in Baltimore, I got an odd feeling that I wasn't really seeing myself. Because I wasn't really seeing myself. (173)

This distributed, flattened-out subjectivity, which causes misrecognition, "a failure to materialize," is, ironically, tied to, and dependent on, the material exchange of *substances*. But sheer materiality, sheer externality seems an insufficient way to describe the self that is produced in the process of Clune's memoir, which ends not unlike the other neuro-memoirs, with a stable and coherent subject whose rationality underwrites the phenomenological descriptions of turmoil that preceded and prepared its present state. The recovered Clune has regained a sense of subjectivity through the "technologies of the self" of habit, embodied sociality, and writing.[110] He now has a career as a scholar and an author, and he lives, he tells us in the epilogue, "in a nice house in a nice suburb" with his wife and "two nice dogs" (257). This is a play on a cliché, to be sure, but there is real gratitude in Clune's praise for the "recovery engine," a "makeshift contraption" which, "once you strap your life to it," will "pull you out of death and into good futures" (257). In Clune's case, as in the others I have discussed, this future includes producing a text about his past that culminates in his present self. Within the realm of the memoir, it seems, even someone intent on forgetting the self cannot but produce a narrative account in which progressively, a transformation occurs, until a self emerges that can speak of its previous trials and tribulations as formative experiences.

---

110 Foucault uses the term "technologies of the self" to describe the mechanisms by which human beings transform their "bodies and souls, thoughts, conduct, and way of being" in the production of subjectivity ("Technologies" 8).

## Chapter Conclusion: Integration and Control

Autobiographical writing, it has been argued, constitutes a "technology of the self" (Gilmore 14, Heehs 228). As such, it produces a textual subject that, on the one hand, is bound to conventions and contracts of social communication (with a readership and certain effects in mind), but also, on the other, embodies authorial attempts to "give an account of oneself," to wrest from the contingency and complexity of human existence a degree of meaning and understanding that can never be total. Both these aspects are epistemically bound by culture: the account in question needs to deploy recognizable forms of expression, and it can only draw from a limited selection of interpretive frameworks. As I have argued, the neuro-memoir is itself the result of the emergence of a new framework, under which the authors assume subject positions that result from medical diagnostics and inquire about the mind-body problem as it presents itself from the standpoint of their respective conditions.

The texts I have been discussing, then, all reveal themselves as machines for "making up people," to use Ian Hacking's phrase. "Making up people changes the possibilities for personhood," Hacking writes ("Making" 165). It is a process which "entails the creation of descriptive or diagnostic categories through expert knowledge; individuals assimilate these categories into their descriptions and practices of the self, and thereby transform them" (Ortega, *Corporeality* 82). It is in this way, I submit, that we need to interpret the authors' attempts to understand themselves in the terms of a materialist anthropology: beholden to one's brain, in thrall to evolutionary demands, susceptible to molecular manipulation, all the while shaping, and being shaped by, one's nervous system. These are thoroughly contemporary ideas, and the project of the neuro-memoir is thus tethered to a particular cultural moment, enabled by novel diagnostic categories and medical concepts that had hitherto been unavailable. But the novelty of these discourses should not distract from the fact that they find their place within a larger project of integration that includes other and older forms of meaning making. As Ortega rightly notes, neuroscience "emerges as *one among several* frameworks individuals have at their disposal to understand themselves and their relations to others" (*Corporeality* 82; my emphasis), and as such, it is not incompatible with other frameworks.

This has in fact been amply demonstrated by my readings. Jamison, Saks, Hustvedt, and Shawn all describe psychoanalysis and dynamic psychology as indispensable. Lewis's attempt to describe "the actual experiences" as well as the underlying brain processes of addiction already implies that by themselves, the latter provide insufficient illustration. Clune's account is as indebted to phenomenological description and aesthetic theory as it is to the materialist idea of "tiny neural tunnels." The neuro-memoir, then, should be regarded as characterized by *integration* rather than *substitution*: the integration of mind and body, of psychology and neurology, of pathology and normality, of contingency and control.

If integration has emerged as one of this chapter's key terms, *control* is another. Each text discussed here presents a variation on the topic of agency, pondering the necessity as well as the limits of control. The frequency with which analogies to postmodern and poststructuralist ideas have suggested themselves in my analysis alerts us to the possibility of reading these texts, and the discourses they reference, as yet another entry in the ongoing debates that pit agency versus structure, freedom versus determination. But since the controversies around social constructivism and the decentering of the subject are themselves part of the background of these books, and sometimes even explicitly acknowledged as such,[111] perhaps the most interesting aspect of a new (or renewed) emphasis on materiality that we find in the neuro-memoir is the attempt to move beyond dichotomous and dualistic thinking. It might be that distinctions between mind and matter do indeed result from a category mistake; surely we find echoes of Gilbert Ryle's famous critique[112] in the authors' insistence that while we can impose a third-person perspective on phenomena experienced in the first person, such descriptions are meaningless by themselves, and that a materialist explanation is merely another mode of description rather than the ultimate or supreme one. As Hustvedt puts it, "What is seen depends on the perspective of the seer" (145).

This leads us back to the question with which I prefaced my analysis: if the neuro-memoir bespeaks a contemporary mode of "cerebral subjectivity," how can we relate this notion to the—potentially antagonistic—concept of the narrative or autobiographical self? As it turns out, the suspicion of antagonism proves to be unfounded: the two ideas are exceedingly reconcilable. Above I have outlined a number of discourses the authors deem vital to the project of accounting for what Shawn calls "the flaws of being human": psychology, phenomenology, aesthetics. Yet the central aspect might be formal rather than methodical: in their autobiographical accounts of their embodied, neural, and chemical conditions, the neuro-memoirists I have assembled here all present their arguments in narrative, literary form. If the cerebral subject and the autobiographical self are not at odds with each other, it is because one incorporates the other. This is the final, and

---

111  To cite just two examples: Jamison illustrates this "decentering" memorably when she writes, "In the mirror I see a creature I don't know but must live and share my mind with" (114), while Saks, who has trained as a psychoanalyst herself and published a book on the hermeneutic view of psychoanalysis, calls attention to the discrepancy between the theory of personhood and responsibility that is operative in judicial contexts (the doctrine of informed consent) and the psychoanalytic view of motivation and the unconscious in *The Center Cannot Hold* (295-96).

112  In *The Concept of Mind* Ryle argues that the mind-body problem is the result of a "category mistake" (6). According to Ryle, there is no such thing as "the mental" (as distinct from the physical); there are only (outwardly observable) behaviors or dispositions toward certain behaviors.

crucial, manifestation of the integrative dynamic informing these texts: in their attempts to come to terms with the conceptual as well as the pragmatic challenges of the mind-body problem, and to formulate alternative modes of subjectivity, narrative is the indispensable form in which their claims are formulated.

With this observation, we grasp the core principle that underlies the revision of subjectivity that occurs here. As I have discussed, the neuro-memoir presents a picture of the self as mutable, susceptible, and elastic to the degree that even the temporary fragmentation or absence of self does not negate its legitimacy: Jamison and Saks wish to be recognized as competent professionals despite their psychotic episodes; Hustvedt and Shawn recount how they learn to tailor their lives to their conditions; Lewis demonstrates via his own biography that addiction need not define one's life, and Clune attests to the resilience of the embodied self, even in the face of the "memory disease." What unites all these revisions, or expansions of subjectivity is an emphasis on transformation. In her study of autobiography, Carolyn Barros names transformation as the defining metaphor of this mode of writing, but as the above examples suggest, this transformation does not exhaust itself in the idea that "I have changed," as Barros proposes (10); rather, its more fundamental implication is that this "I" is always already characterized by a latent mutability, the capacity to undergo change. Its potential describes its essence.

To be sure, biology and materiality affect subjectivity, whether genetically, neurologically, or biochemically; whether as inherited predisposition or as inherent vulnerability. But it neither constitutes not explains the self, a reflective figure that is particularly prone to be summoned by speaking or writing about one's experiences and inner states: "it's this writing that brings it up," as Clune remarks. Barros introduces a triadic structure that applies to all autobiographical writing: "The persona is the spoken or inscribed subject of transformation [...]; the figura is the mode or type of transformation [...]; and the dynamis is the motive force or power to which the inscribed persona attributes the change" (vii). In this model, the beholdenness of the subject to materiality—what I have called the contingency of biology—constitutes the *figura* of the neuro-memoir: its origins, its crises, but also its resolutions always involve the dramatic relation between mind and matter. It is this relation, read through the discourses of present-day medical materialism, that marks these texts as contemporary. As Barros notes, figura "names the particular human story inside the history of the age," and what is striking about the story of the neuro-memoir is how it situates itself on the threshold between older and newer discourses of the mind, between psychological and neurobiological "histories" or ages (13). The textual subjects and authorial figures generated by these texts correspond to *persona*: the "me" in Barros's autobiographical Ur-sentence "something happened to *me*." For all their avowals of the complexity of human subjectivity, this is the least controversial component of Barros's triad as it relates to the neuro-memoir: with the notable exception of Clune, the "I" of autobiography remains a surprisingly stable entity in all accounts—and even in Clune, it proves ultimately inescapable.

The most mysterious element here is *dynamis*, the agency or cause of the change that defines the text. Augustine could still ascribe his transformation to God; for today's neuro-memoirists the explanation is less unequivocal. The nature of the neuro-memoir as I have been tracing it here, its "deep logic," consists in its reconciliation of narrative and neural conceptions of subjectivity, whose revision in these texts occurs via the inclusion of biological, medical, and materialist models of the self in its narrative elaborations. Yet none of the authors assembled here dare to pinpoint precisely where the fulcrum of agency lies in the new, expanded models of subjectivity they put forward. What really motivates the decisive moments of change in these texts? Is it medicine or therapy; insight or askesis; habit or reflection; body or mind? The answer proves elusive. If "change itself is always changing" (Barros viii), and the way in which the "figura" is articulated is itself indicative of the epistemologies and idiosyncrasies of its time, we see the neuro-memoir in mid-stride, one foot in established psychological and literary notions of the self, the other in newly emerging materialist modes of explanation. Looking backward and forward at once. Not settling just yet.

## 4. "Just some kind of nerve impulse in the brain": Substances and Subjects in the Novels of Don DeLillo

> Travelling in thought from the position of participant-observer in the physical and social world 'through' the face and into the machinery that lies behind we are transported, like Alice through the looking glass, to a very different world. We go from a bright place of persons, selves, and subjective experience, to a dark, silent, enclosed, world of physics, chemistry, and biology. It is a mysterious journey.
>
> *Paul Broks, Into the Silent Land*

> One must look into the cerebral cortex, the nervous system, and the digestive tracts.
>
> *T. S. Eliot, "The Metaphysical Poets"*

### Characters and Subjects

When looking for an early[1] and influential example of "materialist minds" in U.S. literature, one can do worse than to turn to the work of Don DeLillo, one of the first American authors of the postmodern era to develop a sustained interest in the biological and neurological determinants of human consciousness.[2] In the novels

---

1  In the framework of this study, which views the mutually implicated developments of information technology, neuroscience, biomedicalization, and evolutionary psychology —all of which begin to pick up speed in the 1990s—as constitutive contexts of a new materialism of the mind, "early" can be understood as predating the nineties.

2  "A neural foundation is insistently present in many postmodern texts," Stephen Burn observes, "but this tendency is palpable perhaps nowhere more consistently than in DeLillo's mid-70s fiction" ("Infinite" 66).

that are commonly held to comprise the first half of his career,[3] we find references to evolutionary biology, to cerebral hemisphericity and modularity, and to a neural (rather than psychoanalytical) unconscious. Mind as machine and the self as mutable and susceptible to pharmaceutical manipulation are recurrent motifs in these texts. Many of the ideas that DeLillo introduces into American literature in the seventies and eighties would prove significant for a younger generation of writers that was to rise to prominence in the nineties, a group that includes Jonathan Franzen, Richard Powers, and David Foster Wallace.[4] Unlike these authors, DeLillo never devotes an entire book or essay to the mind-body problem,[5] but the way in which his novels repeatedly reference the material substrates of subjectivity prefigures the route eventually taken by the younger writers he influenced.[6] While Wallace and Powers will be the subject of subsequent chapters, here I would like to trace the development of DeLillo's engagement with materialist models of mind through a select number of texts leading up to (and including) the 1984 publication of *White Noise*.

In 1981, Robert Nadeau sets the tone for the DeLillo scholarship of the coming decades: here is an author, Nadeau states in his early critical appraisal, who investigates "the tendency of Western man to construct reality in terms of closed systems and symbolics, and thereby renders palpable the "fragmentation of individual identity" (161). This description will acquire the status of consensus opinion among later critics, who, following Nadeau, include DeLillo in a line of American "systems novelists" like Gaddis, Pynchon, and Coover (LeClair, *Loop* xii) and present him as a writer who would "put the existence of the self into question" or even "endorse the view of the self as a nullity" (Goodheart 117-18).[7] Often these assump-

---

3  Critics usually date the beginning of the second stage of DeLillo's career to the publication of either *Libra*, in 1988, or *Mao II*, in 1991—works, in any case, that appeared after DeLillo won the National Book Award for *White Noise*, thus gaining a wider readership. See Olster and Veggian.

4  As Burn has demonstrated ("Infinite" 83 n15), one such motif, Paul D. MacLean's Triune Brain theory, has been deployed by all four authors in different permutations.

5  Franzen meditates on the possible consequences of viewing the self in neurological rather than psychological terms in "My Father's Brain," the relation between brain and mind provides Powers with the plot for *The Echo Maker*, and, as I argue in the penultimate chapter of this study, Wallace's *Infinite Jest* can be read as an extended allegory of, and inquiry into, the cyclical dynamic of mind and body.

6  DeLillo's influence on Wallace, in particular, is well-documented. See Max for an account of Wallace's correspondence with DeLillo, "whom he increasingly turned to as his authority on literary matters" throughout his career (205) and Burn, "Infinite" for a discussion of the way in which Wallace emulated "DeLillo's compositional process of dramatizing specific neuroscientific theories" (68). Powers, for his part, has conceded in an interview that DeLillo has been an "enormous influence" ("Geeks" n. pag.). On the problematic of literary filiation among contemporaries, see Cowart, "The DeLillo Era."

7  See Cowart's suggestion that "DeLillo seems fully to recognize the tenuousness of all 'subject-positions'" (*Physics* 131). Engles argues for an awareness of racial representation, and that DeLillo

tions are linked, so that one begets the other, as when Arnold Weinstein describes "the antics of the individual subject in his encounter with a systemic world" as a key theme of DeLillo's (288), the assumption here being that the individual subject ultimately needs to be seen as dissolving into the systemic world, at which point its "antics" become readable as signs of its own abolition. After all, in a systems theoretical perspective, which speaks of psychic systems rather than selves with interiority and intention, there is little room for the airs of the "classical," liberal humanist subject, which Niklas Luhmann deems "the most ambitious title ever adopted by man" ("Tücke" 48; my translation).[8]

Are we then faced, in DeLillo, with a proliferation of systems at the expense of the self? According to LeClair, the "fundamental subjects of DeLillo's fiction" are not necessarily human beings but "communications loops ranging from the biological to the technological, environmental to personal, linguistic, prelinguistic, and postlinguistic, loops that are both saving and destroying, evolutionary spirals and vicious circles" (*Loop* xi). This view, like Weinstein's notion of the "systemic world," owes a debt to Nadeau's book, which established the "consciousness of systems reality" as an important aspect of postmodern literary production (181). I would like to connect LeClair's mention of biological and evolutionary "loops" to Nadeau's initial formulation and suggest that the latter—perhaps unwittingly—points to DeLillo's engagement with materialist models of mind, which are similarly concerned with how organisms "construct reality" through a process of translation from sense to symbol, while effecting a "fragmentation of individual identity" that rivals postmodern philosophy. In what follows, therefore, I delineate how DeLillo takes up, but also transforms, the materialist anthropologies developed by evolutionary biology, biological psychiatry, and neuroscience. I argue that the motif of "materialist minds" is intimately linked to the themes conventionally associated with DeLillo's work, such as postmodern culture, technology, and science. In keeping with the specific research interest of my project,

---

"counters the white male authorial tendency to create autonomous, individualistic protagonists" (760).

8  Bruce Clarke and Mark Hansen suggest that "[a]utonomy can never be solitary" in such a perspective, in which "the noumenal unity of the humanist subject gives way to a differential observation of the relations of living and nonliving systems and their environments" (6). See also Luhmann's clarification that "concepts like intention, reference, expectation, experience, and action," which have traditionally been associated with individual human subjectivity, "can be assigned either to psychic or social systems" in this theory (*Social Systems* 512 n4). Interestingly, LeClair entirely neglects Luhmann, who is not even mentioned in *In the Loop*. For later accounts that correct this omission, see Chodat, for whom *Underworld* "evokes the presences of Nietzsche and Luhmann" (229) as well as Landgraf, who argues that "Luhmann's rendering of systems theory is uniquely fit to formulize DeLillo's presentation of the mass-media reality of contemporary U.S. culture as a multiplicity of incongruent realities" (86-87).

particularly close attention will be paid to how biological or neurological accounts of cognition are related to "the alien realms beyond and within us" (Keesey 68) and the quasi-Nietzschean "reduction of the self to nonhuman causal forces" (Schweiker 96) that critics have identified as key concerns of DeLillo's. This reduction stands at the center of the various "'post' accounts of the subject," such as posthumanism or poststructuralism (Lundberg 330), but it also occupies a central place in DeLillo's novels—at least according to the critical consensus adumbrated above.

If subjectivity in DeLillo's is typically described as "ephemeral and indistinct," this observation is mainly based on analyses of his characters (Laist 5). Ever since the first *New York Times* review of *Americana*, which identified "an infatuation with rhetoric, but hardly a trace of a man" in the novel (Levin, n. pag.), critics have lamented that Delillo's characters appear "disembodied, at times indistinguishable from one another" (Goodheart 117) or lack "memorably differentiated consciousness" (Tanner 63). Mark Edmundson, drawing on E.M. Forster's dichotomy of character types, suggests that DeLillo's "most extreme figures aren't flat or round; they aren't, strictly speaking, present at all" (119).[9] For commentators like these, the place in which to look for an author's stance on subjectivity is the depiction of character. DeLillo's characters are insubstantial, the reasoning goes, because of their "inevitable absorption in [...] cultural signs," so that American culture becomes the guarantor of an inauthentic and shallow, "decentered" sense of self (Kukich 337). The reduction of internal as well as external reality to the play of "empty" signifiers spells the demise of the deep, authentic self, announcing "the absence of a strong interior" (Edmundson 118). In this reading, the postmodern environment produces the postmodern psyche, and both are united in surfaciality. As the first-person-narrator of *The Names* puts it, "we'd lost our capacity to select, to ferret out particularity and trace it to some center which our minds could relocate in knowable surroundings. There was no equivalent core" (94).

From this perspective it appears as if the only place for the self in DeLillo's work were that of a lacuna.[10] Subjectivity matters only insofar as the author reports on the impossibility of its adequate production: in the co-optive image culture of the present, people—and characters—become "eerily selfless" (Edmundson 119).[11] This assumption enables scholars to take DeLillo, as they have overwhelmingly

---

9   The reliance on Forster's typological model already suggests that the "presence" of DeLillo's characters may be measured by many critics in their distance from realist models of representation, a notion that is reinforced by Michael Wood's observation that they "talk like people who are weirdly able to discuss and picture their lives as they live them, whose intelligence never sleeps and *doesn't pause for realism*" (n. pag.; my emphasis).

10  See Wacker, for whom "subjectivity exists largely as a negativity" in DeLillo (82).

11  See Edmundson, who proposes that "children aren't raised by fathers now—they are raised by power and images. Dialectical encounter, the struggle with fate in which souls are born, [...] is impossible in such a culture" (116).

done, for a quintessential postmodernist, concerned with characters who are less defined by authentic and unique interiority than by an unmitigated absorption into the cultural maelstrom.[12] Hence, his characters are viewed as betraying a "deliberate insubstantiality" (Goodheart 120) that points to what is variously described as the "dispersal of the self into larger systems" (doCormo 2) or the "dissolution of a modernist subjectivity in the mire of contemporary media and technology" (Wilcox 348). This often reduces readings that consider the role of subjectivity to questions of cooptation and resistance: "Generally speaking," Randy Laist writes, "if you want to criticize DeLillo, you argue that his vision is one of social forces overwhelming human subjectivity; and if you want to praise him, [...] you argue that DeLillo's subjects ultimately prevail over their entrapment" (2). While Laist neglects the fact that one can easily find critical assessments of DeLillo that praise him precisely as a prophet of sociocultural and economic domination,[13] one can still observe a distinct tendency in DeLillo scholarship to regard his fiction as "a form of literary activism" (Pass 3 n7).[14]

To sum up: the argument that DeLillo's characters dramatize the hollowing out of the self in postmodernity has been made repeatedly and at length; consequently, there is no need to add to it here. I would rather like to contest and complicate such readings, which seem to me insufficient for a number of reasons. First, character depiction may be the wrong place to look for DeLillo's views on the self. If we concur with the critical consensus that DeLillo's characters are "not fully realized, autonomous individuals but [...] disembodied voices" determined by discursive and social forces and that "both the constraining forces and the narrative plots that describe them are arranged as decentered networks rather than in a traditional top-down pyramid structure of power" (Knight 36)—if, in other words, subjectivity is flattened out and distributed along various discursive elements—then it would make sense precisely *not* to look for it in the "traditional top-down [...] structure of power" that is the human person or character. If, in DeLillo, discourse *produces* the individual (Babaee 31), one would be well advised to direct one's attention not only to the textual function of character but also to the other discursive elements of his novels. Rather than extrapolate a philosophy of the sub-

---

12 For a characteristic description see Wilcox, who views *White Noise* as expressive of "a new order in which life is increasingly lived in a world of simulacra, where images and electronic representations replace direct experience," under whose sign characters (and by implication, extratextual persons as well) depend upon "the proliferation of charismatic images and spectacles of a postmodern society" for their sense of self (346).

13 See, for instance, Anthony DeCurtis's insistence that *Great Jones Street* depicts "a society in which there are no meaningful alternatives, in which everyone and everything is bound in the cash nexus and the exchange of commodities, outside of which there stands nothing" (140).

14 A typical example is Douglas Keesey's view of DeLillo as "anatomizing media man in the hope that he still has a soul" (199).

ject from an author's characters, we might want to examine other aspects of textual production, like the narration itself, and analyze what is being told and what is left out. This approach yields a different picture of how subjectivity is evoked in DeLillo's texts, and it helps us to understand the role that neuro-materialist thought plays in the process.

Second, even if we grant that DeLillo is occasionally staging an "assault on conventional ways of representing character" (interestingly, precious little critical work is being done on the degree to which DeLillo is also *maintaining* crucial elements of "conventional" character representation), we might want to interrogate whether this "assault" necessarily translates to a renunciation of the notion of "true or deep self" (Edmundson 107-8). An oft-repeated criticism of DeLillo is that he reduces his characters to the function of mouthpieces, using them as flimsy pretexts for authorial discourse.[15] However, this impression is the result of artifice rather than accident, so that we need to conclude, as Daniel Aaron does: "No one character in any of his [...] novels can confidently be said to speak for him" (67). In fact, DeLillo himself signals his awareness of the controversy around the notion of character. The term "character," we learn in *The Names*, "comes from a Greek word" that denotes an "engraving instrument or branding instrument"; by virtue of its etymological heritage, it "not only means someone in a story but a mark or symbol" (10).

We are certainly warranted to read this observation as an avowal of the *textuality* of literary character, perhaps even as a repudiation of the very idea of "fleshed-out" characters. Yet this awareness does not preclude the novel's narrator from reflecting on "the boundaries of the self" or "the self and its machinery" (133, 307). It seems, then, that interpreting DeLillo's refusal to fully adhere to the norms of realist character representation as a sign of disinterest in subjectivity per se would be ill advised. After all, the notion of DeLillo's fiction as a staging site for rampant desubjectification is difficult to reconcile with some of the author's own pronouncements. In conversation with Vince Passaro, DeLillo describes the social function of the writer as "the champion of the self" (84), and in his essay "The Power of History," which accompanied the publication of *Underworld*, he writes:

---

15 "Often in the complex orchestration of his ideas, Mr. DeLillo makes his characters name and sing all his tunes for him, speaking in dazzling chunks of authorial essay," Lorrie Moore observes in a typical assessment (n. pag.). It is not coincidental that Moore, herself a writer in the realist tradition, voices this criticism: much of the dismay over DeLillo's "insubstantial" characters can be located along the lines drawn between mimetic and more experimental or expressionistic modes of writing. As Norman Bryson suggests, fear of the grotesque may play a role: "We are normal people and dissociate ourselves from the threat we witness; or we are formless, endlessly malleable creatures, our monstrosity hidden from us only as long as our fiction of a centre, of the norm, remains plausible" (n. pag.). See also Edmundson's distinction of DeLillo from the "identity-novelists," i.e., realist writers with "recognizable" characters, which "work by flattery" (121-22).

"Against the force of history, so powerful, visible and real, the novelist poses the idiosyncratic self. Here it is, sly, mazed, mercurial, scared half-crazy. It is also *free and undivided*, the only thing that can match the enormous dimensions of social reality" (62; my emphasis).

This, I submit, is where critical discussions of DeLillo can profit from a consideration of the ways in which the author ties the question of the self to that of materiality. At times DeLillo invokes the notion of "materialist minds" to produce effects resonant with postmodern philosophy,[16] most notably the "decentering," fragmentation, or mechanization of the subject, but at others he draws on scientific theories about the materiality of mind to underwrite a model of subjectivity that locates the "depth" that his characters purportedly lack in evolutionary and biological ideas, so that the phylogenetic history of humankind guarantees a discourse of the self rooted in materiality as well as symbolicity. We can already observe this tension at work in the author's second novel, *End Zone*, from 1972.

## End Zone

*End Zone*'s protagonist initially seems to conform to the descriptions of Delillo characters as devoid of specificity and interiority. Gary Harkness, the capricious football talent who narrates the book in the first person, states as much on the first page: "Football players are simple folk. Whatever complexities, whatever dark politics of the human mind, the heart—these are noted only within the chalked borders of the playing field" (3). Yet the allusive nature of his narration belies this programmatic externalization that reduces the players to mere functions in a formal system. Even though Gary insists that the typical football player's thoughts are "wholesomely commonplace, his actions uncomplicated by history, enigma, holocaust or dream" (4), the subsequent conversations between the student players at the aptly named Logos College revolve around intricate and esoteric subject matters, while the militarized and militant atmosphere of a United States embroiled in Vietnam and the Cold War forms the ever-present backdrop of Gary's thoughts.[17] "Being made to obey the savage commands of unreasonable men" and "set apart from all styles of civilization as I had known or studied them"

---

16 Postmodernist concepts that have been linked to DeLillo's work include intertextuality (McClure), the simulacrum (Wilcox), the differend (doCormo), and the "postmodern sublime" (Tabbi), just to name a few.

17 Looking back at a period in between enrollments at universities, Harkness notes: "In late spring, a word appeared all over town. MILITARIZE. The word was printed in cardboard placards that stood in shop windows. It was scrawled on fences. It was handwritten on loose-leaf paper taped to the windshields of cars. It appeared on bumper stickers and sign-boards" (20).

(4), his situation resembles that of a draftee overseas in more ways than one, and football becomes analogous to warfare, a conflict during which "strange visions ripple across that turf; madness leaks out" (3).

The historically specific madness of subordinating the self to a system—be it warfare, athletics, or consumer capitalism—is a signature concern of DeLillo's, and in *End Zone*, Gary's anxiety over "human xerography" (19) seem justified insofar as they are expressed in relation to a distinctly materialist imaginary. "Work, you substandard industrial robots. Work, work, work, work," Gary's teammate Bing Jackmin yells at the other players; a moment later, Gary compares one of them to "a retarded computer" (33-34).[18] Curiously enough, this identification of human beings with machinic functions also engenders an inverse dynamic, in which material objects are imbued with consciousness, as when Bing spontaneously develops the idée fixe that the football itself might be conscious: "I sense knowledge in the football. [...] The football knew what was happening. [...] It was aware of its own footballness" (35).

In this first occurrence of "materialist minds" in DeLillo, the reduction of the human to mere materiality and machinic computation authorizes the reverse-engineering of a satirical exercise in panpsychism. It is no coincidence that when Bing returns from the field to report his "strange insight" about the ensouled football, Gary notes that "[h]is eyes seemed to belong to some small dark cave animal" (34). Here DeLillo slyly alludes to Thomas Nagel's "What Is It Like to Be a Bat?"—a classic text in the philosophy of mind, which argues that materialist theories of mental life neglect the import of subjective consciousness. Nagel famously posits, "fundamentally an organism has conscious mental states if and only if there is something that it is like to *be* that organism—something it is like *for* the organism" (436; original emphases). What gets lost in materialist accounts of consciousness is "the subjective character of experience," and thus the very essence of consciousness, the quality that merits our interest in the first place (436).

DeLillo's allusion to Nagel—whom he also invokes in *Ratner's Star*, as we will see—points away from reductionism and toward another function that materialist models of mind assume in his work. If they can be deployed to underscore the alienating effects of instrumental rationality, they can also serve to develop a view of human consciousness as a phenomenon that, while biological in nature, is not amenable to materialist reduction. Consciousness as a capability of biological organisms is a precondition of subjectivity, which cannot exist without perception and cognition. "One key to DeLillo's subjectivity," Curtis Yehnert argues, "is that characters (and readers) are called upon to make sense out of randomness, to give form to formlessness, for it is in the act of creating, of giving meaning to

---

18  The fellow player is similarly reduced to robotic functions, and only described as "Bing Jackmin, who kicked field goals and extra points," devoid of an identity outside the game (33).

the world, that one creates a self" (361). Here Yehnert echoes Nadeau's claim about the importance of reality constructions in DeLillo, but we should also note at this point that this argument tracks closely with the neurobiological notion of the self as emerging from the interaction of the "worlds" of the external environment and internal bodily milieu, the creation of "order out of chaos" (DeLillo, EZ 9).[19]

Antonio Damasio has proposed homeostasis, "the coordinated and largely automated physiological reactions required to maintain steady internal states in a living organism," which necessarily takes place in constant reciprocal interaction with the environment, as "a key to the biology of consciousness" (Feeling 39-40). This is a notion to keep in mind. While End Zone opens up the prospect of de-individuation through machinic metaphors, a crucial passage of this early work takes the form of a parable that imagines a more complex, looped model of mind-body interaction. Here, instead of a reduction of mind to body—the declared target of Nagel's essay—mind develops out of a bodily entanglement with the world.

The parable is doubly mediated: Gary's girlfriend Myna recounts to him "the last part of a trilogy by Tudev Nemkhu," a fictional Mongolian science-fiction author. The story revolves around a race of "half-mollusk creatures called nautiloids" living in the ocean of a planet "in a galaxy not too far from here." The proximity is not only physical: like the ancestors of earth's humans, the nautiloids, who have been communicating "through some intricate ESP number system" leave their maritime habitat for reasons that appear as a reformulation of the contingency of evolutionary pressures: "one day without warning there's a disturbance in the nautiloids' system of communication. Their numerical language gets all garbled." Once on land, a single (and, as we will see, singular) nautiloid breaks out of its shell, at the same time that the "thick foam" encasing the planet also breaks open, letting in light, or rather "electromagnetic radiation," for the first time (162-63). While its companions all eventually return to the ocean, this individual remains on the surface.

This is where things take an interesting turn: the creature is exposed for "many centuries" to the incoming light, which is "infused into the complex brain apparatus of the nautiloid," thus setting off a chain of anatomical changes the author describes "only in terms of chemical formulas, mathematical equations and statements from formal logic." The creature is both "formed of the landscape itself" and reduced to "a mass of equations and formulas rendered into some kind of tangible form," a notion that simultaneously evokes the evolution of organisms in changing environments and their description in the scientific languages of genetics and biochemistry. Just as significantly, "its brain is slowly evolving into phases of light and nonlight"—a process that evokes the deeply binary nature of neuronal processes and cerebral anatomy (162-63). At the most basic level, neuronal processes

---

19  Here and subsequently, End Zone is abbreviated as EZ in parenthetical citations.

are based in the propensity of a neuron to fire or not to fire—a dynamic that constitutes the cornerstone upon which any analogy between brain and computer is
constructed. Brain anatomy is likewise predicated on a binary: the cerebral cortex,
which houses higher cognitive functions like learning, memory, and language, is
separated into two hemispheres—a physical manifestation of the distribution
of brain functions, which provides an important basis for new materialist arguments against "centered" and unified conceptions of the self.

This binary nature of cerebral lateralization also finds expression in the story
of the evolving nautiloid. As a result of its newly formed binary brain, "everything
begins to double. Within the thing's brain mechanism there are now two land-
scapes perceived by two mechanisms. The thing sees itself seeing what is outside
it being seen by itself" (163). This description is extraordinary for several reasons.
First, it traces the emergence of a novel form of consciousness as, essentially, a
consequence of doubling, self-referentiality, and recursivity. Seeing oneself seeing founds the sense of self. This puts one in mind of the idea of re-entry, which
originated with George Spencer Brown and was imported, via Francisco Varela,
into the theory of biological life as an autopoietic (i.e., self-observing and self-sus-
taining) system, and from there on, via Niklas Luhmann, into the study of social
systems. According to Varela, "the physiological and cognitive organization of a
self-conscious system may be understood as arising from a circular and recursive
neuronal network containing its own description as a source of further description" ("Calculus" 5). Given the fact that the recursive sequence of "seeing," rooted
in a "brain mechanism," results here in the genesis of language (about which more
in a moment), we could read the nautiloid story as a parable about the basis of
symbolic systems in biological embodiment. Such a reading also points us to the
possibility that self-referentiality in DeLillo need not be an outgrowth of some
branch of postmodern philosophy; it can also result from the author's interest in
bio-cultural systems and technologies, as evidenced in his description in *Underworld* of "the interplay of terrain and weapons" in the Sonoran desert as "a kind of
neural process remapped in the world" (451).[20]

Second, it credits a plurality of "mechanisms" for the initiation of such processes. This secular creation myth does not begin with a transcendental, unified
subject but with the interplay of elemental (material) forces and substances: biological matter and cosmic radiation. Interactions of the organism with the environment give rise to perceptual and cognitive mechanisms, independently operating procedures that take place both anatomically below and temporally prior
to the sense of self that is their eventual product. Here one feels reminded of the

---

20  See also DeLillo's avowal that the "secrets within systems" inform his work: "But they're almost
    secrets of consciousness, or ways in which consciousness is replicated in the natural world" (De-
    Curtis interview 69).

doctrine of cerebral and cognitive modularity, which views the brain as "more of a sociological entity than a psychological entity," made up of cooperative as well as conflicting mechanisms (Gazzaniga, *Social* 28), and according to which the self with its reassuring sense of wholeness and continuity is no more than a "user illusion" constructed on the neural scaffolding of independently operating brain processes (Dennett, *Consciousness* 311). Viewed this way, the nautiloid allegorizes the fundamental fragmentation of subjectivity implicit in materialist models of mind.

Third, a correlation of the emergence of this auto-referential consciousness is the transformation of a being into an object, as if self-objectification constituted an irrevocable fall from grace: after this point in Myna's recapitulation of Nemkhu's story, the nautiloid is never again referred to as a "creature," but only as a "thing." We can read this reification as an inevitable side effect of the development of self-referential consciousness. To use the language of autopoiesis or systems theory: the ability to make distinctions creates the world and its objects just as much as it creates the self or subject as the position of the observer.[21] Both, in this scheme, can be objects, or "things," as the continuation of the nautiloid story makes perfectly clear. In Tudev Nemkhu's fiction, Myna explains, the "duplication" of brain mechanisms, perception, and consciousness leads, ultimately, to symbolic language:

> Each likeness is a word rather than a thing. When the word is imprinted on the thing's original mechanism, the likeness that was the word's picture instantaneously disappears. The thing's brain keeps on producing likenesses and then delivering words into its own circuitry. The thing perceives everything into itself. It duplicates perceptions and then reduplicates the results. The author finally gives the thing a name. The thing becomes monadanom—the thing that's everything. (163)

Here the parable shifts from an evolutionary and biological to a mythical register. Or, to be more precise, materialist neurology and spiritual mysticism enter into a union: language, which is both representational and symbolic, relying on likenesses as well as words, occurs via a translation and "duplication" process performed by the "circuitry" of the brain. Yet this process is also all-encompassing and immediate, since there is no separation between perception and linguistic

---

21  "The system exhibiting [autoreferential behavior] becomes 'aware' of itself through cognizing the drawing of the distinction between itself and its environment and the understanding of this distinction as an indication what the system is and what it is not" (Reichel 648). This description, in which the discrimination of objects (including other people) precedes self-recognition, is also reminiscent of James Mark Baldwin's theory of mental development, while recursivity is also an important aspect in the models of self-formation developed by social interactionism: see Marks-Tarlow et al.

activity. The nautiloid has become the mystical entity monadanom, a name whose etymological and palindromic construction points to the cyclical and recursive character of its nature: it is simultaneously one and all.

This is the only moment in DeLillo's oeuvre that suggests how a mythical "language before language," which is referenced in many of his works, might actually be imagined.[22] Appropriately enough, it is a deeply bizarre representation, refracted through no less than two distorted surfaces of mediation: a fictional character retells a story within a story composed by a fictional author. DeLillo, a lapsed Catholic, has always been interested in the idea of a prelapsarian language as an unattainable horizon, so it should not come as a surprise that the monadanom also experiences a fall from grace: for a while, "everything is existing inside this complex brain apparatus," but then, "suddenly without warning one of the words erases itself." As its story is heading toward an end, the nautiloid-cum-monadanom is heading towards an uncertain future. "The brain didn't order this and doesn't comprehend it. The word just erased itself. It no longer exists. There is no record of it." The Word of God, the Logos, it is implied, has become unattainable. And just as a return to Eden is impossible, the conditions enabling the nautiloid's evolution toward consciousness are reversed: the layer of foam around the planet closes up again, blocking out the light (165-66). It is fitting that this is where Myna's narration ends as well: "This is as far as I've gotten," she tells Gary (165). The nautiloid/monadanom story is thus marked as an allegory of human prehistory and thrownness, rather than one of human teleology.

Widely disregarded by DeLillo scholars, I would argue that this episode is actually illustrative of the author's portrayal of embodied subjectivity. It is a "microfiction" in the tradition of Borges and Italo Calvino, covering only a few pages but an immense time span, and aimed at effects that are not only "concise, concentrated, and memorable" (Calvino 49), but also, in DeLillo's case, programmatic. Its anticipatory quality consists in the way it ties together the biological, the neurological and the mystical while presenting them as products of the human imagination. The idea encapsulated in this fictional sci-fi story is that perception, cognition, and language—the very building blocks of the self, in other words—are determined bodily and biologically just as much as socially and historically, and it recurs throughout the DeLillo novels that followed End Zone. The evolution of nautiloid to monadanom connects the biological and the transcendent, ending with a situation in which consciousness can no longer be perceived as a holistic unity. Such a unity can at most be intuited, just as the missing Logos can be inferred only from its absence. The biochemical fall from grace experienced by the monadanom

---

22  "DeLillo's major characters," Yehnert observes, "long for the pure, transparent word, for the language that would give them immediacy, return them to themselves, which they imagine as simple and whole" (362).

prefigures a yearning for primordial wholeness that rises up time and again in DeLillo's work, and whose staging site is the organism itself, specifically its brain. In *The Names* James Axton reflects on the mystical potential, or "adductive force," of words to "stir the chemistry of the early brain" (115), a notion that evokes the phylogenetic past as much as the linguistic present. In *Underworld*, Nick Shay imagines the transposition of disused fighter planes onto the desert plane as an embodied symbolism, "a hollow sort of craving lifted out of the brain stem" (451). In *Cosmopolis*, Eric Packer feels the assault of a particularly grubby and bustling the street on his refined senses entering "every receptor and vault electrically to his brain" (65). These are near-mystical, epiphanic moments, but they are experienced via the sensorium of the body and coded neurologically as well as linguistically, as products of a newly constituted "neural imagination" (Massey).

That this neural and evolutionary imagination is an entirely human production is abundantly clear if we look at the way the parable is mediated, with a first-degree fictional character recounting a segment of a book written by a second-degree fictional sci-fi author, a book that, for all the ways in which it encapsulates and anticipates DeLillo's interest in "materialist minds," appears as an absurdly baroque parody of science-fiction writing. This is emblematic for DeLillo's treatment of materialist models of mind, which are never taken at face value in his work but always presented as sutured into the very subjectivities of narrators and characters. *End Zone* is a case in point. Connection to the phylogenetic past is a recurrent motif here, as when Bing informs Gary of the "psychomythical" aspect of their sport: "What we do on the field harks back. It harks back" (34). Gary complains about "that dumb phrase referring to the connection between then and now," but part of his displeasure stems from the fact that, as his last name, Harkness, suggests, he is connected more intimately to the past than he would like. Fittingly, Bing answers with a term even more evocative of the notion of ancestral evolutionary heritage: "Hyperatavistic" (60). That this concept has a distinct evolutionary-biological component is clear, yet it is, as mentioned, always focalized through the novel's characters: Anatole Bloomberg, for instance, states that his "awareness of reptilian antecedents is unnaturally vivid" (48).

## Great Jones Street

Reptilian antecedents also figure in DeLillo's next book, the 1973 *Great Jones Street*. The novel follows the exploits of rock musician Bucky Wunderlick, who withdraws from fame and fortune to spartan lodgings in a New York City apartment building. This building is also the focus of Stephen Burn's article on *Great Jones Street*, in which he claims that the novel is "closely modeled on the concept of the 'Triune' brain, which was being outlined by neurologist Paul D. MacLean at the end of the 1960s" (352). Building upon his earlier work on the evolutionary history of the limbic system in the 1950s and popularized by Arthur Koestler and Carl Sagan in the 1970s, MacLean's triune brain hypothesis has since been largely discredited.[23] It holds that as the product of biological evolution, the human brain is a layered and modular entity, with phylogenetically newer components and functions building upon older ones, so that the "reptilian" brain (the basal ganglia) supports the "paleomammalian" brain (the limbic system), which is followed by the "neo-mammalian" brain (the neocortex). Thus, brain anatomy mirrors evolutionary history as well as the plurality of "agencies" within the brain, yielding what MacLean calls a "schizophysiology."[24] Roughly speaking, in this model the basal ganglia are responsible for survival, i.e., reproduction and fight or flight instincts, the limbic system accounts for nonverbal emotion, and the neocortex houses reason and intellect.

Burn proposes a reading in which the floors of the apartment building and their respective inhabitants correspond to MacLean's hierarchical model of brain functions: the ground floor is inhabited by the widowed Ms Micklewhite and her "deformed and retarded" son, whom Burn interprets as the reptilian brain; Bucky himself occupies the second floor, thus assuming the role of the "emotional battleground of the midbrain" (Burn, "DeLillo" 357); on the third floor lives the writer Eddie Fenig, whose cerebral occupation corresponds to the tasks of his anatomical analogue, the new mammalian brain.  •

There is precedent for such an interpretation: David Cowart had already observed in 2002 that "Bucky is this America's amphibium, the middle ground of contending forces," and that "his lodgings on Great Jones Street suggest a spatial metaphor: blocked cerebration above (the desperate artist Fenig), inarticulate unconscious below (the almost subhuman Micklewhite boy)" (*Physics* 36). Burn expands on this idea, fortifying it with a neurological model to back up his claim that evolution "controls the entirety of *Great Jones Street*" and that "a desperate scramble to escape the fear-dominated impulses of the reptilian brain is one of the motivations behind the text" ("DeLillo" 357).

However, there are some problems with this reading. To begin with, in his eagerness to demonstrate that "the importance of the brain to *Great Jones Street* is fundamental, rather than simply topical" ("DeLillo" 350), Burn at times appears to write and argue in bad faith, selectively quoting from later DeLillo novels to

---

23 "The triune brain has a lot going for it. It is simple, appealing, and logical. Unfortunately, it is also completely wrong," a contemporary science guidebook informs the reader (Trefil 407).

24 "The three evolutionary formations might be popularly regarded as three interconnected biological computers, each having its own special intelligence, its own subjectivity, its own sense of time and space, and its own memory, motor, and other functions," MacLean recapitulates his proposition in an autobiographical sketch (264).

support his reading of the text, and taking quotations out of context. To cite just one example: unlike Burn would have us believe, the phrase "almost a living organism" does not refer to the apartment building that provides the setting for much of the novel, but rather to the literary market. The expression is taken from the monologue with which Eddie Fenig introduces himself to Bucky; in full, the passage reads: "I know the writer's market like few people know it. The market is a strange thing, almost a living organism" (27). Regardless of this context, Burn uses the quotation to create the impression that it supports his thesis. "Examined as an analog of the human brain, this building resembles 'a living organism' with the three levels of the house closely mapping on to the three cerebral levels of the triune brain," he writes, twisting the meaning of the quoted text in a way that borders on willful misrepresentation ("DeLillo" 355).

Questionable citation practices aside, one can also ask how convincing and productive Burn's MacLeanian interpretation actually is. While it is possible to re-read *Great Jones Street* as informed by a neuroscientific imaginary, it is not always plausible. One wonders whether, following Mark Osteen, we could not read the stratified architectural arrangement of the apartment building more profitably as a spatial analogy of Bucky's uneasy relationship with the dynamics of popularity and commodification ("Dedalian" 138-39). After all, Eddie Fenig, whose last name evokes, via the German *Pfennig*, his occupation as a writer of penny dreadfuls, clearly embodies a state of total submission to markets and audiences. In his desperate quest to "pre-empt a corner of the market," Fenig even pitches "pornographic children's literature" as a potential business idea. His willingness to produce writing that "panders to the lowest instincts" and incorporates "elements of primeval fear and terror" (*GJS* 49-50)[25] is obviously difficult to reconcile with Burn's schema, which paradoxically aligns the hack writer with the new mammalian brain (the neocortex), described by MacLean as "the brain of reading, writing, and arithmetic" (qtd. in Burn, "DeLillo" 352). To Burn, Fenig's work "seems to represent higher cortical processes," an interpretation that, in view of the nature of the hack writer's base material, borders on the self-contradictory (356).

At first sight, reading the Micklewhite boy as personifying the reptilian brain appears less counterintuitive. Likened by Bucky to "microlife humming in the floor cracks," the "primal" sound of his moans while dreaming evokes "nature [...] become imbecilic" and expresses "the secret feculent menace of a forest or swamp," clearly drawing on a biological imaginary (51). But Burn's claim that the character embodies the preverbal fight or flight reflexes housed in the brain stem reduces Bucky's observation that "this is what the boy's oppressive dreams brought [...] to the surface, the beauty and horror of wordless things" to the second aspect, horror, while ignoring the first one, beauty. Yet beauty is not a negligible component here.

---

25  Here and subsequently, *Great Jones Street* is abbreviated as *GJS* in parenthetical citations.

When Bucky finally sees the boy in person, he is struck by his "embryonic beauty" and feels compelled to touch him: "There was a lure to the boy, an unsettling lunar pull" (162). This, too, can be interpreted more conclusively as a function of Bucky's personal conundrums than by recourse to cerebral organization. Micklewhite junior exerts an aesthetic fascination over Bucky because he embodies the opposite of rock star celebrity. In diametric opposition to a rock star's libidinal appeal, his appearance is so grotesque it drives away marauders who break into the apartment building (*GJS* 160), and he is irrevocably excluded from the web of capitalist production and consumption that forms the horizon of all Bucky's activities: as his mother sardonically remarks, her husband "wanted to sell the kid to a carnival. But who'd buy him?" (134).

Burn's claim that via the motif of the triune brain, evolution "controls the entirety" of the novel clearly overstates the case. Yet it can be productive if set alongside the observations that "the buying and selling of products is what makes the world of *Great Jones Street* turn," (DeCurtis 137), and that this is "a novel about language" (Veggian 46). In the role of language, in fact, we can locate another aspect that connects the text to the materiality of mind. A number of critics have picked up on the protagonist's strained relation to language, and in fact it is the Micklewhite boy's lack of the linguistic faculty that makes him so fascinating to Bucky, who marvels at the "beauty and horror of wordless things." As Osteen notes, this nonverbal or preverbal quality makes the boy a savant of kinds, in line with a number of similar DeLillo characters whose lack or distortion of speech prompts the texts' protagonists to "try to emulate their quasi-autistic conditions in order to rediscover their voices or acquire new ones" ("Dedalian" 140). Crucially, in *Great Jones Street*, this lack is tied to biological and neurological materiality, a connection that DeLillo also emphasizes in subsequent novels.

Lack of speech is figured here as the muteness of organic nature itself. Bucky muses that the sounds of the boy's dreaming evince a "fundamental terror inside things that grow, things that trade chemicals with the air" (51-52). Consequently, his encounter with him takes the form of an act of reluctant, and uneasy, recognition:

> Standing before him was like witnessing the progress of some impossible mutation, bird to brown worm, but of course he'd been merely deposited there, wet, white and unchanging, completely stagnant, and I began to feel that I was the other point of the progression. [...] One felt nearly displaced by the hint of structural transposition; he was what we'd always feared, ourselves in radical divestment, scrawled across the dark. (161)

In this passage, the boy is simultaneously described as irredeemably *other* and undeniably familiar. Like Thomas Nagel in "What Is It Like to Be a Bat?" Bucky speculates about the nature of an alien consciousness: "I must have seemed a shadow to him, thin liquid, incidental to the block of light he lived in." He then ponders whether he can assign an unfathomable otherness to him: "It would have been better (and even cheering) to think of him as some kind of super-crustacean or diabolic boiled vegetable." But in the end, Bucky needs to admit that this is not a feasible option, because "he was too human for that, adhering to me as though by suction or sticky filaments" (161-62). We see here a somewhat problematic romanticization of the disabled youth as both an unconscious harbinger of a (possibly mystic) pre-linguistic reality and an emblem of the repressed knowledge of the organic nature of human life. Bucky imagines his "embryonic," mute existence as indexing, in "structural transposition," both a component of his own condition—his biological materiality—and its distorted mirror image, the "radical divestment" of the supreme human capability of language.[26]

However, these two aspects—materiality and language—are ultimately linked. If brain damage turns the boy into the personification of the "beauty and horror of wordless things," it is also the pharmacological manipulation of the brain as a material entity via a "lobotomizing drug" (Boxall 39) that allows Bucky to intuit what DeLillo calls "the word beyond speech" (LeClair interview 10). One of *Great Jones Street*'s subplots concerns an experimental drug known as "the product." Reputedly developed by the government to rob subversive activists of their power to speak, the substance is much sought after by all kinds of criminal elements. One of these is the ironically-named Happy Valley Farm Commune, a group that regards Bucky's withdrawal from public view as testament to his agreement with their project of returning "the idea of privacy to American life" (16). When, toward the novel's end, Bucky refuses to comply with the wishes of the commune and commit suicide to ensure his continued silence, he is instead injected with the drug and thus transformed into a "pharmaceutical Philomela" (Cowart). It is this episode, I argue, that presents the novel's most intriguing treatment of the materiality of mind.

The drug's disruptive chemical capacity is helpfully explained by Fred Chess, the radical commune's putative leader: "It's a drug that affects one or more areas of the left sector of the brain. Language sector. [...] It damages the cells in one or more areas of the left sector of the human brain. Loss of speech in other words" (255). Clearly this chemical compound, referred to repeatedly as "the ultimate drug" (57, 227, 228), is described in terms that differ dramatically from the counterculture's customary vocabulary of mind-expanding, consciousness-altering substances. If its effects are consistently rendered in terms borrowed from the

---

26  The notion of language as the supreme human capacity can be traced back to the Aristotelian view of humans as beings that are characterized by their mastery of language, the only animals "endowed with the gift of speech" (*Politics* 28).

neuro-materialist lexicon, the characters' mastery of scientific knowledge and language is far from complete: the drug targets a rather imprecise "one or more areas." This statement has a precedent: earlier in the novel, the rock star-turned-drug dealer Watney discusses the substance in similar terms: "The drug attacks a particular region in the left hemisphere of the brain. That's the verbal hemisphere, it seems. Where the words are kept" (228).[27]

*It seems.* Here DeLillo signals that the materialist science of the mind is an imprecise, perhaps somewhat premature endeavor, and along with his doubly mediated presentation of the monadanom episode (which, after all, figures as sci-fi, not science), such passages create a cumulative, ironical effect that distances his work from the scientific models it appropriates. It makes little sense, then to speak, as Burn does, of *Great Jones Street* as a text engaging in a "straightforward endorsement of its neuroscientific sources" ("Mapping" 39). The novel's characters display only an inchoate knowledge of neuroscientific concepts, and the efficacy of the "product" proves imperfect as well. Osteen has noted that the Micklewhite boy's "wordlessness constitutes the 'pure' form of expression that Bucky has been seeking" throughout the novel (55), but the drug that "destroys the cortical capacity for language" (Cowart 39) is too blunt an instrument to attain this goal. "You'll be perfectly healthy. You won't be able to make words, that's all. They just won't come into your mind the way they normally do and the way we all take for granted they will. Sounds yes. Sounds galore. But no words," Chess informs Bucky before administering the drug (255). Afterwards, Bucky is indeed reduced to sounds, like the Micklewhite boy: Bucky describes how he "stood above the rivers east and west, *wod-or*, this double sound all I could fashion from the sight of sluggish currents in transit to the sea" (258; original emphasis). For a while, the effects are as hoped for: Bucky spends "weeks of deep peace, [...] unreasonably happy, subsisting in blessed circumstance, thinking of myself as a kind of living chant" (264).

If this reads like a return to a prelapsarian plenitude that recalls *End Zone*'s nautiloid/monadanom episode, the connection seems valid. The "product's" desired effect, Michael Valdez Moses notes, "would be to return human beings to a blissful subhuman state, free of [...] logos" (76), and indeed Bucky speaks of his drug experience as an attempt at "permanent withdrawal to that unimprinted level where all sound is silken and nothing erodes in the mad weather of language" (265). As for the nautiloid in *End Zone*, the language capacity is figured as a neural

---

27  It is no coincidence that Watney's description comes on the heels of his avowal that "[p]eople are human beings. They're creatures of infinite capacity. They have immortal souls they do" (228). By juxtaposing this statement, which insists on mind-body dualism, with the subsequent explication of materialist psychopharmacology that suggests the utter inseparability of mind (i.e., language) and body, DeLillo already hints at the defining problem at the heart of the new materialism of the mind.

"imprint," a mechanism of the material brain. When the effects begin to wear off, Bucky recounts, "*Mouth* was the first word to reach me, dropping from one speech mechanism to the other," i.e., from neural to verbal language. The drug's effects, regrettably, are temporary, a fact Bucky registers as a failure, a "defeat." "Several weeks of immense serenity. Then ended," he drily notes (264-65). If a return to an infantile or "reptilian," prelinguistic state is what Bucky aspires to, pharmacology ultimately fails to deliver such "self-entombment" (Dewey, *Grief* 34); a grudging "return to prior modes" is therefore inevitable (*GJS* 264).

Rather than locating a materialist imaginary at the center of the text, as Burn does, I would argue that the materiality of mind is a peripheral, but not insignificant concern for DeLillo in this novel. *Great Jones Street* fulfills an intermediate function with regard to this question: it is looking back, toward *End Zone* and its monadanom parable, and it is looking forward, to *Ratner's Star* and its interest in cerebral hemisphericity, as well as to *White Noise*'s treatment of psychotropic medication, the localization of brain functions, and the "cerebral subject." *Great Jones Street* draws on the biological imaginary of *End Zone*, imagining what the dependence of consciousness on neural materiality (which was only presented in parable form in the earlier novel) might actually look like, and what it might imply. At the same time, its tentative treatments of the relation between brain and logos anticipate the more developed and sustained interest in this relation that we find in *Ratner's Star*, DeLillo's next novel.

## Ratner's Star

At first sight, *Ratner's Star* provides more grist for the mills of those who lament the dearth of DeLillo's character delineation. On closer examination, however, the complaint proves beside the point: austerity of characterization, in this novel, is programmatic and very much an intended effect. *Ratner's Star*, a highly schematic text that DeLillo himself described as aspiring toward "naked structure" (11), is perhaps the author's most overtly intertextual book, modeled structurally on Lewis Carroll's Alice books and formally on the genre of Menippean satire.[28] The essence of the latter form, Joel Relihan writes, "is an otherworldly fantasy in which a naive experimenter travels to an impossible realm in order to learn that the truth is not to be found at the edges of the world but at home and under one's own feet," a truth that is in turn subverted and made comic since, "in accordance with good

---

28 In an overt homage to Carroll's books, the two parts of *Ratner's Star* are titled "Adventures" and "Reflections." Boxall mentions Yeats's *A Vision* as another "guiding text" (60), and Dewey adds *Rasselas, Candide*, and *Gulliver's Travels* to the list of allusions of a novel that also doubles as "science fiction, autobiography, [...] bildungsroman, and cautionary allegory" (*Beyond* 41-42).

Cynic principles, one cannot be dogmatic even about one's anti-dogmatism, and the challenge to accepted authority and received truths cannot honestly take the form of a new authority and a new absolute truth" (109-10). In *Ratner's Star*, which is set in a slightly skewed but still highly recognizable alternate history,[29] this role falls to Billy Twillig, a fourteen-year old math genius and freshly baked winner of the first Nobel Prize in mathematics. Billy is recruited to join Field Experiment Number One, an enormous research installation where a motley crew of scientists and theorists is secretly engaged in the attempt to decode a message from outer space.

Here, somewhere in the remote plains of central Asia, Billy enters the rabbit hole, encountering a seemingly interminable succession of wacky characters who take turns holding forth on their bizarre research projects. Menippean satire provides a venerable generic precedent for this mode of representation. Its form, David Musgrave notes, is characterized by send-ups of the *"philosophius gloriosus, or learned crank,"* a line of attack that accounts for the genre's depiction of "eccentricity, madness, foolishness, extreme behavior or abnormal mental states," qualities which often find expression in a "grotesque iconography, [...] such as comic mésalliances, giants, talking machines, dwarves," and the like (2, 23).

The demented cast of characters Billy meets on his journey indeed fits this category, from his mentor, Robert Hopper Softly, a "child-sized man, [...] pathologically stunted" (*RS* 261)[30] to the titular Shazar Lazarus Ratner, a modern-day Methuselah kept alive in a sterile tent, whose face has to be re-inflated upon "collapsing" at regular intervals. Apart from such "grotesque iconography," little visual information is imparted; declamation wins out over description. This, too, is in keeping with tradition. After all, Mikhail Bakhtin associates the Mennipea with heavily discursive forms like the Socratic dialogue, the diatribe, and the soliloquy (113), while Northrop Frye notes that the form "deals less with people as such than with mental attitudes" and "differs from the novel in its characterization, which is stylized rather than naturalistic, and presents people as mouthpieces of the ideas they represent" (309). We would do well, therefore, to entertain the notion that DeLillo does not present us with "talking heads" out of some sense of loyalty to postmodern philosophy but rather because the rich history of his formal model affords a useful template for satirizing an exclusive devotion to the life of the mind.

---

29  Like the characters, the temporal and geographical setting is never "fleshed out." Boxall suggests the novel's action might take place in 1979 (only a couple of years into the future from the perspective of the novel's publication date in 1976) but the reader repeatedly stumbles over minor alterations to historical reality. For instance, Billy flies aboard a "Sony 747" (1), and there are vague intimations of geopolitical conflict involving, of all places, peaceable Sweden (4).

30  Here and subsequently, *Ratner's Star* is abbreviated as *RS* in parenthetical citations.

It is not surprising, then, that one of the central characters, Maurice Wu, has an intuition of "persistent images of pure form, the sense that he was accompanying himself out of some systemic pattern" (363). After all, attachment to "pure form" and "systemic pattern" is the characteristic mark of the particular pathology—excessive cerebration—that unites the panoply of scientific freaks DeLillo assembles at Field Experiment Number One (FENO). The clamor of voices vying for Billy's attention keeps building to a chorus that echoes the Cheshire cat: "We're all mad here" (65). As Charles Molesworth observes, "the novel suggests that science is futile, an exercise that is largely a displacement of human neurosis" (145). Seen this way, DeLillo appears as a proponent of what Christian Thorne calls the "dialectic of counter-enlightenment," as a postmodern inheritor of the "Pyrrhonists of antiquity and modern Europe" (Thorne 11).[31]

What role does the materiality of mind play in all this? To begin with, a number of FENO scientists actively study the human brain or base their theories on its functions; through their work, the novel is "solidly anchored in the scientific discourse of the early seventies" (Burn, "Neuroscience" 210).[32] Roughly halfway through the novel, Billy meets Dr. Skip Wismer, who is captivated by "the question of what happens in the first few seconds after electrical activity in the brain ceases forever" (241-42). Wismer introduces Billy to his colleague Cheops Feeley, whose name marks him as similarly obsessed with questions of immortality and the afterlife.[33] It comes as no surprise, therefore, that his pet project involves the implantation of a so-called "Leduc electrode" under the scalp to "stimulate and record brain activity" and achieve a union of human consciousness and machinic computation.

The researchers propose that Billy undergo the procedure, thereby combining his intuitive mathematical skills with the massive computational power of "Space Brain," the facility's aptly named supercomputer. "You with your enormous powers of abstraction. Space Brain with its unsurpassed superfine computations," Feeley rhapsodizes, envisioning a "single dynamic entity" as the emergent result of this wedding of man and machine. To this, Billy remarks: "Sounds familiar, this combination" (244). The reason that this vision of a "single dynamic entity" consisting of two functionally specialized components should sound familiar is

---

31  Like his titular character, the DeLillo of *Ratner's Star* appears "drawn to an anti-enlightenment mysticism, drawn to cast a veil over the limits of the universe, to assume that, in the vast symmetrical whole of the universe there are things that remain unknown, and unknowable" (Boxall 55).

32  For the historical sources of these investigations, see Burn, who points out that it is mainly "popular accounts of brain research that underpin *Ratner's Star*," such as journalistic articles published in *The New Yorker* or *The New York Times* in the 1970s ("Neuroscience" 210).

33  Accordingly, Feeley is proud to mention that apart from the Cheops Feeley Medal, "[t]here's a science fair, two research centers and a gypsy health clinic" named after him (243).

that the experiment is effectively modeled on the idea of cerebral hemisphericity, which shapes the novel to such a degree that Burn has suggested reclassifying the novel as a "neurofiction," a generic designation by which he understands a literary work that "carries on a dialogue with the contemporary sciences of mind" ("Neuroscience" 211).

The asymmetry of the brain, its partition into left and right hemispheres with specific functions, became a topic of interest in the 1970s, owing initially to the split-brain research conducted by Michael Gazzaniga and Roger Sperry. In the 1960s, split-brain surgery, or "the surgical section of the corpus callosum," i.e., the band of nerve fibers connecting the two hemispheres of the brain, was sometimes adopted as a measure of last resort in the treatment of epileptic patients (Sperry 428). Gazzaniga and Sperry found that in such patients, whose hemispheres were split off and thus unable to communicate with each other, visual information processed by the left side of the brain elicited a conscious, verbal response, while information processed by the right hemisphere was available to procedural and motor memory but remained at a sub-verbal and subconscious level. Their experiments demonstrated the relative autonomy of the cerebral hemispheres[34] and posited the existence of a "left brain interpreter," a mechanism whose task it is to integrate new information in narrative form (Gazzaniga, "Social" 5). The philosophical implications were clear: agency shifted from the conscious self to subconscious cerebral processes, while self-report was relegated from a subject's ability to meaningfully (and correctly) explain its thoughts and actions to the status of an after-the-fact rationalization, becoming, essentially, a fiction. As a contemporary commentator, looking back on the experiments taking place in the 1970s on the split-brain and blindsight phenomena, writes: "The subject sees absolutely nothing there" (Revonsuo 64). It is the brain, or its "modules," that do the seeing and perceiving, and, in the form of "left brain interpreter," even the speaking. The left hemisphere "edits our experiences, makes them comprehensible and palatable," Paul Broks writes. "It is the brain's spin-doctor" (37).

Sperry and Gazzaniga first made their research available to a wider audience through an article in *Scientific American* 1967 that reported on "how the separation of the hemispheres affects the mental capacities of the human brain" (Gazzaniga, "Split" 25). In the subsequent decade, these ideas began to filter through the media and into the wider cultural imaginary.[35] "In the 1970s," Robert Keith Sawyer explains, "the popular media took hold of these findings, and soon it became

---

34  "The left brain is dominant for language and speech. The right excels at visual-motor tasks" (Gazzaniga, "Revisited" 27).

35  Burn, who has researched the sources of *Ratner's Star* in the archive of DeLillo's papers, notes that perhaps the most important source for DeLillo was *The New York Times*, which "devoted several articles to new breakthroughs" in brain research in the early seventies ("Neuroscience" 215).

widely believed that the left brain was the rational mind, while the right brain was the creative mind" (160). The notion that the right hemisphere is responsible for gestalt stimuli while the left hemisphere assumes analytical tasks also demonstrably informs *Ratner's Star*, a fact that has led Burn to go so far as to speak of a "neural architecture" that underlies the text ("Mapping" 40).

Developing schema and creating a sense of progression is "exactly what the left hemisphere interpreter excels at," writes Gazzaniga ("Revisited" 29)—an observation reflected in the novel by Feeley's admission that since the Leduc electrode "tends to overstimulate the left side of the brain," Billy would likely be struck by "an overpowering sense of sequence" and become "acutely aware of the arrangement of things" after its implantation:

> True, you'll find yourself analyzing a continuous series of acts in terms of their discrete components. Eating a sandwich will no longer be the smooth operation you've always known it to be. You'll experience, should you agree to host the electrode, a strong awareness of your hands, your mouth, your throat, your stomach, whatever's between the slices of bread, the bread itself. [...] You'll be involved in a very detailed treatment of reality. A parody of the left brain. But is this reality of yours less valid than ordinary reality? Not at all. You'll be establishing fresh paths of awareness. (245)

This bizarre preview of the electrode's potential effects suggests two crucial consequences of the materialist mind the character envisions. First, Feeley ascribes a primacy to the brain, which produces the reality of the subject. An altered brain state, it is implied, is no les "real" or valid than its baseline reference value. In Feeley's neuroscientific constructionism, reality and the self become epiphenomena, produced by, and wholly dependent on the material components of the brain. As Hercule Leduc, the (fictional) electrode's inventor, states in the novel: "All of physical reality is a matter of convenience," a view in light of which the vicissitudes of the ego appear as little more than "a style of incessant self-deception" (246-47).

Second, the lateralization of brain function is presented as a possible source of alienation. If the hemispheres cease to function in synchrony, subjective experience ceases to be "the smooth operation" one is accustomed to. "The left hemisphere is the hemisphere of abstraction," Iain McGilchrist's authoritative monograph on the divided brain informs us; its business is the disassembly of phenomena into discrete parts to be analyzed (50). Accordingly, Feeley tells Billy that overactivity of the left side of the brain results in an overly acute awareness of oneself and one's parts as discrete rather than unified. Once implanted, the electrode would cause Billy to cease experiencing himself as an embodied being and turn him into a grotesque exaggeration of the Cartesian central consciousness, painstakingly aware of a transformation of even the most automatic subcutaneous events into conscious decisions and actions: "Every breath you take will be subjected to a thorough sequential analysis. Heart, lungs, nostrils, oxygen, carbon dioxide and so forth," Feeley informs him (245). The envisioned effects of the electrode thus become an intensified version of a more general argument the novel makes: an exclusive focus on the left brain, i.e., language, rationality, and intellect, impoverishes human beings and turns them into the grotesques Billy encounters at FENO, such as the narcoleptic LoQuadro, who is described as "nervously alert, seeming to be engaged in self-espionage, ever attentive to the fluctuations of electric potential in his brain" (65).

Excessive cerebration, we learn in *Ratner's Star*, can be understood as a psychic defense against the knowledge of death. Thus Wismer declares himself "depressed and worried" by the idea of death, the "sheer allness, the sheerness of it all," and Leduc tells Billy: "We are most a victim of the principle of intelligence when we try to conceal our lonely terror" (241, 247). One of the ways in which DeLillo advances this point is through allusions to Descartes, a figure often identified as the source of the mind-body problem. DeLillo has stated that with *Ratner's Star*, he sought to write a "cult history of seminal figures in mathematics (LeClair interview 11), and in chapters 4 and 5, Descartes serves as the text's guiding light. This is already signaled by the chapter headings, whose titles, "Expansion" and "Dichotomy," reference the concept of *res extensa* and mind-body dualism respectively. Over the course of these two chapters, Billy meets Soma Tobias, who by virtue of her aptronymical name and her status as the architect of FENO's building is associated with body-as-matter. Conversely, he also learns more about the facility's supercomputer, the brain inside the building's body that "continues to expand," and "refuses to be contained," thus representing the immaterial mind of Cartesian philosophy (65).

Yet the allusions do not stop there: Billy himself shares several characteristics with Descartes. Like Descartes in his small cabin in wintry Ulm, Billy has a series of "three dreams" during which the world appears to him as "comprehensible, a plane of equations, all knowledge able to be welded, all nature controllable," and like the seventeenth-century philosopher who experienced his oneiric vision while enlisted in the army of the Duke of Bavaria, he is not only "a dreamer," but "a soldier in repose" (64). The significance of these parallels consists in Billy's function within the text as the uncorrupted "naive experimenter" who stands at the center of both Menippean satire and the bildungsroman. As such, it is Billy's task to "overcome a Cartesian mind-body dualism that plagues most of FENO's self-involved scientists," as Osteen suggests (70).

What is more, many of the researchers Billy meets resemble Cartesian caricatures. Like LoQuadro, "engaged in self-espionage," many characters convey what DeLillo has called "a kind of fragmented self-consciousness." There is a "mechanical element" to his characters, DeLillo has stated (LeClair interview 5), and nowhere is this more clearly visible than in *Ratner's Star*: in a dark satire of Cartesian mechanicism, the characters intone phrases like "My mouth says hello" or "I don't think my ears are hearing" (6, 437), as if the aspects of the social, sensory body amounted to little else but an assemblage of machinic components that are as amenable to control and observation as they are prone to malfunction. The "Convergence Inward" that spells the title of chapter 6 references the life of the mind led by the scientists, a trajectory that is "both symptom and cause of their alienation" (Osteen 72).

DeLillo portrays this alienation as *cerebral* in the literal sense of the word. Toward the end of the novel, the mathematician and logician Edna Lown, "in the grip of scientific rapture," which turns "[t]he past, the whole chromium world" into nothing more than "meek recollection, the negative image of colleagues, family and friends," is described as:

> entering herself just as surely as if she'd been able to bend her arms into her mouth and swallow them to the shoulders; arms, legs, torso; a bewitchingly comic meditation technique; leaving the head balanced on a cushion, head and skull, abode of the layered brain, everything we are and feel and know; the universe we've made. (329)

This is simultaneously an invocation of neuroscientific idealism—the brain as all-encompassing and all-productive—and a "bewitchingly comic" representation of Billy's possible fate: *in extremis*, Cartesian rationalism means "becoming a brain without a body" (Osteen 70).[36] Billy's fate, however, is far from settled. A large share of the novel's considerable humor derives from Billy's incredulous and laconic responses to the absurd situations and propositions he is confronted with. Upon being told by Feeley that he is "definitely the person we want" for the brain electrode experiment, Billy begs to differ: "my head stays shut," he declares. And for good reason: DeLillo leaves little doubt that this endeavor, too, is an inherently absurd one. To drive the point home, we are treated to an exchange between Feeley and Billy about the scientific prize named after the older researcher, which is "given for work that's crazy in places," and contains a particularly high "madness content." True to his name, Feeley then proceeds to finger Billy's scalp, locating a "mathematics bump" on his skull. DeLillo here aligns Feeley's ostensibly cutting-edge neuroscientific research with its coarse and thoroughly discredited nineteenth-century predecessor, phrenology (243). Here as elsewhere, Billy's curt retorts establish him as a sane person in an insane environment.

---

36  Anticipating Billy's potential development, a classmate who sees him reading advanced mathematical texts, "sometimes two at a time," remarks, "What I got sitting downside me here is getting to be nothing but two eyes and a head" (136).

What marks this environment as thoroughly deranged is its exclusive focus on the activities of the left hemisphere: the whole research center functions as a "parody of the left brain." In true bildungsroman fashion, Billy's mission is to learn from this environment, to avoid following in the mad scientist's footsteps, to minimize the "madness content" of his own embodied psyche. This task, too, is couched in brain rhetoric. Halfway through the novel Billy visits Henrik Endor, formerly "a celebrated mathematician and astrophysicist" who has since abandoned scientific inquiry. Frustrated with his failure to decode the transmission, he has resigned himself to a hermitic existence in the desert, where he lives in a hole in the ground, eating worms and larvae. Equally crazed as the other scientists, Endor nonetheless functions as an important counterweight to their pursuits. Whereas FENO is occupied with "symbolic structure" and [t]he purest of pure science," Endor is "trapped in matter," as one of his former collaborators puts it (96).

This opposition between the scientists and their estranged colleague repeats the dualism of the Cartesian separation between mind and matter, yet it would be inadequate to associate the earth-bound Endor exclusively with (geological or biological) materiality: he, too, is an aficionado of cerebral hemisphericity, informing Billy that "[w]hatever order can be conceived by the left-handed mind is yours to impose elsewhere" (194). More precisely, Endor's function is to remind us of the role of the right hemisphere. To advise the "naive experimenter," he launches into a litany of exhortations spanning an uninterrupted one and a half pages, to which Billy replies in characteristic curtness, "All that?" The gist of Endor's counsel becomes apparent toward the end of his monologue:

> Nothing less than sanity itself must be tipped into the scheme. Compulsions, tumults, fevers, epileptic storms. What is unlearned, along with your craftiest fabrications. Remember the savage and what he accomplished in his instinct for pure space and the mathematics of motion. Inventor of the boomerang. Yes, he pulled the string on space itself. The right side of his brain outprocessed the left. Intuition and motion and the conquest of time. It's the object of your labor, lad, to join the hemispheres. Bring logical sequence to delirium, reason to the forager squatting, language and meaning to the wild child's dream. (195)

This segment, which begins by endorsing the primitivism of the "savage" along with a Rimbaudian derangement of the senses that recalls the Romantics, ends with an appeal to strive toward synthesis, to "join the hemispheres" and thus unite intellect and intuition. Like Bucky in *Great Jones Street*, Billy is an in-between figure, but unlike Bucky, he is suspended not between art and commerce but between "the rigors of logic" as "a ruthlessly precise system of symbolic notation" (*RS* 272) and what the novel's narrator calls "holism, a state of unqualified being"

(329). Here and elsewhere, however, the text strongly hints at the possibility that non-linear creativity itself might be a neural process, as when Billy speculates about "whatever neocortical region nurtures the intuition, that contrapuntal faculty his mathematics relied on" (129).

But whereas logic and language are associated repeatedly with the risk of becoming "left-brain crazy" (RS 259), a less alienated form of being would appear to involve an acknowledgement of all that which rational science attempts to fend off or suppress. The text's Cartesian scheme links phenomena like ambiguity, uncertainty, contingency, decay, and death with the body, which resonates with the "screech and claw of the inexpressible" (RS 22). As Jean Venable, a central author figure in the novel, reflects: "all fiction takes place at the end of this process of crawl, scratch and gasp, this secret memory of death" (394). The mind, on the other hand, is associated in this scheme with the realm of language, of the symbolic, of mastery and the idea that ultimately, everything can be understood and expressed.

DeLillo scholars have pointed out that the scientists, who are "driven by a hunger for knowledge, by a frantic need to know everything, to divine the mechanics of the universe" (Boxall 55), are motivated, in the final analysis, by the desire to fend off death, and that Billy's uneasy relationship with the bodily, his aversion to excretions and anxiety over the sexual act might spring from similar sources (Dewey, *Beyond* 42-43). While the materiality of the mind is linked in *Ratner's Star* to a view of human beings as largely the products of their brains, as "cerebral subjects" in the sense proposed by Ortega/Vidal and Ehrenberg, the materiality of the body indexes a more primordial and less determined mode of existence.

As I hope to have demonstrated, for long stretches the novel appears to subscribe to a resolutely neuro-materialist imaginary that envisions the various capacities and capabilities of humans as predicated on the characteristics of their cerebral architecture. However, an important point of emphasis of my analysis here has also been that DeLillo consistently frames such avowals as the opinions and ideas of his crazed characters, thus undercutting the impression that he views brain research as a sufficient explanation for human subjectivity. As Burn notes, "DeLillo's treatment of neuro-rhetoric—whether borrowed from MacLean, Sperry, or elsewhere—is neither simply a passive transcription of their claims, nor an attempt to borrow whatever scientific authority accrues to their viewpoints" ("Infinite" 67); rather, his appropriation, in *Ratner's Star*, of materialist models of mind "probes the limits of neuroscience's explanatory power" ("Mapping" 39).

The novel's most emphatic endorsement of a self that is not expressible, let alone quantifiable solely in terms of cerebral anatomy comes toward the end, in a section entitled "I Am Not Just This." The narrative voice, easily identifiable as Billy's own, insists on its essential inexpressibility, in the book's only instance of first-person narration, worth citing here in its entirety:

> There is a life inside this life. A filling of gaps. There is something between the
> spaces. I am different from this. I am not just this but more. There is something
> else to me that I don't know how to reach. Just outside my reach there is something
> else that belongs to the rest of me. I don't know what to call it or how to reach it.
> But it's there. I am more than you know. But the space is too strange to cross. I can't
> get there but I know it is there to get to. On the other side is where it's free. If only
> I could remember what the light was like in that space before I had eyes to see it
> with. When I had mush for eyes. When I was dripping tissue. There is something
> in the space between what I know and what I am and what fills this space is what I
> know there are no words for. (370)

This subjective record of self-reflection proposes that true, transcendental subjectivity relies on a connection between the ineffable—the stuff of mysticism—and
biology, the primordial oneness of child and womb. It exceeds both the realm of
the linguistic "I" (not least, the avowal "I am more than this" refers to the first-person pronoun we find on the page) and that of consciousness itself. It is the stuff
of intuition and transcendence, which neither science nor language, the products
of the left brain, can attain: "I can't get there but I know it is there to get to" is a
proposition neither science nor logic can prove. But by saying he is "not just this
but more," Billy also means that he cannot be reduced to mere matter, or studied with scientific methods: his subjectivity is irreducible to objective description.
This realization marks a turning point for Billy. When, shortly after this passage,
he comes across an underground river, his reaction, and the register in which the
narration records it, suggest that he has acquired a different mindset than the scientists, "those who drove hooks into nature" (RS 34), and that he might have even
overcome his own "fear of the body's fundamental reality" (RS 37).

> It came flowing past him, carrying clay, silt and organic debris, carrying limestone
> to redeposit, straight on past, leaving him only a hint of its animal presence, that
> complex and adaptive motivation that directs living things toward the strange-
> ness, beauty and freedom of repeated sequences. Naturally he put his hands in
> the water. It was cold enough to make him tremble and when he cupped his hands
> and brought some water to his lips to drink he felt some seconds later a brief asser-
> tion of pain behind his right eye. Mildly frightening. When it subsided, he simply
> listened to the river, feeling no special need to see it, photograph it or take samples
> home to study. He had *tasted* it, after all. (373; original emphasis)

Like the "I Am Not Just This" section, this passage, embedded in a section titled "I
Take a Drink," is nearly without parallel in the rest of the novel; almost nowhere
else does the steady succession of dialogue and stream-of-consciousness renderings let up and allow for a detailed description of subjective, phenomenological

experience. The implication is clear: Billy is able to experience and accept rather than investigate and dissect nature, becoming one with it (drinking the water resembles an act of communion) instead of transforming it into symbols and forcing it to conform to a need for "an overarching symmetry" (*RS* 49). The "underground river" evokes the river Styx and the Greek underworld; it bears deathly associations as it bears along "organic debris" awaiting its "redeposit" in cycles of growth and decay. But for Billy, this no longer translates into a knowledge that has to be repressed at all costs; instead, it signals the "beauty and freedom of repeated sequences." Consequently, the experience becomes bearable: "Mildly frightening," Billy concludes laconically.

Mild fright would appear as a significant improvement, preferable to the "unnamable horror" Billy still feels when confronted with the thought of bodily decay and mortality at the beginning of the novel (6-7). As a polysemous generic hybrid and ambiguous modernist allegory, *Ratner's Star* allows for multiple readings and interpretations, but read as a scientific satire or bildungsroman (two of its most dominant generic templates), the novel seems to make an argument against the coldly analytical examination of thought, including its material substrates, and in favor of an embodied, *phenomenological* account of subjectivity that is able to confront rather than suppress the experience of being-in-the-world as well as being-toward-death.[37] DeLillo's position here resembles that of neuropsychologist Paul Broks, who proposes that minds emerge from "the spaces between things," i.e., "process and interaction, not substance," and that "we"—the conscious, feeling subjects of human experience—are embodied but nonetheless "nowhere traceable within the physical structures of the body" (56, 95). That DeLillo makes a similar argument in large part by drawing on, discussing, and most irreverently *playing with* neurobiological knowledge speaks to the considerable amount of creative and artistic leeway that literary authors command in deploying materialist models of mind.

However, there is a caveat to this observation, for DeLillo subscribes to the idea that fear has primal, biological origins which have left their evolutionary mark on the human nervous system. "The fear in DeLillo's fiction," Tom LeClair points out, "is primal, hard wired, and universal, pulsing up from the brain stem" (142). This observation leads back to the layered, evolutionary model of the brain advanced by MacLean and to the related idea of modularity, according to which certain instincts and emotions bypass cognition and volition, generating instead immediate and automatic reactions that are only accessible to consciousness in retro-

---

37 The need for such an accounting is also palpable in recent writing on the implications of neuroscience for conceptions of the self. Paul Broks's assertion that "we are not only physically *embodied*, but also *embedded* in the world about us," that the mind needs to be understood as "distributed beyond biological boundaries," is a typical example here (101; original emphases).

spect. In *Ratner's Star*, DeLillo plays with the idea that such primordial dynamics underlie and continue to shape the modern psyche. To this end, the text makes use of an extended spatial metaphor that associates what lies below—all manners of subterranean locales or deeper strata—with the equally "hidden" workings of the brain in general and the evolutionary subconscious in particular.

In a telling turn of phrase we learn that Billy's father "spent nearly half his conscious life" underground, as a safety inspector for the New York subway system. When he takes a seven-year-old Billy into the tunnels to show him his place of work, part of his rationale is that he intends to "introduce his lone son to the idea that existence tends to be nourished from below, from the fear level" (4). The idea appears to take hold: as Billy explores the FENO complex, the narrator often records Billy's somatic awareness, feeling "his own fear uncurl from his stomach" or noticing how a "fear bubble traveled upward through his respiratory system" (95-96). In all these instances, "cavernous fear" is described as an autonomous nervous reaction that rises up from the depths of bodily existence (*RS* 249).

If, in the spatial matrix of the novel, the underworld is associated with the phylogenetic emotional traces buried in the right brain (the seat of emotion according to the popular split-brain scheme of the 1970s), the scientists' "left-brained" attempts to pursue the inverse route—to close the distance to the stars above—suffers a significant and symbolic setback. This is foreshadowed on the one hand by the express hope that the message will "tell us something important about ourselves," as Endor, himself a subterranean figure, announces (91), and on the other hand by Billy's intuition that "there is always a danger linked to the science of probing the substratum" (18). As it eventually turns out, the message did not come from above, from outer space; instead, it came from below, from the primordial past, as a transmission from an ancient human civilization that had reached a more evolved level than that of the modern, contemporary world but subsequently vanished: a case of "counterevolution" or "reverse evolution" (*RS* 327, 388).

The prospect of learning "something important about ourselves" is, of course, a frequently mentioned aspect of new materialist anthropologies. Countless books on the brain, the nervous system, or embodiment per se promise to inform us about our true nature.[38] "When we see the brain we realize that we are, at one level, no more than meat; and, on another, no more than fiction," neuropsychologist

---

38  We can think here of titles such as Jean-Pierre Changeux's Neuronal Man, Daniel Dennett's Consciousness Explained, Joseph LeDoux's Synaptic Self: How Our Brains Become Who We Are, Thomas Metzinger's The Ego Tunnel: The Science of the Mind and the Myth of the Self, as well as books that take an opposing position, like Jeffrey Schwartz and Rebecca Gladding's You Are Not Your Brain, Alva Noë's Out of Our Heads: Why You Are Not Your Brain, and Other Lessons from the Biology of Consciousness, or Francisco Varela, Evan Thompson and Eleanor Rosch's The Embodied Mind: Cognitive Science and Human Experience.

Paul Broks writes (63). And even though the self is "nowhere traceable within the physical structures of the body," it is embodied nonetheless, and therefore "we are a natural product of [the world's] material evolution: science, intellect, emotions, moral codes and all" (Broks 143). In close alignment with such materialist anthropologies, in *Ratner's Star* this "something important about ourselves" will be discovered not by a star-gazing scientist but by a spelunker who stumbles across the fate of present-day humanity by literally "probing the substratum" of the prehistory of the species while digging for and examining skulls.

Along with Billy, who at the end of the novel finally figures out that the message refers to a particular time (the moment of an unscheduled and scientifically unexplainable solar eclipse that calls analytical inquiry itself into question), it is archaeologist and anthropologist Maurice Wu who solves the riddle of the stellar transmission. It is Wu who unearths the skulls of obviously highly evolved human ancestors: "Man more advanced the deeper we dig" (*RS* 321). If Billy's task is "to join the hemispheres," Wu is similarly preoccupied with the constraints and characteristics of the cerebrum:

> What we need, he believed, is a way to reinvent the human brain. As now constituted it can be viewed in cross-section as a model for examining the relative depths of protohistoric and modern terror. Cycles and swamp terrains of fear and periodically recurring depressions and earliest wetland secretions of dread (brain stem and midbrain), not to mention Mr. Mammal as paranoid grandee of the grassy plains, that (limbic) region of emotional disorganization, falling sickness, psychosomatic choking, another way of saying terror of the veldt, he thought, which is fear not really of lurkers in long grass but of the veldt itself, its terrifying endlessness, its obliteration of both singularity and pluralism, its lack of soul-cozying nooks, its tendency to disappear into itself, leaving us, he thought, with the geometry, music and poetry of our evolved, cross-referencing and highly specialized outer layer of gray tissue (cerebral cortex), not to mention celestial mechanics, medicine, the research and development of wars, not to mention voiceless cries in the night, utterly neomammalian in this last activity, a cortical subclass of fear itself [...]. (381)

In a significant deviation from previous narrative modality, this breathless passage then abruptly shifts into the consciousness of another character, the writer Jean Venable, so that we are left with the impression that the distinctions between individual characters begin to dissolve, a twist of technique that is very much in keeping with the idea of the biological universality of human consciousness and its products, which is adumbrated here in Wu's reflection on the evolutionary brain. Yet even more striking is the way in which Wu's imaginary journey through the Triune Brain's sections manages to redescribe both the lowest, "earliest wetland secretions of dread" and the highest cultural and cognitive achievements of humanity, from music to medicine, as outgrowths of cerebral architecture, thus connecting "protohistoric and modern terror." Here it is not only individual subjectivity that is dependent on a "highly specialized outer layer of gray tissue," but the collective consciousness of the human race as such.

LeClair is certainly right that DeLillo here "investigates the rolling effects of the brain's fear, illustrating its obsessions and self-destructive loops" (142), but the framing of this episode should also alert us to its less serious, more playful aspects. Its setting—a warren of underground caves—allegorically indexes the fathoms of the human skull, but the inhabitants of these caves also point toward the impossibility of determining the depths of the brain in an exhaustive or final manner. The caves house scores of megaderma—"false vampire" bats. With Wu pondering "[c]razed bat consciousness," we are reminded of Thomas Nagel's seminal essay, which argued for the ultimate unfathomability of subjectivity, its inaccessibility to third-person observation. It surely is significant that Wu, who deduces advances in intelligence from "increased cranial capacity" (321) and infers the qualities of "Mr. Mammal" from a cross-section of his brain, finds himself overwhelmed when reflecting, like Nagel, on the interiority of bats. His orderly thoughts on the intricacies of echolocation fail when he observes the bats begin to take flight.[39] "Wu began to laugh. He didn't know what was going on. [...] It was an incoherent event" (395).

Likewise, Wu's perception of the cave as "a living madness," filled with a "sense of insane life" hints at the limits of analytical, scientific inquiry (395). DeLillo's irreverent stance toward brain research, which he mines for metaphors and motifs while never accepting it as gospel, never lets us forget that for all its cumulative insights, the history of the science of mind is also littered with false starts and dead ends, and that it has, occasionally, been as insane as the subjects it purported to study. It is not for nothing that Maurice Wu, descending into a "living cave," which reminds him of "the valves and piping of the body," and from there into a "small chamber" that evokes the narrow confines of the human skull,[40] finally finds himself "at the edge of the guano deposit" (380-82). Playing on the slang term for "crazy, mad, insane," Wu, figuratively burrowing down into the history of the brain, makes there a most unglamorous finding: "Countless decades

---

39  Donald R. Griffin's 1944 finding that bats use echolocation has in fact been retrospectively awarded the status of a defining discovery in the history of neuroscience: see chapter 11 of Gross. It also provided an important impetus for Nagel's essay (Nagel and Griffin taught together for a time at Rockefeller University).

40  The association of skull and brain with enclosures or confined locales is an extended motif in the novel, as witnessed in the following description of Billy's room, or "canister," at FENO: "The room is extensively shielded from outside interference. The walls, the floors, and all the furniture are equipped with extremely superfine sensing devices" (263).

of accumulated bat shit" (313). Consciousness might depend on the material brain, DeLillo seems to imply, but it also just might be "batshit insane."[41]

While he stops demonstrably short of presenting materialist models of mind as final or satisfactory explanations, DeLillo is nonetheless consistently devoted to the idea that humanity's phylogenetic history provides a link between "proto-historic and modern terror." The brain, or rather the nervous system in its entirety, provides the source for much of the "magic and dread" that Osteen views as so central to the author's oeuvre. This is a motif that already figured in *End Zone* and *Great Jones Street*, is fleshed out in *Ratner's Star*, and reappears with a vengeance in *White Noise*.

## White Noise

DeLillo's interest in the implications of viewing human beings as "complex molecular systems" (*RS* 389), which has been building up throughout his earlier works, is most pronounced in *White Noise*.[42] Despite the fact that a quotation from *White Noise* has by now been used as an epigraph for a paper in neuroeconomics (Camerer et al.) and cited in a review of Eric Kandel's *In Search of Memory* in the neurology journal *Brain* (Cornwell), literary critics have largely neglected the ways in which this text engages with neuroscientific thought and its portrayal of "materialist minds." The novel continues to display the fascination with cerebral architecture and the localization of brain functions that I have traced through the earlier novels, and it notably expands on the idea, introduced in *Ratner's Star*, that fear might have a neural, evolutionary ontology. But *White Noise* also introduces additional concerns that anchor the text in its cultural moment, the early 1980s.

Whereas *Ratner's Star* was mainly influenced by the functional asymmetry of the brain that was a "hot topic" in the 1970s (Broks 32), in *White Noise* the Gladneys confront a related but expanded set of new materialist ideas that emerged in the subsequent decade, such as the ability of psychotropic drugs to alter psychic

---

41  "batshit, n. and adj." OED Online. Oxford University Press, September 2015. Web. 21 September 2015.

42  To be sure, it also resurfaces occasionally in his later writing: in *Mao II*, migraine is experienced as "an electrochemical sheen, [...] brain-made, the eerie gleam of who you are," while the connection between cult leader Sun Myung Moon and his followers penetrates the skin, so that he becomes "part of the structure of their protein." His followers "know him at molecular level," DeLillo writes. "He lives in them like chains of matter that determine who they are" (78, 6). Likewise, a "college boy" is described as "a land animal with a major brain" in *Underworld* (52). Yet such passages are essentially isolated occurrences, not sustained thematic preoccupations, so that it makes sense to have *White Noise* mark the cut-off point of my inquiry into the functions of the idea of the materiality of mind and self.

life and the reduction of the self to patterns of electrochemical signals. In a telling detail, the later novel focuses not on an elite group of scientists engaged in cutting-edge research but a suburban family ensconced in a cocoon of quotidian normality. The new materialism appears to have migrated from avant-garde laboratories to "Middle America" and the everyday lives of its inhabitants.[43]

The sources of this migration are to be found, on the one hand, in the introduction of noninvasive brain imaging technologies like CT and MRI scanning, which further cemented the idea of cerebral localization (since it enabled viewing the experimental "activation" of different brain regions in real time and in a live subject), and, on the other, in the increased scientific and popular attention to neurotransmitters and drugs that worked by influencing specific neurological pathways and receptor sites in the central nervous system.[44] By the 1980s, a renewed awareness of the mind's material substrate—clusters of neurons and the electrochemical communication between them—was firmly in place, along with a radically expanded scope of psychiatric and pharmaceutical intervention, which no longer restricted itself to treating pathology but began to target "the minimization of sadness and anxiety" through the systems of neurotransmission (Rose and Abi-Rached 123). The latter development was accompanied by the 1980 publication of the DSM-III, which dispensed with the psychoanalytic etiological framework of previous editions and adopted a purely descriptive, "neo-Kraepelinian" approach that has been instrumental in legitimizing pharmacological efficacy as an ontological marker of disorders and diseases.[45]

Accordingly, in *White Noise* we still find the spatial association of depth with layered brain processes that DeLillo introduced in *Ratner's Star*, as when Jack ponders the fact that brand names might be "[p]art of every child's brain noise, the substatic regions too deep to probe" and describes his own descent into "deep-dwelling crablike consciousness" (155), but the novel is more significantly marked by the ways in which the workings of the brain now breach the surface of cultural consciousness. This theme is introduced early in the book, when Jack's son Heinrich entangles him in knotty conversations about the nature of perception and consciousness.

---

43  "A sign of the development and rapid expansion of a scientific discipline is its impact on popular culture. *White Noise* depicts neuroscience, albeit through a fantastically distorted lens, from the vantage point of the mid-1980s as a coming discipline," Cornwell observes (304).

44  In their overview of the development of the neurosciences, Rose and Abi-Rached note that "the fundamental shift in the visibility of the living brain was linked to the development of computerized tomography (CT) scanning in the 1970s and magnetic resonance imaging (MRI) in the 1980s" and that the fist "studies to quantify neurotransmission and neurochemistry in humans were published in the 1980s" (13, 71).

45  The paradigm shift initiated by the DSM-III has been called a "revolution" in psychiatric practice. See Mayes and Horwitz.

In these dialogues, Jack assumes the role of the pragmatic realist, while Heinrich argues with scholastic pedantry and zeal for postmodern relativism. An initial exchange concerns the question whether "it's raining *now*, at this very minute." Jack insists on defining the phenomenon in the terms of ordinary language philosophy: "It's the stuff that falls from the sky and gets you what is called wet." In turn, Heinrich lists a whole catalogue of qualifications that would make the statement untenable, from the impossibility of the "view from nowhere"[46] ("What truth does he want? Does he want the truth of someone traveling at almost the speed of light in another galaxy?) to the cultural specificity and indeterminacy of linguistic signification ("What if this guy [...] comes from a planet in whole different solar system? What we call rain he calls soap. What we call apples he calls rain."), the vicissitudes of temporality ("Is there such a thing as now? 'Now' comes and goes as soon as you say it.") and the general difficulty of moving from subjectivity to objectivity in the post-Newtonian world ("Don't you know about all those theorems that say nothing is what it seems? There's no past, present or future outside our own mind. The so-called laws of motion are a bog hoax."). Frustrated and resigned, Jack can only conclude, "A victory for uncertainty, randomness and chaos. Science's finest hour" (22-24).

Randy Laist is surely right to assert that "[t]he kind of knowledge Heinrich has mastery over is a very 80's kind of knowledge, the kind that deconstructs the possibility of knowledge itself" (84); reading this passage one has little difficulty grasping why *White Noise* has entered English curricula everywhere as a paradigmatic expression of the postmodern condition, characterized by "the decline of the unifying and legitimating power of the grand narratives" (Lyotard, *Postmodern* 38). Timothy Melley correctly identifies a clash of "postmodern relativism and social constructionism against [...] commonsense analytic empiricism" in this passage ("Technology" 78). Yet two things have typically been overlooked here. First, the dialogue, like much else in DeLillo, is *funny*: as Kenneth Gergen—something of an expert on social construction himself—helpfully notes, Heinrich's sophistry is hilarious, in the best sense of the word (3). This is no small matter: like the framing of *Ratner's Star*'s scientists' zany projects by Billy's laconic incredulousness, the fact that DeLillo chooses to refract this "very 80's kind of knowledge" through the voice of a precocious twelve-year old has to count for something, as does the fact that later in the novel, Heinrich seems to shed his skepticism toward knowledge production when Jack sees him happily reciting information he learned at school to a group of fellow evacuees in the wake of the "airborne toxic event" (130-31). Clearly, we are meant to read this exercise in exactitude as resting on a less than pure commitment to epistemological consistency.

---

46  See Nagel, *View* for the concept of the "view from nowhere," i.e., a scientific description that excludes the subjective, first-person perspective.

Second, Heinrich's dismissal of certainty also extends from the "objective" world to the realm of subjectivity and self-knowledge, an extension that points toward the contiguity of postmodern conceptions and critiques of the subject and a new materialist reassessment of the self. Asked where he wants to spend his holiday, Heinrich answers his father's query with more questions:

> Who knows what I want to do? Who knows what anyone wants to do? How can you be sure about something like that? Isn't it all a question of brain chemistry, signals going back and forth, electrical energy in the cortex? How do you know whether something is really what you want to do or just some kind of nerve impulse in the brain? Some minor little activity takes place somewhere in this unimportant place in one of the brain hemispheres and suddenly I want to go to Montana or I don't want to go to Montana. How do I know I really want to go and it isn't just some neurons firing or something? Maybe it's just an accidental flash in the medulla and suddenly there I am in Montana and I find out I really didn't want to go there in the first place. I can't control what happens in my brain, so how can I be sure what I want to do ten seconds from now, much less Montana next summer? It's all this activity in the brain and you don't know what's you as a person and what's some neuron that just happens to fire or just happens to misfire. (45-46)

It is telling that Heinrich ends his statement by projecting the logical extreme of his merciless neural determinism: referring to the incarcerated mass murderer with whom he corresponds and plays chess through mail, Heinrich asks, "Isn't that [i.e., misfiring neurons] why Tommy Roy killed those people?" It is also telling that having reproduced Heinrich's tirade, the first-person narration breaks off for the space of an empty paragraph: faced with these questions, Jack does not even have a response.

There is no need here to rehearse the all-too clear implications of Heinrich's new materialist theory for Jack's cherished humanist assumptions about individual agency, responsibility, and free will.[47] The reader realizes that the existential problem of making decisions and facing the prospect of regret is no less a central aspect of adult existence for being amenable to formulation in a neuro-materialist register; consequently, she is sure to be nowhere near as devastated as Jack. I would rather note at this point that DeLillo is among the first American authors

---

47  Assumptions, one feels compelled to add, that largely drive his failed transformation into a "killer" in the book's final section, where Jack vows to take initiative and fulfill a "plan" that keeps changing as it is being executed. It is no coincidence that in this desperate attempt at self-willed action, Jack's narration unwittingly cycles back to his exchanges with Heinrich, as when he senses "molecules active in my brain moving along neural pathways," or reflects, "I knew for the first time what rain really was. I knew what wet was" (306, 310).

to spell out the problematic consequences of neuroscientific determinism in their work, and that he does so in a way that invites reflection on the interconnections between the new materialism of the mind and the "relativism" and *Subjektkritik* that characterize postmodernism.

Paul Civello reads DeLillo as working in the vein of literary naturalism, defined as literature that dramatizes "a rift between the self and the material world—in this case, the postmodern, 'built' environment that has grown in complexity beyond humanity's comprehension." According to Civello, DeLillo's fiction dramatizes the "collapse of the old cause-and-effect scientific paradigm"—as expressed in Heinrich's disdainful mention of the "so-called laws of motion"—and the emergence of a world in which "[t]here is no separation between subject and object, and therefore no 'objective' reality" (4). Seen this way, neuroscience itself becomes an aspect of postmodernity, a technology-fueled research field whose findings cycle back through cultural channels to effect the submission of subjectivity itself to the framework of technoscientific explanation: if the subject is reconceptualized as a material object, it really becomes "all a question of brain chemistry."[48] *White Noise* thus appears as an early example of "the contemporary novel's neurological turn" and as confirmation of Stephen Burn's assessment that "a surprising number of themes and concepts cursorily ascribed to postmodernism are shared by the contemporary sciences of mind" ("Mapping" 35-36).

Epistemological uncertainty and relativism, DeLillo suggests in *White Noise*, may have a lot do with cultural postmodernity, but they also flow from a new materialist attitude toward psychic life. In fact, the two can be linked, as the book's third section, "Dylarama" makes abundantly clear. Critics have pointed to the ways in which DeLillo appears to subscribe to the Weberian notion of the disenchantment of the world, which in his rendering divests modern humans of a meaningful relation to their own mortality.[49] It is this absence that incites the "deep terrible lingering fears" (*WN* 198)[50] that pervade the novel as well as the defenses (Hitler as a figure "larger than death") and new forms of cathexis—to consumerism, to media representation—it offers as compensations.[51] Secular-

---

48  See Moses's contention that "[t]he society which encourages the production of Dylar"—which I examine below—"is one which tends to understand all human beings on the model of a thing" (78).

49  For comments on the relation between DeLillo and Weber, see Cowart 35 and McClure 104. For his ideas about modernity's repression of mortality, DeLillo relies heavily on Ernest Becker's 1973 book *The Denial of Death*.

50  Here and subsequently, *White Noise* is abbreviated as *WN* in parenthetical citations.

51  Apart from the obvious shared interest in simulations and media, this connection may be one of the reasons why *White Noise* has been linked so insistently to the work of Jean Baudrillard, who reflects on the relation between postmodern environments and death in his *Symbolic Exchange and Death*.

ization and demystification thus prepare the ground for the "paradoxical way in which scientific enlightenment reverts to new forms of mythology" (Moses 72). As convincing as these interpretations are, we need to note that the novel's most explicit attempt at safeguarding against the awareness of death—the next best thing in the absence of true immortality—arrives in the form of a psychotropic drug.

For Jack, the experimental (and unapproved) medication Dylar represents another occasion for anxiety over the postmodern, new materialist human condition. "Every emotion or sensation has its own neurotransmitters" Jack's wife Babette informs him, so that the makers of Dylar were able to isolate the "fear-of-death part of the brain," which the drug targets, and, ostensibly, anesthetizes.[52] To Jack's mind this extended model of modularity, in which brain functions are no longer only dependent on hemispheric allocation, as they were in *Ratner's Star*, but rather are reformulated in neurochemical terms and thus made amenable to pharmaceutical intervention, opens a Pandora's box of philosophical and ethical conundrums. "Everything that goes on in your whole life is a result of molecules rushing around somewhere in your brain," Babette tells him, which predictably causes Jack to fret, "Heinrich's brain theories. They're all true. We're the sum of our chemical impulses. [...] It's unbearable to think about" (200). However, he then does go on to think about it:

> What happens to good and evil in this system? Passion, envy and hate? Do they become a tangle of neurons? Are you telling me that a whole tradition of human failings is now at an end, that cowardice, sadism, molestation are meaningless terms? What about murderous rage? A murderer used to have a certain fearsome size to him. His crime was large. What happens when we reduce it to cells and molecules? (200)

Here, Jack rehearses a catalog of concerns that have become commonplace in debates about the implications of neuroscientific research for existing ethical and judicial practices and philosophies, recently codified in the fields of "neuroethics" and "neurolaw."[53] The irony, of course, is that this is not what Babette is telling him at all. Not only is Jack the only one worrying here (Babette's laconic response is, "Can I sleep now?"), but his worries also turn out to be unfounded: after all, the drug does not work. This is an important point, since it further undercuts the alarmist tone with which Jack reacts to "this system." That the Dylar episode should end in inconclusive disappointment comes as no surprise, embedded as

---

52  The drug's mechanism, Moses observes, can thus be called "psychobiological" (75).

53  See Eagleman, "Trial," Rosen, and chapter 6 (aptly entitled, "My Brain Made Me Do It") of Gazzaniga, *Ethical*.

it is in a novel that presents all kinds of authority (parental, professional, spiritual) as tenuous.[54] Fittingly, the source of most of our information about Dylar is Jack's colleague Winnie Richards, who blankly states, "I do neurochemistry. No one knows what that is" (188).

So while Burn is certainly correct in observing that Delillo's fictions "ask questions about the impact the ascendance of the neurosciences might have on our hierarchies of value" ("Mind" 200), we should also note that *White Noise* asks these questions in a deliberately silly, satirical manner. For all DeLillo's sustained interest in the biological basis of human emotions, he presents materialist discourses about the mind not as a privileged mode of knowledge production but as merely another variation of general ignorance. "Do you know how complex the human brain is," Babette asks Jack. "I have some idea," Jack replies. "No, you don't," Babette shoots back (192). As Winnie Richards, the closest thing to a scientific authority the novel has to offer, freely admits, "I have only a bare working knowledge of the human brain," which she describes as "like a galaxy that you can hold in your hand, only more complex, more mysterious" (189).[55] We are certainly not supposed to lend too much credence to Heinrich, the novel's most vocal advocate of neuro-determinism, who at one point proposes that happiness may be reduced to "just a nerve cell [...] that's getting too much stimulation or too little stimulation" (182). His suspicion, voiced earlier in the novel, that "no one actually knows anything" might be closer to the mark (149).

## Chapter Conclusion: "The old human muddles and quirks"

In its prospective implications (the reduction of human, social meanings "to cells and molecules" that Jack fears) and in its actual effects (the transformation of Willie Mink into a babbling stream of signifiers, the human equivalent of televisual discourse), Dylar performs a decentering of the subject that Delillo casts as a consequence of both postmodernism and the new materialism of the mind: in the image of the Dylar tablet, Moses observes, postmodern technology "merges with the technology of psychobiology" (76).[56] The psychotropic drug thus indexes a view

---

54  On the representation of authority, see Conroy, who examines how the novel calls into question "four master narratives of cultural transmission in Jack Gladney's universe: the familial, the civic, the humanist, and the religious" (98).

55  Richards's simile echoes an oft-used illustration of the brain's complexity that draws on the vastness of outer space as an analogue, as when neuroscientist David Eagleman invites us to consider that "there are as many connections in a single cubic centimeter of brain tissue as there are stars in the Milky Way galaxy" (*Incognito* 2).

56  The Willie Mink episode also illustrates the conflation of postmodernism and medical materialism in another way: Mink's inability to distinguish signifier from signified, which causes him

of "materialist minds" as a manifestation or an aspect of postmodernity: both have their roots in an Enlightenment belief in the efficacy of technology, and both generate largely coterminous effects. When Heinrich describes "brain chemistry" as "signals going back and forth" he may just as well be speaking of the man-made, electronic environment synecdochically evoked by the novel's titular "white noise" (45).[57] DeLillo consistently portrays the human ability to intervene in natural processes as fool's gold, partly because attempts to do so tend to backfire, but mainly because they generate a misplaced sense of hubris along with questionable effects on human consciousness.[58] As my analysis has shown, the flattening of subjectivity, its dispersal over a range of external or internal systems of communication, is portrayed in the novel as a potential effect not only of medialization but also of medicalization. The fragmentation of the concept of character, its deconstruction into recursive constituents, which is often cast as an exclusive effect of postmodernist thought, is here shown to derive instead from new materialist ideas about the mind.

On the other hand, DeLillo also seems interested in the relation between subjectivity and the nervous system as a phenomenon in its own right. I have traced this interest here through four novels, over the course of which it has most often manifested itself either as an investment in the effects of the longue durée of evolutionary history on the contemporary cerebral subject or as an awareness of the ways in which the biological specifications of the human mind make it susceptible to material manipulation. For all the ways that *White Noise* presents materialist minds as products of the postmodern condition and the associated configurations of the cultural imaginary, many of the author's earlier books contain variations of the idea that core aspects of postmodernity, like runaway technology and the nev-

---

to hit the floor and crawl for cover when Jack speaks the words "Hail of bullets" (311), may well be modeled on a neurological condition resulting from damage to the amygdala. Paul Broks describes the case of a patient, who, "minus amygdala," became oblivious to real threats while showing "excessive fear in response to an innocuous TV program" (154). Given his interest in the neurological basis of fear, one should not discount the possibility that DeLillo was aware of similar cases.

57  "We have indeed secreted a human age out of ourselves as spiders secrete their webs: an immense, all-encompassing ceiling of secularity which shuts down visibility on all sides even as it absorbs all the formerly natural elements in its habitat, transmuting them into its own man-made substance," Fredric Jameson writes. *White Noise* would appear as an ideal illustration of this notion, especially since it filters its ideas through the consciousness of Jack Gladney, whose anxious stocktaking of his situation resonates strikingly with Jameson's observation that "[t]he world of the human age is an aesthetic pretext for grinding terror or pathological ecstasy" and that "in its cosmos, […] we continue murmuring Kant's old questions—what can I know? What should I do? What may I hope?" (*Valences* 608).

58  As Moses is right to note, for DeLillo, "the danger of technology is greater on the metaphysical than on the physical side" (71).

er-ending "rationalization" and optimization of economic processes, might have their basis in the characteristics of neural architecture, whose functional asymmetry has, in some accounts, been identified as underlying and driving social and cultural developments.[59]

What unites these two different aspects of DeLillo's portrayal of "materialist minds" (first, as an aspect of postmodernity; second, as an aspect of human embodiment) is the consistency with which his novels present the "cerebral subject" as an anthropological figure that is always mediated through culture and discourse and human concern. It is important to note that more often than not, the manner in which DeLillo focalizes and filters his interest in the materiality of the self through his characters can best be described as ironical. In this way, paying attention to the representation and the functions of materialist minds in DeLillo's novels can help us to recall the fact that much of his work—and certainly the texts I have discussed here—is as silly as it is serious. That DeLillo is not least an exceedingly funny writer, a master of a distinctly American brand of parodic and comedic literature, is often neglected in academic accounts of his work, which for obvious reasons prefer to focus on his more controlled, historical novels like *Libra* and *Underworld*. This is not to say that DeLillo does not take the ideas with which he infuses his fiction seriously. Perhaps the best way to phrase it is to say that irony and interest balance each other out, or that the former is a way of rendering the latter.

In fact, such a balancing-out may well lie at the heart of DeLillo's engagement with materialist models of mind. The novels under consideration here do not subscribe to the notion that the brain holds the key to explaining human behavior, but they also do not incorporate biological perspectives simply to subject them to ridicule. Stephen Burn has argued that the function of such a perspective is "to remind the reader that their own experiences take place within biological constraints: that is, the boundaries of their cerebral hardware," and that DeLillo attempts "to outline a general, species-level, neural model," but it seems to me that this assessment overplays the degree to which the writer aspires toward the function of the scientist or the philosopher ("Mapping" 40, 42). While it is correct, and useful, to point out the ways in which DeLillo acknowledges the import and implications of notions like cerebral modularity and hemisphericity, we need to remain aware of the considerable levels of irony and contextualization through which he filters these ideas.

---

59  See, for instance, Iain McGilchrist's 2009 book *The Master and His Emissary*, which advances the thesis that differences between the modes of functioning of the cerebral hemispheres can be traced in their effects on human culture, so that in the Western world we may be seeing the highly problematic "triumph of the left hemisphere" (209).

Perhaps, then, it would be more accurate to say that as a literary author, DeLillo is interested in the limitations and the possibilities of neuro-materialist perspectives, which he considers with both creativity and constraint. Raymond Williams's *The Long Revolution*, an early example of the use of neurological concepts in reflections on human subjectivity, provides an intriguing analogy. Here, drawing on the work of neurophysiology pioneer J. Z. Young, Williams develops the idea of a cerebral creativity that, ironically, is based on constraint. The nervous system is a product of evolution, which limits and focuses its capabilities; at the same time, the dispersed and fragmented sensory input it allows has to be assembled into a sense of a coherent whole for us to experience, which is a creative act of gestalt formation: "The brain of each of us does literally create his or her own world" (32). For Williams, cultural meaning results in equal parts from "the human brain as it has evolved, and the interpretations carried by our cultures," and those interpretations include the changing views of the relation between mind and body (34).

Similarly, DeLillo portrays "materialist minds" in both senses of the term: his fiction not only ponders the implications of the notion that the self is constructed along the specifications of its material substrate but also consistently identifies such speculations as productions of the human imagination. The materialism of the mind is itself a product of the mind, just as the "structure of the atom was conceived in a dream" (*RS* 265). We can think here of Jack Gladney, experiencing a heightened sense of reality at the end of *White Noise*, making use of the brain theories he encountered earlier to cast his epiphany in new materialist terms: "I continued to advance in consciousness," he marvels, "I understood the neurochemistry of my brain." Needless to say, this transcendent state, during which Jack imagines himself as "a Buddhist, a Jain, a Duck River Baptist," i.e., as simultaneously enlightened and aloof, turns out to be yet another delusion (310). When he is shot by Willie Mink, his fantasies of advanced understanding and a "higher plane of energy" come to an abrupt end: "The pain was seering. [...] The extra dimensions, the super perceptions, were reduced to visual clutter, a whirling miscellany, meaningless. [...] The old human muddles and quirks were set flowing again. Compassion, remorse, mercy" (313).

It is surely relevant that here as in *Ratner's Star*, a turning point is marked by images of fluidity—the flow of water and blood, respectively—and by a renewed awareness of corporeality and mortality that bears decidedly positive, life-affirming connotations.[60] In fact I would like to contend that DeLillo introduces an opposition between the analytical, third-person perspective onto the materiality of mind, which threatens to arrest the brain in time and isolate it in space, and a phenomenological, first-person insight into the subjective experience of embodiment, which is more attuned to the ever-changing states of its engagement with

---

60  I am thinking here of the "I Take a Drink" section, discussed above.

the world and others. This opposition also significantly informs two authors whom DeLillo influenced and who will be the focus of the next two chapters: David Foster Wallace and Richard Powers.

# 5. Between Agency and Automatism: David Foster Wallace's Infinite Jest

> As a result of these relentlessly churning thoughts about symbols and meanings, patterns and ideas, machines and mentality, neural impulses and mortal souls, all hell broke loose in my adolescent mind/brain.
> *Douglas Hofstadter, I Am a Strange Loop*

> Machines have less problems. I'd like to be a machine.
> *Andy Warhol*

## An Informing Fear

In 1989, six years before the publication of David Foster Wallace's magnum opus *Infinite Jest*, the author's novella "Westward the Course of Empire Takes Its Way" contained a suggestive sentence:

> Like many *Americans of his generation in this awkwardest of post-Imperial decades*, an age suspended between exhaustion and replenishment, between input too ordinary and input too intense to bear, Sternberg is deeply ambivalent about being embodied; an informing fear that, were he really just an organism, he'd be nothing more than an ism of his organs. (254; original emphasis)

By registering a latent unease about the relation between subjectivity and corporeality and connecting it to a nationally and historically specific situation in a language that itself avows its cultural datum, this fragment from the earlier, shorter story adumbrates a set of concerns that would significantly shape the novel that was to follow.[1] A character, claimed as representative of a larger cultural contin-

---

1 In *Infinite Jest* we find two remarkably similar sentences connecting national belonging to existential disquiet. Early in the novel, the narrator says of the novel's putative protagonist: "Like

gent, is described as laboring under a peculiar kind of ontological uncertainty about his status as a subject: his simultaneous existence as mind and matter, as consciousness and "organism," causes him to worry that the former might be reducible to the latter.[2] This condition is linked not only to the various forms of "input" that characterize a putatively "post-Imperial" information age, but also, via the binary of "exhaustion and replenishment," to American literary history.[3] The sentence thus suggests that at the turn of the 1990s, American literature and culture can be correlated with a specific anxiousness about the biological basis of subjectivity.

If this connection was only hinted at in the earlier novella, it is fully developed in the later novel. As I argue in this chapter, a historically specific "ambivalence about being embodied" also constitutes the "informing fear" of *Infinite Jest*, a work that likewise asserts connections between individual and cultural pathologies. Contained within the book's gargantuan heft of 1079 pages is a satiric depiction of a dystopian "Organization of North American Nations" (O.N.A.N.) in the throes of rampant addiction, a grotesque *Gegenwelt* in which afflictions like "social isolation, anxious lassitude, and [...] hyperself-consciousness" as well as "poverty of affect" strike grizzled drugs addicts and fledgling tennis talents alike (*IJ* 503).[4] Formally as well as thematically, the text signaled that it had something substantial to say about the relation between U.S. society and subjectivity.[5] This impres-

---

most North Americans of his generation, Hal tends to know way less about why he feels certain ways about the objects and pursuits he's devoted to than he does about the objects and pursuits themselves"; roughly 600 pages later, we are informed that "[o]ne of the really American things about Hal, probably, is the way he despises what it is he's really lonely for: this hideous internal self, incontinent of sentiment and need, that pules and writhes just under the hip empty mask, anhedonia" (54, 695).

2   In a regrettable irony, such a reduction has actually been taking place in the aftermath of the author's death in 2008. In a recent collection on the philosophical underpinnings of his work, one critic wonders whether Wallace was "genetically predisposed to substance abuse and/or emotional instability" (Bustillos 123), while another blames "his neurotransmitters" for his suicide (Bolger 32), speculations which go some way toward reducing the writer's life and death to "nothing more than an ism of his organs."

3   The reference here is to John Barth's essays "The Literature of Exhaustion" (1967) and "The Literature of Replenishment" (1979). Wallace's novella is in fact an extended parody of and programmatic answer to Barth's 1967 short story "Lost in the Funhouse."

4   Here and subsequently, *Infinite Jest* is abbreviated as *IJ* in parenthetical citations.

5   What is more, the text's formal and thematic designs mutually reinforce each other, so that "the grueling aspects for the reader of Infinite Jest (1079 pages, including 96 pages of footnotes) [...] mirror the novel's somber depiction of American culture as a spiral of obsessions and compulsions, a labyrinthine system from which there is no escape" (Giles 334).

sion of the novel as a significant cultural intervention was also openly encouraged by the publisher, Little Brown and Company, in the run-up to its publication.[6]

For the most part, journalistic and scholarly articles on the novel have adhered to this understanding of the text as a culturally significant "intervention." The medical connotations of this term are apt here, since the notion of *Infinite Jest* as "simultaneously challenging and therapeutic" has figured prominently in its reception (Baskin, n. pag.). In fact, this medical register, particular evident in tropes of pathology, diagnosis, and treatment, has accompanied the novel both in anticipation and in retrospect: Jonathan Franzen's blurb for the first edition praised the book as "addictive in its comedy and endless invention, detoxifying in its profound, clearheaded sadness," while Wallace's posthumous biographer, D.T. Max, contends that *Infinite Jest* "didn't just diagnose a malaise. It proposed a treatment" (214).[7] In what follows I critically interrogate this notion and examine how Wallace as well his commentators construe the novel as an inherently therapeutic endeavor.

The installation of the "therapeutic paradigm" (Aubry) as a frame for the text is inseparable from the question of "materialist minds," since pathology in *Infinite Jest* is figured, philosophically and pragmatically, as a problem of how to imagine—and how to *live*—the mind-body relation.[8] Embodied existence and experience, particularly the mutability of mind through material manipulation and the susceptibility of the nervous system to chemical substances, are key concerns of the novel: in braided narrative strands, the text traces how substance addiction and behavioral conditioning transform subjectivity in pathological ways, leading to isolation and depression, and how such self-alienation can be overcome by the social and spiritual rituals codified in the tenets of Alcoholics Anonymous (AA). Simultaneously pursuing "the path through madness," "the path through the nerves," and "the path through the brain," the novel thus engages extensively with medical materialism, the "new style of thought" identified by Rose and Abi-Rached as the molecular-materialist approach to the question of the self (30-31).

Stephen Burn has suggested that in *Infinite Jest*, Wallace is interested in "the essential ways that medical language and especially neural theories invade and reorder our relationship to ourselves" (Burn, "Webs" 64). This contention is supported by even a cursory reading: in the novel, characters describe themselves as

---

6  Prior to the publication of *Infinite Jest*, Little, Brown initiated a well-targeted promotion campaign, sending out postcards to key personnel in the media and publishing industry that cryptically hinted at the imminent arrival of a momentous work. See Aubry, *Reading* 120-21, and Bruni.

7  Max also points out that this "treatment" was to be a specifically literary endeavor, so that *Infinite Jest* appears situated in a genealogical line that the biographer rather floridly describes as Wallace "proposing to wash Pynchonian excess in the chilling waters of DeLillo's prose and then heat it up again in Dostoevsky's redemptive fire" (213-14).

8  "Living in your body" is a problem the novel's characters are demonstrably concerned with (*IJ* 158).

"webs of nerves pulsing and firing" (168) while avant-garde films dramatize the dynamic of neuroplasticity, depicting how "memory neurons [...] in the Inferior frontal gyrus of a man's [...] brain fight heroically to prevent their displacement by new memory neurons as the man undergoes intensive psychoanalysis" (987 n24). Most strikingly, however, the effect of the book's central imaginative conceit, a film so spellbinding that its viewers succumb rather than turn their eyes from the screen,[9] is explained by analogy to "a biomedical experiment" in which rats are taught to press a lever to directly stimulate so-called "*p*-terminals" in the brain, said to house the receptors for "all the various neurotransmitters of pleasure." As a result, the rats ignore all other stimuli in their "fatal addiction to the electric pleasure" and ultimately die of dehydration. While this episode has a historical basis,[10] the novel dramatically expands on it, imagining a scenario in which people line up for human testing, "willing to trample one another to undergo invasive brain surgery and foreign-object implantation" in the pursuit of pleasure: "By free choice, of course" (470-73). The lethally addictive film (variously referred to in the novel as "*Infinite Jest*," "the *samizdat*," or "the Entertainment") thus links to agency, autonomy, and the perversion of pleasure, but it does so specifically by invoking a "cerebral subject" whose conscious thoughts and actions appear as subservient to its biological and neural priorities.[11]

This last point directs us toward an important aspect, for the deadly video cartridge functions as a "limit case" not only for "questions about the philosophical and ethical implications of pleasure," as Laura Catherine Frost argues (240), but also for questions about the relation between the material body's dictates and the mind's free will. The "Entertainment," itself a rewindable, repeatable media artifact enabling looped, cyclical (and, for all intents and purposes, *infinite*) viewing, generates a feedback loop that metonymically stands for the whole range of addictive cycles the novel addresses. "Wallace is interested not only in chemical dependence," David Dunning observes, "but also in the psychological dependencies that can attach to *any* enjoyment" (4; my emphasis). In this respect his novel would appear to reflect the ubiquity of addiction discourse in the contemporary

---

9   The film's viewers, we learn, "lose even basic-survival type will for anything other than more viewing" (*IJ* 507). Left to their own devices, they starve to death like the laboratory rats.

10  Wallace's source for this episode is the well-known rat brain research conducted in the 1950s by James Olds and Peter Milner, the validity of which has since been called into question. For a summary of their findings, see Olds; for a contemporary assessment, see Kringelbach and Berridge.

11  The conceit of the *samizdat* and its neurological effects is also an overt reference to DeLillo, an author Wallace revered and, later in his career, corresponded with. In its devastating effects on viewers' faculties, the lethal film resembles the "lobotomizing drug" that in *Great Jones Street* occasions clandestine pursuits and machinations similar to those we encounter in *Infinite Jest*. See also Burn (*Guide* 111 n13) for the potential neurological effects and allusions of the "Entertainment" and its handlers.

United States.[12] Yet *Infinite Jest* presents the omnipresence of addiction not only as an assemblage of practices but also as a cognitive habit: after running down an extensive list of "abusable" behaviors,[13] the narrator discloses that "most Substance-addicted people are also addicted to thinking, meaning they have a compulsive and unhealthy relationship with their own thinking" (200, 203). This vicious cycle of cognition, also described here as "Analysis-Paralysis" (203), links the susceptibility of the nervous system with the corruptibility of thought itself, so that the biomedical conception of addiction as an organic disease and the problem of linguistic and cognitive self-reflexivity appear mutually implicated.

Timothy Melley reads this universalization of addiction through Eve Kosofsky Segdwick, according to whom the common denominator of present-day addiction discourses consists in their shared emphasis on the insufficient exercise of individual will.[14] Like self-reflexive thought in *Infinite Jest*, "the assertion of will itself has become addictive," Sedgwick has argued (qtd. in Melley, "Terminal" 39). In other words, modern Western societies, particularly the U.S., idolize free will[15] to the point that the doctrine of unencumbered choice becomes contradictory and counterproductive: "Paradoxically, the compulsion to sort addictions from freely willed acts increasingly erodes the distinction between those terms" (Melley, "Terminal" 39). *Infinite Jest* reads like an illustration of this idea, portraying as it does "a whole system [...] founded on your individual freedom to pursue his own individual desires," whose internal logic of escalation transforms desire into addiction (*IJ* 423).

Since it subverts freedom of choice, which according to Wallace, "is part of what America's all about," addiction functions here as the antipode to freedom ("Deciderization" 299). Melley views both the compulsive need to make such distinctions and the increasing difficulty of making them as indicative of what he calls "agency panic"—a term he uses to describe a particularly postmodern kind

---

12  Timothy Melley argues that the "most striking feature of America's general discourse on addiction [...] is just how general it has become: Americans now account for all sorts of ordinary human behavior through the concept of addiction" ("Terminal" 38).

13  Residents of drug rehab facilities, the narrator states, soon learn that "sleeping can be a form of emotional escape and can with sustained effort be abused. [...] That purposeful sleep-deprivation can also be an abusable escape. That gambling can be an abusable escape, too, and work, shopping, and shoplifting, and sex, and abstention, and masturbation, and food, and exercise, and meditation/prayer, and sitting so close to Ennet House's old D.E.C. TP cartridge-viewer that the screen fills your whole vision and the screen's static charge tickles your nose like a linty mitten" (202).

14  "Addiction, under this definition, resides only in the structure of a will that is always somehow insufficiently free, a choice whose voluntary is insufficiently pure," Sedgwick writes (131).

15  On this point, see also Hayles, who describes the "privileging of autonomy" as a "very American virtue" ("Illusion" 676).

of "intense anxiety about an apparent loss of autonomy or self-control" (*Empire* 12) that ultimately gives rise to questions about the "autonomy and individuality of persons" ("Terminal" 39). This anxiety, Melley believes, is a direct result of American commitment to the tenets of liberal individualism, that long-standing conception of the self as "a rational, motivated agent with a protected interior core of beliefs, desires, and memories," which agency panic attempts to conserve (*Empire* 14).[16]

Informed by what Zadie Smith calls Wallace's "fear of automatism" (264), *Infinite Jest* can profitably be read as a text that situates itself within this area of conflict, addressing conceptions of the self that view its essential freedom and autonomy as prerequisites of its very existence as well as those that regard the neural, biomedical, and chemical susceptibilities of subjectivity (such as addiction) as serious hindrances to its flourishing. The separation of compulsion from an ideally unencumbered will is often achieved by mapping these terms onto a mind-matter dichotomy: the body is external, unfree, subject to the laws of physics, while the mind marks a sovereign domain of inner freedom, that kingdom of "infinite space" that is also paradoxically "bounded in a nutshell" in *Hamlet*, the most important intertext of Wallace's novel. To put it differently, Sternberg's "informing fear that, were he really just an organism, he'd be nothing more than an ism of his organs" can be rewritten as the "agency panic" that pervades *Infinite Jest*. Melley's interpretation of agency panic as a reaction to a felt waning of traditional models of personhood certainly is not too far off the mark here, and can be connected to the novel's cultural context.

Rather ominously, Stephen Burn describes Infinite Jest as an attempt to "measure the depth of the modern self during the twilight hours of modern identity" (*Guide* 32), while Paul Giles argues more specifically that "developments in information technology, as well as in scientific fields such as biology and genetics, permeate Wallace's fiction to such an extent that the liberal humanist centers of gravity that structured the worlds of Bellow and Updike now seem but a distant cultural memory" (328).[17] The biomedical paradigm that had become part of

---

16  Melley refers here to C. B. Macpherson's concept of possessive individualism (*Empire* 14-15) and points out that the universalization of addiction can only occur if one adopts a series of foundational assumptions: "First, one must believe individuals *ought to be* rational, motivated agents in full control of themselves. This assumption, in turn, entails a strict metaphysics of inside and outside; that is, the self must be a clearly bounded entity, with an *interior* core of unique beliefs, memoires, and desires easily distinguished from the *external* influences and controls that are presumed to be the sources of addiction. Finally, one must view control as an indivisible property, something that is possessed either by the individual or by external influences" ("Terminal" 39; original emphases).

17  Whether one reads this distance as an insurmountable barrier separating radically different eras or as a cathectically charged gulf that produces nostalgic affection for the past surely is its

American culture in the 1990s presents a major challenge to an author dedicated to preserving traditional humanistic values in a hostile cultural environment. This prospect of a reduction of mind to body/brain was certainly not a welcome one for Wallace, who had dedicated his undergraduate thesis to refuting Richard Taylor's 1962 paper "Fatalism," which posited by way of philosophical logic that human decisions and actions have no bearing on the outcome of events, i.e., that free will is an illusion. In his thesis, Wallace pronounces this "a strange and unhappy metaphysical doctrine that does violence to some of our most basic intuitions about human freedom" and presents an intricate argument to disprove Taylor's assumption (146). It has been argued that the problem of human freedom remained a central interest of Wallace's that also constituted the core of his later, literary work.[18] What is certain is that problems of determinism and subjective agency visibly shape *Infinite Jest*, a text that investigates and challenges the validity of what Wallace calls "our sense of ourselves as intelligent free agents" ("Deciderization" 305).[19]

## Wallace Scholarship and the Therapeutic Paradigm

If *Infinite Jest* can be understood as a literary treatment (in both senses of the word) of the "Epidemics of the Will" identified by Sedgwick, it is important to emphasize that this reading is itself predicated on several preliminary assumptions. In fact, one of my central concerns in this chapter is to complicate the prevailing picture of the therapeutic ethos of Wallace's "encyclopedic account of America's addiction to addictions" (Melley, "Terminal" 39). A concern with pathology and therapy has become a staple of Wallace studies[20] that sees particularly heavy use in critical readings of *Infinite Jest*. As I have already mentioned, for Aubry the novel

---

own question. Giles thinks that Wallace's writing "sought effectively to remodel the idea of a romantic subject across an extended communal domain, one bearing a residual attachment to traditional American values" ("Swallowed" 4); Burn likewise detects in Wallace "at least a partial nostalgia for traditional conceptions of selfhood" and observes that the word *soul* continues to "carry a notably powerful valence in his fiction" (*Guide* 109 n9).

18  See Hirt and D. Kelly.

19  Leland de la Durantaye observes that for Wallace, the question of free will "links together all his works, all his most passionate thinking" (21). Finding himself in agreement, Burn notes that "in the minds of his contemporaries, Wallace is particularly connected to an examination of freedom," which "is a concept that runs right through" the author's career (*Guide* 5).

20  In his introduction to the recent collection *Consider David Foster Wallace*, David Hering announces "the commencement of what I suppose we should call Wallace Studies" (9). In the same vein, Adam Kelly has stated that given the steadily increasing number of academic publications, the term "Wallace Studies" no longer seems hyperbolic ("Death" n. pag). See also Fest ("Inverted" 125 n1) and Howard.

conforms to what he calls "the therapeutic paradigm" (*Reading* 17), the tenets of which "affirm the American faith in individual agency" (Introduction 15). In broad outline, the therapeutic paradigm refers to the understanding of psychobiological phenomena, patterns, and behaviors as legitimately subject to the expertise and interventions of several specialized discourses and knowledge formations operating under a medical or psychological rubric and aiming at some sort of recovery functional improvement. It is a certain way of constructing subjects, lifeworlds, and narratives, but—and this point is crucial for my analysis—neither is it the only one, nor should its claims be regarded as beyond suspicion.

In "Epidemics of the Will," Sedgwick—one of Aubry's sources—has shown how certain practices and preferences are refigured as pathological behaviors and identities, thereby underlining the historicity of what are now deemed addictions—an ontological ascription that obfuscates its historically contingent production (129-30). Likewise, Jennifer Fleissner has called attention to the mechanism by which a focus on the etiology of a given symptom tends to "fold it back into realism's governing narrative structure" and to fix it within the purview of medical materialism ("Symptomatology" 391). This goes to show that in literature as in language, the classification of specific phenomena as pathological or an addiction is not without alternatives. Rather, it is contingent upon a pre-judgment, a willingness to view matters through the rationalistic lens of science and medicine, which in turn informs the course one's engagement with a given phenomenon will take. Addiction in *Infinite Jest* is a metaphor, and metaphors, Ansgar Nünning reminds us, "not only serve to structure how we understand cultural transformations, they also project 'mininarrations' onto them, thereby providing ideologically charged plots and explanations of historical changes rather than 'neutral' descriptions" (233).

I contend that the dominant view of *Infinite Jest* as "addictive" or "therapeutic" (or both) is one such mininarration, circulated within a critical community attentive to the author's self-descriptions, and reinforced at every turn. Zadie Smith provides a paradigmatic assessment of Wallace when she writes that his work:

> pitched itself as a counterweight to the narcotic qualities of contemporary life, and then went a step further. It questioned the Jamesian notion that fine awareness leads a priori to responsibility. It suggested that too much awareness—particularly self-awareness—has allowed us to be less responsible than ever. It was meant for readers of my generation, born under the star of four interlocking revolutions, undreamed of in James's philosophy: the ubiquity of television, the voraciousness of late capitalism, the triumph of therapeutic discourse, and philosophy's demotion into a branch of linguistics. (268)

Smith's characterization here is representative in its assumption that Wallace's artistic project rests on an understanding of the contemporary world as pathological, and in need of therapeutic intervention. Her use of the term "narcotic," drawing as it does on medicine and pharmacology for its metaphorical source domains, hints at the dominant explanatory model associated with Wallace's brand of cultural critique. However, if one accepts this "mininarration," the game is rigged: by conceiving of certain phenomena—in the case of *Infinite Jest*, drug use and the waning of affect may serve as examples—as pathological, writers (of fiction, medical literature, philosophy, criticism, etc.) invariably skew their accounts or narratives toward a concern with recovery, recuperation, the restoration of an equilibrium. Here, the adoption of the therapeutic paradigm also leads to a curiously curtailed view of American culture as inherently pathological.[21]

Pathologizing a phenomenon often entails ignoring its historical and cultural contexts and causations, as Jennifer Fleissner points out in her essay on literature and obsessive-compulsive disorder ("Obsessional" 110). In Wallace criticism, the opposite seems to be the case: the ubiquity of addiction and pathology is itself seen as an indication that historical and cultural factors are everywhere at play. Wallace certainly has done little to discourage this view—not coincidentally, *Infinite Jest* imagines a high school class called "The Personal Is the Political Is the Psychopathological" (307)—but it is also reinforced by the inordinate critical attention to what Adam Kelly, in his overview of Wallace scholarship, calls "the essay-interview nexus," the core of which is formed by the author's extensive interview with Larry McCaffery as well as the essay "E Unibus Pluram: Television and U.S. Fiction," both published in a 1993 special edition of the *Review of Contemporary Fiction* ("Death," n. pag.).[22] Perhaps the most-quoted sources in Wallace criticism, these pieces are frequently used to support a specific reading of the author's work.

"E Unibus Pluram," which Wallace himself called "a try at a comprehensive diagnosis," laments the exhausted possibilities of postmodernism (McCaffery interview 127).[23] Self-reflexivity and metafiction in particular, Wallace argued,

---

21   "Taken as a whole," Lee Konstantinou writes, "Wallace's oeuvre might be seen as a single long survey of the different forms individual human suffering can take in a postindustrial or postmodern society" (104).

22   By now this dominant mode of reading is meeting some opposition: Kelly's unwillingness "to reduce Wallace's ideas to a set of tenets drawn mainly from [...] the 'essay-interview nexus'" ("Development" 268) is shared by Bradley Fest, who posits that "Wallace criticism has focused at times almost exclusively on [his] comments regarding irony and sincerity" (Review 102) as well as by Burn, who detects in critics "a tendency to hang on the master's words" and laments that "a near-deification has allowed [Wallace] to define the terms of his own critical reception too completely" (Review 467).

23   Wallace's critical appraisal of the perceived shortcomings of his postmodern predecessors should not be understood to extend globally to postmodernism as a literary style, but rather

were catalyzing and exacerbating late-capitalist alienation rather than challenging it.[24] In the McCaffery interview, Wallace wagered that "we'd probably most of us agree that these are dark times, and stupid ones" (131), a sentiment he followed up in a later interview with the observation that "what it's like to live in America around the millennium" is to experience "a stomach-level sadness" or "a kind of lostness" ("*Salon* Interview" 59). If Wallace was visibly concerned with diagnosis—a term he uses four times in the McCaffery interview alone—he also avowed an interest in treatment: "In dark times, the definition of good art would seem to be art that locates and applies CPR to those elements of what's human and magical that still live and glow despite the times' darkness," he proposed to McCaffery (131). Art and literature are thus seen as capable of alleviating culturally produced but individually experienced alienation. According to Jonathan Franzen, Wallace had been "very explicit, in our many discussions of the purpose of novels, about his belief that fiction is a solution, the *best* solution, to the problem of existential solitude" ("Farther" 44; original emphasis) and in the McCaffery interview, Wallace describes literary fiction as potentially "nourishing, redemptive," pronouncing it a veritable antidote to existential human loneliness (127).[25]

Under the twin signs of pathology and therapy, these statements enable, even encourage, a view of Wallace's essays and interviews as informing his literary production. Perhaps it is the ease with which these two discursive fields can be mapped onto each other that accounts for the widespread critical tendency to understand Wallace's practice by what he preached; in any case, the author's own assumptions seem to have a way of insinuating themselves into the metadiscourses that aim to explain his work. We find a typical example in Mary Holland's description of Wallace as a writer "who penned not only fiction but also manifestos for fiction," and in her claim that we "cannot help but read [*Infinite Jest*] only in the context of the agenda that Wallace so clearly and passionately articulated

---

as directed at a nationally circumscribed movement. When Wallace speaks of postmodernism, he is thinking primarily of American authors: he mentions "Barth and Coover and Burroughs, even Nabokov and Pynchon" as fitting the role of "a real enemy, a patriarch for my patricide" (McCaffery interview 146). The insularity of this reduction has been noted by Staes, who objects that there are differences even between American postmodernists, and that "ironic self-reflexivity has been an often-used strategy by writers dealing with problems of representation since well before the 1960s" (412).

24 In keeping with the essay's focus on television and advertising, Wallace notes that "it is now *television* that takes elements of the *postmodern*—the involution, the absurdity, the sardonic fatigue, the iconoclasm and rebellion—and bends them to the ends of spectation and consumption" (64; original emphases). See Burn, "End," for an overview of similar positions among American writers and critics in the 1990s.

25 That same year, Wallace actually used a similar phrasing in his interview with Hugh Kennedy and Geoffrey Polk, calling "good writing" an "anodyne against loneliness" (16).

shortly before its publication and by considering its success in implementing that agenda" (57). Viewed this way, the author's interviews and essays not only become paratexts that augment the primary text they attach to,[26] but also compel critics to read the primary text "*only* in the context of their agenda" (my emphasis).[27]

*Infinite Jest* certainly lends itself to such readings: at times, the narration seems to echo Wallace's authorial assessments, as when it links loneliness to the observation that "the lively arts of the millennial U.S.A. treat anhedonia and internal emptiness as hip and cool" (694). Little wonder, then, that early Wallace scholarship often focused on the ways in which the novel connects psychological alienation to the postmodern media environment and its concomitant regimes of specularity and irony.[28] Recently, Stephen Burn has proposed a different approach: identifying in the text a "monistic thesis that does away with appeals to *soul* or *spirit* in its insistence that mind is simply an emergent phenomenon of the biological matter of the brain" (*Guide* 50), he locates in *Infinite Jest* not an alienation born from the excesses of postmodernism but rather "a loneliness that stems from our entrapment in the mind" ("Webs" 80). While Burn's valid observation about Wallace's timely interests in materialist minds[29] also provides the starting point for my analysis, I believe that neither his interpretation nor the well-established narrative of *Infinite Jest* as a diagnostic/therapeutic intervention are convincing in themselves. Instead, it will be necessary to combine their respective claims: we should recognize how Wallace uses the fraught relation between mind and matter, which always plays out at the level of the individual, as a metaphor for degrees of alienation and authenticity, which always have distinctly cultural components. To begin with, the idea of the self as contained within the skull provides Wallace with a potent figure of isolation, as I shall argue in the next section.

---

26  I am using the term paratext here to convey the idea of Wallace's nonfiction as informing his fiction. In the classificatory scheme introduced by Gerard Genette, an essay would, strictly speaking, be categorized as a text in its own right, whereas an interview would be understood as an epitext. For this distinction, see chapters 13 and 14 of Genette.

27  For a more nuanced version of this statement, see Cohen, who deems it impossible "to fully understand *Infinite Jest* without reckoning in what Wallace was feeling and thinking about writing and about himself as a writer at the time he wrote it" (59).

28  See Boswell, Cioffi, and Scott for typical examples of this approach.

29  Burn deems it "perhaps not entirely coincidental that as *Infinite Jest* was published in the middle of the 1990s it shares that decade's fascination with science's materialist accounts of the mind" (*Guide* 51).

## "A machine in the ghost": Hal Incandenza

If there is a character that epitomizes what Don DeLillo calls the "spiraling sense of isolation" in Wallace's work, it is Hal Incandenza ("Informal" 23). A "potentially gifted ten-year-old tennis and lexical prodigy" (*IJ* 30),[30] Hal is the son of James O. Incandenza, heavy drinker, founder of the Enfield Tennis Academy (E.T.A.), and director of the titular, lethal "Entertainment."[31] This makes him both a central character in the novel's convoluted plot—he is arguably one of the two protagonists—and an allegorical personification of some of the text's key concerns. Memorably, *Infinite Jest* begins with Hal narrating, in present tense and the first person, the catastrophic failure of his admission interview for an athletic scholarship at the University of Arizona. The interview ends in disaster because Hal (mysteriously, at this point) appears to be largely unable to control his bodily movements or his vocal expressions. When prompted to speak, he only emits what appear to the admissions committee as "*Sub*animalistic noises and sounds" and performs what they see as an "awful reaching drumming wriggle," evoking, for one committee member, "a vision of hell," and causing another to exclaim, "We witnessed something only marginally *mammalian* in there" (14-15; original emphases).

The verdict is clear: "This boy is damaged" (*IJ* 14). But what caused the damage? Since the first scene of the book is chronologically its last, taking place roughly a year after the end of the narration that follows it, the whole of *Infinite Jest* can be read as a literary jigsaw puzzle that, upon completion, yields the story behind Hal's disintegration.[32] Not for nothing does this initial section end with Hal envisioning the aftermath of his "breakdown," with a hospital employee receiving him and asking, "what's your story?" (17).[33] Yet the text is deliberately ambiguous about the ultimate cause of Hal's plight, which has led readers and critics alike to speculate about what might have taken place in the lacuna between the end of the novel and its beginning. Has Hal taken the mythically powerful drug DMZ, experienced the progressively debilitating effects of Marihuana withdrawal, or been exposed

---

30  The character of Hal Incandenza is notably influenced by DeLillo's Billy Twillig from *Ratner's Star*: among other parallels, both are *Wunderkinder* who react to their bizarre environments with baffled incredulity.

31  James O. Incandenza's drinking (or lack thereof) and filmmaking appear to be somehow linked: Hal's father's ghost—another obvious *Hamlet* allusion—explains at one point that he "spent the whole sober last ninety days of his animate life" at work on the titular film, providing yet another link between addiction and entertainment (838).

32  In a telling simile, Wallace himself has described *Infinite Jest* as "a very pretty pane of glass that had been dropped off the twentieth story of a building" (qtd. in Caro 53).

33  Emily Russell links this opening gambit of the text to its commitment to the therapeutic paradigm: "Hal Incandenza's profound failure to communicate," she argues, causes us to "read the novel with the disability-inspired impulse for diagnosis, for cause" (159).

to the "Entertainment" itself? Or does the solution lie in the batch of (apparently hallucinogenic) mold he accidentally ingested as a child (*IJ* 10-11)?[34] For my purposes here, the "correct" answer is not even that important; what matters more is that Hal's ruinous state in the novel's first pages represents a more pronounced version of the persistent issues he grapples with throughout the book. Rather than searching for some ultimate catalyst, then, it will be instructive to try to determine the nature of these underlying issues.

In a novel that "creates cycles within cycles within cycles," as Katherine Hayles describes it, one of the most significant cycles is that of genealogical reproduction, which links the Incandenza family to the larger themes of the book ("Illusion" 684). In particular, we can trace *Infinite Jest*'s concern with materialist models of mind to the male line of the Incandenza family, for Hal's problems with athletics, addiction, and artifice are shown to originate with his father's father. Here familial and cultural heritage intersect in an allusion to Cartesian dualism and the "fundamental Western division between mind and body that our society, for all its sophisticated caveats, still endorses" (Luhrmann 8). In one of the earliest scenes in the novel's chronology, Hal's grandfather, James Incandenza Sr., tries to impart to the necessary perspective for becoming a "truly great" tennis player to his son James Jr. (Jim):

> The trick will be transcending that overlarge head, son. Learning to move just the way you already sit still. Living in your body. [...] Son, you're ten, and this is hard news for somebody ten, even if you're almost five-eleven, a possible pituitary freak. Son, you're a body, son. That quick little scientific-prodigy's mind [...]: son, it's just neural spasms, those thoughts in your mind are just the sound of your head revving, and head is still just body, Jim. Commit this to memory. Head is body. Jim, brace yourself against my shoulders here for this hard news, at ten: you're a machine a body an object, Jim [...]. (159)

Stephen Burn interprets this monologue as a refutation of Cartesian mind-body dualism in favor of a materialist paradigm that subsumes consciousness into corporeality and lays the groundwork for an "erasure of self" that is ultimately bequeathed to Hal (*Guide* 55).[35] While the elder Incandenza's conviction that his

---

34 Attentive readers of *Infinite Jest* can also speculate about a combination of these factors: in the opening scene, Hal explains his state by saying, "Call it something I ate" (10), and later we learn not only that DMZ is synthesized from an "obscure mold that grows only on other molds," but that its effects are "*temporally*-cerebral and almost ontological" (170; original emphasis).

35 "The elder Incandenza collapses the Cartesian distinction between mind and body, and offers an account of consciousness that leaves little space for traditional conceptions of selfhood. This reductionist strategy is recognizably materialist" (Burn, *Guide* 49).

son's sense of himself can be reduced to the "neural spasms" produced by his body does indeed appear to conflate soma and subjectivity, I would like to complicate Burn's claim in two ways. First, I argue that the monologue remains well within the Cartesian paradigm as Burn understands it; second, I propose that Incandenza Sr.'s ideology exacerbates rather than abolishes the separation of mind and body. To tease out the implications of this interpretation for the novel as a whole, we first need to correct, or at least qualify, Burn's reading of the passage as "anti-Cartesian."

Burn neglects several crucial moments that offer valuable clues about the nature and implications of the philosophical views that are being espoused here. One such moment occurs immediately before the quoted passage. James Incandenza's father works up to his remarks about neural spasms and the head-as-body by inviting his son to consider the family car:

> Jim, it's a machine. It will do what it's made for and do it perfectly, but only when stimulated by someone who's made it his business to know its tricks and seams, as a body. The stimulator of this car must know the car, Jim, feel it, be inside much more than just the … the compartment. It's an object, Jim, a body, but don't let it fool you, sitting here, mute. It will respond. If given its due. With artful care. It's a body and will respond with a well-oiled purr once I get some decent oil in her and all Mercuryish at up to 95 big ones per for just that driver who treats its body like his own, who feels the big steel body he's inside, who quietly and unnoticed feels the nubbly plastic of the grip of the shift up next to the wheel when he shifts just as he feels the skin and flesh, the muscle and sinew and bone wrapped in gray spiderwebs of nerves in the blood-fed hand just as he feels the plastic and metal and flange and teeth, the pistons and rubber and rods of the amber-fueled Montclair, when he shifts. (159)

Nicely illustrating *Infinite Jest*'s method of hiding circular dynamics within loquaciousness, Incandenza Sr. not only compares car to body, but, in a breathless series of back-and-forth shifts, each introduced by the conjunction "just as," also compares body to car. However, the resulting ontological uncertainty should not distract us from the fact that the analogy between the "big steel body" and the one made from "skin and flesh" keeps the mind-body division intact, even as it rewrites the Cartesian cogito as a "stimulator" of "spiderwebs of nerves."

It is obvious that the passage does not convey an impression of true oneness or a primordial, inseparable connection that truly would "collapse the Cartesian distinction between mind and body." Instead we are presented with an account of feeling one's way into a certain mechanism or process. One is reminded of Bourdieu's description, in *The Logic of Practice*, of the "feel for the game"—a metaphor derived, appropriately, from the domain of sports and play—as a "proleptic adjustment to the demands of a field" (66). Through practice, i.e., sensorimotor and behavioral conditioning, an actor/player acquires the ability to automatically, prereflectively, act in such a way as to favorably manipulate events taking place within the limits of the respective "game." Bourdieu speaks of the "almost miraculous encounter between the *habitus* and a field, [...] which makes possible the near-perfect anticipation of the future inscribed in all the concrete configurations on the pitch or board (44; original emphasis). This would appear to be what Jim's father means by a great tennis player's "appreciation of angle, a prescience re spin," when he advises "living in your body" as the recipe for athletic success: "Total physicality. No revving head. Complete presence" (160). While this may sound like a transcendence of mind-body dualism, it is crucial to recall the metaphor of car and driver that James Incandenza Sr. uses to illustrate his philosophy.

This image evokes steering, piloting, a "cockpit of the soul" as well as a "soul-pilot" (Broks 41), and it sustains the distinction between inside and outside, mind and body, or *anima* and *machina*. Jim's father urges him to "know the car," to "feel it," thereby suggesting that true mastery requires complete presence. But this notion of genuinely "inhabiting" one's chosen exterior vehicle, whether car or body, upholds the Cartesian distinction between two ontologically distinct essences. Car and driver do not merge to become a heretofore-unknown third form; it is still the driver who is piloting the car, no matter how ingrained the mechanics of driving might have become for him. If what we mean by Cartesian dualism is the distinction between mind and body as two essentially different substances, with the mind as master over the body, then Incandenza Sr. does not offer up a refutation of Cartesian dualism; rather, he argues for its perfection.[36]

The real subject of the monologue can thus be described as the means and mechanics of mastery, the exercise of willed control over inanimate objects. This becomes apparent when Jim's father speaks of a tennis ball as "the ultimate body. Perfectly round. [...] But empty inside, utterly, a vacuum. [...] It will reflect your own character. Characterless itself. Pure potential" (160). The ball, like the car, functions as a metaphor for the body. All three "objects" are imagined as empty shells that need to be controlled by a separate agency —the player, the driver, the mind. The point of this instruction is not to transcend the mind-body divide; it is for the mind to seize control over the body, a fact that is explicitly, and typographically, emphasized: "exert some goddamn *control* is the whole point," Incandenza Sr. explains (161; original emphasis).

The lengthy monologue also incorporates less than thinly veiled references to Descartes and Gilbert Ryle's critique of Cartesianism. Incandenza Sr. tells his son

---

36 Once we accept that this is the case, Burn's claim that the passage calls into question "traditional conceptions of selfhood" becomes tenuous, since mind-body dualism has been described as a cultural dominant in Western societies: see Luhrmann 6 and Grosz 93.

what he wants him to become: "A player. A body in commerce with bodies. A helms-man at your own vessel's tiller. A machine in the ghost, to quote a phrase" (160). This misquotation of Ryle, which inverts the positioning of "ghost" and "machine" in his famous phrase, simultaneously announces the idea that the self might be as mechanic as it is autonomic, and reveals the ultimate goal of Incandenza Sr.'s athletic philosophy: the player's body is supposed to become unconscious, machine-like, to the point that most elements of play can occur automatically. The phrase "a machine in the ghost" thus evokes not just the philosophical behaviorism of Ryle, but behavioral conditioning, the technique by which the "mechanical" reiteration of physical routines comes to shape bodily and mental processes.[37]

As we have seen, James Incandenza Sr. appears as dedicated to the notion of the self as a "pilot in his ship" (Descartes 33) and the "dogma of the ghost in the machine" (Ryle 27) as he is to a reduction of the self to electrical activity in the brain. These are essentially irreconcilable positions, since one assumes a central intelligence in control of the body's actions, while the other views the biochemical processes of the body itself as preceding and causing the illusion of such a central intelligence. This contradictory dual allegiance, along with the fact that the mono-logue references both Descartes and his behaviorist critic, suggests that the posi-tion staked out here is fraught with a tension that prefigures the contradictions in which Hal will find himself entrapped.

If we compare James Incandenza Sr.'s monologue with Descartes's work, an inconsistency becomes apparent. Neither in the *Discourse on Method* nor in the *Meditations on First Philosophy* does Descartes unreservedly subscribe to the pilot-ship (or helmsman-vessel) model Incandenza propagates.[38] In the *Discourse*, Descartes says of the soul, "it is not enough for it to be lodged in the human body like a pilot in his ship, unless perhaps in order to move its members, but rather that it must be more closely joined and united to the body in order to [...] constitute a true man" (33). So while body and soul (or mind) can heuristically be conceived as separate entities, a "true man," a flesh-and-blood human being as opposed to a thought experiment, is fully embodied. In other words, the mechanistic model of a guiding intelligence operating a non-sentient machine is insufficient; a deeper interconnection between mind and body is required. The latter is supplied, or at least suggested, in the *Meditations*, where we find a similar qualification. Here, the immediacy of sensations provides proof of a fundamental interconnection:

37  For a concise account of Ryle's *The Concept of Mind* as initiating behaviorist philosophy, see Bailey 419. For the influence of scientific mechanics on psychological behaviorism, see L. Smith 264.
38  Wallace's use of the terms "helmsman" and "vessel" likely originates in older translations of Descartes texts—more recent translations tend to use the terms "pilot" and "ship."

By means of these sensations of pain, hunger, thirst and so on, nature also teaches not merely that I am present to my body in the way a sailor is present in a ship, but that I am most tightly joined and, so to speak, commingled with it, so much so that I and the body constitute one single thing. For if this were not the case, then I, who am only a thinking thing, would not sense pain when the body is injured; rather, I would perceive the wound by means of the pure intellect, just as a sailor perceives by sight whether anything in his ship is broken. (98)

Here we see that contrary to popular opinion, Descartes does not fully subscribe to the pilot-ship model, which would limit interactions to a steering apparatus of some kind, but instead proposes a more integrated and global kind of connection predicated on the idea of "commingling" or "intermingling" (*permixtione*).[39] This is the first sign that James Incandenza Sr.'s endorsement of the pilot-ship model rests either on questionable assumptions or willful misrepresentation. That he references both Descartes and Ryle in the same sentence, thus conflating their positions, only serves to underline this impression. After all, Gilbert Ryle's phrase "ghost in the machine," which appears in his 1949 book *The Concept of the Mind*, was meant to emphasize what the author regarded as the absurdity of Cartesian dualism, or, as he called it, "the official doctrine" (1). Yet Ryle's critique, some scholars have noted, is itself based on an unfair reduction.[40] Cartesian dualism, or "Cartesianism" is often used as a shorthand that refers to both a simplified understanding of Descartes's original work and the followers this understanding attracted, as expressed in Stefan Brandt's remark that the "conflation of Descartes's original writings with the popularized versions of his concepts constitutes a common misunderstanding in mainstream cultural criticism" (102).[41] That James Incandenza Sr. approvingly quotes Ryle's (inverted) phrase in conjunction with Descartes's vessel/helmsman image suggests not only his rather tenuous grasp of the philosophical assumptions on which he bases his athletic pedagogy, but also that the idea of the self as helmsman or ghost in the machine is already an instable construction in itself: the "Cartesian dualism" Burn invokes is not really Cartesian after all.[42] From the start, then, Incandenza Sr.'s doctrine is based on a fallacy.

---

39  Descartes also reiterated this position in *Passions of the Soul*, where he famously identified the pineal gland as the seat of mind-body interconnection (Stent 143).

40  A number of scholars have criticized Ryle's account as misrepresenting Descartes's position for the same reasons I have outlined above: see for instance Alanen, Baker and Morris, and Cottingham.

41  For a knowledgeable and detailed discussion of the conceptual differences and problems of the terms "Cartesian dualism" and "Cartesianism," see Brandt 97-107.

42  Slyly referencing the title of Ryle's first chapter, Lilli Alanen notes that despite its popularity, the Rylean representation of Descartes's position "has not much in common with the view Descartes actually held. It could be called the 'myth of the Cartesian myth'" (45).

His doctrine, which James O. Incandenza then institutionalizes at the Enfield Academy, is thus marked as inherently confused and logically flawed.[43] Burn's claim that "Rylean materialism has become the dominant philosophy of the academy" neglects the degree to which this philosophy is still infused with Cartesianism ("Machine-Language" 45). By reducing the mental to the corporeal, it attempts to develop a fully materialist perspective in which "the head is still just body," but in doing so, it remains trapped within the framework of a misinterpretation of Cartesian dualism. Ironically, Ryle issues a warning against just such reductions in his book: "The 'reduction' of the material world to mental states and processes, as well as the 'reduction' of mental states and processes to physical states and processes, presuppose the legitimacy of the disjunction 'Either there exist minds or there exist bodies (but not both)'" (12). Since Wallace was well read in philosophy and demonstrably familiar with Descartes, we are well justified in assuming that he deliberately fashioned Incandenza Sr.'s reduction of subjectivity to soma as a confused pseudo-materialist dualism that functions as a troubling inheritance for Hal.[44]

Since machinelike functioning is the tennis academy's declared goal for its players, Hal is not alone in this respect; dehumanization, or "self-forgetting," is part of the program (*IJ* 635). Thus an assistant coach informs his charges that the "repetitive movements and motions" of the game are supposed to "sink and soak into the hardware, the C.P.S." until "the mechanics are wired in" (117-18). The novel presents the players as the subjects of intense cognitive and behavioral conditioning that aims at teach them to ignore what the narrator calls the "hot narrow imperatives of the Self—the needs, the desires, the fears, the multiform cravings of the individual appetitive will" (*IJ* 82). Wallace's portrayal of the tennis academy is both an homage to DeLillo, who similarly traces the transformation of an athlete's subjectivity in *End Zone*,[45] and testament to a cultural and historical moment in which the material manipulability of subjectivity has become an urgent topic. As a result, Burn notes, "materialist references consistently cluster around the players at E.T.A." (*Guide* 51). In an apt illustration of this dynamic, the coaching staff tell a female player:

---

43  Steven Moore has pointed out that in an earlier draft of the novel, James Incandenza's Latin motto for the tennis academy was originally "LARVARDUS PRODEO—a slip for Larvatus prodeo, 'I advance masked,' which was the young Descartes' motto" (n. pag.).

44  The author's knowledge of Descartes can be verified: asked about his formative influences by Laura Miller, Wallace named the *Meditations* and the *Discourse* as among the "stars you steer by" (62).

45  *End Zone*'s Gary Harkness faces a similar situation in which he encounters a charismatic yet loony coach, finds himself "reduced in complexity," and is driven by a constant regime of physical and mental conditioning to experience a distinct unease about his machinelike existence.

What actually we do for you here is to break you down in very carefully selected ways, take you apart as a little girl and put you back together again as a tennis player who can take the court against any little girl in North America without fear of limitation. [...] One possible way of couching it is to choose to say that we will take apart your skull very gently and reconstruct a skull for you that will have a highly developed bump of clarity and a slight concave dent where the fear-instinct used to be. (520-21)

This description, which rewrites the deconstruction of personality as material manipulation, i.e., brain surgery, aptly illustrates the absurdity of conflating self and soma. It not only displays an inherent brutality barely mitigated by the coach's assurances that the breaking down and taking apart will occur "very carefully" and "very gently"; crucially, it also likens the process to the discredited discipline of phrenology. Wallace exposes the E.T.A. "sporting philosophy" (Burn, *Guide* 55) to ridicule here, and he does so in a highly intertextual way: the references to phrenology and the "fear-instinct" are, again, obvious allusions to DeLillo, who used the nineteenth-century pseudoscience as an ironic foil for dystopian neurological experiments in *Ratner's Star*.[46]

If E.T.A. is a factory that turns youth into unthinking machines whose most useful skill consists in "shutting the whole neural net down" (*IJ* 96), Hal represents the pinnacle of this transformation into *l'homme machine*.[47] Thus the narrator describes him as "far more robotic than [fellow player] John Wayne," (694) who already qualifies as a "grim machine" (*IJ* 438). His portrayal is meant to evoke the idea of the human mind as a computer, an idea that had entered the cultural mainstream by the 1990s.[48] Thus, when Hal describes his own eyes in the opening passage as "two pale zeros" (8), he is alluding to the binary code of computation, a

---

46  See chapter 3.

47  "The body is but a watch," nineteenth-century materialist Julien Offray de La Mettrie writes, and the human animal is "but a collection of springs which wind each other up" (135). Wallace intentionally invokes such mechanicist imagery when his narrator says of an E.T.A. player, "if you could open Stice's head you'd see a wheel inside another wheel, gears and cogs being widgeted into place" (635).

48  Christoph Koch reminds us that the metaphor of the mind as a computer is part of "a long line of technological metaphors that extends back from parallel and von Neumann computers, telephone switchboards, steam engines, clocks, and waterworks, all the way back to wax tablets in ancient Greece" (232 n2)—a point also made by Daugman (10). The severe criticisms this idea has received since the 1990s (see Dreyfus; Edelman) can be interpreted as a sign that it is already moving toward obsolescence. Current scholarship in cognitive science also increasingly views the incarnate nature of mind and consciousness as the foundation for a more extensive view of embodied cognition: "The whole body (and not only the brain) in its interaction with the environment has become the subject of interest," Oliver Kauffmann emphasizes (49). On this point, see also Gallagher.

description that echoes his "robotic" self-description. Not coincidentally, his name recalls the computer HAL 9000 from Kubrick's *2001: A Space Odyssey*; both Hal and HAL simulate human behavior, and both "shut down" progressively. This view of the body as a machine and the mind as a computer is clearly not an unproblematic one for Wallace.[49] In *Infinite Jest*, computational and mechanistic tropes serve to emphasize Hal's lack of quintessential human qualities: "he finds terms like *joie* and *value* to be like so many variables in rarified equations," the narrator observes, casting Hal as endowed with a computational rather than a human consciousness, "and he can manipulate them well enough to satisfy everyone but himself that he's in there, inside his own hull, as a human being" (694; original emphases).

This telling description provides the blueprint for what Wallace sees as the curse of postmodern hyper-awareness, namely the notion that, given encyclopedic knowledge of all possible language games,[50] an actor is capable of anticipating and performing any given social exchange without truly engaging in it on an affective level. Under such a regime of discursive preemption, Zadie Smith observes, no actual social communication can take place, since "*all* exterior referents have been swallowed up by language and loop back into the self" (270; original emphasis). The result is solipsism, the condition Hal experiences as being alone "inside his own hull."[51] As the novel's "hidden boy" (*IJ* 838), Hal functions as the allegorical embodiment of a peculiarly postmodern deadlock that locks the self in cycles upon cycles of self-consciousness.[52] Hal does not suffer from a lack of interiority, as Burn's formulation of the "loss of self" (*Guide* 52, 54) would have us believe; rather, he is *all* interiority, shut off against the outside world.

"Wallace's subjects are more often cultural subjects than human subjects," James Wood writes (28), and the character of Hal in particular seems to serve such metaphorical purposes. Representing "the logical terminus of a hyper self-consciousness that transforms the head into a cage" (Baskin, n. pag.), his pathology is not only a philosophical but also an allegorical one, referring simultaneously to sterile postmodern metafiction that only ever addresses itself—thus Hal's trajectory toward pure, in-bent self-reflexivity—and to postmodern culture at large. Hence the popular reading of the novel as depicting "what happens when recursivity, through the society of consumption and mediation, becomes pathological—

---

49  Thus, the computer metaphor is linked to drug use: for the E.T.A. players, the narrator states, recreational getting high means "to basically short out the whole motherboard and blow out all the circuits and slowly recover and be almost neurologically reborn and start the gradual cycle all over again," a routine that works only as long "your basic wiring's ok to begin with" (53).

50  The reference here to Ludwig Wittgenstein is fitting: his work arguably constitutes the biggest philosophical influence on Wallace. See Boswell 21-64.

51  For readings of Wallace's portrayal of solipsism, see Holland and Horn.

52  Hal's "addiction, and accompanying hyperreflexivity and endless irony, are typical of the society portrayed in *Infinite Jest*," Allard den Dulk points out (215).

trapping one within the self" (Holland 68). Taking his lead from Fredric Jameson, Wallace presents *Infinite Jest*'s parodically exaggerated postmodern environment as inherently hedonistic, image-centered, and anemic. Under postmodernism,[53] Jameson suggested back in 1984, one can discern a "shift in cultural pathology": the alienation of the subject that had been the reigning malaise of modernism now gives way to its all-out dissolution or fragmentation. Jameson describes this "end of the autonomous bourgeois monad or ego or individual"—it appears to matter little what term we use—as a "decentering" of the subject that produces a shift in emotional valence: the "waning of affect" is replaced with the "liberation from every [...] kind of feeling [...], since there is no longer a self present to do the feeling" (14-15).

Wallace stages a curious version of this postmodern pathology, in which the waning of affect coincides with an anxiety over its disappearance, and the alienation that Jameson considers a relic of the past coexists with the dissolution of the feeling self he posits as paradigmatically postmodern. Initially, *Infinite Jest*, with its quintessentially postmodern pleasures of the surface and ironic references to cultural codes, might appear to map the very shift Jameson delineates. Populated by often grotesque figures that bear little resemblance to the "round" characters of traditional realism or the complex representation of consciousness in high modernism, the text seems to reject the humanistic category of the subject, replacing it with a biomedical self whose "essence" splinters out into a network of various pathological habits and compulsive behaviors.[54]

Yet this description already suggests a crucial divergence from Jameson's model, for the latter views the abolition of affect as liberating, whereas in *Infinite Jest* it figures as an all-encompassing entrapment, symbolized in the frequently invoked figure of "the cage" (*IJ* 222-24). The novel's characters exist not in a utopia of excess signification and jouissance, but in a netherworld of psychobiological agony that is presented as a direct consequence of the deep psychic lack resulting from the loss of the notion of the true, authentic self. When Hal tells his brother Mario about his fears, he says, "I feel a hole. It's going to be a huge hole, in a month. A way more than Hal-sized hole. [...] And the hole's going to get a little bigger every day until I fly apart in different directions" (785). Ironically, the opposite comes to pass. Hal ends up not flying apart but constricting, becoming so bound up in himself that even his own body becomes foreign territory to him. Rather than depict-

---

53  I am using the preposition "under" (rather than "in" or "during") deliberately here to signal Jameson's notion of postmodernism as a comprehensive cultural regime—or, to stay in the Jamesonian register, a "totalizing" one (*Postmodernism* 400).

54  Gerhard Hoffmann's description of *Infinite Jest*'s characters as "distanced, flattened, even obscured" and "fantastic in their threatened condition" is a typical expression of this view (643).

ing the disappearance of the subject, Wallace examines the anxiety that this idea incites.

Hal, who is described as utterly devoid of feeling, is still capable of experiencing at least one emotional response. Ironically, it is nostalgia for affect: "One of the really American things about Hal, probably," the narrator muses, "is the way he despises what it is he's really lonely for: this hideous internal self, incontinent of sentiment and need, that pules and writhes just under the hip empty mask, anhedonia" (695). Wallace allegorizes the plight of a contemporary subject that can neither establish meaningful, sincere connections with others nor experience the elation of indulging in the play of surfaces that Jameson suggests as the end result of postmodern culture. *Pace* Jameson, it is not true that there is "no longer a self to do the feeling" in Hal—there might no longer be feelings, but there is still a self that mourns its inability to feel. This is a crisis of interiority, not a celebration of its absence, and it is presented as a generational phenomenon[55] that can be traced back to the ways in which postmodern culture changes what Wallace has called the *"cognitive* texture of our lives" (Lipsky 39; original emphasis). In a passage that goes some way toward illustrating the difficulty of distinguishing Wallace's non-fiction from his fiction, the narrator invites the reader to consider the following:

> It is of some interest that the lively arts of the millennial U.S.A. treat anhedonia and internal emptiness as hip and cool. [...] The U.S. arts are our guide to inclusion. A how-to. We are shown how to fashion masks of ennui and jaded irony at a young age where the face is fictile enough to assume the shape of whatever it wears. And then it's stuck there, the weary cynicism that saves us from gooey sentiment and unsophisticated naïveté. (694)

In light of passages like this one, it is understandable why Paul Giles laments that "the polemical qualities of Wallace's nonfiction essays intrude into the moralizing narrative voice of *Infinite Jest*" ("Sentimental" 335)—one barely needs to point out the parallels to the ideas Wallace put forward in the "essay-interview nexus." The way the passage links "emotionless" art and loss of affect also has led at least one critic to suspect that Wallace was familiar with Jameson's theory about postmodernism's affective valences and may have been alluding to it in *Infinite Jest* (Burn, "Webs," n28).[56] In an ironical inversion typical of the text's method, contempt of for "gooey sentiment" is construed first as a prerequisite for fitting in, for becoming

---

55  The text positions Hal as representative of his generation: "Like most North Americans of his generation, Hal tends to know way less about why he feels certain ways about the objects and pursuits he's devoted to than he does about the objects and pursuits themselves" (54).

56  For an account of Jamesonian echoes in Wallace's novella "Westward," see Luther.

part of contemporary American youth culture, but then immediately re-cast as the very instrument of isolation that accounts for the rampant sense of alienation and dehumanization that pervades the novel.

Hal appears to be well aware of the progressive reduction of his humanity. On the telephone with his brother, he describes his academic-athletic existence as thoroughly robotic: "I eat, sleep, evacuate, highlight things with yellow markers, and hit balls. I lift things and run in huge outdoor circles. [...] I am out of all loops but one, by design"—a phrase that emphasizes this reduction and the fact of arti-ficial isolation, the deliberate refusal to take part in the social world (1016 n110).[57] Given the alignment of tennis with regimes of behavioral conditioning and the reduction of the self to a specialized machine in the service of individual perfor-mance and success, tennis cannot very well be considered, as Hayles does, as an "effective counter-measure" against cultural pathology ("Illusion" 693). If anything, the E.T.A. *program*—a telling term in itself, bearing connotations of machinic functioning and external control—and its effects on Hal appear as one of many vicious cycles woven into the fabric of the text. The E.T.A. program may mitigate against the confinement within the self that Wallace critiques, but ultimately it is complicit in a regime of alienation: "excessive data-gathering, addiction, annular fusion technology, and athletic training lead to a dizzying circularity from which there is no escape" (Mullins 236). Again, Hal best illustrates this principle.

Though he exhibits symptoms of "Analysis-paralysis" all through the book, it is during the "Eschaton" match that Hal's condition takes a pronounced turn for the worse. Watching from the sidelines, Hal gets high with his friends and ends up in a "paralytic thought-helix" (335) so powerful that even as a fight breaks out between his charges, the "Little Buddies," he can do nothing but sit and watch in silent amazement:

> Troeltsch says he for his own part wouldn't be just sitting and lying there if any of the Little Buddies under his personal charge were out there getting potentially injured, and Hal reflects that he does feel a certain sort of intense anxiety, but can't sort through the almost infinite-seeming implications of what Troeltsch is saying fast enough to determine whether the anxiety is over something about what he's seeing or something in the connection between what Troeltsch is saying and the degree to which he's absorbed in what's going on out inside the fence, which is a

---

57  Apart from its obvious connection to the novel's preoccupation with infinite recursion, the con-cept of the loop also hints at a popular concept of its critical reception, namely the category of the "systems novel"—a characterization first developed by Tom LeClair to describe the work of Don DeLillo, which, as we have seen functions as an important intertextual reference point for Wallace. For the systems novel, see LeClair, *Loop*; for the influence of DeLillo, see Burn, "Webs," as well as Natalini.

> degenerative chaos so complex in its disorder that it's hard to tell whether it seems choreographed or simply chaotically disordered. (341)

It is amid this confusion that Hal experiences the first symptoms of dissociation from his own body, losing the immediacy of affective reaction. Watching the Eschaton match escalate into a violent brawl, Hal is "suddenly aware that Troeltsch and Pemulis are wincing but is not himself wincing and isn't sure why they are wincing and is looking out into the fray trying to determine whether he should be wincing" (342). Toward the end of the passage, this process reaches its pinnacle in a "completely and uncomfortably bizarre" moment when Hal "feels at his own face to see whether he is wincing" (342). The narrative thus carefully aligns Hal's mental self-absorption with his proprioceptive degeneration, so that he slowly turns into an allegorical embodiment of the very caricature of Cartesian dualism first evoked by James Incandenza Sr. and subsequently codified as E.T.A. philosophy. Hal is pictured here as slowly retreating into the shell of his own body and assuming the role of the Cartesian "helmsman" who can steer his ship but possesses no immediate sensory connection to its physical form. The terminal point of this process is the novel's opening scene, which is worth quoting at length here:

> I am seated in an office, surrounded by heads and bodies. My posture is consciously congruent to the shape of my hard chair. This is a cold room in University Administration, wood-walled, Remington-hung, double-windowed against the November heat, insulated from Administrative sounds by the reception area outside, at which Uncle Charles, Mr. deLint and I were lately received.
> I am in here.
> Three faces have resolved into place above summer-weight sportcoats and half-Windsors across a polished pine conference table shiny with the spidered light of an Arizona noon. These are three Deans – of Admissions, Academic Affairs, Athletic Affairs.
> I do not know which face belongs to whom.
> I believe I appear neutral, maybe even pleasant, though I've been coached to err on the side of neutrality and not attempt what would feel to me like a pleasant expression or smile.
> I have committed to crossing my legs I hope carefully, ankle on knee, hands together in the lap of my slacks. My fingers are mated into a mirrored series of what manifests, to me, as the letter X. (1)

The scene is constructed so as to evoke the near-complete separation of Hal's subjective interiority from the external world, including his own body. Hal "believes" he appears neutral, but has no way of telling anymore; his self-alienation has escalated to the point that he needs to be "coached" on how to assume even the blankest of facial expressions. Likewise, he no longer experiences his extremities as belonging to his phenomenological *corps propre*[58] but as external objects that "manifest" themselves to his consciousness instead of being given and felt a priori. The disconnect between mind and body now also extends to how Hal perceives his social environment: other people appear only as "heads and bodies," which "resolve into place" like images on a screen. Like the room he is sitting in, Hal's self is "insulated" from the outside, and like the room, his inside is "cold," in the sense that it appears devoid of anything but cool, detached observation. Not least, the insulated nature of the room, its atmosphere of temperature-controlled stasis, evoke the similarly "walled-off" and homeostatically controlled confines of the human skull.

Hal's declaration "I am in here" thus takes on a double meaning. He is located inside the room, but like the Cartesian cogito, he is also located inside his body, or, more precisely, inside his head. When he finally attempts to speak, he is "calling into the darkness of the red cave that opens out before closed eyes," and when he opens his eyes, he "looks out" through his own eye sockets (*IJ* 11-12). If such descriptions bring to mind Daniel Dennett's Cartesian theater, the effect is intended.[59] In the opening scene, the terminus of Hal's pathology is represented as a Cartesian caricature: Hal has become a "homunculus" trapped inside a body.[60] In a dark irony, Hal is granted his wish: if earlier he thought that inside of him, "there's pretty much nothing at all," and regretted that he "hasn't had a bona fide intensity-of-interior-life-type emotion since he was tiny," now his own interiority is all he has left (*IJ* 694).

This is certainly one of the text's supreme ironies: if the horror of becoming "posthuman," i.e., animalistic or machinelike haunts the text, it is precisely recourse to the quintessential quality of traditional humanistic models of selfhood—interiority, self-reflection, consciousness—that ultimately accounts for Hal's banishment from the human realm. He protests that he is "not a machine,"

---

58  Maurice Merleau-Ponty used the term *corps propre* to designate one's own body as the subjective basis of lived experience (*Leib*), as opposed to one's own body as it is perceived as an object (*Körper*), which is why the term has usually been translated as "living body" or "lived body." For a full account, see Merleau-Ponty.

59  The "Cartesian theater" is a term in the philosophy of mind coined by Daniel Dennett to reveal the implicit, residual materialism of Cartesian mind-body dualism, the idea that "we" are "inside" our own heads. See Dennett, *Consciousness* 39 and 107. Susan Blackmore notes that the term describes "not just the analogy of the mind with a theatre, but the notion that somewhere in the mind or brain there must be a place and time at which everything comes together and 'consciousness happens'" (15). The head figuratively becomes the location from which the conscious mind looks out onto the world.

60  In Dennett's critique of the Cartesian model, "homunculi" are the fictive "little men" in the brain that stand in for the conscious subject of experience (*Consciousness* 14-15).

that he is not just a creātus, manufactured, conditioned, bred for a function"; not coincidentally, his claim to true humanity is predicated on sensibility and *Bildung*, the classical markers of humanistic distinction: "I have an intricate history. Experiences and feelings. I'm complex. I *read* (11-12; original emphasis). Yet all his complaints are in vain; the committee does not hear his passionate pleas but only garbled sounds; it is his claim to an authentic self that seals his fate as "some sort of animal" (*IJ* 14).[61]

Whether we read Hal's estrangement from both his own and the social body as an allegory of postmodern literature and/or culture, as a symptom of an untenable philosophy of mind, or, following the tenets of "surface reading," simply as a narrative event to be connected to the rest of the plot,[62] it is striking that Wallace tells Hal's story in constant reference to, and interplay with, Descartes's foundational theory of the relation between mind and matter. The portions of *Infinite Jest* that focus on E.T.A. and Hal appear to fulfill a double function: on one hand they present an indictment of mind-body dualism in which the conflation of subjectivity and materiality is condemned just as roundly as the reduction of the self to Descartes's "thinking thing." On the other hand, this sweeping indictment of "mind over matter" as well as "matter over mind" is not an end in itself but instead serves to convey the novel's central concerns with the interconnections between addiction, compulsion, consumerism, and postmodern literature and culture. More than just vaguely registering "the impact of therapy, pharmacology and the terminology of clinical psychology," as Catherine Toal has it (306), *Infinite Jest* specifically engages with the questions the new materialist view of human mind generates. In this way, the text registers the discrepancy between the "different notions of what it is to be a person" implicit in biomedical and psychodynamic approaches (Luhrmann 5).

The novel stages this as a conflict between the concept of the subject as someone who possesses interiority, free will, an authentic self, and agency, and the opposing view of humans as biologically determined, thoroughly physical beings, "hardwired" like machines or computers and wholly subject to the laws of physics. Yet this contrast remains linked at all times to the novel's general concerns; it refers not only to its own historical specificity but also, through metaphoric connections, beyond itself, to cultural and literary meanings, whereby it becomes polysemous, open to different and diverging readings. A provisional finding of my

---

61  This ironic reversal, in which the anxious prospect of being reduced to mere materiality comes true because of its intense rejection, has led some critics to identify a "strain of anti-intellectualism" in *Infinite Jest* (Aubry, "Selfless" 214).

62  For an account of "surface reading," which foregoes the "hermeneutics of suspicion" for a more straightforward engagement with the manifest content of texts, see Best and Marcus as well as Felski, "Suspicion" and "Suspicious."

analysis here can thus be summed up as follows: in direct contradiction of Roth's reductive description of the "neuronovel," *Infinite Jest* demonstrates how, rather than arresting ambiguity and short-circuiting the play of interpretation, biomedical or materialist models of mind (as computer, as biological machine, or as a site of pathology) can itself assume ambiguous and allegorical functions.

## "Now they've got you, and you're free": Don Gately

If Hal Incandenza personifies the perils of mind-body dualism, self-consciousness, ironic detachment, and the prioritization of encyclopedic knowledge over affective attachment (or *ratio* over *emotio*), the novel's other protagonist is in many ways his polar opposite. Don Gately is a petty criminal of working-class background who succeeds in overcoming his addictions through the communal sociality and proto-spirituality of twelve-step programs, thanks to their insistence on unreflective *praxis* and "mindless" submission. Wallace portrays Gately, who is "almost twenty-nine and sober and just huge," as a hard worker, simple but kindhearted. He functions as a stabilizing and benevolent presence at Ennet House, the recovery home that employs him as a "live-in staffer," where he performs menial tasks (*IJ* 277, 196). Along with his impressive physique and dedication to duty and service, his inclination to take "zero in the way of shit" marks him out for guardianship and self-sacrifice: he narrowly survives a gunshot wound sustained while protecting the residents of the halfway house from a pair of thugs (*IJ* 55, 613).[63]

A somewhat idealized figure,[64] Gately display both selflessness and a stubborn determination to remain sober; large portions of the final part of the novel revolve around his refusal to ingest morphine-based painkillers while hospitalized, despite excruciating pain. This has led a number of critics to consider Gately's "metamorphosis" (Cioffi 165) as a redemptive, "heroic" effort (Boswell 137) that represents the novel's key instantiation of hope.[65] Since it is a twelve-step program that enables Gately to break the cycle of addiction, the novel, "for the most part, reads as an apology for AA" (Aubry, *Reading* 113). Accordingly, the text's portrayal

---

63  Accordingly, Nicoline Timmer reads Gately as a "parent figure" (161).

64  As Aubry notes, the readers who are susceptible to *Infinite Jest*'s aesthetic appeal are also "precisely the ones likely to suffer from the problem that it explores: a combination of emotional detachment and cerebral sophistication" (*Reading* 100). A corollary of this is that for the typical *Infinite Jest* reader (young, white, male, middle-class), Gately is a figure of the social other, prone to romanticization.

65  LeClair's idea of the novel as "a hopeful monster," for instance, is largely based on the character of Gately ("Prodigious" 34). A notable exception is Mary K. Holland, who argues that the novel's dynamics of solipsism and narcissism are too powerful to read Gately's "valiant" struggle as significantly transformative (234).

of AA has become a point of some contention: does Wallace unabashedly beat the drum for the organization, or does he assume a more distanced, critical position? Given *Infinite Jest*'s highly allegorical quality, one suspects that Gately's story might aim at more than the validation of twelve-step programs.[66] Accordingly, I will argue that the question of whether AA "works" is ultimately less important than the way the program is framed and contextualized, and the functions it fulfills within the text.

AA's *raison d'*être is addiction, which *Infinite Jest* paradoxically depicts as an embodied, holistic phenomenon that deeply divides the self. In effect, addiction poses the relation between mind and matter as a dilemma: through material manipulation—the ingestion or injection of substances—subjectivity itself is splintered, separated into a part of the self that craves drugs, and another part that wants to quit them. The result is a pathological state the narrator dubs a "peritonitis of the soul" that causes the addict to wonder, "why can't I quit if I so want to quit, unless I'm insane?" This schizophrenic situation is described as an untenable double bind: "You are, as they say, Finished. You cannot get drunk and you cannot get sober; you cannot get high and you cannot get straight" (*IJ* 346-47). In accordance with the tenets of AA, addiction figures in *Infinite Jest* as "the Disease" or "the Spider," an autonomous entity worthy not only of capital letters but of the utmost caution: Gately learns that it is "fiendishly patient" and "envisions his brain struggling in a silk cocoon" (355, 887).

Though rooted in materiality, the realm of "substance," addiction affects the comparably less substantial sphere of volition and agency—it appears, to use Nietzsche's phrase, as a "malady of the will" (613).[67] The will, historically understood as the capacity linking mind and body in human action (Valverde 2), is irrevocably compromised for the addict, requiring its relinquishment:

> The will you call your own ceased to be yours as of who knows how many Substance-drenched years ago. It's now shot through with the spidered fibrosis of your Disease. His own experience's term for the Disease is: *The Spider*. You have to Starve The Spider: you have to surrender your will. [...] You have to want to surrender your will to people who know how to Starve The Spider. [...] If you don't obey, nobody will kick you out. They won't have to. You'll end up kicking yourself out, if you steer by your own sick will. (*IJ* 357; original emphasis)

---

66  See Jacobs, who calls *Infinite Jest* an "aesthetic allegory" (284), LeClair, who describes it as a "metafictional allegory" ("Prodigious" 33) as well as my own analysis, in the previous section, of the allegorical functions of the character of Hal.

67  "Malady of the will" is originally Nietzsche's phrase for the underlying psychological deficiency he believes gave rise to Buddhism and Christianity, implying that religious belief fills a lack of personal, autonomous will and motivation (613).

Such a view of addiction as colonizing the will effectively destabilizes distinctions that are fundamental for Western conceptions of subjectivity, like inside and outside, mind and body, self and other, rendering obsolete the classical conception of the subject as the master of its intentions. In other words: "Not all compulsion comes from without" (*IJ* 320). Addiction, to invoke Hamlet, "puzzles the will." This line of thinking continues the critique of consciousness encapsulated in the novel's portrayal of Hal. In fact, we learn that consciousness exacerbates the problem of addiction: "It's the newcomers [to AA] with some education that are the worst [...]. They identify their whole selves with their head, and the Disease makes its command headquarters in the head" (*IJ* 272). *Infinite Jest* thus produces a far-reaching critique of the cogito, inverting the Cartesian ideas it alludes to by casting reason as the handmaiden of the passions, and rejecting the famous Freudian dictum "Where id was, there ego shall be" (112) in favor of a "surrender" of will. Wallace was avowedly suspicious of the claim "that etiology and diagnosis pointed toward cure, that a revelation of imprisonment led to freedom" ("Unibus" 67). But if insight and understanding fail to produce positive effects, what does?

"If the problem originates in the presumption of autonomy that is the founding principle for the liberal humanist self," as Katherine Hayles suggests in her essay on the internal logic of *Infinite Jest*, then what is required is a "reconceptualization of subjectivity" that does away with the emphasis on autonomous, conscious function ("Illusion" 693). And indeed the novel seems to provide something very similar: after all, Gately's road to sobriety is marked not by freely willed decisions but by the compulsive repetition of ritual behaviors, "very basic rote automatic get-me-through-this-day-please stuff" (*IJ* 443) like going to meetings, cooking and cleaning, and, perhaps most importantly, getting "creakily down on his mammoth knees in the A.M. every day" and invoking a higher power he does not believe in. Unable to muster religious belief, Gately is "just going through the knee motions," but is told that his lack of authentic, inner belief does not matter: "All that mattered was what he *did*. If he did the right things, and kept doing them for long enough, what Gately thought and believed would magically change" (*IJ* 466; original emphasis). And in fact, it does: eventually, as a result of the AA regimen, the craving for drugs is "mysteriously magically removed from Don Gately" (466).

There are obvious parallels between Ennet House and E.T.A. here: the tennis players are similarly encouraged to perform "repetitive movements and motions for their own sake" and to adopt "Going Through the Motions" as their motto (117-18).[68] Just like at the halfway house, life at the tennis academy is characterized by "[l]imits and rituals" (*IJ* 120). In both cases, an institutionalized framework of embodied practice, based in mindless repetition, is used to modulate and ulti-

---

68 See also Freudenthal's claim that "[c]ompulsiveness links together the novel's family, halfway house, and political-economic plots" (195).

mately transform subjectivity itself; Hayles's characterization of the novel's two programs as Foucauldian "technologies of the self" seems entirely apposite here ("Illusion" 693). We might call this process "conditioning," a phrase the narration itself employs frequently in reference to the tennis academy (e.g., *IJ* 49, 79, 95), or "habit," a term that emphasizes that addiction and recovery operate by similar, embodied mechanisms,[69] but there is also an argument to be made that in its portrayal of "programmable" human subjects the novel points toward the new materialist notion of neuroplasticity.

Somewhat predictably, this transvaluation of the self as no longer guided by an inner core of autonomous consciousness but instead dependent on externality, on others and material practices, has led some critics to welcome what they see as the novel's commitment to an alternative conception of subjectivity capable of supplanting older, ostensibly outdated formulations. Thus Hayles identifies in *Infinite Jest* a critique of "an ideology that celebrates an autonomous, independent subject who is free to engage in the pursuit of happiness" ("Illusion" 692-93), while Elizabeth Freudenthal believes the novel "depicts a world in which people are most able to cope with their world when they view themselves as dynamic objects in relationships to other people and objects" and sees in Gately's unthinking performance of physical tasks a "generative embrace of materiality" (204-205).[70] One problem with these readings is that they tend to conflate the different aims and results that the prioritization of matter over mind have at Ennet House and E.T.A: in light of what happens to Hal, Hayles's characterization of both tennis and AA as "effective counter-measures" against the novel's pathologies of the self can only qualify as a misreading ("Illusion" 693).[71] Another problem is that they ignore or neglect the apparent contradictions of *Infinite Jest*'s "materialist minds."

Given Wallace's unease about materialist models of the self it appears counterintuitive that liberation should come in the form of yet another "program" predicated on the force of habit and behavioral conditioning. In fact, the narration registers this unease by noting that "the term *Program* resonates darkly, for those who fear getting brainwashed" (369; original emphasis) and that Gately "feels like

69  "As with drug addiction itself, the routine prescribed by AA becomes stronger the more it is repeated, until the will is gradually bound over to a different and less fatal substance (North 170).

70  Freudenthal describes this alternative conception of subjectivity as "anti-interiority," a "mode of identity founded in the material world of both objects and biological bodies and divested from an essentialist notion of inner emotional, psychological, and spiritual life" (195).

71  See also Mark McGurl's assessment that "whether it is a nursing home, a halfway house, Alcoholics Anonymous, a tennis academy, mammoth federal bureaucracy, or the university, the 'institution' in Wallace is first and foremost a communal antidote to atomism, a laboriously iterated wall against the nihilism attendant to solitude." In contrast to Hayles, however, McGurl is attentive to the fact that "these institutions are also importantly specific in their social ends" ("Institution" 38).

a rat that's learned one route in a maze to the cheese and travels that route in a rat-ty-type fashion and whatnot," which connects suggestively to the text's earlier discussion of neurological animal experiments (443). The book certainly presents the "intensely social" AA group as a structural antipode to the tennis academy's focus on individual achievement (360), but such metonymic connections reinforce the impression that there is real ambivalence in Wallace's portrayal of AA's recovery regime. Nowhere is this ambivalence more palpable than in a key sentence, worth quoting in full, which renders Gately's experience with the program in Wallace's signature style:

> And so you Hang In and stay sober and straight, and out of sheer hand-burned-on-hot-stove terror you heed the improbable-sounding warnings not to stop pounding out the nightly meetings even after the Substance-cravings have left and you feel like you've got a grip on the thing at last and can now go it alone, you still don't try to go it alone, you heed the improbable warnings because by now you have no faith in your own sense of what's really improbable and what isn't, since AA seems, improbably enough, to be working, and with no faith in your own senses you're confused, flummoxed, and when people with AA time strongly advise you to keep coming you nod robotically and keep coming, and you sweep floors and scrub out ashtrays and fill stained steel urns with hideous coffee, and you keep getting ritually down on your big knees every morning and night asking for help from a sky that still seems a burnished shield against all who would ask aid of it—how can you pray to a "God" you believe only morons believe in, still?—but the old guys say it doesn't yet matter what you believe or don't believe, Just Do It they say, and like a shock-trained organism without any kind of independent human will you do exactly like you're told, you keep coming and coming, nightly, and now you take pains not to get booted out of the squalid halfway house you'd at first tried so hard to get discharged from, you Hang In and Hang In, meeting after meeting, warm day after cold day...; and not only does the urge to get high stay more or less away, but more general life-quality-type things—just as improbably promised, at first, when you'd Come In—things seem to get progressively somehow better, inside, for a while, then worse, then even better, then for a while worse in a way that's still somehow better, realer, you feel weirdly unblinded, which is good, even though a lot of the things you now see about yourself and how you've lived are horrible to have to see—and by this time the whole thing is so improbable and unparsable that you're so flummoxed you're convinced you're maybe brain-damaged, still, at this point, from all the years of Substances, and you figure you'd better Hang In in this Boston AA where older guys who seem to be less damaged—or at least less flummoxed by their damage—will tell you in terse simple imperative clauses exactly what to do, and where and when to do it (though never How or Why); and at this point you've started to have an almost classic sort of Blind Faith in the older

guys, a Blind Faith in them born not of zealotry or even belief but just of a chilled conviction that you have no faith whatsoever left in yourself; and now if the older guys say Jump you ask them to hold their hand at the desired height, and now they've got you, and you're free. (350-51)

Clearly, the intricately constructed and absurdly long sentence aims to re-enact the strenuous recovery process by making us wade through lines upon lines of subordinate clauses, holding us in its grip like an addiction, only to release us unannounced and abruptly at the very end, just as Gately is—miraculously, surprisingly—released from his dependence. Yet in the process, the narration contains some noteworthy allusions. Phrases like "sheer hand-burned-on-stove terror" and metaphors like that of the "shock-trained organism" clearly evoke behavioral conditioning, a rather bleak template for a reconceptualization of subjectivity that would replace the inner self with a matrix of appetitive and aversive stimuli. In such a scenario, "faith in your own senses" would indeed be misplaced, as would the notion of agency: nothing left to do then, but to "nod robotically." And yet we are reminded that this state of affairs is still "better, realer," than its alternative, while paradoxical pairings like "convinced" and "maybe" prepare the ground for the supremely contradictory conclusion that "they've got you, and you're free."[72]

But is it really true that Wallace "undermines the concept of will" in *Infinite Jest*, as Emily Russell claims (156)? Perhaps it would be more accurate to say that freedom of choice is curtailed, while individual *willpower* is sustained as an ideal. In keeping with the dominant ideology of twelve-step programs, Wallace presents recovery as the result of a conscious willed effort that has to be reiterated daily—aptly summed up in the AA motto, "one day at a time." When, toward the end of the novel, Don Gately lies in a hospital bed, recovering from a gunshot wound, he actively chooses to suffer excruciating pain rather than accept an analgesic. Lying there, he realizes that he:

could just hunker down in the space between each heartbeat and make each heartbeat a wall and live in there. Not let his head look over. What's unendurable is what his own head could make of it all. What his head could report to him, looking over and ahead and reporting. But he could choose not to listen; he could treat his head like [...] clueless noise. He hadn't quite gotten this before now, how it wasn't

---

72  In his reading of this passage, Aubry emphasizes the interpretive leeway the sentence's internal contradictions afford readers: "Wallace's sentence encourages, through its overt registration of its own tensions, the reader's interpretative freedom, a freedom to doubt the validity of the final word 'free.' [...] Hence the reader, like the AA participant, is, after some serious labor, put in a position to choose actively to embrace the positive though paradoxical account of AA's coercive mechanisms as a means of achieving liberation" ("Selfless" 211).

just the matter of riding out the cravings for a Substance: everything unendurable was in the head, was the head not Abiding in the Present but hopping the wall and doing a recon and then returning with unendurable news you then somehow believed. (860-61)

Obviously, this is a different model for overcoming pain and addiction than the biochemical one, which consists in "riding out the cravings for a Substance" through the embodied rituals of AA. What is being described here is the conscious decision to act or think a certain way, a deliberate choice that requires the exertion of individual volition. I would make the case that this is not an isolated scene but a paradigmatic one: in the world of *Infinite Jest*, battling addiction or mental illness is cast as an exercise in willpower. Accordingly, methadone clinics are mentioned exactly once in the text, and in the only instance where psychiatric drugs make an appearance, they are disqualified for essentially falling under the dreaded rubric of "substances," much like painkillers.[73] As Wallace has stated in another context, "only the human will can defy, transgress, overcome, love: *choose*" ("Fire" 169; original emphasis).

At the same time, we cannot ignore that choice figures here essentially as a feat of *physical* endurance, the will to "hunker down in the space between each heartbeat" and subsist by "abiding" in the present, despite the pain it causes.[74] And we cannot get around the fact that the concept of the will manifests here as a deeply contradictory idea, grounded simultaneously—and paradoxically—in a lack of choices and in the freedom to choose. "The bitch of the thing is you have to *want* to," the narrator says of the AA program, a formulation that leads the very notion of autonomous volition ad absurdum (357; original emphasis). In other words, *Infinite Jest*'s addicts have no chance, so they take it. Evidently, for Wallace, freedom and will are not inseparable: in his posthumous novel *The Pale King*, a character muses, "If I wanted to matter—even just to myself—I would have to be less free, by deciding to choose in some kind of definitive way. Even if it was nothing more than an act of will" (224).

---

73  The medication regime of Kate Gompert, a minor character who mostly serves to discuss the phenomenology of depression, is described as follows: "On Prozac for a short time, then Zoloft, most recently Parnate with a lithium kicker. [...] Bi-Valium discontinued two years, Xanax discontinued one year—an admitted history of abusing prescribed meds" (69).

74  One can correlate this description with the experience of reading *Infinite Jest*, which requires a similar willingness to suffer vicariously in order to empathize, to figuratively "work hard" in order to arrive at insights that the author—as an authority figure that resembles the authoritarian structure of AA—may or may not provide. This could be described as an essentially theological arrangement; Zadie Smith's observation that Wallace requires *"faithful* readers" rings true here (290, original emphasis). See also McGurl, "Institution" for a critical assessment of Wallace that portrays him as, essentially, an institutional-minded disciplinarian.

Thus we are confronted with a situation in which the will oscillates between freedom and limitation, just as the willing subject appears caught between mind and matter. Perhaps it is possible to explain, if not solve, these aporias by putting them in relation to each other. We can take our cue from the observation, made by many critics, that Wallace is clearly invested in what Hayles calls the "reconceptualization" of subjectivity.[75] As we have seen, a large part of this reconceptualization consists in a complex critique of the Cartesian model, yet Wallace is also disinclined to replace it with an entirely materialist paradigm. Both, we take it, qualify as "epistemological errors," a term that figures prominently in a text that may have served as inspiration for *Infinite Jest*'s "paradoxical," looped representation of embodied phenomena like addiction, subjectivity, and the will.

In "The Cybernetics of the 'Self': A Theory of Alcoholism," Gregory Bateson argues that the situation of the alcoholic is characterized by an "unusually disastrous variant of the Cartesian dualism, the division between Mind and Matter, [...] between conscious will, or 'self,' and the remainder of the personality." This "occidental error" (321) is so profound that recovery cannot occur under its predicates; instead, "a change in epistemology" is needed (319). AA and Bateson's cybernetics both work to this effect and are united in key assumptions, like the need to reject the idea of the addict as "captain of his soul" (318), a suggestion that closely maps onto *Infinite Jest*'s extensive use of the "helmsman" metaphor. Wallace may have encountered Bateson's work through his reading of R. D. Laing, who draws on Bateson's concepts in his book *The Divided Self*, which Wallace studied closely during the composition of *Infinite Jest* (Burn, "Webs" 72).

At any rate, Wallace's likely familiarity with Bateson would go a long way toward explaining *Infinite Jest*'s refutation of the "myth of self-power" (Bateson 318) and its portrayal of the interrelation between subjectivity and material practices.[76] In Bateson's theory, the mind is produced by material entities and processes,[77] but the self cannot be pinpointed to a particular biological location. Instead, it emerges out of the interaction of organism and environment: "The total self-corrective unit which processes information, [...] 'thinks' and 'acts' and 'decides,' is a system whose boundaries do not at all coincide with the boundaries either of the body or of what is popularly called the 'self' or 'consciousness,'" Bateson writes. Thus, "to explain or understand the mental aspect of any biological event, we must

---

75  See also Burn's observation that the "search for an adequate understanding of the self" can be considered one of the novel's "obsessive explorations" (*Guide* 45).

76  Along with Borges, Bateson could also have been the source for Wallace's play on the idea that "the map is not the territory," which figures prominently in the Eschaton episode and is discussed by Bateson in his essay "Form, Substance, and Difference."

77  Bateson is convinced that "any ongoing ensemble of [material] events and objects which has the appropriate complexity of causal circuits and the appropriate energy relations will surely show mental characteristics" (321).

take into account the system—that is, the network of closed circuits, within which that biological event is determined" (325, 323).

This redescription of the mind as "both flesh and not" (to invoke the title of one of Wallace's most popular essays), as an embodied system operating an and through feedback loops, resonates strongly with Wallace's presentation of his characters as networked nodes whose functioning depends less on their individual consciousness than on the systems to which they make themselves available.[78] "Attachments are of great seriousness. Choose your attachments carefully," Marathe, one of the novel's spokespersons for a less individualistic mode of existence, advises (107). The turn away from the self may also account for *Infinite Jest*'s method of surrounding two protagonists with several other "main" characters and a supporting cast of countless minor ones. Here the text may merely be practicing what it preaches, distributing agency across various characters and interlocking mental-material systems instead of bundling it in a clearly designated, classical "hero."[79] In a continuation of this dynamic, *The Pale King* arguably no longer has any protagonist at all (McGurl, "Institution" 47).

Recourse to Bateson can also help us understand the functional difference between the tennis academy and the halfway house in *Infinite Jest*. Both aim at producing a "change in epistemology," but E.T.A. remains linked to the regimes of entertainment and competition. To become a professional is called "making it into the Show," and Hal informs the younger players that tennis is "an individual sport," so they are "all on each other's food chain" (49, 112) In contrast, "the single purpose of AA is directed outward and is aimed at a noncompetitive relationship to the larger world," as Bateson writes (342), and Wallace, who is similarly sympathetic toward the program, draws on this altruistic idea of AA to complement, or even counteract, his allegory of cultural pathology with an ideal of social connection.

The former, as we have seen, is conveyed through Hal's story, which literalizes the condition the author once described as "being marooned in [one's] own skull" (McCaffery interview 127). Wallace viewed this self-centeredness as an existential condition, "our default setting, hard-wired into our boards at birth" (Wallace, *Water* 38), but he also believed it was exacerbated by the pressures of postmodern culture, or rather by those of its aspects—science, technology, and media— that Mark McGurl, in an attempt to define Wallace's target more precisely, calls

---

78  See also Burn's observation that the novel's multiple narrative strands "are designed to suggestively interact, illustrating how individual action effects and is shaped by a larger community," though his choice of the term "community" ignores the possibility, of non-human factors, which Bateson makes a point of including (*Guide* 38).

79  Intriguingly, the text itself touches upon the problem of the hero by incorporating a cultural studies paper that discusses the shift from the "classically modern hero of action" to the "'*post*'-modern hero" and imagines the eventual arrival of the "hero of *non*-action, the catatonic hero"—a designation fit for Hal himself, given his trajectory toward paralysis (140-42).

"technomodernism" ("Institution" 32).[80] Conversely, Gately's story is often read as exemplifying the values and virtues that might counteract this self-absorption: sociality, sincerity, and, however tentatively, spirituality.[81] When Gately realizes that "it wasn't just the matter of riding out the cravings for a Substance," the narration hints at this allegorical aspect, which Wallace confirmed: "The book isn't supposed to be about *drugs*, getting off drugs," he confided to David Lipsky. The drug theme, Wallace explained, functioned only as "a kind of a metaphor" (81; original emphasis). And it is indeed tempting to read AA's "pragmatic utopianism," its insistence on an "alternative set of values," as an alternative to everything the novel deems pathological (Aubry, "Selfless" 212, 206). At the same time, AA's injunction to "check your head at the door" is not entirely unproblematic; the narration itself registers its implications as "almost classically authoritarian, maybe even proto-Fascist" (374).

This contradictory portrayal of AA as both autocratic and liberating has drawn much critical ire; it also accounts for strikingly disparate readings of the novel.[82] Essentially, we can distinguish between the optimists, who read Wallace's portrayal of AA as a programmatic instantiation of his ideas about the need to transcend narcissism and self-absorption, and the pessimists, who emphasize its darker, dehumanizing aspects. Yet for all their avowed differences, both camps share common ground in that they accept the terms set forth by Wallace for the reception of *Infinite Jest*; that is, they read the novel by placing it in the binary frame of pathology and therapy that forms the basis of the author's cultural critique. I would like to propose that instead of restricting our interpretive freedom to the limits of the therapeutic paradigm in this way, we should subject its operative assumptions to analysis.

"The most American thing about Wallace," Adam Kirsch observes, "is his conviction that his unhappiness is a specifically American condition" (198). Perhaps just as "American," one wants to add here, is the way he attempted to make the experience of a small, materially privileged, predominantly white stratum of society into a universal quality of American life in general. "Wallace's 'infinity' of sympathetic imagination is terminally white middle-class suburban," Mark McGurl points out ("Institution" 43). Kirsch's and McGurl's statements aside, the dubious

---

80  For the concept of technomodernism, see also McGurl, *Program* 56-68.

81  See Aubry, who suggests that in his portrayal of AA, Wallace emphasizes the "sustaining forms of empathy, conviction, and emotional solidarity" (*Reading* 99), and Hayles, who proposes that "Gately's struggle reveals what it means to attempt on a daily basis to shed the illusion of autonomous selfhood and accept citizenship in a world in which actions have consequences that rebound to the self because everything is connected with everything else" ("Illusion" 693).

82  Catherine Toal detects in Wallace's work the normative conviction "that concepts and processes of formation can only be rigidly disciplinary, prescriptively 'corrective'" (317); others diagnose "conservatism" (Baskin, n. pag.) or "anti-intellectualism" (Aubry, "Selfless" 214).

yet fundamental supposition that a particularly postindustrial sense of aimlessness and alienation has become culturally endemic is still underexamined in Wallace criticism. I would like to read it here as a sign of the author's internalization of a biomedical perspective and a binary mode of thinking that categorically distinguishes between illness and health.

Timothy Aubry identifies in *Infinite Jest* a problematic dichotomy: "On one side there is drug abuse, irony, excessive self-obsession, mass-culture entertainment, hedonistic pursuit of pleasure, and on the other side there is AA-sponsored sobriety, sincerity, empathy, difficult art, and authentic feeling" ("Selfless" 213). It is precisely because Wallace posits debilitating pathology as a universal condition, I contend, that he ends up advocating a therapeutic intervention that does away with what it meant to salvage, namely the agency and wholeness of the human subject. Upon closer examination, what Paul Giles calls Wallace's "hortatory idiom" ("Swallowed" 6) is justified by an imagined state of constant emergency.[83] By authorial fiat, in the world of *Infinite Jest* it is *always* high time; the shift toward the pathological is always already in full swing, so that radical therapeutic intervention appears as the only hope. Familial dysfunction is a particularly persistent given—almost without exception, *Infinite Jest*'s characters seem to have been misunderstood, mistreated, or abused as children.[84]

In this sense, it is true that, as Catherine Toal laments, Wallace "avoids advocating a model of formation [...] that might be an alternative to all the exhausting technologies of the self found in *Infinite Jest*" (320). The a priori existence of pathology creates a curious situation in which health or normality are nowhere to be found yet constitute the ever-present horizon of the characters' projects:[85] *Infinite Jest* constantly and relentlessly "limns states of personal emergency" (Blair 15), and the radical disavowal of the self that characterizes the "emergency measure" of AA can only appear as a feasible alternative in light of the manifold crises that strike the novel's troubled characters. One is reminded here of Nünning's observation that the mere mention of the term "crisis" (whose etymological origin in medical discourse is apt here) serves to legitimize certain modes of action that might otherwise appear more controversial (251-52).

Here, too, Bateson is of interest, for the way he expresses AA's *raison d'être* strikes a similar chord: "There are no alternatives" (341). This is both a banal cli-

---

83  The importance of this idea can be glimpsed in the fact that as late as 2007, Wallace still believed that "we are in a state of three-alarm emergency – 'we' basically meaning America as a polity and as a culture" ("Deciderization" 313).

84  I refer here to Elaine Blair's description of *Infinite Jest* as "a novel in which every parent betrays his child in one way or another, and every child is estranged from his parents, and there are certainly no mutually devoted spouses or couples in love or loyal friendships" (16).

85  "Perhaps the most profound effect of the medical model of disability lies in the exaggerated value of 'fixing,'" Emily Russell states in a related observation about *Infinite Jest* (154).

ché and an appropriate characterization of the internal logic that drives Wallace's therapeutic ethos. In *Infinite Jest*, there is a compelling reason for addicts to submit to the coercive demands of twelve-step programs. Typographically set apart from the surrounding body of text, it is rendered concisely in what the narrator calls "AA's real prime directive":

> Do not ask WHY
> If you don't want to DIE
> Do like your TOLD
> If you want to get OLD
> (143; sic)

This purposely crude motto reveals one of the novel's central assumptions: addiction is viewed a priori as a *lethal* pathology, which in turn legitimizes the rigors of the "program." Failure to comply with its commands is presented as the route to certain death. This, however, is a hard pill to swallow if we assume that AA is supposed to provide a model for socially and psychologically beneficial epistemological reorientation. Are the problems of postmodernity truly so grave as to warrant an analogy with the death drive of addiction?

Once we ask this question, it becomes apparent that *Infinite Jest*'s reconceptualization of subjectivity is predicated on a number of problematic assumptions. Truly entering into what Zadie Smith calls the "procedure" (276, 279) or the program of the novel means accepting, among other things, the notion that postmodern literature amounts to sterile metafictional play, that popular entertainment is psychologically harmful, that contemporary U.S. culture is inherently pathological and desensitized in a historically unprecedented way, that a whole host of cultural phenomena and behaviors are best understood as addictions, that addiction is per se lethal and tied to self-reflection (rather than, say, the wish to escape the self), and that faith in authorities and institutions might be socially restorative and psychologically liberating.

## Chapter Conclusion: "Configured for a recursive loop"

Intended or not, I would argue that the deeply unsatisfactory assumptions[86] that underlie the novel's canonical interpretations as both diagnosis and cure ultimately refer us back to the text's recursive loops of structure and meaning and to the way they generate contradictions, paradoxes, and, most importantly, ambi-

---

86  I concur on this point with Mark McGurl, who notes that Wallace's critique of American culture, "while advanced with considerable verve, and unusually well attuned to the vicissitudes of iron-

guity. In an ironic reversal, it is the very tenuousness of the ideas Wallace used to frame his work and direct its reception that now account for greater interpretive freedom in our repeated readings of *Infinite Jest*. McGurl is right to remark that "there is much to be gained from our refusal [...] to enter into Wallace's project and finish it on his terms" ("Institution" 49), and I believe we are justified in doing so, since the instability uniting the author's own assumptions and the dominant strain of Wallace scholarship, which operates by adopting these assumptions, also finds expression in the text itself. Taking Wallace's cue, critics have overwhelmingly described the book as a conditioning and training apparatus akin to E.T.A. and Ennet House, an ethical endeavor whose critique of self-involved fiction aspires toward the status of what Kenneth Burke called "equipment for living," that is, a text that issues "implicit commands or instructions of one sort or another" (Burke 304). Yet such readings ignore how the text's circular dynamics perpetuate ambiguity and paradox.

After all, how else are we to make sense of the fundamentally self-divided and self-contradictory dynamic that suffuses the novel?[87] If we think back to the extravagantly long sentence whose meandering construction and contradictory conclusion Wallace uses to convey the paradoxical process of recovery, are we within our rights to attempt to twist this linguistic tapeworm into the straight line of an arrow pointing toward liberation and escape? Reading the sentence this way certainly does not do justice to its intricate twists and turns, the way it fashions what should be a linear progression from the "cage" of addiction toward the freedom of sobriety into a baroque loop of mutually contradictory meanings. The circular dynamics and meanings of *Infinite Jest* imply a radical indecisiveness. And while we can read the novel as attempting to salvage or resuscitate sociality and the self, we can also read it as irrevocably fragmenting these concepts by unmasking their intrinsic paradoxes. In the final analysis, I submit, the novel reveals not so much Wallace's authorial agenda as our own projections and judgments of what we perceive his agenda to be.

By way of conclusion, I would like to expand on this thought and argue that Wallace's (re)conceptualization of subjectivity and the mind-body relation cannot be separated from those dynamics—recursion, infinity, the loop—that also account for the text's ambiguous allure. It is a testament to the novel's successful implementation of its self-referential and self-contradictory program that it creates division not only between readers but also between readings. In my repeated encounters with the book, I certainly have shifted back and forth between inter-

---

ic distance, amounts finally to a highly conventional morality tale about the ill effects of narcissism and TV" ("Institution" 30).

87  "The mind is divided against itself," Blakey Vermeule summarizes the novel's fundamental dynamic; "there's no real way out of the trap of division" (118-19).

pretations. Over the years, I have read *Infinite Jest* either as an attempt to salvage a humanistic conception of selfhood or as a devastating critique of subjective consciousness, alternating between pathology and therapy, but never quite settling on either. Intentional or not, the novel does not provide us with unequivocal instructions on how to read it. Whether we describe it as a program, a world, an experience, an activity, an entertainment, or an addiction, it remains a linguistic machine that produces spirals of meaning that we refuse or agree to enter at will, and whose cycles within cycles are, I contend, modeled upon perhaps the most primordial feedback loop of all: the mind-body system.[88]

For an illustration of this idea, we can turn to the novel's depiction of addiction and recovery. Both are presented as cyclical, recursive processes, or feedback loops, in which every turn of the screw reinforces the dynamic it inscribes. The more severely addicted one is, the harder it becomes to refrain from consumption; the farther removed one is from addiction, the easier it becomes not to relapse. Yet this self-reinforcing loop is, crucially, distributed along the mind-body continuum: addiction is a psychological as much as a physiological habit, and one's internal (emotional, cognitive) experience is dependent upon the actions and material manipulations of the body. This is why both the "conditioning" of athletics and addiction and the "de-programming" of recovery are depicted in *Infinite Jest* as embodied processes whose fundamental workings are inaccessible to consciousness and impervious to its commands.

This "looped" conception of mind and body, in which subjectivity is located on neither side but emerges precisely from their perpetual interaction, is itself a manifestation of the book's titular infinity. We can think of this dynamic as akin to a Möbius strip, the closest visual approximation of the idea of infinity (Figure 1). "The Möbius strip," Elizabeth Grosz explains, "has the advantage of showing that there can be a relation between two 'things'—mind and body—which presumes neither their identity nor their radical disjunction." It is a model that illustrates that "while there are disparate 'things' being related, they have the capacity to twist into one another" (209-210).

---

88  We can think here of Umberto Eco's understanding of the novel as "a machine for generating interpretations" ("Postscript" 2).

*Figure 1: The Möbius strip.*

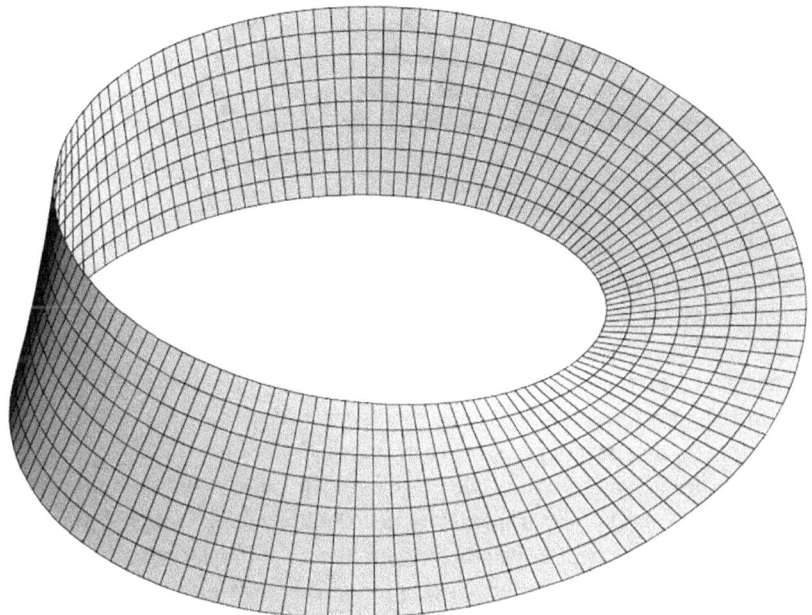

Such a conception of subjectivity may have come naturally to Wallace, who was trained in mathematics and logic and considered Douglas Hofstadter's *Gödel, Escher, Bach: An Eternal Golden Braid* "a great book" that he "actually shoved [...] excitedly at people in the eighties" (Eggers interview, n. pag.). Applied to the novel as a whole, this idea accounts for much of what has been described as characteristic of Wallace's method: the obsessive backtracking, the intractable double binds, the anguished self-consciousness, the compulsive tendency of the narration to bend in on and cycle back through itself. Here we can recall Hayles's description of *Infinite Jest* as consisting of "cycles within cycles within cycles," and complement it with David Hering's observation that Wallace "employs the triangle, the circle and the cycle to describe processes of recollection, narrative construction, addiction and personal choice" (n. pag.). The triangle Hering has in mind is a so-called Sierpinski triangle (Figure 2), which Wallace himself has identified as the structural model for *Infinite Jest* (Silverblatt interview, n. pag).

*Figure 2: The Sierpinski triangle.*

This fractal figure encapsulates Wallace's method of programmatically suffusing his novel with a fixed set of motifs and patterns, which may appear in small, iso-lated episodes as well as in larger themes or structures.[89] By repeating the same construction over and over, the triangle can, in theory, expand indefinitely. Like the Möbius strip, then, the Sierpinski triangle illustrates how reiteration, looping, and recursion can produce self-referential, potentially infinite series. And like the Möbius strip, its fractal shape has been used to illustrate the self-similar structure of the mind-body system, which can be conceptualized as building upon neuronal nets that gain complexity by copying their recursive patterns.

While these figures serve to illustrate both the relation between mind and matter and the novel's formal characteristics, their recursivity also tells us some-thing about the effects of Wallace's constructions. For the notion of infinite cir-cularity is also an apt description of the production of ambiguity and of a reading process that can never be concluded. Overall, *Infinite Jest* favored "clarification of questions > solutions," as Wallace presented the equation in a letter to his edi-tor (qtd. in Max 193). The narration's many lacunae, along with its constitutive method of cycling back on, and calling into question, its own pronouncements, amount to an aesthetics of perpetual ambiguity. *Infinite Jest* not only "eludes total mapping" (Burn, *Guide* 34); it is indeed "configured for a recursive loop" (*IJ* 52) and meant to be read over and again so as to yield, and sustain, multiple, alternative interpretations. Wallace's text, then, does its title justice: upon closer examina-tion, it reveals neither beginning nor end, like the looped relation between mind and matter that it envisages.

---

89    See also Greg Carlisle's description of the production of Sierpinski triangles as "an iterative pro-cess of cutting smaller triangle-shaped holes out of larger triangles" (20).

# 6. Neural Narrative: Richard Powers's *Galatea 2.2* and *The Echo Maker*

> One has to be bilingual, switching from the language of neuroscience to the language of experience; from talk of "brain systems" and "pathology" to talk of "hope," "dread," "pain," "joy," "love," "loss," and all the other animals, fierce and tame, in the zoo of human consciousness.
>
> *Paul Broks, Into the Silent Land*

> We remain strange to ourselves out of necessity, we do not understand ourselves, we must confusedly mistake who we are...
>
> *Friedrich Nietzsche, On the Genealogy of Morality*

## Contemporary Contexts of Consciousness

In a 2001 interview, Richard Powers proposes that it is impossible to "understand a person completely in any sense, unless that sense takes into consideration all of the contexts that that person inhabits." This assumption informs how the author views his artistic medium and method: "If you think of the novel as a supreme connection machine," Powers submits, "then you have to ask how a novelist would dare leave out 95% of the picture" ("Generalist" 104). In what follows, this programmatic statement will serve not as an already accepted aesthetic doctrine but as a reference point, a metaphor we can, and should, interrogate. Why does Powers choose the proliferation of "contexts" as the poetic yardstick against which to measure his work, why does he conceive of the novel as a "supreme connection machine," and, most importantly, what kind of work does this machine actually perform?

To answer these questions, we can begin by examining the "contexts" that Powers considers vital for fiction, and how critics and commentators have described their functions in his writing. Beginning with these contexts rather than the texts themselves is justified because, as we will see, the discursive exchange between artistic production and its critical assessment acquires special significance in Powers's case. More than perhaps any other living American author, Powers attempts to facilitate, maintain, and direct the "follow-up communications" produced by his work, particularly those that take place between the realms of literature, science, and the social.[1]

Lamenting the humanities' "intellectual hyper-specialization" and their lack of an "understanding of life science," Powers proposes that "a literary critic's work would only be enhanced by a more sophisticated sense of, say, evolutionary paleontology, or molecular biology, or cognitive science, or cosmology" ("Generalist" 103-104).[2] The contexts Powers wishes to see included in literary fiction and criticism thus appear to map neatly onto one side of the infamous "two cultures" divide.[3] Powers believes humanists need to acquaint themselves with science because contemporary culture is "shaped by runaway technology, by the apotheosis of business and markets, by sciences that occasionally seem on the verge of completing themselves or collapsing under their own runaway success" ("Generalist" 104).

There is more than a hint of the topical here, with the modifier "runaway" twice intruding into the description to convey a sense of frantic activity. Understandably, some critics suspect "a very smart and very marketable move" in the author's conflation of "avant-garde science" and "everyday social concerns" (Sielke 240). Not coincidentally, scholarly work on Powers has overwhelmingly focused on his ability to master the discourses of contemporary technoscience.[4] Joseph Dewey provides a typical assessment of Powers as an author endowed with an "encyclopedic command of arcane knowledge" and the "metaphors of contemporary sci-

---

1   I borrow this concept (German: *Anschlusskommunikation*) from Niklas Luhmann's systems theory, where it describes the principle or possibility of the reaction to communications by further communications; textual production in general is viewed here as responding to the need for continued communicative acts in formations of knowledge production (Luhmann, *Aufsätze* 116).

2   It is curious that Powers voices this concern at a time when the neo-naturalist turn in the humanities was already underway and cognitive science was beginning to be more frequently invoked in literary study. For classic contributions already available at the time Powers gave the interview, see Fludernik, Spolsky, and Turner, *Literary* and *Reading*.

3   The term was coined by C. P. Snow in his 1959 Rede Lecture, which was later published in book form (see Snow, *Cultures*), and, after much public debate and a controversial reply from F. R. Leavis, followed by the publication of a "Second Look" at the trope (see Snow, "Cultures"). For contemporary assessments of the debate, see Kimball as well as chapter 3 of Kucharzewski.

4   See, for instance, LeClair, "Prodigious," Neilson, and Dewey, *Understanding*. The compound word "technoscience" refers to the relationality of technology and science as well as their social embeddedness. The term is also used to refer to a development in the philosophy and sociology of science: the "science studies" approach pioneered by Donna Haraway and Bruno Latour. For collections of work in this tradition, see Aronowitz as well as Ihde and Selinger.

ence" (*Understanding* 3), while Jim Neilson praises him for his "extraordinary abil-ity to acquire and convey expert knowledge in diverse fields" (8).

Powers's attempts to merge scientific knowledge and aesthetic procedures have attracted the attention of thinkers like Bruno Latour and Daniel Dennett. Dennett has contributed a highly complimentary "Letter to Richard Powers" to a recent scholarly collection of critical essays on Powers's work, in which he approv-ingly notes that the author has "managed to find brilliant ways of conveying hard-to-comprehend details of the field [of artificial intelligence], details people in the field were themselves having trouble getting clear about" ("Astride" 152). In the same volume, Latour praises Powers as an author of *"scientifiction"*[5] ("Powers" 273, original emphasis) and effectively claims him as a colleague when he dubs him "the novelist of 'science studies,' the field to which I belong" ("Powers" 264).

This recognition has not remained unreciprocated: Powers has published and given talks together with Latour,[6] and identified Dennett's "multiple drafts model" as a source for his novel *The Echo Maker* (Burn interview 174). Here we see the dynamic of follow-up communication in full effect: Powers writes books that "are not merely *about* scientific ideas but that [...] *are* science as much as fiction" (Kucharzewski 272; original emphases), and thus provide points of intersection[7] with other commentators, who then refer back to Powers, reinforcing his autho-rial image as a synthesizer of the first order. This makes for a situation in which there is curiously little disagreement over Powers's project: it has become hard to tell whether Powers echoes the scholars who study his work or vice versa. Ste-phen Burn describes Powers as an heir to American postmodernists, a writer who examines "the individual's life amid the dense-informational texture that char-acterizes modern existence" (Introduction xxviii), but Powers has already antici-pated this assessment by stating that his books "work by saying you cannot under-stand a person minimally, you cannot understand a person simply as a function of his inability to get along with his wife, you cannot even understand a person through his supposedly causal psychological profile" ("Generalist" 104).[8]

---

5  Before conferring the label on Powers's writing, Latour used the term "scientifiction" to describe the writing style he employed in his book *Aramis, or the Love of Technology*, a text belonging to a "hy-brid genre [...] devised for a hybrid task" (i.e., doing justice to "scientific worlds" as *possible* worlds) that blurs the line between fact and fiction (*Aramis* xiii-ix).

6  See Latour and Powers.

7  Fittingly, a recent volume of critical essays on Powers is titled *Intersections* (Burn and Dempsey).

8  Further illustrating the accord between the author and his exegetes, this statement then makes its way into Dewey's monograph on Powers in slightly paraphrased form: "The individual cannot be understood [...] solely as a function of domestic relationships or employment or by geography or culture. Rather, the individual must be measured by the widest range of contexts—historical, political, technological, aesthetic, sociological, economic, relational, even genetic and molecu-lar" (*Understanding* 13).

Together with his insistence on widening the scope of "contexts," Powers's mention of "supposedly causal" psychological dynamics hints at a revised view of human psychology and, one is tempted to say, ontology: as Joseph Tabbi writes, "'the human measure' is itself changing—or being newly discovered—at basic perceptual and subperceptual levels" (*Cognitive* x). In this emerging view, which Powers seems to share, we are not only social and psychological "characters" but also, importantly, biological organisms whose sense of self is based on the brain, floridly described by Powers as the "bewilderingly complex fiber in its impossible live weave" (*GA* 40).[9] Powers considers this promising terrain for humanists: "Why wouldn't a literary scholar want to know everything that neurologists are discovering about the way the brain works?" ("Generalist" 103). His conviction that the biological needs to complement the psychological aligns the author with recent advocates of cognitive literary studies, who base their research agendas on cognitive science and the neurosciences—fields that, as Alan Richardson notes, "have largely abandoned the Saussurean and Freudian approaches to language and mind that still set the terms for most literary theory" (39).

Along with these approaches, they have also largely abandoned the "humanist or Enlightenment idea of man on which the presentation of character in the novel is based" (Lodge 2), so that we should not be surprised that conceiving of "*mind as machine*"—the major conceptual move of cognitive science according to Margaret Boden's history of the field—also entails aesthetic transformations (9; original emphasis). In his caustic reduction of dynamic or depth psychology, the dominant model of novelistic character in the twentieth century, to a "supposedly causal" ascription best used to register banal bourgeois disequilibrium ("his inability to get along with his wife"), and in his preference for cognitive science as a more "scientific" model of mind, Powers can also be associated with the shift from the psychological novel to the "neuronovel" that Marco Roth has recently delineated.[10]

Characterized by Roth as a move "away from environmental and relational theories of personality back to the study of brains themselves, as the source of who we are" (n. pag.), this shift is what brings Powers's work within the purview of the present study, for in two of his most acclaimed novels, *Galatea 2.2* and *The Echo Maker*,[11] the "contexts" with which Powers seeks to complement character psychology are precisely those "sciences of mind" that seek to account for human cognition and experience in materialist terms. In this respect, Powers, like DeLillo and Wallace before him, positions himself as an author ineluctably, and ostentatiously,

---

9  Here and subsequently, *Galatea 2.2* is abbreviated as *GA* in parenthetical citations.

10  The neuronovel is characterized by Marco Roth as the kind of novel "wherein the mind becomes the brain" (n. pag.).

11  *Galatea 2.2* was a finalist for the 1995 National Book Critics Circle Award, while *The Echo Maker* was a Pulitzer Prize finalist and won the 2006 National Book Award.

shaped by his cultural moment. As John Johnston points out, "the 1990s saw an energetic resurgence of interest in the study of consciousness, both among philosophers and scientists working in the fields of cognitive science, neuroscience and AI" (326) and Powers, whom Tabbi calls "our time's most systematic literary researcher of cognition," can be considered the American author most overtly occupied with these themes (*Cognitive* 59).

*Galatea 2.2*, published in 1995, and *The Echo Maker*, from 2006, are concerned with consciousness as a process that is based on material substrates and amenable to scientific study, though their respective disciplinary and metaphorical approaches to this topic differ, dependent as they are on the then-prevalent theoretical model.[12] Thus, while Powers draws on cognitive science and artificial intelligence in *Galatea 2.2*, the book already announces an interest in the topics of neuroscience and evolutionary biology, which would only become "available" to the author later, upon the composition of *The Echo Maker*.[13] Tabbi has pointed out that "emerging sciences of the mind have produced detailed descriptions of [...] agents, modules, and distributed neural networks *in us*," and with *Galatea 2.2*, Powers begins an investigation into the poetic affordances of these new descriptions (*Cognitive* x; original emphasis). "We seemed to be on the verge of a new evolution in consciousness," *Galatea 2.2*'s narrator-protagonist muses (242), and he already suspects, in this earlier text, that the function of consciousness "must be in part to dummy up and shape a coherence from all the competing, conflicting subsystems that processed experience"—a theme that will find its definitive treatment in the later novel (217-18).

While investigating Powers's use of the scientific discourses surrounding the physical correlates of consciousness, I will pay close attention to the interrelation of the formal and thematic aspects of his novels, which, as we will see, are closely connected to this topic. This interrelation is widely understood as central to the author's method: Stephen Burn has described Powers's books as "arranged to stress homologies between form and content" (Powers, Burn interview 164), Jan Kucharzewski sees him "deal with science both on the level of form and on the level of content" (25), and Powers himself has stated that "complete commensurability between form and content at the level of the individual sentence is really what writing is all about" (Berger interview, n. pag.). Assuming such an interrela-

---

12 Tabbi notes that "[e]very Powers novel has its concept, and its technology: photography in *Three Farmers*; mathematics in *Prisoner's Dilemma*; genetics in *Gold Bug*; medicine in *Operation Wandering Soul*; and so forth" ("Afterthoughts" 224).

13 See Powers's comment on the genesis of *The Echo Maker*: "The field of neuroscience has made such incredible strides since I began writing that *it finally seemed possible* to try to weave a dialogical novel around the very specific new views of the brain that have emerged from laboratories over the last couple of decades—the distributed, modular, massively preconscious, multiply recursive, narrative-dependent model of the bundled 'I'" (Burn interview 175; my emphasis).

tion between form and content, we can then not only ask how harmonious these homologies really are, but also inquire after the aesthetic transformations that a thematic concern with the materiality of mind might entail.

If cognitive science and neuroscience inform a novel's themes and plot, what consequences does this have for its characters and narrators, and perhaps for the dynamics of narrative itself? As Bruno Latour has pointed out, Powers's texts investigate and perform "the problem of the progressive emergence of individuals," a term we can understand as applying to living persons and literary characters alike. "Powers asks what it is for a character to exist at all, when so much of existence depends upon the things one is attached to—the most important connection being to the biological basis of life itself," Latour writes ("Powers" 265). This prompts the question, what is a literary character—indeed, what is a literary text—when conceived of as an entity to be understood "from the ground up," as it were: constructed on "the biological basis of life itself"? Does such a method further dispel the "old myths of depth" which Alain Robbe-Grillet describes historically as the psychological basis of literature (23)?

In this area of inquiry, *Galatea 2.2* and *The Echo Maker* are ideal objects of study: taken together, these novels, and their "brain plots" (Stedman)[14] represent perhaps the most sustained engagement with the materiality of mind in contemporary U.S. literature.[15] Like his contemporary David Foster Wallace, whose magnum opus *Infinite Jest* would be published within a year of Powers's career-summarizing autobiographical fiction *Galatea 2.2*, Powers produces narratives in which habitual modes of thinking about subjectivity are challenged by attempts to no longer understand mind as fundamentally dissimilar from matter and to develop a "materialist model of consciousness" (Bould and Vint 89). Yet despite their similar backgrounds and concerns, Wallace and Powers are vastly different authors.[16]

---

14  In her useful overview of the relation between neuroscience and the contemporary novel, Gesa Stedman defines "brain plots" as "revolving around mental illness, the workings of the mind and how experts and victims deal with these issues" (113).

15  See, for instance, Stephen Burn's assertion that amongst the postmodernists, "Powers has most successfully mined the interface between neuroscience and fiction" (*Franzen* 26).

16  Since the beginning of their careers, Powers's and Wallace's names have been mentioned in the same breath, often in an attempt to position them as contemporary heirs to the "encyclopedic novel" or the "systems novel" of the postmodern era; Ickstadt regards Pynchon, Gaddis, McElroy, and DeLillo as Powers's "ancestral line" (23). For an early comparison of Powers and Wallace, see LeClair, "Prodigious"; for a recent study that compares Powers and Wallace with Jonathan Franzen, see Burn, *Franzen*. For the encyclopedic novel, see the original conception of "encyclopedic narrative" in Mendelson, "Encyclopedia" and "Encyclopedic" as well as later adaptations of the concept in Clark, Moretti, and Ercolino. For Powers as an author of "encyclopedic fictions," see Strecker. For the systems novel, see LeClair, *Art* and *Loop* as well as Powers, "Rounds," for the author's own sense of belonging to this tradition.

Whereas Wallace unfolds a veritable panorama of pathology against the backdrop of the sinister "conditioning" effects produced by addiction and athletic training, Powers draws directly on the scientific discourses that describe mind as brain in order to fashion "neuronarratives"[17] with a distinctly optimistic bent: as Dewey observes, "pessimism is never the last word in Powers's fiction" (*Understanding* 108). It is telling, and typical, that Powers appropriates the term "hopeful monster," originally coined by Tom LeClair to describe Wallace's *Infinite Jest*, to refer to his own work (*GA* 256). In order for his work to register as ethically responsible and morally uplifting,[18] Powers instrumentalizes scholarly discourse to engineer what I call the "apotheosis of narrative": a representation of literature as universally important and, what is more, *necessary*. Through his novels and their discursive framing, the author engages in acts of revaluation that seek to afford a privileged position to literary language and humanistic explanatory models at a historical moment when they appear at risk of being supplanted by science and technology.

To understand this process, I will frame my analysis—here in the introduction and later in the conclusion—by reference to Jane Tompkins and Pierre Bourdieu. The concept of "cultural work" is useful for my purposes since, like Tompkins, I am interested in literary texts not as productions that "escape the limitations of their particular time and place," but as artifacts that provide "powerful examples of the way a culture thinks about itself, articulating and proposing solutions for the problems that shape a particular historical moment" (Tompkins xi). However, I would hesitate to subscribe to the notion that texts produced around the turn of the millennium can still be said to reflect their national or economic culture as a whole, both because the idea of literature as reflection or representation is intrinsically problematic and because contemporary market dynamics work in favor of niche specialization and media proliferation, so that literature can no longer be regarded as the royal road to a nation's psyche—a situation that presents itself as markedly different in the case of Tompkins's archive, which covers a much earlier period.

For this reason I have decided to complement Tompkins's concept of cultural work with Bourdieu's field theory, which holds that the work that is performed by a (cultural, social) agent in a given field is not merely reflective of its larger environment but also directed at dynamics of power and prestige *within* the confines

---

17  For an analysis of *Galatea 2.2* and *The Echo Maker* as "neuronarratives," i.e., as "works of fiction that incorporate advances in cognitive studies as a prominent theme, that compel novelists to struggle with consciousness as 'content' and to reassess the value of narrative fiction," see G. Johnson.

18  See Berger, who sees Powers as providing "the basis for an ethics that arises from but goes beyond the study of literature" (114).

of its specific distribution of internal rules.[19] It is particularly Bourdieu's notion of the *intellectual field* as a "matrix of institutions and markets in which artists, writers, researchers and academics compete over valued resources to obtain legitimate recognition for their artistic, literary, academic or scientific work" (Swartz 226) that will be of interest here, as I argue that through their investment in "materialist minds," Powers's novels aim to ensure a position of cultural prestige for literary fiction.[20]

Balancing out the notion of "cultural work" with what, in a pun on Bourdieu, we might call "fieldwork," effectively sidesteps both the danger of treating the texts under consideration as unproblematic reflections of extraliterary reality, possessing the primacy of cultural interpretation and cultural capital,[21] and that of treating literature itself as a totally self-contained semantic system.[22] Instead, literary texts become "nodes within a network" of discourses (Tompkins xvi), nodes whose specific functions and dynamics can only be explained with reference to the dynamics of power and recognition that affect their producers, which can in turn be studied and analyzed. While Powers would certainly be all in favor of the first part of this description (literature as part of a larger system of world-descriptions) he might be comparably less keen on its caveat (literature as a strategic play in a contest for recognition), which places him under the kind of critical scrutiny that does not exhaust itself in the act of retracing an "essay-interview nexus" the author can, to an extent, control and manipulate in his own favor.[23] In other words, what I hope to achieve in this chapter is a balanced description of the textual dynamics of Powers's novels, their placement within economic and intellectual fields, and the interrelations between these aspects. In this way, I hope to draw attention to the texts not only as self-contained mimetic systems but also as

---

19  On the concept of the field, see Bourdieu and Wacquant. For his accounts of the artistic and cultural fields, see Bourdieu, "Field of Cultural Production," "Historical Genesis," and "Literary Field."

20  A cogent account of the notion of the intellectual field can be found in an interview Bourdieu gave to the *Norddeutscher Rundfunk*: see Bourdieu, "Intellectual Field."

21  Such primacy is still afforded to literary texts by Tompkins, whom Dorothy Hale describes as, *pace* Foucault, "reprivileging to the novel as an object of cultural study [...] in order to accomplish her goal of political legibility" (445).

22  On this point, see Bourdieu, "Field of Cultural Production," where he submits that by "defining the literary and artistic field as, inseparably, a field of positions and a field of position-takings we also escape from the usual dilemma of internal ('tautegorical') reading of the work (taken in isolation or within the system of works to which it belongs) and external (or 'allegorical') analysis, i.e., analysis of the social conditions of production of the producers and consumers which is based on the–generally tacit–hypothesis of the spontaneous correspondence or deliberate matching of production to demand or commissions" (34).

23  I discuss Adam Kelly's concept of the "essay-interview nexus" in the context of my analysis of *Infinite Jest* in the previous chapter.

networked cultural artifacts that form part of an American culture understood as "something that keeps *happening*—something that keeps ensuring the continuation of its own existence, enlisting for this purpose different players and products, ambitions and commitments, affiliations and identifications," as Frank Kelleter has recently described it (*Serial* 4; original emphasis).

## "An owner's manual for the brain": Galatea 2.2

*Galatea* 2.2 tells the ostensibly "posthumanist" story of a character named Richard Powers, who teaches the interpretation of literary texts to an artificial intelligence (AI), which may or may not acquire consciousness in the process. Narrated in the first person by Richard,[24] the text has pronounced autobiographical components, discussing, among other things, the genesis of Powers's previous books, but remaining, as the book cover assures us, "a novel." As its title suggests, *Galatea* 2.2 brings together two kinds of language: literature and computer code. While the title's first part calls to mind Ovid and the Pygmalion myth,[25] its numerical addendum invokes the convention of using rational numbers to identify successive versions of software. This juxtaposition introduces a number of interconnected problems that embodied subjectivity runs into in *Galatea* 2.2 and *The Echo Maker*, such as invention, poïesis, doubling, authenticity, and the relation between fiction and reality, or world and self.

Some have argued that Powers's main interest in *Galatea* 2.2 lies in the posthumanist problem of "disembodied" artificial intelligence (Adams 148), but to do so is to insist too much on the text's literal dimension and to neglect both that the AI "represents more than disembodiment" (Wald, n. pag.) and that the book is presented to us as the work of Richard, a quintessential "man of metaphor" (Saltzman, *Mad* 106). As befits a novel chronicling the construction of consciousness out of literature, almost every aspect of *Galatea* 2.2, from its characters' names and dialogues to its setting and situations, is "freighted with allegorical dimensions" (Dewey, *Understanding* 101).

For one thing, the text allegorizes anxiety over the "two cultures" of knowledge production: upon the novel's publication, Sharon Snyder described Richard as "the latest in a series of emissary figures [...] who brave the crossing of C. P. Snow's 'two cultures divide' between the humanities and the hard sciences" (88).

---

24 From here on, I will distinguish between author and narrator/protagonist, by referring to the former as "Powers" and the latter as "Richard."

25 With its academic setting, interest in language and focus on the asymmetrical power relations between the sexes, Powers's novel also alludes to George Bernard Shaw's reworking of the Pygmalion story.

This bridging, however, is notably asymmetrical: Richard is recruited by his alma mater for a one-year stay at the imposingly scientific-sounding "Center for the Study of Advanced Sciences," where he assumes the function of "token humanist" (4). The Center serves as a spatial metaphor for the prestige and sophistication of modern science, dwarfing Richard's writerly identity. It is huge, a "block-long building" whose "chief virtue" is "sheer size," and it houses research areas "so esoteric" that Richard is unable to "tell their nature from their names. Half the fields were hyphenated" (5).[26] His erstwhile workplace at the university compares unfavorably with the overfunded glamour of the research complex: "The Center possessed 1,200 works of art, the world's largest magnetic resonance imager, and elevators appointed in brass, teak, and marble. The English Building's stairs were patched in three shades of gray linoleum" (75). The absurdity of this juxtaposition leaves little doubt that we have entered the realm of the allegorical, with the novel setting out to satirize the widening gap between the humanities and the sciences in terms of cultural and academic prestige.

More to the point, the novel's setting also evokes its governing metaphor: with its inhabitants "busily skimming its interior like electrical firings," the center functions as a "magnified analog for the neurochemistry of the brain," as Arthur Saltzman points out (Mad 98).[27] If this sounds familiar, it is because we have encountered this conceit before, in DeLillo's Ratner's Star. That novel's FENO complex seems to serve as the model for Powers's Center, with its parallelization of built and brain architecture and its assembly of zany "theorists, experimentalists, technicians, magicians," who have "a probe attached to every conceivable flicker" (GA 6). This description doubles as an accurate characterization of Powers's intensely allusive novel, whose zeal for thematic complexity can cause confusion.[28] Powers mixes autobiography, bildungsroman, and metafiction to tackle a host of themes, from consciousness and mental disability to romantic relationships and the existence of evil. As a consequence, it is not only at the end, when twists and epiphanies pile up with increasing frequency, that the author's method appears somewhat "congested and over-excited" (Lodge 27).

Assuming a more benevolent stance, one can also read the text's multifunctional overload as an allegorical performance meant to resemble the operations of the human brain, which, after all, "does things in massive parallel" (GA 67). This

---

26  Richard's helplessness in the face of hyphenated disciplines here echoes DeLillo's campus satire in White Noise, whose Winnie Richards states, "I do neurochemistry. No one knows what that is" (188).

27  To reinforce this notion, the narrator describes the researchers "firing messages back and forth to intercontinental colleagues" (15).

28  Late in the book, Richard imagines a story "that could grow to any size, could train itself to include anything we might think worth thinking," an obvious, if somewhat grandiose, self-referential description of Powers's project in Galatea 2.2 (315).

is the foundational idea of connectionism, an approach to modeling the human brain that gained popularity in the 1980s and '90s. Yet its origins reach back even further, to the post-WWII discoveries that almost any conceivable message can be translated into binary code and that synapses, either firing or not firing, operate just like a binary code. Together these ideas made it possible to think of the human brain as analogous to an information processor.[29] Complemented by Hebbian theory, often paraphrased as the "law" (*GA* 75) that dictates that "cells that fire together, wire together," these assumptions led to the development of connectionist theory, which assumes that complex systems can "emerge" from interconnected networks of simple units.[30]

In this framework, learning and memory were thought to "depend largely on a change in weights at individual synapses, which altered the probability that activity at that synapse would contribute to firing its postsynaptic neuron" (Smythies 1). Or, as Richard explains the process of "simulated thought":

> Neural networks no longer wrote out procedures or specified machine behaviors. [...] Rather, they used a mass of separate processors to simulate connected brain cells. They taught communities of these independent, decision-making units how to modify their own connections. Then they stepped back and watched their synthetic neurons sort and associate external stimuli. [...] Nowhere did the programmer determine the outcome. She wrote no algorithm. The decisions of these simulated cells arose from their own internal and continuously changing states. [...] By strengthening or weakening its own synapses, the tangle of junctions could remember. (14-15)

Neural nets thus implement the mechanics of synaptic weights along with the massive parallel-distributed processing (PDP) capabilities of the human brain (Wilson, *Neural* 5). Even though connectionism necessarily "simplifies neurobiology" (Hogan 33), artificial neural networks were seen as a promising new approach to simulating the brain-based processes of learning, possibly of thought itself. This (admittedly simplified) picture has seem significant modifications since at least the 2000s,[31] but it is still a passable description of the state of the "field-imag-

---

29 See Hayles, *Posthuman* 57-59, on the role of the "McCulloch-Pitts neuron" in this conceptualization.

30 For Hebbian theory, see Hebb; for connectionism, see Rumelhart and McClelland, whose 1986 book *Parallel Distributed Processing: Explorations in the Microstructure of Cognition* Richard alludes to in the novel as "the famous two-volume study nets. The connectionist bible" (74).

31 Smythies goes so far as to call the "classic picture" of synaptic clefts as semipermanent structures that effect learning (solely) through differential weights has been proven "wildly inaccurate" by recent research, which has revealed, among other things, the importance of neuronal pruning, i.e., the removal of synapses and new synaptic growth (2-3).

inary" of cognitive science at the time Powers wrote *Galatea 2.2.*[32] Powers appears upfront about this discursive source; his first-person narrator suggests that the novel only became possible once the scientific ideas it builds on became "available." Richard relates that he had given up "thinking about thought" because the debates about the material basis of the mind appeared "deadlocked," until new developments in the sciences of mind, such as brain imaging and neural networks, changed his perspective: "overnight, [...] everything changed. The impasse broke" (28).

Because of its interest in materialist approaches to the study of the mind, the novel has been described as engaging with "eliminative materialism"—the notion that cognition and subjectivity can be understood as (or reduced to) the activity of neurons (Chodat 6). However, Powers's use of brain science is more complicated than that: the brain, Richard muses, "emerged to exceed the chemical sum passing though its neuronal vesicle." In accordance with the tenets of connectionism, he describes it as "a model-maker, continuously rewritten by the thing it tried to model." His subsequent flash of inspiration, "Why not model *this*, and see what insights one might hook in to," is already an apt description of the book itself, summarizing as it does the operative idea informing its method of grounding recursion, self-referentiality, and metaphoricity in neuroscientific discourse (29; original emphasis).

A chance encounter with Philip Lentz, a researcher in neural networks, provides Richard with the occasion to operationalize the computational modeling of mind as a metaphor. Lentz's work fascinates him: "Repeated inputs and parental feedback created an association and burned it in. Reading that fact tripped an association in *me*" (15-16; original emphasis). In keeping with the "parental" dynamic of learning via "feedback," memory and pedagogy figure as important motifs throughout the text.[33] Richard comes into his new role as private tutor to an AI when he is embroiled in an argument between Lentz and his colleagues at a bar. After adding to the book's preoccupation with the "two cultures" split by asking him what "passes for knowledge" in his "so-called discipline," Lentz wagers that with Richard as his "research assistant," he will be able to fashion a neural net capable of passing an English exam; it would have to produce a textual interpretation that proves indistinguishable from one written by a human author (43-46). We later learn that the wager is a ploy, an elaborate practical joke to test "the credu-

---

32   I borrow the concept of the "field-imaginary" from Donald Pease, who defines it as a "location for disciplinary consciousness" and "the field's fundamental syntax—its tacit assumptions, convictions, primal words, and the charged relations binding them together" (11).

33   Most importantly, the novel links learning and the brain through metaphor, as when Richard imagines Hebbian Law "as a teacher prowling her class, slapping the wrists of bad students and rewarding the good until they all stood up and pledged coordinated allegiance" (75).

lity of a techno-illiterate humanist" rather than the machine's capability (*GA* 314), but it is clear from the beginning that Richard needs little in the way of encouragement to believe in the possibility of textual-machinic consciousness. When Richard reads about a precursor experiment, in which a neural net had learned to read aloud, he is captivated: "The story grabbed me. I wanted the *image*, the idea of that experiment," a statement that, in keeping with the novel's self-referential aesthetic, simultaneously describes a state of affairs within its diegetic world and the kernel of its own construction (31; original emphasis).

Success or failure of the experiment is to be determined in a manner typical of the AI field: "Standard Turing Test. Double-blind. Black-box both respondents" (46-47). This inclusion of the classic mechanism for distinguishing human intelligence from machinic simulation has caused many critics to read *Galatea 2.2* as informed by posthumanist thought.[34] If, following Neil Badmington, we regard Descartes as "one of the principal architects of humanism" ("Approaching" 3), it is not hard to see why the posthuman has long been an important reference point in scholarly accounts of Powers's work. In the *Discourse*, Descartes distinguishes human beings, who possess reason, from animals and automata, which do not (31-32). For Descartes, the "universal instrument" of reason outclasses the purely mechanistic, soulless behavior ascribed to animals, and provides the basis for human freedom and expression (*Discourse* 32).

By this logic, any non-human being that could reason would explode Cartesian humanism and establish a properly posthuman situation, as would an unmasking of human beings as "complex biological machines" (Broks 188). And in fact, Descartes's assertion that a machine could be mistaken for an animal but never for a person since it "could not arrange its words differently so as to respond to the sense of all that will be said in its presence, as even the dullest men can do" (*Discourse* 32) can be seen as effectively prefiguring the Turing Test, the procedure proposed by Alan Turing to "crystallize the questions surrounding the possibility of an intelligent artifact" (Shieber 1).[35] Viewed by some as the ultimate instantiation of the posthuman, machine intelligence is one way of destabilizing the "ontolog-

---

34  See Campbell, who understands the identification of mind with brain as a quintessentially posthuman move; Fitzpatrick, who reads the novel as containing posthumanist ideas so that the "primacy of the humanist project" is "safely restored" ("Exhaustion" 554); Silva, who similarly sees Powers as attempting to recuperate humanism in an ostensibly posthumanist setting; Miller, who thinks the novel "represents less the triumph of humanity over its machines than the new growth made possible by the very examination of this opposition" (399); and Hayles, who dedicates a chapter in her 1999 landmark study *How We Became Posthuman* to Powers's novel.

35  An even more approximate anticipation of the Turing Test can be found in what philosopher Jack Copeland calls "de Cordemoy's Principle," named after a 17th-century Cartesian: "If all the experiments that we are capable of making show that *x* uses speech as we do, then *x* has a soul (i.e., thinks)" (Copeland 528).

ical hygiene" that ostensibly separates humans from animals and machines and, through definition by negation, determines the human subject (Graham 11-13).[36]

A problem of authenticity ensues: who is the "real" human? Turing himself, in his original 1950 article, called the test an "imitation game," a phrase that evokes a crucial characteristic of its setup (433). As Stuart Shieber reminds us, the Turing Test is supposed to determine whether a given artifact is "indistinguishable from a person with regard to what [Turing] took to be the pertinent property, *verbal behavior*" (1; original emphasis). Strictly speaking, then, the test does not detect intelligence or sentience but rather rewards a successful act of rhetorical impersonation. In other words, the test safeguards the "ontological hygiene" that separates man and machine while simultaneously destabilizing it, and it does so via a process that, in itself, provides proof of indistinguishability rather than authenticity, the key quality "central to modern concepts of individualism, autonomy, and uniqueness" (Haselstein et al. 10).

In *Galatea 2.2*, this pattern provides the template for a number of scenes of de-authentication, in which the lines between the real and the simulated, or the fictional, begin to blur, scenes that the book presents as resulting from exposure to "materialist minds." "I had learned too much neuroscience," Richard realizes at one point: "The more I read about how the mind worked, the flakier mine became" (194). Since neuroscience teaches that the world is only ever present to us as representations in the brain, as neural "maps" of sensory input and cognitive feedback, subjectivity itself starts to splinter. Thus, when Richard describes the final days of his favorite professor, who is mortally ill, the vicissitudes of personality are conveyed through a neural metaphor. Drawing on neuroscience's view of the self as produced by "topographically organized sensory maps" (Damasio, *Descartes* 239), Richard writes: "Near the end, the medications did change him. But even then, his topographies fought to keep themselves intact" (203).

A related phenomenon is memory, the "strengthening or weakening" of synapses by which a "tangle of junctions could remember," which, as Richard learns, is at base a physical, biochemical process: "memories are laid down when the thumb-sized basal forebrain bathes the hippocampus in acetylcholine" (GA 70). Since memory is assumed to have both a material, i.e., neural, basis and the ontological status of a mediated representation, it becomes a process whose physicality connects human and machine, while its illusory effects link life and fiction.[37] Thus the story of the verbal training and literary education of the neural net's succes

---

36  On the question of humanist "ontological hygiene," see also Bourke and Sheehan/Sosna.

37  Ian Hacking identifies two new "sciences of memory," cellular-level neurology and artificial intelligence research, both of which preoccupy Powers (*Rewriting* 199); Sidonie Smith has pointed out how these new fields reinforce a view of the self as "materially activated and materially enacted" (91).

sive "implementations," alphabetically named from A to H, is juxtaposed with the narrator's memories of his failed relationship with his ex-girlfriend, whom Richard, in another of the text's doublings, only refers to as "C."[38] Both are Richard's "inventions," it is implied, constructed simultaneously by his memory and the text we are reading.[39] This sense of authorial projection is brought to the fore when Richard names "Imp H" Helen, anthropomorphizing his invention even more (179).

But these alphabetical and neuronal constructs also experience their own ontological uncertainties. When Richard recounts C.'s desire to travel to the Netherlands, the homeland of her parents, the contrast between the "phantom of childhood" and the "real village" produces a "lifelong gap that held her at arm's length from her own interior" (157). This condition of alienation applies to the neural net even more drastically, since it lacks sense organs and has to rely exclusively on the linguistic symbols it encounters in the books Richard reads to it, which are "simulations" themselves.[40]

As a result, "Helen" remains stuck on the level of the signifier: "The symbols these shameless simulations played on had no heft or weight for her, no real-world referent," Richard concludes (190). In an ironic reversal, it is the material machine, fashioned fully from electrodes and silica, that lacks any sense of connection to the physical world, a deficit that distinguishes her from the biological organism that is the human individual:

> Helen had to use language to create concepts. Words came first: the main barrier to her education. The brain did things the other way around. The brain juggled thought's lexicons through multiple subsystems, and the latecomers, the most dispensable lobes, were the ones where names per se hung out. In evolution's beginning was not the word but the place we learned to pin the word to. Little babies registered and informed long before they invented more mama by calling her such. (248)

Here Richard adopts a view of psychic life informed by neurobiology and evolutionary psychology, in which the materiality of embodied experience precedes the

---

38  The novel also presents machinic memory as analogous to cultural memory and the process of literary tradition: "Each machine lived inside the others—nested generations of 'remember this.' [...] E's weights and contours lived inside F's lived inside G's, the way Homer lives on in Swift and Joyce, or Job in Candide or the Invisible Man" (171).

39  This interplay between the narrative "present" and past functions as this book's "contrapuntal narration," which Dewey describes as Powers's characteristic method: "Two (and sometimes three) narrative braids are offered polyphonically, told side by side," so that they "complement and deepen each other" (*Understanding* 11).

40  Helen's name obviously also alludes to Helen Keller's related story of the coinciding development of language and subjectivity. See Berger as well as Chodat, "Naturalism" 694.

formation of cultural concepts and a linguistic imaginary phylogenetically as well as ontogenetically. For this reason, Wes Chapman regards Powers as implicitly siding with the critique of the "Standard Social Science Model" (SSSM) put forward by John Tooby and Leda Cosmides, which in the view of the authors "denies that human nature—the evolved architecture of the human mind—can play any notable role as a generator of significant organization in human life" (qtd. in Chapman 245 n7).[41]

Even though he has in fact voiced such concerns in interviews,[42] in *Galatea 2.2* Powers does not so much contrast the social with the natural as merge the two spheres into one complex and contradictory "world" that functions as the novel's ultimate horizon of meaning. Richard is convinced that knowledge is sensory as well as social: "Knowing entails testing knowledge against others. Bumping up against them. [...] We take in the world continuously. It presses against us. It burns and freezes" (*GA* 147-48). Helen's lack of contact and conflict with the physical-social world therefore crucially impoverishes her understanding. As a species of one, a *sui generis* entity, she lacks both embodiment and an evolutionary history, the mechanism by which biological needs are developed and answered; consequently, the matrix of feeling and interest that arguably provides the basis for any sense of self fails to take shape.[43]

"We know the world by awling it into our shape-changing cells," Richard muses (302). Along with memory, *experience* thus becomes the text's key criterion for authentic subjectivity, but Powers makes clear that this notion will have to include a phylogenetic dimension, the "experience" of the species. In a statement that illustrates the seamless continuity of the author's novels and his own paratextual commentary, he explains that "the actively narrating conscious brain is

---

41  Together with Barkow, Cosmides and Tooby have published *The Adapted Mind*, one of evolutionary psychology's foundational texts, which the editors characterize as providing "the necessary connection between evolutionary biology and [...] social and cultural phenomena" (6). *The Adapted Mind* has consequently become an important source for neo-naturalist attempts to describe the mind as "an empirical entity, a substance with tangible form and describable content" (Kelleter, "Tale" 173).

42  "The standard social science model of everything being culturally constructed in some ways has it backwards," Powers states elsewhere. "Something must, in fact, construct culture, and something other than 'culture' does give language its shape, even before language shapes our sense of self. Part of me wants to say that that something is a couple of billion years of evolution. Yet that view has been so simplified and so abused in the past that the humanists are rightfully on their guard about it. Still, there's no denying that we all have bodies and that there are more similarities between our anatomies and their attendant bodily states than there are differences" ("Generalist" 102-103).

43  The question of *interest* is central to conceptions of the human, which need to account for "the fact that we are beings to whom things matter" (Taylor, *Human* 2). See also chapter 7 in Kucharzewski.

not arbitrary; it is itself the evolutionary product of several billion years of bumping up against the world" (Neilson interview 16). We also find this notion in the
novel, whose digital Galatea "had trouble with values, because she had no fear of
self-preservation, no hierarchy of hard-wired pain," as the narrator informs us
(250). This "erasure of embodiment" underlies Hayles's discussion of the novel's
posthuman credentials, as it nicely illustrates her thesis that posthumanism is not
a far-off potential outcome of some speculative scenario but rather "already with
us" when we conceive of information as disembodied, and cognition as constructible (*Posthuman* xi).[44]

But Helen is not only a figure of the posthuman, she is also a metaphor for
what Powers sees as the disagreeable effects of poststructuralist thought on the
literary environment. When Richard sums up the state of literary study at the
turn of the twentieth century, he might as well be speaking of the disembodied
AI, who has no existence aside from linguistic protocols: "Meaning doesn't cir-
culate. Nobody's going to jailbreak the prison house of language" (91). Helen is
made of words as Pygmalion's Galatea was made of marble, and Powers, who says
he wrote the novel in part "to poke fun at the high sanctimoniousness of literary
theory" ("Generalist" 102) clearly intends Helen's artificial person as a personification of readers who insist, with Derrida, that "there is nothing outside of the text"
(158).[45] Instead, he aligns his poetics with the likes of Mark Turner, who proposes
that "acts of language, including literature," are always and everywhere "acts of a
human brain in a human body in a human environment" (*Reading Minds* vii-viii).
The book can thus be seen as endorsing cognitive science's turn from representational, symbol-based computation to modes of embodiment, i.e., the interdependency of mind, body, and environment, a turn that, as Powers repeatedly reminds
us, also bears implications for the question of literary construction.[46]

---

44 See Hayles in her prologue: "The important intervention comes not when you try to determine
which is the man, the woman, or the machine. Rather, the important intervention comes much
earlier, when the test puts you into a cybernetic circuit that splices your will, desire, and perception into a distributed cognitive system in which represented bodies are joined with enacted
bodies through mutating and flexible machine interfaces. As you gaze at the flickering signifiers scrolling down the computer screens, no matter what identifications you assign to the
embodied entities that you cannot see, you have already become posthuman" (*Posthuman* xiv).

45 That Powers's critique of "sanctimoniousness" gives short shrift to the diverse and heterogeneous discourses of postmodernism has already been pointed out by Chapman, who considers
"the novel's engagement with poststructuralist or postmodernist theory [...] often evasive," and
its targets ill-defined as, variously, "literary theorists, criticism, lit crit, lit critters, poststructuralism, postmodernism, pomo, and the like" (226-27). Powers, Chapman concludes, is "playing a
double game, critiquing poststructuralist assumptions while eschewing substantive engagement with its conclusions" (244).

46 For proponents of this shift in cognitive science, see A. Clarke; Thompson; and Varela et al.

The publication of *Galatea* 2.2 coincided with the first wave of cognitive literary critics, and Chapman reads it as in some significant aspects anticipating their
ideas by "sketching out in fictional form a theory of literature rooted in cognitive
science," whose "central premise" is that "cognition is embodied, and therefore so
is reading" (227, 234).[47] However, I would argue that the interesting question here
is not how familiar Powers was with cognitive literary theory when he composed
the novel[48] but rather his method of turning the findings of cognitive science and
neuroscience into metaphors for literary activity, a method that is predicated on
analogizing brains, books, and machines. When the characters discuss "symbolic
grounding" and sarcastically remark that according to "the" literary theorists, "a
human's real-world interface is problematic at best," (126) postmodern theory and
literature appear, paradoxically, to be caricatured through the ascription of positions that the text itself propounds: after all, we are informed repeatedly, and by
different characters, that we "take in the world" via "chemical symbol-gates" and
that consequently, symbols are "all that remains of the real" (148, 204).

If this is how matters stand, it is not immediately comprehensible why "the
pomo and the cultural studies and the linguistic-based solipsism," which the novel's representative postmodern academic—the graduate student "A.," momentarily breaking character—lambasts as "verbal wanking off," should be so much
more deplorable than the basic mechanisms of perception and cognition (255).
Both, it would seem, are detached from the real. The reason, we suspect, has to
do with Powers's conviction that "art without the real-world referent is valueless,"
as Dewey, somewhat drastically, phrases it (*Understanding* 91). We human beings,
who in contrast to Helen are "bathed in a stream of real-world data," may know
the "real" world "only through synapses," but at least our neural representations
stand in a relation to the world; they achieve referentiality, even if only at a remove
(*GA* 27-28).

Helen, then, both is and is not like us, which affords Powers the opportunity
to seize upon the similarities and differences between what historian of cognitive science Margaret Boden calls "minds and mindlike artifacts" (168) as metaphorical illustrations of his ethical and poetological ideals. The key term here, I
would argue, is *construction*. In *Galatea* 2.2, Powers presents self-referentiality—back-propagation in artificial neural networks; autobiographical memory in
human beings; intertextuality in literature—as the very stuff of poïesis. The idea
of crafting something, be it a self, an "intelligence," or a novel, out of preexist-

---

47  See also Worthington, who states that Richard's and Lentz's project "grapples with the question of what actually constitutes consciousness: whether interaction with the physical world is
   necessary to construct a conscious subject or whether, as poststructuralists would have it, consciousness is formed completely within and by language" (124-25).

48  See the second footnote in this chapter.

ing materials underlies the book's parallel process of teaching man and machine alike. What is more, the AI's "shaped evolution, the lay of her synapses," and the scientific ideas they are based on, serve to express Powers's signature concerns about the construction of texts, lives, and worlds (GA 302). Like Helen's computer consciousness, human subjectivity is built on machinic processes; it is only that our brains are biological machines endowed with "natural" rather than artificial intelligence. Yet both kinds of brains are constructed, and both constructions produce illusions, an assumption that, to Powers's mind, also applies to literature.

The self-referential project of Galatea 2.2 aims at presenting literary language and lived life as mutually constitutive. "We spend our years as a tale that is told" Richard states, drawing on the bible for legitimization (311).[49] Yet the "tale" acquires a neuro-materialist connotation here, since in keeping with its scientific sources, the novel understands subjectivity itself as a neural construction.[50] This much becomes apparent when Richard and Lentz discuss "operationalism," the notion that a successful run of the Turing Test means that "you pass off your simulation as functionally equivalent to the thing you're simulating." When Richard expresses his worry about the dividing line between the mere "imitation" of consciousness and "the real thing," Lentz dresses him down: "Awareness is the original black box. [...] The brain is already a sleight of hand, a massive, operationalist shell game. [...] Experience is a Turing Test—phenomena passing themselves off as perception's functional equivalents" (275-76; original emphasis).

Galatea 2.2 tells a story about the quest for the technical (re)creation of consciousness, but as the above passage demonstrates, it also tells a story about the technical nature of consciousness itself. Mark Hansen has drawn attention to the "essential technicity of being," by which he means the fact that embodiment and technicity "furnish the (double) condition of the human as a form of life" (79). Yet it is not only that the body is always already technological and prosthetic, as Stiegler and Wills as well as Hansen have pointed out.[51] More to the point, materialist accounts of mind often discuss consciousness itself as reliant upon, or even consisting of, different (and functionally differentiated) "modules" in the brain's "hardware" that can be seen as technical processes in their own right. Tabbi's men-

---

49  The line is from Psalm 90:9 in the King James Bible; in other translations "as a tale that is told" has also been rendered as "like a sigh" or as "according to the word," both of which dramatically transform the meaning of the quotation.

50  See Broks's summary of the reigning dogma in neuroscience, which holds that the brain "constructs a model of the organism of which it is a part and, beyond this, a representation of that organism's place in relation to other, similar, organisms: people. As part of this process it assembles a 'self,' which can be thought of as the device we humans employ as a means of negotiating the social environment" (51).

51  See Wills 1995 and 2008 as well as Stiegler 1998 and 2008.

tion of the "agents, modules, and distributed neural networks *in us*" (cited above) is apt here.

Modular theory as conceived by Jerry Fodor in the early eighties in its "earliest and strongest version" holds that mind and brain are made up of a "collection of relatively independent processing devices called modules that receive distinct kinds of information at peripheral levels (eyes, ears, fingers, for example), then operate over and produce successively richer (i.e., more integrated) structures of meaning" (Spolsky 20). One can tell from Spolsky's description that Fodor's theory rests on the reduction of mind to brain, on the brain's hierarchical architecture, on the computational paradigm that views the brain as a processor of information, and on the view that thought amounts to mental representation.[52]

Such conceptions clearly inform *Galatea 2.2*, where Lentz views the brain as "just a glorified, fudged-up Turing machine" and Richard describes the "input layer" of a neural network as "fronting the boundless outdoors" (71, 15). In such a model, which conceives of the interaction of mind and world as analogous to the subject-object divide, albeit on the dramatically more microscopic level of brain modules, a rupture or rift between self and environment is built into the conceptual framework. Consciousness, which is "inside," has no direct contact with, and no direct knowledge of, the outside, which first has to filter through the senses and the nervous system up to the technical information-processing machinery of the mind before being represented for the benefit of Fodor's "central processor."[53] The "I" of consciousness is thus not only separated from the noumenon of the external world but *constructed* by a collection of unconscious, technical, lower-level processes. As Patricia Waugh puts it, "mind is a shadow that falls across and processes a world of immediacy from which it is ever locked out" ("Thinking" 76). In this scheme, our "natural" sense of self betrays us; consciousness itself becomes, dependent on one's interpretation, a poietic process, a construction, or an inauthentic impostor.

These ideas authorize "neuroscience's view of the self as unreal, as an illusion produced by the brain" (Ortega and Vidal, "Brains" 344). In Powers's novel, they are mainly advanced through Lentz, who characterizes consciousness as "a deception" and describes his own personality as "a lot of little delta rules running recurrently, evaluating and updating themselves" (88, 113). Yet epiphenomenalism and reductionism are not limited to Lentz.[54] Since Richard largely adopts these doctrines, they suffuse the whole of the book and surface regularly, as when Richard

---

52  See Fodor (60-68) for the concept of mental representation.

53  For the notion of central processing, see part IV, "Central Systems" in Fodor.

54  Brian McLaughlin defines epiphenomenalism as the doctrine "that mental phenomena are caused by physical phenomena but do not themselves cause anything" (275).

says of an early "implementation" that "the way its linked nets responded to input reminded me too much of my own little rickies" (91).[55]

It should be noted, however, that all these bold statements are themselves metaphorical constructions, and as such they work in both directions: minds evoke machines; machines evoke minds. When Richard asks A. for instructions on how to play pinball, she replies, "I just kind of whack at it, you know? The lights. The bells and whistles." Her reply immediately (and predictably) spurs the meta-phor-mad narrator to fashion the episode into yet another allegory of machinic mental functioning: "Volition was moot musing. The little silver ball did what it wanted" (282). Here we get Powers's metaphoric method in its purest form: the respective book's central conceit (in this case, connectionism) serves as the source domain from which terms are liberally borrowed to describe a variety of phenom-ena. There are few limits to this process in *Galatea 2.2*, so that over the course of the book, connectionism is invoked to characterize not only the human mind and its development, but also romantic relationships and the writing and reading of literary texts, as well as their academic study.[56]

Thus, love is rewritten as a phenomenon involving a kind of neuronal behav-iorist conditioning. "You can only say, 'Yes, to everything,' once. Once only, before your connections have felt what everything entails," Richard muses wistfully, redescribing love as "the feedback cycle of longing, belonging, loss. Anti-Heb-bian: the firing links get weaker" (152). But the language of cognitive science also informs Richard's description of his chosen profession. "Creating a world from memory" is yet another endeavor that bears resemblance to physical processes occurring in the brain. "I meant to reverse-engineer experience," Richard recol-lects. "Mind can send signals back across its net, from output to in" (160). *Galatea 2.2* suggests a confluence of function between brains and texts: the imagination, we learn, is what links neurons and narrative, both of which produce fictions. Literary narrative does this, Powers proposes, through representation as well as enactment: "a book both mirrored and elicited the mind's unreal ability to turn inward upon itself" (141).

It is but a short step from this idea to the notion of the text itself as an analogue of both mind and machine. Ortega and Vidal observe a substitutionality at the heart of the "neuroliterary field," which they describe as "characterized by its the-

---

55  "The function of consciousness must be in part to dummy up and shape a coherence from all the competing, conflicting subsystems that processed experience. By nature, it lied," Richard mus-es, providing additional proof that the narrator, if not the author himself, has come to accept the idea of consciousness as an illusion (218).

56  This allegorical abundance can prove wearisome for readers: with palpable exasperation, David Lodge notes that Powers "will never use one metaphor when a dozen will do" (27), while James Wood describes his writing as "at once showy and anxiously explanatory" ("Brain," n. pag.).

matic structure: brains in literature/literature in the brain" (330). *Galatea 2.2* provides ample illustration of this reciprocal relation: it is not only that theories about the brain provide convenient sources of metaphoric imagery; Powers also locates metaphoricity at the heart of the brain's operations. When Helen cross-references the phenomena of old men losing their hair with that of trees shedding their leaves to form the counterintuitive—and quintessentially poetic—expression, "The trees bald," Richard experiences an epiphany about the centrality of metaphor to the cerebral processes that produce meaning:

> Associations of associations. It struck me. Every neuron formed a middle term in a continuous, elaborate, brain-wide pun. [...] To fire or not meant different things, depending on how the register aligned at a given instant and which other alignments read the standing sum. [...] These weird parallaxes of framing must be why the mind opened out on meaning at all. Meaning was not a pitch but an interval. It sprang from the depth of disjunction, the distance between one circuit's center and the edge of another. (154-55)

Here, Richard is not only "using literary language to explain the brain," as Anne DeWitt has it (207), but installing the mechanism of metaphor—the substitution of one sememe for another—at the center of the brain's biochemical transactions.[57] One feels reminded of Paul Broks's proposition that for all its materiality, the meanings that the brain generates, which include the construction we call the self, are ultimately the products of difference: "Minds emerge from process and interaction, not substance. In a sense, we inhabit the spaces between things. We subsist in emptiness" (56). But Powers's conception of neural meaning production also bears a strong resemblance to Mark Turner's notion of "conceptual blending," a process that makes use of difference to create new concepts out of the comparison and combination of preexisting elements:[58] it is the disparity between one neural "sign" and others that produces the meaning of the "brain-wide pun."[59] Since in this construction the circuits themselves perform the dual function of writer and reader, tasked with both producing and interpreting their own patterns, substitution and self-reference coincide: "Every act of depicting depicted itself, as read by some other set of overlapping signal lights" (155).[60]

---

57  The definition of metaphor is Umberto Eco's (109).

58  See Turner's example of talking animals (*Literary* 11).

59  See also Chapman's comment that the novel "insists that all cognition is figural on more than one level" (240).

60  See also Tabbi, who paraphrases the plot of the novel in the terms of systems theory: "a system becomes conscious of itself, and consciousness then re-enters the system as information, changing the system irreversibly" (*Cognitive* 65).

Curiously, Powers emphasizes that this self-referential representation of one's own internal states as material for further representational acts is a process common to both (human) minds and machines. Despite the book's insistence that Helen's mode of being is different from ours, the underlying neural *modus operandi* is assumed to be identical. As Richardson notes, Powers is eager to "assert the centrality of 'literary' subjects like metaphor and imagination to language and to mental life generally" (39). "Recursive by nature," machinic cognition and human consciousness are aligned by Powers's effort to render them both analogous to his own literary method (*GA* 28).[61] In Powers's ascription of the simultaneity of representation and enaction to both literature and cognition in equal measure, we glimpse the crucial function materialist theories of consciousness perform in his poetics.

Powers has described the mimetic and self-referential aspects of fiction in terms of the modular, evolutionary brain, stating that "the war for the soul of the novel has raged from the moment that narrative need first took hold in our kludged-up rejiggering of the mammalian brain. [...] Limbic versus cortical, affective versus thinky" ("Children" 8). Elsewhere, he has contrasted mimeticism, which "willfully takes the symbol for the symbolized" with postmodernism, which calls "attention to itself as an artifice," in order to present his own work as a third term that mediates between the poles of this binary, a "bastard hybrid, *like consciousness itself*, generating new terrain by passing 'realism' and 'metafiction' through relational processes, inviting identification at one gauge while complicating it at others" ("Making" 308; my emphasis). Powers is drawing here on one of the core tenets of (second-wave) cybernetics, systems theory, and autopoiesis, namely the notion that "in order for living things to be able to cognize, their organization must be one where mutual reference is mandatory, where the key logic is that of recursive functionals" (Varela, "Ages" xvi). The result is a metaphorical equation of first-order representations (realism; perception) and second-order observations (metafiction; self-reflective cognition) from the domains of literature and psychic life.

With this observation, we have arrived at a fundamental motif of Powers's fiction, the "reconnection" of life and literature. A book, Powers suggests, "may finally locate its greatest worth in its ability to refresh us to the irreducible complexity of the analog world" ("Being," n. pag.), a sentiment duly echoed by his exegete Dewey, who describes the author's texts as addressing the "rich ad-lib of the enterprise of living itself, the stunning mystery of animated matter" (*Understanding* 14). To achieve this lofty goal, *Galatea* 2.2 takes a three-pronged approach: arguing for the centrality of bodily life to language (literary and otherwise), emphasizing the

---

61  As Wald notes, "Powers's novel sets up resonances between the process of writing fiction, the process of self-creation, and the investigation of cognition" (n. pag.).

referentiality of literature, and installing literary mechanisms at the physical center of psychic life, i.e., the brain.

What motivates Richard to anthropomorphize Helen, to animate and breathe life into his Galatea, is a visit to Lentz's wife Audrey, who has been spending her days in a nursing home since a stroke left her brain damaged. In accordance with the "two cultures" paradigm, the characters dutifully perform the roles assigned to them: the humanist Richard observes that Audrey's "soul had pulled up stakes from behind her features," while the scientist Lentz sums up his wife's condition by saying that "database" and "retrieval" are "still intact"; "It's just meaning that's gone" (166, 168). Once more, Richard has an epiphany: "I knew now what we were doing. We would prove that [...] one could back up one's work in the event of disaster. [...] We could eliminate death. That was the long-term idea" (170). Here the posthumanist theme of artificial intelligence gives way to the quintessentially *transhumanist* fantasy of transcendence,[62] which ironically "humanizes" not only Lentz's research but also the neural net. "Imp G became Imp H, in seamless conversion, after I met Audrey Lentz," Richard recalls, and shortly after, he attributes a gender and a name to Imp H: "You're a girl [...]. You are a little girl, Helen" (171, 179).

Powers suggests here that even computer code, the most virtual of languages, is rooted in worldly concerns and the lived facts of vulnerability and mortality, as is the novel's central conceit, the quest for a virtual model that would yield an "owner's manual for the brain" (*GA* 6). Jon Adams may be right to suspect that the "fragility of the brain, the vulnerability of mind to matter, worries Powers," (144), but he appears no less preoccupied with the relation between the "disengaged" aesthetic realm of literary language and the "world's infinite density" (*GA* 243). According to James Berger, *Galatea 2.2* shows that "the contexts of formal self-relation and intertextual reference [are] never complete, and that literary texts [point] beyond the literary world toward social realities [...] and toward the non-textual, sensual and social world." (130). This idea emerges toward the end of the book, when Helen, who functions as an "elaborate analogy for the canon," expresses her dissatisfaction with the selective diet of canonical literature she has been fed (Berger 119).

In keeping with the text's pedagogical motif, Helen's literary education eventually runs up against the problem of the social and political dimensions of literature, and like a child gradually awakening to knowledge of the world's evils, she exchanges innocence for curiosity. "It was Huck Finn [...] that made me real-

---

62  On the distinction between critical posthumanism and transhumanism, see Herbrechter, who in his preface helpfully defines transhumanism as the hope that "technoscientific developments might transform us in a not too distant future into a new digital species with fantastic new potential" (viii).

ize [Helen's] childhood had ended," Richard states, as the Twain classic prompts Helen to ask, "What race am I? [...] What races do I hate? Who hates me?" (230). The AI, we take it, has mastered semantic and grammatical operations to the degree that she can develop an interest in thematic aspects, in *content*. From this point on, Richard can no longer hide "the world's violent misgivings" from her (270). Learning about a selection of canonical works, which Richard calls "the long list of irrelevant classics I'd memorized for my master's," has merely stalled Helen in her inevitable procession toward discovering a world in which "tanks were everywhere" (GA 102, 242).[63]

Rather simplistically, Powers contrasts Kantian, disinterested aesthetic contemplation with an incomparably more urgent extraliterary reality. "In taking her through the canon, I'd left out a critical text," Richard realizes. "She needed to know how little literature had, in fact, to do with the real" (313). To close the "gaps in her worldliness" (GA 230), Richard feeds Helen a digest of several decades' worth of news stories and UN reports. The overwhelming sense of injustice and violence proves too much for Helen, who retreats into stunned silence after announcing, "I don't want to play anymore" (314). This is a curious passage in the way it upholds a clear distinction between the "reality" of reportage and the fictionality of literature, whose invented dramas and tragedies presumably were too "irrelevant" to stir Helen's sense of moral outrage. Still, to assume that Powers argues here for the primacy of the real world vis-à-vis literary language is to fall prey to a "false dichotomy," Saltzman notes, "for according to *Galatea 2.2*, word and world is the association connectionism forges first" (109). True to this idea, the novel ends with an affirmation of the power of narrative.

In the final analysis, symbols, and, by implication, books, do have an intimate connection to the "real" world, Richard finds: "The symbols a life forms along its way work back out of the recorder's office where they wait, and, in time, they themselves go palpable. Lived" (204). Richard's insistence on the "lived" nature of symbols may put us in mind of Lakoff and Johnson's work on conceptual metaphors, which was gaining popularity when Powers was writing the novel,[64] but the passage's potential sources are less interesting than its use of metaphors from cognitive science as a means of tracing how symbols, which "form" in a primary

---

63  See also Eckstein and Reinfandt: "The world of literature as portrayed in Galatea 2.2 is precisely not capable of offering a totality of knowledge, but is presented as a fairly autonomous realm, opposed to, rather than interlinked with, the realm of experience" (98).

64  See Lakoff and Johnson, *Metaphors*, for the authors' classic work on the role of preconscious metaphors in perception and cognition. Also of interest in this context is Lakoff and Johnson, *Philosophy*, where the authors draw on more recent cognitive science to work out how basic metaphors derive from bodily experience.

process of representation, undergo a qualitative change from linguistic to lived upon re-entry into the psychic system.[65]

Diverging from a mimetic understanding of fiction, Powers proposes that literature and life model rather than imitate each other. Each provides a language or context for the other to draw on, in a process that is mutually constitutive and open-ended. The nexus where the two meet, however, is the brain; *Galatea 2.2*'s metaphoric zeal produces a fundamental conflation of literary language and neural narrative. In a published dialogue with Bruno Latour, Powers has expressed his "vested interest in manufacturing artificial, intelligent creatures that create the illusion of being fully independent and alive," and *Galatea 2.2* can be read as an extension of this analogy that posits artificial intelligence, human consciousness, and literary language as in some way commensurate (177). Crucially, this conflation rests on an understanding of narrative as an a priori process of consciousness—a thesis borrowed from cognitive science and neuroscience—and it leads to a view of literature as a meta-system that not only contains or represents but performs or models cognitive processes. In his interview with Sven Birkerts, Powers explicitly avows this notion: "By the end of the book, the book itself becomes a kind of artificial intelligence. The Galatea in the book, Galatea 2.0, is superseded by revision 2.2, the one that you've been reading" (n. pag.).

But for this "update" to take effect, Powers first needs to re-awaken his virtual Galatea from her self-induced slumber, and then kill her off. If "politics imploded her," what puts Helen back together is a mystic plea for the power of narrative (319). Richard tells the mute Helen that "plot was mind's brainchild," that the "gist of religious truth" is narrative at heart, that "care had to lie to itself, to carry on as if persistence mattered" (320-21). The novel thus "ends on a note of religious mysticism, negative theology, and something like Kierkegaard's Christian existentialism" (Lodge 27). That Lodge cannot be more specific here is no fault of his own; Richard's "desperate, eleventh-hour fix" (*GA* 277-78) is simply too vague and, as Lodge is right to lament, "congested and over-excited" (27) to convey anything beyond the mere impression that mystical, transcendent ideas are being deployed here against the existential horror of Yeats's "dying animal." Yet for all his narrator-protagonist's frantic invocations of the "immaterial in mortal garb" and the "rest mass of God," Powers fails to produce more here than what the text itself calls "miraculous banality" (*GA* 320).

The book's ending disappoints in part because, as Saltzman notes, it reiterates "the lesson of every Powers novel" about the redemptive potential of narrative

---

65  The novel explains back-propagation as For the concept of re-entry, see Luhmann, "Postmodern" 172-73.

(99).[66] But it also fails because its flimsy construction borders on the self-contradictory. In a span of a mere ten pages, Richard learns that he has been the butt of an elaborate practical joke ("It wasn't about teaching a machine to read"?), Lentz inexplicably declares himself eager to proceed with the test ("Tell her something. Anything. [...] Just get her back here"), Richard coaxes Helen back by appealing to some vague sense of transcendence ("how body stumbled by selection onto the stricken celestial"), the test is somehow performed despite the fact that all involved are now aware it was never meant to be taken seriously, Helen shuts herself off immediately afterwards, and Richard has the all-important epiphany that returns him to writing (318-328).

In fact, the latter is contingent upon the former: Helen effectively sacrifices herself to provide Richard with the inspiration for his next book: "She had come back only momentarily, just to gloss this smallest of passages. To tell me that one small thing. Life meant convincing another that you knew what it meant to be alive" (GA 327). After much handwringing about the material basis of subjectivity, Richard "seems to learn that the self must be construed relationally," as Bould and Vint argue (100), but one has to acknowledge that this is a profoundly unequal relationality: Helen, fed up with her disembodied state, interprets a key passage from Shakespeare's *The Tempest* by denouncing her incomplete state: "You are the ones who can hear airs. Who can be frightened or encouraged. You can hold things and break them and fix them. I never felt at home here. This is an awful place to be dropped down halfway" (326).

Helen proves her independence here, but at a price: her final refusal is "represented simultaneously as an incredibly powerful means of exerting her agency [...] and as a death sentence" (Worthington 129). Helen's "AI suicide" (Silva 208) thus prepares the way for a demonstration of the primacy of the "fully human" over the machinic pretender and the supremacy of the analog book over the digital computer. Richard is inspired to take up writing again "after having it proven [...] that being half human is worse than not being human at all" (Fitzpatrick, "Exhaustion" 554).[67] This is a convenient solution in more ways than one: it simultaneously removes the problem of "posthuman" consciousness from the equation, reasserts the status of the "natural" human being, and installs narrative as the key quality

---

66  See also Wood, who laments that "Powers always discovers the happy and humane mixture, in which human beings are revealed to be a combination of the unfree and the free, the chemical and the non-chemical, the given and the found, the animal and the human" (n. pag.).

67  "The humanist writer, in confronting the computer and sensing his imminent demise, imagines not simply the marginalization of print in an electronic age, but the demise of the hierarchies that have supported his dominance," Fitzpatrick argues. "In representing this anxiety in text, the writer is able not only to protect print from its putative death but to 'save' humanism as well" ("Exhaustion" 525).

of the latter. As Eckstein and Reinfandt acerbically summarize: "Helen commits virtual suicide. Richard Powers writes another book" (100).

We may well be organic automata, Powers implies, but our ability to produce fictions distinguishes us from machines and safeguards our freedom. Fiction, myth, religion all become compensations for a "thinking organ" that "could not help but feel itself to be more inexplicable than thought" (*GA* 320). *Galatea 2.2* "permits us to envision the persistence of the power of narrative, particularly literary narrative," in an "affirmative light," Jeffrey Pence writes (344). As I have shown in this section, this affirmation of literary narrative proceeds in close conjunction with a parallelization of brain and book. Powers envisions his text as a self-operating machine that bridges the gap between life and literature and the "two cultures" by locating their final synthesis in the brains of its readers, who add yet another layer of representation and referentiality to the textual-artificial brain that is *Galatea 2.2*.[68] In this way, the book aims at what I call the apotheosis of narrative, an ultimately self-serving operation that safeguards the relevance of the literary author in the wider cultural and intellectual field, and, as we are about to see, also significantly shapes his later novel *The Echo Maker*.

## "The brain is the ultimate storytelling machine": The Echo Maker

> A moral man, Phineas Gage
> Tamping powder down holes for his wage
> Blew his special-made probe
> Through his left frontal lobe
> Now he drinks, swears, and flies in a rage.

This anonymously authored limerick recounts the fate of railroad construction foreman Phineas Gage, who in 1848 suffered an accident that immortalized him in psychological and neurological literature. A charge set to clear away rocks for railroad tracks exploded prematurely, propelling his tamping iron, a large metal rod used to "tamp down" the blasting powder into holes in the rock, straight through his skull, taking bits of his brain along with it. Though Gage survived and made a stunning recovery, he was not left unchanged by the injury. Given the state of medical knowledge at the tine, "little could be said about the changes the injury produced in his behavior, and even less about the parts of his brain that were injured," as the authoritative history of the case reminds us (Macmillan 1), but even at the time, the attending physician suspected the case to be "exceedingly

---

68  See Tabbi, who describes *Galatea 2.2* as a textual artifact "whose truths are primarily cognitive rather than representational" (*Cognitive* 76).

interesting to the enlightened physiologist and intellectual philosopher" (Harlow, qtd. in Macmillan 387). In a follow-up report published twenty years later, the same doctor noted striking changes in Gage's personality that took hold within a year of the accident:

> The equilibrium or balance [...] between his intellectual faculties and animal pro-
> pensities, seems to have been destroyed. He is fitful, irreverent, indulging at times
> in the grossest profanity (which was not previously his custom), [...] impatient of
> restraint or advice when it conflicts with his desires, [...] capricious and vacillat-
> ing, devising many plans of future operation, which are no sooner arranged than
> they are abandoned in turn for others appearing more feasible. [...] Previous to his
> injury, [...] he possessed a well-balanced mind, and was looked upon by those who
> knew him as a shrewd, smart business man, very energetic and persistent in exe-
> cuting all his plans of operation. In this regard his mind was radically changed, so
> decidedly that his friends and acquaintances said he was "no longer Gage." (Har-
> low, qtd. in Macmillan 414-15)

The accident and its aftermath drastically demonstrated the reliance of mind upon matter and suggested that physical injury might not only affect but annihilate the self, to the point that Gage was deemed "no longer Gage." Because of the apparently radical change in behavior, the case is widely "judged to be the first and possibly most important to reveal something of the relation between the brain and complex personality characteristics." As a result, Phineas Gage has become "the classic example of the personality changes that are the hallmark of frontal lobe pathology" (Macmillan 1, 315). Thus the renowned neuroscientist Antonio Damasio dedicates the first fifty pages of his 1994 book *Descartes' Error* to the Gage story and its implications for the relation between brain and mind. Profoundly literary itself,[69] Damasio's account installs Gage as a narrative archetype that anticipated its "modern counterparts" who, through localized lesion or trauma, see their emotional systems disturbed, their reasoning compromised (Damasio, *Error* xiii).[70]

---

69  Damasio begins his account in the style of a raconteur: "It is summer of 1848. We are in New En-
    gland. Phineas P. Gage, twenty-five years old, construction foreman, is about to go from riches
    to rags." Interspersed throughout his retelling are references to Edgar Allan Poe, to emphasize
    the macabre nature of the tale, and Nathanael West: Damasio imagines Gage having "come to
    California to die" at the end of his life, like the California transplants in *Day of the Locust* (*Error* 3,
    10).

70  In keeping with his central idea that emotion is a prerequisite for, and not a hindrance to, ratio-
    nality, Damasio hypothesizes that Gage's frontal-lobe injury damaged or removed brain circuits
    responsible for emotional regulation, thus compromising his cognitive capacities: "Part of a re-
    gion which our recent investigations have highlighted as critical for normal decision-making,
    the ventromedial prefrontal region, was [...] damaged in Gage"; "it was selective damage in the

In this respect, Phineas Gage is also an ancestor in spirit of Mark Schluter, the central character of Richard Powers's 2006 novel *The Echo Maker*. Having swerved off the road for unknown reasons that the book uses as an occasion to set up a "whodunit" mystery story, the 27-year old crashes his truck and is hospitalized with cerebral trauma, causing his sister Karin to leave her job and head home to Kearney, Nebraska, to care for him. Like Phineas Gage, Mark quickly recovers his physical health, but it soon becomes apparent that the accident has left him with a case of Capgras delusion, "one of the rarest and most colorful syndromes in neurology" (Ramachandran 1856). Like Gage's frontal-lobe injury, Capgras involves the disturbance of affective ascriptions: "The Capgras sufferer almost always misidentifies his loved ones. A mother or father. A spouse. The part of his brain that recognizes faces is intact. So is his memory. But the part that processes emotional association has somehow disconnected from them" (*EM* 61).[71]

Mark refuses to recognize Karin as his sister; to him, she has become "Kopy Karin," an agent of ominous forces he can only suspect but not understand (*EM* 86). Soon, the range of his misrecognition expands to include his dog and his modular home. A concomitant of Mark's condition is anosognosia, i.e., the lack of awareness of one's own pathological state that often accompanies psychotic disorders: "nothing *inside* Mark felt changed. [...] *Mark* still felt familiar; only the world had gone strange" (*EM* 301; original emphases). The discrepancy between familiar and unfamiliar states is papered over by confabulation, the invention of narrative to explain what confuses consciousness: "A story to link the shifting self back to the senseless facts" (*EM* 164).[72] However, the mechanism underlying anosognosia and confabulation is revealed as central not only to psychotic repression but human consciousness in general. When Karin recruits the assistance of Dr. Gerald Weber, a famous cognitive neurologist modeled after Oliver Sacks, he is quick to point out that at its core, consciousness is concerned most of all with sustaining and "naturalizing" or hiding its own operations: "The self's whole end was self-continuation," and "a single, solid fiction always beat the truth of our scattering" (*EM* 301, 164).

This may sound familiar and call to mind Freudian concepts like repression, compensation, and defense mechanisms, but here, the need for narrative closure is explained as a biological imperative. "What is particularly striking about the operations of the conscious human brain is the necessity for integration, for a uni-

---

prefrontal cortices of Phineas Gage's brain that compromised his ability to plan for the future, to conduct himself according to the social rules he previously had learned, and to decide on the course of action that ultimately would be most advantageous to his survival" (32-33).

71  Here and subsequently, *The Echo Maker* is abbreviated as *EM* in parenthetical citations.

72  Personal confabulation is a term originally coined by neurologist Todd Feinberg, who defines the phenomenon in his chapter on "mything persons" as follows: "In personal confabulation, the patient misconstrues an actual event in his or her life or creates a wholly fictitious narrative about life, in which they play the starring role in another identity" (55). See also Hirstein.

tary picture, for construction, and for closure," Gerald Edelman writes (*Sky* 37), and it is a characteristic of such deep-seated neural mechanisms that they are "not unconscious so much as *nonconscious*, inaccessible to psychoanalytic techniques," as Charles Harris points out in his article on Powers's "neurological" (as opposed to psychological) realism (241; original emphasis). The biologist and neuroscientist Edelman is one of Powers's avowed scientific sources for *The Echo Maker*,[73] and his attempt to explain consciousness as originating in biological processes and principles informs the book's governing trope of the self as a "useful fiction" devised by low-level physical processes.[74] In keeping with this conception, Mark's "uninterrupted, unthinking trust in his shattered self" (*EM* 167) is presented as the automatic behavior of a "neuronal machine sitting inside a Darwinian animal struggling for its life" and obeying a universal, organic urge for survival and self-protection that holds true across species (Latour, "Reality" 9). As Daniel, Karin's conservationist ex-boyfriend, explains, "Hiding is natural. [...] A bird will do anything, not to reveal that it's hurt" (62).

Human kinship with birds and other animals is a recurrent theme in *The Echo Maker*, announced early on and sustained throughout. As Karin drives up to Kearney, she notices "a lone male" on a country road, who "tracks" through the snow and "turned and snarled as she passed, repelling the intrusion" (5). Later, when she visits Mark's bedside, she is struck by her brother's "animal eyes" and the way his fingers "feather" toward her (7). This emphasis on biology and "animality" illustrates how *The Echo Maker* builds on, but also differs from, *Galatea 2.2*.[75] While the latter assumed a "cybernetic approach" to the problem of consciousness, the former redeems Powers's promise to himself to "come back to it again someday from a biological side" (Owens interview, n. pag.).[76]

Both books take place over the course of a year and unfold plots that touch on the conflict between the "two cultures," or between psychodynamic and neurological conceptions of psychic life. In the earlier novel, the conflict already surfaces intermittently, as when a disgruntled colleague of Lentz's asks himself if "the man

---

73  See Powers, Burn interview 176.

74  For all its currency in contemporary neuroscience, the notion of the self as a "useful fiction" can be traced back as far as Locke's *Essay Concerning Human Understanding*: see Martin and Barresi 295.

75  See Wolfe, *Animal* and *Posthumanism* for the concept of animality.

76  As with *Galatea 2.2*, Powers emphasizes that the book has been made possible only once scientific discourses had progressed enough to allow for the material to be processed in literary form: "The field of neuroscience has made such incredible strides since I began writing that it finally seemed possible to try to weave a dialogical novel around the very specific new views of the brain that have emerged from laboratories over the last couple of decades—the distributed, modular, massively preconscious, multiply recursive, narrative-dependent model of the bundled 'I'" (Burn interview 175).

is just trying in his own warped way to be loved" or if the problem is rather that "his limbic system is diseased," thereby weighing psychological against neurological explanatory models (80). In the later book, we witness a similar divergence of perspectives when Dr. Weber meets his younger colleague Dr. Hayes, who functions as the novel's champion of eliminative materialism, much like Lentz did in *Galatea 2.2*. Weber, a writer of "neurological novelistic books" whose name evokes the weaving of stories, believes in the power of narrative, and that Capgras "still manifested in psychodynamic processes—individual response, personal history, repression, sublimation, and wish-fulfillment that couldn't be reduced entirely to low-level phenomena" (*EM* 359, 191). Hayes, on the other hand, sees "only structure" and is taken aback by the idea that something "more than neurons" might be involved (131-32).[77]

What is more, both books revolve around the necessity of embodiment for consciousness. As Damasio, whom Powers also invokes as inspiration,[78] suggests: "Mind is probably not conceivable without some sort of *embodiment*" (*Error* 234; original emphasis). Where *Galatea 2.2* had tackled this issue by way of negative illustration and imagined a machine that lacks a bodily sensorium, *The Echo Maker* approaches the topic by emphasizing the continuity and contiguity of human and animal modes of being. Humans, Powers suggests, define themselves in opposition to their environment and their fellow animal sojourners, yet they are everywhere connected to them, physically and temporally, an idea that is rehearsed in a number of variations throughout the book.

The novel's chapters are preceded by evocations of the lives of the sandhill cranes that frequent the Nebraskan countryside where the book is set. In these sections, the birds are presented as social beings—they fly in families, as lifelong mates with one or two offspring—with intimate connections to their lifeworlds, "places recovered from previous years, by a crane map, inside a crane's head" (97). Lest kinship structures and memory do not suffice to render animals homologous with humans, we are also informed of the presence of "symbols in the birds' heads, something that says *again*," (98; original emphasis). In any case, we are meant to realize our deep familiarity with the birds, as Karin does toward the end of the novel: "Those birds danced like our next of kin, looked like our next of kin, called and willed and parented and taught and navigated all just like our blood relations. Half their parts were still ours. Yet humans waved them off: *impostors*" (348; original emphasis).

---

77  In accordance with this clash between recent reductionist models the brain and older, psychological conceptions of the mind, Mark's experience can either become a "trauma-induced case" or "the strange case of The Man Who Doubled his Sister" (*EM* 173, 128).

78  See Powers, Burn interview 176 and Michod interview, n. pag.

In passages like these, the novel shares in positions simultaneously developed by current critical theory, which also finds that linguistic analysis is not the only way to decenter the human subject: we see in animals "what we consider most special about our status as a species—that we speak, we reason and comprehend, we produce knowledge, we hide ourselves or cover our tracks, we know ourselves, we deceive," Elizabeth Grosz argues. "The conditions for the emergence of all these qualities, and every other distinctively human capacity are already there in animal existence" (*Becoming* 17). Nowadays, "even sympathetic Derrideans" agree on the need to move from language to biology, Jeffrey Nealon observes (147), and *The Echo Maker* proves curiously consonant with attempts by scholars like Elizabeth Grosz or Catherine Malabou to further diminish the hegemony of human subjectivity through appeals to evolutionary and physiological discourses.

This is one reason the novel has been read by some, in yet another parallel to *Galatea 2.2*, as propounding or performing posthumanist ideas.[79] However, instead of inquiring whether Powers is "still" a humanist or "already" a posthumanist author, it may be more productive to discuss the characteristics and the functions of the novel's ostensibly posthumanist sensibilities. Much of these can be ascribed to Powers's sources, like Edelman's Darwinist account of "how the mind relates to matter," which posits "an intimate relation between animal functions [...] and the development of the brain" and adopts as its central postulate the decidedly non-anthropocentric statement, "In the course of evolution, bodies came to have minds" (*Bright* 5-7, 15). If the novel's vision of inter-species familiarity, based on a concept of evolutionary continuity ("Half their parts were still ours") is one obvious toehold of such sentiments in the text, another is the directly related idea of both brain and mind as modular and constructed.

Joseph LeDoux, whom Powers has called "the most interesting" of his influences (Burn interview 16), says about the brain that "all three levels [hindbrain, midbrain, forebrain] are represented in all vertebrates, and even the evolutionarily advanced forebrain is structured according to a common underlying organizational plan that is applicable to every vertebrate species" (*Synaptic* 35). Out of this foundational idea of cerebral constructedness, Powers develops a "polyphon-

---

79  Most critics who have discussed the novel's posthumanist credentials have been content to provide rather simple assessments, casting Powers either as a humanist or a posthumanist— the former often less stringently defined than the latter. Even where this model is not strictly adhered to, the binary opposition of its constituent terms is kept intact. To cite just a few examples: Nicola Brindley, who understands the posthuman (somewhat vaguely) as a "process of redefining what it means to be human in the twenty-first century," considers both the humanist and the posthumanist option for Powers before declaring Donna Haraway's "non-humanism" as "the place where Richard Powers could most comfortably be situated as an author" (n. pag.). Quentin Miller sees Powers as seeking to "redefine humanism" (384); T. J. Lustig likewise identifies a "vestigial" humanism in Powers (135).

ic"[80] account of the deconstruction of subjecthood in which three main characters (Mark, Karin, Weber) are forced to come to terms with the modularity, mutability, and vulnerability of what LeDoux calls the "synaptic self." Accordingly, *The Echo Maker* has garnered much scholarly attention as a document illustrating "conceptions of the (human) subject as they evolve from the fictional universe of 21st-century North American literatures," as Sabine Sielke phrases it (239).

This is an unsurprising reading insofar as the text itself loudly insists on it. Its epigraph, taken from Soviet neuropsychology pioneer A. R. Luria, reads, "To find the soul it is necessary to lose it," and the novel resolutely follows through on this programmatic premise, deconstructing the idea of the self for several hundred pages only to reconstruct it at the very end. Since this is the 21st century, however, this deconstruction is neurological rather than linguistic, and it occurs on two fronts simultaneously, by emphasizing the opacity of the self and by calling into question the immediacy of experience. The book's main vehicle for the distribution of this kind of information is Weber, who learns from his patients that the self is "not one, continuous, indivisible whole, but instead, hundreds of separate subsystems" (171), and teaches his students that "[t]he job of consciousness is to make sure that all of the distributed modules of the brain seem integrated. That we always seem familiar to ourselves" (363).

By rendering Weber's professional opinion on the functions of consciousness and the nature of the self, the book rehearses, again and again, a litany already familiar from *Galatea 2.2*: at the level of modular brain processes, one is faced with an undeniable fragmentation of agency. Here as in the earlier novel, the brain is conceptualized as consisting of functionally differentiated parts whose complex interplay somehow gives rise to the unified experience of consciousness. The difference this time around is that this division of cognitive labor is understood strictly in evolutionary terms. Fodor's ideas about modularity of mind are thus filtered through those of evolutionary psychology, so that personality is no longer deconstructed into sets of "delta rules" (*GA* 118); instead it is conceptualized as the amalgam of acquired experience and the primal dictates of "the herd in the head" (*EM* 323).

In accordance with this reconceptualization, metaphors of mind undergo a transformation. Consciousness is no longer a computer but an organic system: "We're more like coral reefs [...]. Complex but fragile ecosystems" (*EM* 186). Clearly, at this level of analysis, where a single process like vision requires "careful coordination between thirty-two or more separate brain modules," immediacy gets

---

80  Powers is fond of describing his poetics as "polyphonic," a term he appropriates from Bakhtin. *The Echo Maker*'s polyphony consists in the text's focalization through the three main characters, whose individual dictions color their respective passages. On the polyphonic in Powers, see also Ickstadt.

lost (*EM* 149). As Weber explains, "what we took for a priori, absolute apprehension of real space in fact depended upon a fragile chain of perceptual processing. 'Left' was as much *in here* as *out there*" (125). In this view, we never experience the Kantian "things-in-themselves" but only hastily and retrospectively assembled representations, constructed by electrochemical processes occurring on a neural, preconscious level forever inaccessible to us. This explains why one of Powers's favorite notions is that internal experience is "cobbled up" from external events. Thus we learn in *The Echo Maker* that multiple "layers of brain stood in between, cobbling up from raw signals the reassuring illusion of solidity" (258), just as in an interview, Powers informs us that "we're disembodied sensibilities cobbled into our bodies" ("Two Geeks", n. pag.).

In accordance with the ruling orthodoxy of contemporary neuroscience, the brain has to *represent* models of the external world—the first degree of separation of self from world—which then provide the ground on which the brain can act, make decisions, and so on—the second degree of separation, since it is not the human subject that thinks, acts, decides, but the modular brain itself.[81] The subject, now doubly removed or alienated from him- or herself, can thus be said to fall victim to a twofold illusion: the illusion of an objective external reality which is really only a subjective construction, and the illusion of being the locus or origin of his or her own cognition, perception, volition, and emotion. Faced with this double remove, the search for the authentic subjectivity, let alone the soul, becomes a Sisyphean endeavor. Like David Hume, looking for his self in introspection and declaring it nowhere to be found, Powers appears to argue for the ontological unreality of the self.[82] His preferred way of expressing this idea is to state that the self is a fiction, a formulation that establishes an analogy between literature and subjectivity:

> if neuroscience concludes anything, it's that sensing and feeling and thinking and perceiving and hundreds of other seemingly separate processes are all conjoined in a huge, dynamic, and continuously revised narrative network. The brain is the ultimate storytelling machine, and consciousness is the ultimate story. Our neurons tell our selves into being. (Michod interview, n. pag.)

---

81  This is demonstrably the argument put forth by Joseph LeDoux, who says, for instance, that it is "possible for your brain to know that something is good or bad before it knows exactly what it is" (*Emotional* 69).

82  "For my part, when I enter most intimately into what I call *myself*, I always stumble on some particular perception or other, of heat or cold, light or shade, love or hatred, pain or pleasure. I never can catch *myself* at any time without a perception, and never can observe any thing but the perception" (Hume 165; original emphases). Recourse to Hume's "bundle theory" of perception is common in arguments against the existence of the self: see for instance Hood ix.

Armed with this interpretation of neuroscientific research, Powers is free to "universalize" Capgras in *The Echo Maker*, where the syndrome becomes a convenient metaphor for just such processes of neural storytelling. This notion is rehearsed in *The Echo Maker* in a variety of permutations. "Even baseline consciousness has about it something hallucinatory," Weber concludes (206), while Karin eventually realizes that "the whole race suffered from Capgras" (347). A deep-seated anxiety that invention might equal inauthenticity pervades the book, much as it had already informed *Galatea 2.2*, and for similar reasons. As soon as the self is viewed as constructed, or consciousness as constructible, knowledge and reality appear to be up for grabs. Thinking about his wife, Weber muses, "What did he know about her? Nothing at all. Nothing but what his prefrontal cortex might spin out of thin air and flotsam from the hippocampus" (367).

Ever willing to disclose the ideas and inspirations behind his books, in an interview Powers readily names the most important source for this idea of the fundamental commensurability of self and fiction. Asked whether he can identify affinities between *The Echo Maker* and Daniel Dennett's multiple-drafts theory of consciousness, Powers happily responds, "I see more than affinities: I see strong equivalences! *The Echo Maker* is in many ways a narrative working-out of those ideas" (Burn interview 174). The author's passionate response, accentuated by an exclamation mark, might warrant a short excursus to clarify just what ideas of Dennett's Powers "works out" in his novel. For this purpose, we can turn to Dennett's 1991 book *Consciousness Explained*, which Patricia Waugh locates "at the heart of first- and second-generation cognitivism" ("Thinking" 78).

Taking his cue from Hume, Dennett begins his discussion of "the reality of selves" by asking, "who is this *I* that has looked in vain for a self" and observes that "we" can both be said to exist, since there has got to be someone asking the above question, and *not* to exist, since demonstrably, there are no "entities, either *in* our brains, or *over* and *above* our brains, that control our bodies, think our thoughts, make our decisions" (413; original emphases).[83] So Dennett begins to a construct a "middle-ground position" by first submitting that selves need to have come about in a certain way, historically: there needs to be, Dennett says, a "true story to be told about *how there came* to be creatures with selves" (413; original emphasis). This "true story," it turns out, is a biological one. Thus Dennett moves from the animal kingdom—amoebas making distinctions between themselves and their environment; beavers building dams, and birds nests, and spiders webs—to the constructions of the human realm, where "[e]ach normal individual of this species makes a *self*. Out of its brain it spins a web of words and deeds, and, like the other creatures, it doesn't know what it's doing; it just does it" (414-16; original emphasis).

---

83  Until specified otherwise, all following in-text citations in this section are taken from *Consciousness Explained*.

There are two observations to be made here, one being that Dennett feels the need, at this early stage of his argument, to introduce the qualifier "normal," the other that his humanity-animality analogy is based in no small part on behaviorist and neo-Darwinian assumptions. Dennett invokes both B. F. Skinner's "negative reinforcement" and Richard Dawkins's "extended phenotype" to prepare the ground for his ideas, which should alert us to the fact that this "true story" is by no means without presuppositions or ideological bent (415).

Sustaining the animal analogy, Dennett explains that unlike a spider, "an individual human doesn't just exude its web; more like a beaver, it works hard to gather the materials out of which it builds its protective fortress" (416). Apart from the curious fact that the individual human being's fundamental contiguity with his fellow animals has caused him or her to become a gender-neutral "it," we can note here that this is an essentially poïetic understanding: the self is not created out of whole cloth but produced, crafted out of preexisting materials. Lest he be misunderstood, Dennett hastens to add that this linguistic-sounding "web of discourses" is "as much a biological product as any of the other constructions to be found in the animal world" (416).

However, the notion of *discourse* also propels Dennett to his first qualification that distinguishes humans from animals. No surprise here: as in other famous accounts of human identity, it is language, or, at any rate, symbolic activity. "We, in contrast [to animals], are almost constantly engaged in presenting ourselves to others, and to ourselves, and hence *representing* ourselves—in language and gesture, external and internal," Dennett writes (417; original emphasis), and if he takes pains to distance himself from "the deconstructionists" (410), the reason might be that he is about to formulate a thought that does have a poststructuralist ring to it. For what happens "when we let in these words, these meme-vehicles," Dennett informs us, is that "they tend to take over, creating us out of the raw materials they find in our brains" (417).[84]

So after the heyday of poststructuralism, we are once more spoken by language, only this time around it is biology rather than "discourse" that is doing the talking. Similar to the neo-Darwinist account of evolutionary biology, this is fundamentally a *blind* process: "Our tales are spun, but for the most part we don't spin them; they spin us. Our human consciousness, and our narrative selfhood, is their product, not their source" (418). The effect of all this spinning and representing and all these "words, words, words," (417), according to Dennett, is to produce the impression of unified agents in the absence of ontological proofs for their existence, and as "[t]hese strings or streams of narrative issue forth as *if* from a single

---

84  Dennett borrows the concept of the meme from Richard Dawkins. See chapter 11 of Dawkins for details. See also Deacon for a critique of Dawkins on semiotic grounds, as well as Robinson for a critique of the concept as "parascientific" (*Absence* 66).

source," we can observe that "their effect on any audience is to encourage them to (try to) posit a unified agent whose words they are, about whom they are: in short, to posit a *center of narrative gravity*" (418; original emphasis).[85] The implication here is that just like gravity, we cannot see the self but still observe its effects.

This is a crucial point for Dennett (and for Powers, as we will see), but before we move on to examine how it is that "our tales spin us," we should pause and take note of the fact that the concept of the center of narrative gravity rests, again, on essentially behaviorist assumptions. There really is no interiority here, just an "audience" who draw inferences about blackboxed agents from the observation of behavior. This replacement of individual interiority for a consensual attribution of agency is what underlies Dennett's chosen name for his method, heterophenomenology.[86]

How are we to imagine the process by which words (or "memes") spin us or even *produce* us in the first place? The key here is Dennett's "multiple drafts model." Espousing a modular view of the brain, about which we have heard quite a bit by this point,[87] Dennett argues against what he calls the "Cartesian theater"—the notion that there is a place in the brain where everything "comes together" to be experienced by consciousness: a "finish line" in the brain, as it were (106). Instead he submits that "all varieties of perception—indeed, all varieties of thought or mental activity—are accomplished in the brain by parallel, multitrack processes of interpretation and elaboration of sensory inputs. Information entering the nervous system is under continuous 'editorial revision'" (111).

This model has two important implications. First, as in all representationalist theories, experience is never direct. Perception, which for obvious reasons is the favorite example for theorists arguing against immediacy of experience or "oneness" with the world, is "a product of many processes of interpretation—editorial processes, in effect" (112). Here perception—and, by implication, consciousness itself—becomes a process of *mediation* that precludes the subject from ever catching sight of the noumenon. Second, the multiple drafts model fragments the assumed agency of a unified subject into an array of interrelated but autonomously operating parallel processes. Such a dispersion of central agency into mul-

---

85  For another look at the self as the "center of narrative gravity," see Dennett 1992.

86  According to Dennett, heterophenomenology constitutes a *"neutral* method for investigating and describing phenomenology. It involves extracting and purifying texts from (apparently) speaking *subjects*, and using those texts to generate a theorist's fiction, the subject's *heterophenomenological* world. [...] Maximally extended, it is a neutral portrayal of exactly *what it is like to be* that subject—in the subject's own terms, given the best interpretation we can muster (*Consciousness* 98; original emphases). Note that judgment is being withheld on the key point of the ontological status of the "apparently" speaking subject and that this "phenomenological" description is assembled exclusively from manifest "texts" instead of subjective perceptions.

87  See my discussions of Fodor and Barkow et al.

tiple neural sites of computation or modular agencies, obviously entails a rethinking of concepts like free will and personal responsibility.[88]

So far, so familiar. Where Dennett believes his theory adds something new is this: "Feature-detections or discriminations *only have to be made once*. That is, once a localized, specialized 'observation' has been made, the information content thus fixed does not have to be sent somewhere else to be *rediscriminated* by some 'master' discriminator. In other words, it does not lead to a *re-presentation* of the already discriminated feature for the benefit of the audience in the Cartesian Theater" (113; original emphases). This, too, has consequences. Since several agencies or "editors"—after all, someone or something needs to do the editing—are involved in this highly volatile and provisional process, all of them operating in accordance with their own specific terms of reference, aims, and techniques, and since there is no chance for revision in this staccato flow of mediation, we can never be sure that the output—what we "get"; the actual content of our consciousness—is accurate or not.[89] We are, it seems, at the mercy of our modules.[90]

What are the consequences of Powers's enthusiastic adoption of Dennett's ideas? In a first step, we can note that Powers adopts three of Dennett's basic assumptions. First, we encounter in *The Echo Maker* the notion that human consciousness is not only necessarily "natural," but that it needs to be understood in an evolutionary framework before it is viewed in cultural terms. Thus we are told with some certainty: "The evolutionary psychologists had that much right, at least. Older creatures still inhabited us, and would never vacate" (*EM* 231). Second, Powers incorporates Dennett's multiple-drafts model into his novel by citing it almost verbatim: "*Me* is a rushed draft, pasted up by committee, trying to trick some junior editor into publishing it" (415; original emphasis). Third, Powers struggles under the weight of the epistemological implications of the representationalist paradigm, which precludes anything like direct experience and instead installs a regime of mediation in which consciousness operates forever at a remove from physical reality. Powers's depiction of a world in which "[t]he senses were a metaphor at best" accounts for anguished passages in which his characters worry about the impossibility of immediacy and ruminate on how impressions are "never hot or cold, solid or soft, left or right, high or low, but only the image, the store. Only the play of likeness cut by chemical cascades" (*EM* 229, 364). As we will see, this

---

88 For a "reconstruction" of Dennett's multiple drafts theory that examines its assumptions and consequences more closely, see Akins.

89 See on this point also Dennett and Kinsbourne's comment that "[t]he 'stream of consciousness' is not a single, definitive narrative. It is a parallel stream of conflicting and continuously revised contents, not one narrative thread of which can be singled out as canonical—as the true version of conscious experience" (145).

90 This thought has prompted at least one explicator of Dennett to remark that rather than *Consciousness Explained*, this is a "deconstruction" of consciousness (Cunningham 82).

lingering sense of inauthenticity prepares the ground for the novel's ending, which attempts to resolve the problem of solipsism created by Powers's adoption of neuroscientific epistemology, a move that suggests that the author might share Weber's wish to find the self "at some level *above the module*" (190; original emphasis).

But a humanistic yearning to salvage the self is not the only consequence of the revised model of subjectivity that informs *The Echo Maker*. If brain science "launched the book's plot events, provided material causes, and shaped the characters' conscious understanding of their crises," as Powers has stated (Michod interview, n. pag.), its challenge to existing models of mind also poses problems for the literary representation of consciousness: after all, how does one evoke on the page the "riot of free agents" (*EM* 347) that constitute psychic life in the new materialist paradigm?

"Apart from the 'crane'-sections the text consists of the shifting accounts of Mark, Karin, and Weber, alternating between three third-person narrations," Laura Bieger says of *The Echo Maker*'s narrative construction (206). That is, the novel contains three different instances of focalization, and one instance of "pure" narration that consists solely of authorial description.[91] We can read this narrative presentation in light of the assumptions of Dennett's heterophenomenology, as an attempt to provide an account of "*what it is like to be* that subject—in the subject's own terms" at the same time that such an account is supposed to consist exclusively of transcriptions, of "texts," i.e., outwardly manifested, recorded, and observable behavior.[92] In accordance with this notion, readers of *The Echo Maker* are provided with renderings of the characters' interiority, transcribed in the words of the narrator, so that owing to the third-person perspective, we do approach something like Dennett's "neutral portrayal."[93] In keeping with this idea, we only ever view each character's physical appearance through the eyes of another, focalizing, character.

This limited third-person perspective may seem like a fairly conventional narrative mode commonly associated with the realist novel (Barrish 51; Palmer

---

91  Here we get the narrator describing the world of the birds, imparting zoological information about their behavior, incorporating bits of crane mythology, and engaging in authorial commentary: "When the surface of the earth is parched and spoiled [...], this world will start its slow return. [...] Nothing will miss us. [...] Cranes or something like them will trace rivers again. When all else goes, birds will find water" (443).

92  See Cunningham's remark that consciousness, "on Dennett's view, should not be understood by its phenomenal 'feel' but by the *behavior* it controls—linguistic or otherwise" (84; my emphasis).

93  See also Bieger's observation that "what we are reading cannot be taken as a direct transcription of subjective accounts of the three protagonists" because these transcriptions "orchestrated by the novel are synchronized by the poetic *choice*" inherent in third-person narration (211; original emphasis).

275), but in his interview with Stephen Burn, Powers claims otherwise. When Burn observes that *The Echo Maker* seems to him to "less explicitly interrogate the codes of realist fiction" than the author's previous works, Powers counters with a lengthy exposition of the ideas behind the book's formal composition:

> Because almost all of the book presents itself as a plausible, externally self-justify-
> ing narrative on the part of these three protagonists, it's easy to read the book as if
> it is purely mimetic or conventionally realistic fiction. [...]
> But once you take seriously the double-voiced narration and realize that every-
> thing you've read is focalized closely through participants who have all just demon-
> strated their utter unreliability (third-person unreliable narration!), another possi-
> bility arises—fiction exposed from *inside* the conventional. There is no place *except*
> the map, and yet we make the map together, by reading ourselves into one another,
> through conventions and codes, all of them provisional. (178; original emphases)

There are a number of implications to unravel here. First, Powers appears wary, defensive even, about the possibility that his book might be understood as "purely mimetic or conventionally realistic fiction." Second, he claims for his text an inno-vative mode of narrative presentation, namely "third-person unreliable narration." Third, he wishes us to read the text as "exposing fiction"—that is, highlighting its own fictionality—"from inside the conventional." And finally, he conflates text and extratextual reality, saying that both are a matter of constructing consensual "maps" through provisional "conventions and codes." In what follows, I would like to question the first two assumptions; the third will provide the transition to my discussion of the novel's ending.

Reading Powers's explanation, it is not clear just how the characters in *The Echo Maker* demonstrate "their utter unreliability" once we "take seriously the double-voiced narration." Powers borrows this concept from Mikhail Bakh-tin, who uses it, among other things, to describe a mode of telling in which two voices—that of the narrator and that of a character—merge in a single utterance.[94] A typical, short example from *The Echo Maker*, chosen at random, reads: "She kept reading to Mark: all she could do." (50). Here, the first part of sentence is pure narration, whereas the second part cannot be unambiguously attributed to either narrator or character. Another term for this would be free indirect discourse, or "consonant psychonarration" In Dorrit Cohn's terminology.[95] "I wanted to try writ-

---

94  In *The Dialogic Imagination* Bakhtin defines double-voiced narration, or heteroglossia, as "anoth-
      er's speech in another's language, serving to express authorial intentions but in a refracted way"
      (324); in *Problems of Dostoevsky's Poetics* he speaks of double-voiced utterances as having "the au-
      thor's ironic stamp" on them (96).

95  See Cohn 26-32.

ing a book that was almost completely double-voiced interiority presented as if it were externally narrated. Since the self is the ultimate reified story, this seemed the perfect book to try out that approach," Powers says (Burn interview 175-76). By describing as "double-voiced interiority presented as if it were externally narrated" what in narratological terms qualifies as third-person limited point of view, focalized through three different characters, and by saying he wanted to "try out that approach" (as if it had never been done before), Powers effectively claims as an innovation a narrative mode that has been in use since the nineteenth century.[96]

But why would this type of narration be unreliable? Clearly, the fault cannot lie with the narrator; after all, readers do not automatically distrust information given in free indirect discourse. And in fact, Powers tells us as much: he says the characters demonstrate *their* unreliability. How so? Given that we need to trust the narrator when he tells us that a certain character said or did something, the only possible domain of unreliability within the narrative is the realm of the characters' thoughts, feelings and perceptions, i.e., their interiority and motivations. This is a realm about which they could be deluded, and it is here that we are thrown back upon Powers's idea of the self as "the ultimate reified story."

If one subscribes to this understanding, it becomes justifiable to call the characters in *The Echo Maker* "unreliable" focalizers. "Third-person unreliability" would then mean that the characters' "reports" of their interiority and subjective experience were not "the things themselves" but only retrospectively assembled rationalizations of low-level, unconscious neural processes, and therefore not to be trusted. But before we grant this notion the status of a revolutionary narrative device, we should pause to ask: by this standard, what narration is *not* unreliable? It would seem that this is merely a matter of neurophilosophical perspective rather than a genuine literary technique. Powers appears to be doing little more here than swapping the Freudian unconscious of modernism for a contemporary, neural unconscious. Both function as powerful forces influencing characters' thoughts, feelings, and actions, but the latter lends itself less readily to literary representation: at the current stage of research, the modules and mechanisms of neuroscience are too general, too coarsely grained to rival the power of psychodynamic concepts to capture human experience.

Thus the neural processes that underlie the characters' behavior are exceedingly basic; aside from the deep-seated desire to "hide," to keep up a respectable, coherent façade in front of others as well as oneself,[97] the novel only gestures

---

96  And Powers should know: in the same interview he speaks of his familiarity with a number of narratologists, "such as Mikhail Bakhtin, Gérard Genette, Mieke Bal, Algirdas Julien Greimas, and Shlomith Rimmon-Kenan," which renders his claim for innovation even more curious (174).

97  In keeping with the biological imperative of survival, characters in the novel are repeatedly referred to as "self-protecting" (48, 120, 437).

vaguely toward romantic, or sexual, affects. It turns out that Weber returns to Kearney again and again not only to see Mark but also his Mark's nurse Barbara, with whom he eventually strikes up a short-lived affair. Likewise, Karin spends the book torn between two men, unable to sort out her urges, slowly working up toward the realization that her life has been merely "[o]ne small deceit laid on after another" (*EM* 407). Powers suggests that what makes these small personal deceptions neurobiological is that they remain shielded from conscious awareness for so long: "the *first person* is always the last to know" (*EM* 423; original emphasis).

These are hardly insights that require neurological knowledge, to which they are tied only in the most tenuous of ways. While presenting characters' thoughts in smooth syntactic and temporal order can with some benevolence be interpreted as a good fit for a novel preoccupied with consciousness as creating a "whole, continuous, and stable" illusion, realist conventions are ill-suited to convey a sense of the underlying "frenzied mass" of modular processes that the novel can only *name* but never evoke (*EM* 347). As readers, we only ever get access to the smooth surfaces of the character's phenomenal consciousness, modularity's finished product, as it were, and these are rendered even more conventional by Powers's writerly sensibilities, which tend toward the sentimental and the melodramatic.

In fact, Powers's determination to combine the third-person narration of subjective experience with the epistemic challenges of the neurochemical self lead to some awkward descriptive passages. Upon kissing Barbara, Weber "surges on the dopamine, the spikes of endorphins, his chest jerking. [...] He slips down into limbic back alleys, corners that survived when the massive neocortex came through like a superhighway" (428). Since dopamine, endorphins, and "limbic alleys" are precisely the kinds of things would seem to contradict rather than reveal singularity, passages like these are a far cry from the "neo-phenomenological" literature Patricia Waugh envisions as a response to the biomedical age that would "rescue the singularity of human experience from phantom objectivity" ("Turn" 24-25). It is not the case, then, that "the 'big' of biological determination" would "render the social as relatively 'little,'" as Lustig suggests in his article on *The Echo Maker*; rather, biological determination is tacked onto a sentimental version of the social (135).[98]

While it might indeed be worthwhile to try to develop a literary aesthetic capable of combining the insights of neuroscience with an understanding of neuroscience's "subjects" as human beings that think and feel, little is gained from having them feel only within the narrow bounds of heterosexual mating, which connects

---

98  Lustig's use of the big-little opposition refers back to Jim Neilson's identification of a number of binaries in Powers (described by Lustig as "'little versus big,' 'public versus private,' 'personal agency' versus 'cultural construction,' 'narrative' versus 'cognition'") that underwrite the "bi-directional" nature of his work (130).

biological accounts of behavior with the romantic conventions of nineteenth-century realism. The latter is not substantially transformed by the mere act of naming
the neurotransmitters involved in the interaction; if anything, the awkward juxtaposition of Powers's "fondness for the most stolid elements of old-fashioned realism" (Wood, n. pag.) and the contemporary neuroscientific lexicon emphasizes
the conventionality of the writing, which has prompted even former champions of
Powers to declare themselves dissatisfied.[99] Renouncing, or at least moderating,
his previous investment in the author, Joseph Tabbi now questions "whether the
form of the sentimental novel, which Powers maintains, is adequate to the knowledge base he purports to master." While "cognition and its evolution offer ample
mystery and a wide sky of unknowns," Tabbi writes, "it is not clear that fiction's job
is to fill those empty spaces with human sentiment" ("Afterthoughts" 226).

It appears then, that Powers's attempt to engage with neuroscientific theories about the self "from *inside* the conventional" prevents him from developing
a fictional form that could legitimately be called innovative. It is precisely the
constraints of typical realist fiction—third-person narration, a "stable" diegetic
reality, characters that conform to established conventions of psychological veri-
similitude—that work against the author's ambition to produce a new kind of
"neurological novel" whose aesthetics would be commensurate with its neurophilosophical underpinnings. "The scandal of an innermost multiplicity—of brain
parts, and beneath them, of axons and dendrites in their several billions [...]—is
a scandal that confronts the residually humanist novel in its innermost recesses,"
Julian Murphet writes, but *The Echo Maker* "refuses that confrontation in its form"
(192).

It may be that it is not an easy task to integrate the neurological scale into
the conventions of literary realism, which is why Powers fails to develop a narrative form capable of accommodating first-person phenomenal consciousness
and its third-person scientific explication in equal measure. That Powers puts forward such an elaborate exegesis of his own formal operations, and that he feels
prompted to do so in response to a question pointing out the rather obvious fact
that his novel is written in a realist register, would suggest that perhaps the only
way for his text to appear not only thematically topical but formally experimental
may be to retroactively present it as the product of sophisticated aesthetic considerations. Were he not to speak at such length about his work's form and "frame
it didactically with massive explanatory comment," its avant-garde credentials
would not be nearly as apparent (Ickstadt 27).

Lustig and Peacock pose a valuable question when they ask whether "linear
narrative, faced with the complexities of neurological systems and the ungrasp-

---

99  In 2002, Tabbi still celebrated Powers as an author of timely "cognitive fictions"; in 2008, Tabbi's
    "afterthoughts" on *The Echo Maker* take a distinctly more critical turn.

able nature of consciousness" might risk "looking increasingly outmoded and more suitable, perhaps, to some kind of Whiggish liberalism" (10). In a somewhat counterintuitive manner, *The Echo Maker* confirms this suspicion: Powers is unwilling to sacrifice either the centrality of narrative to human life or the fundamental primacy of human subjectivity. The novel's ending demonstrates this problem and discloses the author's normative ideas, since here, the "perspectivist" method of rendering information through the divergent perspectives of characters' consciousnesses gives way to a narrative mode heavily marked by authorial intervention.

In roughly the last seventy pages, the strict regime of tripartite focalization that has been sustained for most of the novel falters. Powers suddenly introduces two new perspectives, as the narration is now also focalized through Karin's boyfriend Daniel (390-95) and Mark's nurse Barbara (437-40). We can indeed read this, with Bieger, as a consequence of Powers's desire for "messaging," his need to convey "openness to community and environment" and "selfless" existence not only as ideas but as ideals, for the new perspectives go hand in hand with a succession of epiphanies distributed across different characters, all of which deliver curiously similar "disclaimers of selfhood" toward the end of the novel (Bieger 213, 203). Thus Karin discovers that she is "no one," which enables her not only to commit herself to the correspondingly "selfless" work of caring for the environment,[100] but also to experience life as occurring "everywhere—microscopic, vegetative, humming," suggesting all-encompassing connection and unity across the biome instead of an atomizing differentiation into individuals (418).

In keeping with this theme of de-individuation, toward the end of the novel Powers appears to engage in an all-out deconstruction of human subjectivity, which is disassembled into its smallest physical constituents. Consciousness is envisaged as traceable all the way back to the cellular level, to cells that, after eons of evolution, "exploded into hopes and dreams, [...] theories of other minds, invented places as real and detailed as anything material, themselves matter, microscopic electro-etched worlds within the world." In this view, human subjectivity is material "all the way down": at heart, consciousness consists of "[m]atter that mapped other matter" (364).[101] Such descriptions prepare the ground for the characters' "depersonalizations," which Powers presents as a consequence of their realizing that the self is a "painting traced on a liquid surface" and the brain a "set of changes for mirroring change" (*EM* 382).

---

100  "It's the most fulfilling work I've ever done," Karin declares; "Bigger than myself? How about bigger than anyone" (329).

101  This description is part of a lengthy passage in which Powers imagines the evolution of consciousness from "an ancient cell" through interactions with energy, a passage that, when read closely, betrays an indebtedness to DeLillo's "monadanom" section in *End Zone* (see chapter 3).

Like Karin, Weber experiences an epiphanic breakdown of personality, concluding that he has "[n]o whole left to protect, nothing more solid than braided, sparking cells" (451). This insight arrives on a cross-country flight, and it illustrates how Powers attempts to replace the classical humanist idea of man as the crown of creation with a seemingly posthumanist panorama of "life itself." It is fitting that Powers's neo-Darwinian novel works up to a scene in which Darwin's conception of "the world of the living—which equally incorporates the animal, the vegetal, and the human alongside protozoa, bacteria, and viruses" (Grosz, *Becoming* 13) underwrites a final review of the biological contexts of human consciousness:

> Even the sealed cabin around [Weber] has grown septic with life. Everything is animate, green and encroaching. Dozens of millions of species seethe around him, few of them visible, even fewer named, ready to try anything at once, every possible cheat and exploitation, just to keep being. He stares at his shaking hands, whole rain forests of bacteria. Insects burrow deep inside this plane's wiring. Seeds abide in the cargo hold. Fungus under the cabin's vinyl lining. Outside his little window flap, frozen in the airless air, archaea, superbugs, and extremophiles live on nothing, in darkness, below zero, simply copying. Every code that has stayed alive until now is more brilliant than his subtlest thought. And when his thoughts die, more brilliant still. (448)

Note that the posthuman "zoe" or "bios" is conceived here by human consciousness, and made to conform to its categories.[102] So the bacteria and microbes try, cheat and exploit, motivated by some kind of élan vital or will to live. It is only at the end of the paragraph that the human is being edged out by the informational, in the form of single-cell organisms that blindly persist by "simply copying." Here as in *Galatea 2.2*, life is at its most fundamental level genetic or computational "code," which not only rivals but outshines human cognition in its Darwinian ability to adopt. In the end, the certainty that biological life will continue after Weber's personal death, which stands metonymically for the end of human consciousness itself, evokes a quintessentially posthumanist decentering of the human.

We are reminded here of Lytotard's "Postmodern Fable" that imagines a posthuman narrative "concerned only with energy and matter as a state of energy," in which cosmic energy rather than a human or anthropomorphic character functions as the "hero" or agent of the story (98).[103] But this would be taking matters too far, for in *The Echo Maker* the consolation of this prospect is that life itself will still be "brilliant," and in this way still be judged according to human criteria. Powers

---

102    For the concepts of "zoe" and "bios," see Braidotti and Esposito, respectively.

103    See Herbrechter 4-7 for a discussion of Lyotard's fable as emblematic of a posthumanist imaginary.

presents us with a scenario in which the possibility that the human might be transitory is mitigated by the possibility that something analogous, something equally "brilliant," might continue. This, I submit, is not so much a demystification of what Marilynne Robinson calls humanism's "romance of the self" (10) as it is a neo-romantic re-enchantment of the natural world absolutely in line with a "transcendental pretence" that projects the categories produced by the human self onto the universe as such.[104] No wonder then, that Weber's epiphanic insight continues by shifting its focus from the microbiological onto the human sphere.

> But something else is messaging, too soft to hear. Through the plane's plastic windows, the lights of unknown cities blink beneath him, hundreds of millions of glowing cells linked together, swapping signals. Even here, the creature spreads countless species deep. Flying, burrowing, creeping things, every path sculpting all the others. A flashing electrical loom,[105] street-sized synapses forming a brain with miles-wide thoughts too large to read. A web of signals spelling out a theory of living things. (450)

The sense that is being conveyed here, of communication designated for a human recipient, may be in line with the novel's sustained focus on the ways in which reality can only ever be the product of epistemic processes of world-making, but it also underlines that this notion ultimately sustains an anthropocentric view of the ecosphere. Indubitably, these passages are about scale: we move from the microscopic to the macroscopic, and while the "messaging" of microscopic life can only be intuited for all its subtlety—it is "too soft to hear"—the "thoughts" of life on the macro-scale are "too large to read." Yet this romantic legibility of nature *is* being postulated, so the implication is that it might be accessible to a degree, at least to the poetic sensibilities of the literary author.[106] Following the writer's romantic intuition, we end up with a brilliant code, a brain with thoughts, and a web of signals, "spelling out a theory." It seems that there is no escaping the symbolic.[107]

---

104   The concept of "transcendental pretence" is Robert Solomon's. He describes it as having "two central components: first, the remarkable inner richness and expanse of the self, ultimately encompassing everything; and secondly, the consequent right to project from the subjective structure's of one's own mind" (1-2).

105   Powers here alludes to the early neurophysiologist Charles Sherrington's influential description of the brain as "an enchanted loom where millions of flashing shuttles weave a dissolving pattern" (178).

106   This is true in a double sense: Powers is certainly "authoring" these notions, but they are also focalized in the novel through Dr. Weber, who is, of course, an author in his own right.

107   See Ickstadt, who notes that *The Echo Maker* "may dramatize Powers's distrust of any notion of a self-reliant self; yet it also reveals his Emersonian awareness of an infinite network of relations: of mind and nature, of mind in nature—a unity pervading all particularities that constantly

This is of course very much in concordance with a humanist point of view, according to which, as Alain Robbe-Grillet writes, "it is not enough to show man where he is: it must further be proclaimed that he is everywhere." Robbe-Grillet holds that "metaphor is never an innocent figure of speech," and he tells us that "anthropomorphic analogies [...] reveal an entire metaphysical system" (53). Powers's metaphysical system, it would seem, is governed by an avid desire for correspondence and congruence and—the term "metaphysical" is apt here—a *belief* that because of such harmonies, man is in a sense indeed everywhere, for the code of life renders everything commensurable, human beings included. The "neural metaphor" that Powers grafts here onto an aerial view of human life "conjoins [...] individuality and dynamic collectivity: we are all cells in the great body of the city, and world," so that system and consciousness are reconciled (Gotman 79). This is indeed an image of a "vast, yet single cooperative organism," as Dewey has described Powers's vision of the world, and it is not only a "humane" vision but also a deeply anthropomorphic one (*Understanding* 70, 148). The mystic undertones of these passages are in fact reminiscent of the promise, ascribed by Žižek to "third culture" authors, that "egotistic individualism will be replaced with a transindividual cosmic awareness" (22). We would certainly be justified in regarding *The Echo Maker*, and perhaps Powers's whole oeuvre, as informed by "a new Romanticism" as much as a new naturalism (134).[108]

This impression is reinforced by the book's systematic reconstruction of human subjectivity in an intersubjective register. Not content to "lose the self" altogether (a prospect already rendered impossible by his unswerving attachment to realist modes of representation), Powers endeavors to formulate an alternative conception of subjecthood, grounded on the twin pillars of narrative construction and intersubjective recognition. "Just a scared struggle to build a theory big enough for wetware to live in" is one of the book's memorable descriptions of subjectivity (*EM* 274), but it is also an apt description of the book itself, which first invokes and then assuages the anxieties that a neuroscientific debunking of the self elicits. Curiously, the connection that Dennett establishes between cognitive modularity and narrative dynamics simultaneously provides the problem and the solution for this anxiety. For if, as Weber observes, "neuroscience had proved that symbols were real" and there truly is "[n]o place else to live," then an agreeable arrangement within this symbolic realm might be all that is left (354). Here we come back to Powers's claim that "we make the map together, by reading ourselves into one another, through conventions and codes, all of them provisional." Powers's insistence that there is "no place *except* the map" does away with postmodern

---

unfolds in an open-ended process of creation in which fiction and the fiction-making brain take part" (40).

108  See LeClair, "Prodigious," for a description of Powers as adopting a "new naturalism" (20).

"nostalgia for nostalgia, for the grand older extinct questions of origin and telos" (Jameson 156), instead encouraging us to stop worrying and love intersubjective constructivism: our brains might "invent" the world and everything in it (including ourselves), but at least we are all inventing it together.

As Bieger has pointed out, self-conceptions in *The Echo Maker* are curiously congruent with Paul Ricoeur's concept of narrative identity, and in fact the notion of an omnipresent narrative production informs an *ethics* of story construction that Powers wishes to extract from his neurological narrative.[109] If there is "no place else to live" but the realm of the symbolic, the logic goes, we might as well consider this our "true" habitat, and since symbols are only intelligible by virtue of their communicability, a life coterminous with narrative is by definition intersubjective. This, at any rate, is how Powers attempts to curb the danger of solipsism inherent in the representationalist paradigm of his neuroscientific sources. "Story was the storm at the cortex's core," Weber muses, but this fundamental primacy of narrative need not spell inauthenticity, since it cuts both ways: "We told ourselves backward into diagnosis and forward into treatment" (414). There is a curious slippage here, from accepting the tenets of a neurophilosophy that denies the self any reality to an ethics of narrative responsibility that demands that "we" who are spun by our tales also spin tales ourselves that are in some way desirable or beneficial rather than harmful and destructive.

Thus Mark describes himself—with refreshing simplicity—as "some totally invented asshole," but he, too, needs to experience some communion with nature and remark that it is "not all so bad," gesturing "out the window, approvingly: the Great American Desert. The inch-deep river. Their next of kin, those circling birds" (420). As far as subjecthood is concerned, the novel ends on a markedly optimistic note: "If all forged, then all free. Free to play ourselves, free to impersonate, to improvise, free to image [sic] anything. Free to weave our minds through what we love" (*EM* 426). This is quite a turnaround for a novel that only 45 pages earlier recounted the famous Libet experiment, which is widely cited in support of arguments against free will, and concluded that "[t]he *we* that does the willing is not the *we* that we think we are" (381; original emphasis).[110] Faced with so many claims for the benefits of depersonalization and the awe-inspiring omnipresence of biological life, we might indeed be excused for calling the end of Powers's "case for wonder" (Houser 403), this paean to "Emersonian awareness" (Ickstadt 40) as

---

109  See Bieger 3-5.

110  In the 1980s, neuroscientist Benjamin Libet conducted experiments that appeared to prove that a neural "readiness potential" preceded a voluntary decision by test subjects to perform a flick of the wrist. This finding has often been taken up to argue that free will is an illusion, retrospectively introduced into cognition. For the original account, see Libet; for a cogent critique of the adoption of Libet's findings in philosophy (particularly in affect theory), see Leys.

rather too "tidy" and "comforting" (C. Harris 249)—or, at any rate, as trying too hard to be just that.

There is a curious sense of resignation here at the end of the novel, perhaps best expressed in the final scene that Karin and Mark share. Recently recovered thanks to pharmacological intervention and newly aware of what has happened to him, Mark is nonetheless left shaken, imbued with epistemological doubt: "This is what scares me: if I could go so long, thinking...? Then how can we be sure, even now...?" (447). After his experience with Capgras, he is no longer certain that anything he experiences is more than a construction of his individual, susceptible consciousness. Yet when Karin starts to cry, he consoles her by directing her gaze through the window and on to the world outside, saying, "It's not all so bad, huh? Just as good, in fact. In some ways, even better. [...] I mean us. You. Me. Here. [...] Whatever you call all this. Just as good as the real thing" (447).

This, then, is the final, conciliatory note Powers strikes after his book-length depiction of the "scared struggle" of "wetware." The boundary between inside and outside, symbolized here by the "plate-glass window" through which the siblings gaze out onto a "the Great American Desert," is rendered less prohibitive simply by ignoring the ontological difference that it installs in the first place (447). Thus, the desert of the real becomes "just as good as the real thing," and the danger of solipsism, that specter haunting epistemology after Descartes, is kept in check by the idea that narratives can be validated through a mechanism of mutual recognition: "You. Me. Here." Ever since *Galatea 2.2* and throughout most of *The Echo Maker*, Powers has been developing the notion that a construction might be an illusion, yet here he reverses the idea. "Instead of 'interrupting' the world image that keeps us comfortable within our own illusions, as he himself prescribed, [Powers] makes cognition into a staging site where people can come together and understand one another better," Joseph Tabbi concludes, and asks: "All this brain-power, all this conceptual cogency, and for what? To tell stories of remembered childhoods and loves unrequited, unfulfilled, and unpursued?" ("Afterthoughts" 228-29). I contend that apart from perpetuating the "most stolid elements of old-fashioned realism," Powers's invocations of "brain-power," i.e., the human brain's characteristics and capacities, may indeed serve another function as well, which I would like to discuss in conclusion to this chapter.

## Chapter Conclusion: The Apotheosis of Narrative

"The identity, which we ascribe to the mind of man, is only a fictitious one," David Hume, ancestor of today's neuroscientific deniers of the self,[111] argued in the eighteenth century, a position that has since been rehashed regularly (169).[112] As we have seen, Powers's work aligns itself with various accounts that reject the "reality" of the self. For all its nods toward modularity, the dominant mode of *Subjektkritik* in *Galatea 2.2* was still more closely associated with its postmodern variant, operating under the paradigm of the essential inseparability of text and self-enunciation. Here in the earlier novel, we still saw Powers playing with the ontological ambiguities of a narrator who speaks of "a portfolio that now seemed the work of someone else," or of having "another fiction" in him (3; 328). This changes in *The Echo Maker*, where self-referentiality is traded in for mimetic representation and the characters' ontological instability is no longer rooted in their status as (meta)fictional constructs but in the neurological "illusion of solidity" that underlies their self-perceptions (258). Yet both books end with paeans to the power of narrative as a force capable of creating "a place wide enough to live in" (*GA* 321), a poïetic principle operating at the neural level that warrants both regeneration and freedom: "We are every second being born" (*EM* 450).

To discuss Powers's apotheosis of narrative, I would like to return to the concepts I have introduced at the beginning of this chapter—Tompkins's notion of cultural work and Bourdieu's field theory. But before doing so, a word about terminology may be in order, since understanding Powers in terms of Tompkins's theory of cultural work might seem somewhat counterintuitive. After all, the rather well-adjusted Powers clearly is not out to "redefine the social order," nor do his upscale literary productions, aimed at an educated readership, strike one as designed to "win the belief and influence the behavior of the widest possible audience" (Tompkins xi).[113] I therefore propose to adopt a "toned-down" version of

---

111  Mark Johnson claims Hume as having anticipated the insights of current neuroscience and describes "naturalistic accounts of mind" as proceeding from Hume through James to Damasio (13). Likewise, David Williams considers Hume's thought "strikingly similar to what neuroscientist Antonio Damasio has shown in his research" (91), while Bruce Hood imagines the historical Hume as a fellow Scot contemplating "the self illusion" in a "dull, drizzly, [...] Edinburgh" (x).

112  "The self does not really exist as something truly real," Raymond Tallis sums up, "because: it is not available to introspection (Hume); it is not a thing (Existentialists); it is a soluble fish in a sea of general meanings or representations (postmodernists); and/or it cannot be found in the brain or its activity (neurophilosophers)," an enumeration to which one could also add Buddhism and Indian philosophy ("Saving," n. pag.).

113  The desire to be "enshrined" in a "literary hall of fame," on the other hand, may be more familiar to Powers (Tompkins xi).

cultural work in this concluding evaluation of Powers's project.[114] After all, Powers, too, has "designs" upon his audience and seeks "to make people think and act in a particular way," even though his designs and his audience are more narrowly circumscribed than those of the early American writers Tompkins discusses (xi).[115]

But how can we describe Powers's "designs" and the cultural work they aim to perform? Tompkin's insistence that "forms of non-fictional discourse, when set side by side with fiction, can be seen to construct the real world in the image of a set of ideals and beliefs in exactly the same way that novels and stories do" is suggestive here (xv), for it points us toward Powers's intellectual contexts, which do, in fact, exist "side by side" and in a mutually constitutive relation with his work. Drawing on the "two cultures" trope that Powers so often invokes, we could describe the non-fictional discourse that surrounds it as marked by the attempt to establish a "third culture," a unitary language capable of uniting the humanities and the sciences.

Powers's champions have long claimed for his novels a quasi-scientific, or quasi-philosophical, status as "science as much as fiction" (Kucharzewski 272). We need only think of Latour's praise of Powers as "the author of science studies" or Daniel Dennett's description of Powers's novels as "scientific fiction" and "a contribution to the scientific imagination" ("Letter" 161). Arguing in the same vein, Sarah Birge claims that "neurofiction" provides a valuable source of knowledge for scientific and medical practitioners, so that literature "provides a model of what it might be like to be someone else, synthesizing information into a compelling story that helps us better understand social interactions" (96-97). Needless to say, Powers himself perpetuates such views: in a *Harvard Book Review* interview he contends that "[a]ll arts and all sciences are components of that speculative, recursive, self-revising process of making and testing meaning" (n. pag.).[116] Seen this way, the cultural work of Powers's novels consists in contributing to a process of knowledge-production in which scientific and literary discourses are essentially on equal footing. However, I would like challenge this idealistic image on a number of grounds.

---

114  I am not the first to do propose such an approach: it is testament to the adaptability of Tompkins's concept that it has in recent years seen use in studies of American iconography, magical realism, and sports writing.

115  Tompkins's project of developing a "new kind of historical criticism" that would not neglect popular (and populist) or "sentimental" works of fiction previously deemed inappropriate due to "glaring artistic defects" is obviously larger in scope than Powers's target audience (xii-xiv).

116  See also John Johnston's claim that Powers's novels "model and reflect new forms of postmodern subjectivity […] by serving as exemplary instantiations of a contemporary psychic apparatus, registering and material and semiotic processes which are not yet entirely assimilable" (*Information* 8).

First, Powers's wide-ranging metaphoricity rests on the wholesale acceptance of the scientific theories it operates with. Amid all the enthusiasm for a fertile exchange between science and literature, it is important to note that "in overrelying on the neural metaphor, a seductive, protean image to describe every sort of conjunction," authors like Powers, "depend on scientific discovery, and on science's 'objective' truth" (Gotman 75). Indeed, one of the problematic aspects of Powers's project is his wholesale acceptance of certain tenets of cognitive neuroscience. If Susan Blackmore, a leading researcher in the field of consciousness studies, admits that after interviewing the most important experts in her discipline, she can neither claim to understand the phenomenon better than before, or even be sure that it exists at all (Introduction 10), Powers's conviction that consciousness is best understood as an epiphenomenon of low-level brain processes appears not only strikingly steadfast but somewhat credulous.

Second, Powers claims vast erudition for himself, as when he mentions in an interview that the authors he reads in his research "tend to be the practitioners, rather than subsequent general-readership folks" (Burn interview 176), but this claim seems overblown: all of the scientists he mentions have published books for a popular audience, and the comprehension of scientific and medical discourses in *Galatea 2.2* and *The Echo Maker* never transcends the level of sophistication of precisely the "general-readership folks" that Powers deems below his standards. In its facile assumption that constructedness of the self is tantamount to its "unreality," *The Echo Maker* resembles nothing more closely than the popularizations of neuroscience one finds in books like Bruce Hood's *The Self Illusion*.[117] If we take into account Powers's "well-behaved" reliance on scientific research, the cultural work of his texts seems to consist mainly in the popularization of "third culture" tropes—a "soft posthumanism" that renders posthumanist ideas like the modularity of consciousness commensurate with humanistic assumptions about the freedom of narrative invention.[118]

Third, Powers presents us with a biased rather than a balanced account of the state of research in a given field, since he tends to concentrate on the theories that enable him to make the points he wants to make. Thus *Galatea 2.2* and *The Echo Maker* are heavily influenced, as we have seen, by the connectionist paradigm and the notion that consciousness is the product of the evolutionary development of

---

117  Upon closer inspection, we even find that Hood and Powers cite the same experiments in support for their thesis that the self is an "illusion": see Powers, *EM* 381-82 and Hood.

118  See Tabbi, who notes, "Powers's mastery of information is no less deep or extensive than Pynchon's, but he is *much better behaved*, much more inclined to keep his imagination within the frame of what science allows and technology licenses. Powers is much more disciplined than his literary predecessors, when it comes to processing information from other fields. But it is a discipline that serves these scientific fields and these professional discourses better than it serves the semi-autonomous development of literature" ("Afterthoughts" 227; my emphasis).

the human brain. However, contrasting voices, for example those that argue for an embodied cognition not wholly locatable within the confines of the skull, do not figure in these texts at all.[119] Thus opposing viewpoints, which are a crucial part of scientific practice, are swept under the rug. If Dennett describes Powers as making "a contribution to the scientific imagination," one suspects it might be because his writing favors Dennett's model to the exclusion of alternative accounts, but one might question how "scientific" such slanted presentations really are.

Fourth and last, knowledge production with the means of literature seems to be of secondary importance to Powers, whose metaphorical impulse is primarily directed by his belief in the power of literature and informed by the goal of "keeping the faith in fiction" (Sielke 258). A good example is what Kélina Gotman calls the "neural metaphor"—the mapping of physiological and neurological functions onto other conceptual realms—which according to Gotman "offers a seductive portrait of society and human life: networked, changeable, full of flows of information and capital and goods, conveniently biological as well as subject to a form of free will" (72). In both *Galatea 2.2* and *The Echo Maker*, consciousness is transposed from the realm of human beings to that of computers, the ecosphere, and—finally and most importantly—literature itself, where it is recharged with human agency and freedom. Perhaps Powers's project is best understood not as quasi-science or quasi-philosophy but as appropriating the prestige and explanatory power of science and technology, as well as their attendant philosophies, in order to elevate the humanistic *technē* of literature, which is seen as losing ground to the sciences.

Ickstadt is right to note that if Powers wants to safeguard the efficacy of his fictions, he "has to rely on the reader's ability to read right" (27). But on an even more fundamental level, he has to inspire belief in the continual social and aesthetic relevance of literature, and it is the production of this belief that his entire oeuvre aims at. One can hardly avoid the suspicion that the "astonishing number of interviews that have accompanied the publications of his novels" is directly related to this aim (Ickstadt 27). In the end, the cumulative effect of Powers's rampant metaphoricity is to refer back to the author's own poetics, which he readily explains at every opportunity, lest readers lose sight of it. The function of his work as quasi-scientific is thus everywhere subordinated to his roving metaphorical impulse, and this metaphoricity always recurs back to ideas about literary narrative as inherently valuable, which makes Powers's oeuvre almost uniformly interpretable: hence the many scholarly accounts of his work that see all his novels as

---

119   I am thinking here particularly of thinkers working in the phenomenological tradition, like Alva Noë, Evan Thompson, Francisco Varela, or Dan Zahavi.

pursuing one coherent and identifiable project.[120] I thus argue that the author's main concern—and the ultimate rationale behind his "apotheosis of narrative"—lies in elevating the status of literary fiction, a move that can be explained by Powers's location within a "field of cultural production" suffused with anxiety about the status of literary fiction in a changing media ecology.

"Given that the work of art exists as such (i.e., as a symbolic object endowed with meaning and value) only if it is apprehended by spectators possessing the disposition and the aesthetic competence which are tacitly required, one could say that it is the aesthete's eye which constitutes the work of art as a work of art," Pierre Bourdieu writes ("Historical" 257). For the "aesthete's eye" to recognize something as art, rules and guidelines must be in place. Here Bourdieu's field theory is instructive, since the patterns and "commonly held assumptions" (Tompkins xvi) Powers draws on are codified within, and according to, the field of "high" literature in the United States at the turn of the millennium, its dynamics and unwritten rules.

Powers produces the kind of literature, James Wood remarks acerbically, that "gets prizes, or gets nominated for prizes [...] precisely because it is hiding in plain sight: it sounds like every other middlebrow realist novelist, and so probably something like the Novel itself" (n. pag.). In fact, one of the recognizable templates that Powers's fiction follows is that of the nationally significant novel of ideas, the "Great American Novel," an artistic ideal that has remained curiously impervious to the postmodern dispelling of master narratives. In his study of the "G.A.N." phenomenon, Lawrence Buell invites us consider "the spate of doorstop books of the late 1990s that tried to sum up the century, or at least the half-century" (3).[121] Powers would have to be included in this list, if not for *Galatea 2.2* and *The Echo Maker*, then certainly for *The Gold Bug Variations* and *The Time of Our Singing*, books which similarly weave expansive narratives around twentieth-century American history and can be understood as "compendious meganovels [...] acting and interacting in relation to epoch-defining public events or crises"—in this case, the deciphering of the human genetic code in the 1950s and the race riots of the 1960s, respectively (Buell 8).[122] Powers himself certainly subscribes to the notion of

---

120 Such overall assessments of Powers's project often invoke its inherent humanism. See, for instance, Tabbi's remark that Powers "has been eagerly claimed by literary humanism as a sustained attempt to reintegrate the alienated self" (*Cognitive* 62), or Burt's description of Powers's work as informed by a "scientific humanism" whose "subject is not collapse but convalescence" (n. pag.).

121 Buell mentions David Foster Wallace, John Updike, Philip Roth, Don DeLillo, Neal Stephenson, and Jonathan Franzen by name, painting the quest for the "G.A.N." as an exclusively male pursuit.

122 Additionally, these works fulfill Buell's "doorstop" criterion, weighing in at 640 pages each in the hardcover editions. Generally, Powers's novels rarely drop below the 350-page mark.

literature as "carrier of the DNA of the national imaginary" (Buell 464), seeing as he does "the archive of literature as the race's high-level genome" (Neilson interview 20).

The elevation of the novel from a form of popular entertainment to the status of high (or "fine") art can, in the U.S. context, be traced back at least as far as Henry James, and such "elevations" have since seen periodical rearticulations that depended for their rhetoric and character on their specific historical contexts, as Mark McGurl has shown.[123] In Powers we see a contemporary variety or manifestation of this recurrent impulse to boost the prestige of "literary" fiction. Needless to say, elevation can only occur in relation to a point of reference, so it might be worthwhile to inquire after the cultural objects Powers against which Powers defines his work. The most telling statement in this regard comes from his interview with Jim Neilson, where he states that *Galatea 2.2* allowed him "one last intimate occasion to address the issue that ties all of my books together: the apology for fiction in a postfictional age" (22).

In 1913, G. H. Mead could still say that "the Western world has lately done much of its thinking in the form of the novel," but throughout the late twentieth and early twenty-first century the role of the novel as the central arbiter of cultural relevance has increasingly been called into question (147). This is the background against which to understand Powers's oft-repeated claims for the potential and relevance of the novel form. It is no coincidence that Powers's description of the novel as a "supreme connection machine" evokes the world wide web: "The internet is merely the latest of the competitors that print culture has been pitted against since the late nineteenth century," Kathleen Fitzpatrick reminds us (*Anxiety* 3). While the "death of the novel," or its transformation into something hitherto unrecognizable, has been proclaimed or prognosticated with some regularity throughout the twentieth century, from Walter Benjamin's "Krisis des Romans" to Alain-Robbe Grillet's *Pour un Nouveau Roman* and Jon Barth's "The Literature of Exhaustion," the trope gained new currency around the turn of the millennium with the advent of new media, and subsequently exerted a significant influence on literary authors susceptible to worries about the novel's cultural relevance.[124] Looking back, we could say with Fitzpatrick not only that in the 1990s, "the death

---

123  See McGurl, *Novel*.

124  A typical example is Sven Birkerts, who in his tellingly titled 1994 book *The Gutenberg Elegies* postulates "a deep-down connection between our cognitive and communications behaviors and our imaginative and affective being," and proposes that "we have to ask whether the historically sudden emergence of an electronic network, rapidly binding us all into a web of signals and data, has begun to change us at an affective level, has not blocked off emotion with distraction" (245).

of the novel is alive and well," but also that professions of an "anxiety of obsolescence" can serve strategic functions (*Anxiety* 26).[125]

In his study *Cognitive Fictions*, Joseph Tabbi identifies "a new mode of writing
about the self when measures of both selfhood and literary evaluation are up for
grabs," noting that electronic environments have "brought to the foreground writers who work self-consciously with narrative as an artistic medium—one medium
among many possible media struggling for representational primacy" (ix). As
Fitzpatrick points out, such self-conscious preoccupations with the ostensible
vulnerability of the novelistic medium can serve to circumscribe a "protective
space" around literary production—specifically "high" literature—that functions
as a mark of distinction for precisely those authors most invested in its ongoing
existence and relevance (*Anxiety* 4, 26). Thus for Jonathan Franzen, high cultural
literacy, manifest in the production of letters and literature, is aligned with an
image of human beings as more than the sum of their physical parts. Invoking the
*Phaedrus* and assuming himself "at the other end of the Age of the Written Word,"
Franzen muses:

> The will to record indelibly, to set down stories in permanent words," "seems to me
> akin to the conviction that we are larger than our biologies. I wonder if our current
> cultural susceptibility to the charms of materialism—our increasing willingness
> to see psychology as chemical, identity as genetic, and behavior as the product of
> bygone exigencies of human evolution—isn't intimately related to the postmod-
> ern resurgence of the oral and the eclipse of the written: our incessant telephoning,
> our ephemeral e-mailing, our steadfast devotion to the flickering tube. ("Brain" 33)

It is striking, in fact, that Powers, Wallace, and Franzen—each of whom has signaled interest in the implications of a materialist imaginary—have all put forth
poetological theories about the status and the function of the novel in a new
media regime.[126] Developing their work in relation to American authors like Barth,
Coover, and Gaddis, themselves adherents of a literary style "self-conscious about
its identity as a period, conscious of its own historicity," these writers inherited
the self-consciousness of the earlier postmodernists (McHale, n. pag.).[127] Despite
their many substantive differences, they all share in what William Paulson calls

---

125   An important aim of Fitzpatrick's study is also to draw attention to the possibility that such
      claims might serve to preserve white male hegemony in literary production. See Fitzpatrick,
      *Anxiety* 49-50.

126   See Franzen, "Perchance" and "Difficulty," as well as Powers, "Being," "Conversation," "Dia-
      logue," "Making," Burn interview, and Wallace, McCaffery interview and "Unibus."

127   On the three writers as sharing a common cultural and literary-historical background, see
      Burn, *Franzen* 16-17.

the "cultivation" of literature "as practices of resistance to the hegemony of electronic information processing systems" (21).[128] As a result of attempts to install the
sphere of "serious" literary fiction as a "protected space" (Fitzpatrick *Anxiety* 26),
theories about the role and function of the novel "have never been so robust (or so
commercially viable) since the rise of modernism" (Tabbi and Wutz 19).

To clarify: I do not mean these observations as a moralizing ascription of
ulterior motives. As McGurl emphasizes, we can see the literary career as a "thoroughly self-interested game" à la Bourdieu, but we can also regard it as a Hegelian
struggle for recognition, the dialectical dynamics of which underline that these
"projects of individual authorization are in fact always collective endeavors," two
perspectives that do not have to be mutually exclusive (*Novel* 20). We should therefore read Powers's "positioning" both as a collective endeavor in the sense that it
would afford the same privileges to fellow practitioners of the writing profession,
and as an individual quest for distinction and cultural as well as financial capital
that entails strategizing and calculating market dynamics. Both efforts can only
be understood against the background of the literary field of late-nineties U.S. fiction.

Locating Powers's work within this historical and cultural context enables us
to understand his use of the "neural metaphor," which draws on materialist models of mind to establish a correspondence between the narratives of consciousness,
self, and literature, as a strategic move intended to safeguard literary fiction's status as an epistemological instrument of the first order.[129] Seen this way, recourse to
neuroscientific and biomedical discourses functions and the idea that "the brain is
itself the ultimate narrator as well as the supreme focalizing protagonist" (Powers,
"Lakehouse" 459) function as a "containment strategy" that ensures the relevance
and social interest of the author's literary production (Tabbi, "Afterthoughts" 227).
This also helps explain the Powers's appeal for academics. For illustration, we can
turn to Lustig and Peacock's recent volume on *Diseases and Disorders in Contemporary Fiction*. Here the interest U.S. literary authors take in neurological symptoms

---

128 That the postmodernists' heirs insist on the autonomy and value of literary fiction has to do
not only with the audiovisual media ecology of the nineties, but also with the critique of postmodernism as having been absorbed, reified, and rendered ineffectual by the mass media,
which was widely circulated at the time: see for instance Hal Foster's description of a nineties
culture in which "market and media are all but symbiotic" (122) and postmodernism, "treated
as a fashion [...] became *démodé*" partly because it was "emptied out by the media" (206; original
emphasis). This idea had previously been put forward by David Foster Wallace in his famous
account of the complicity of television and advertising in using postmodernist techniques for
interpellation effects ("Unibus"). Not coincidentally, Wallace's magnum opus *Infinite Jest* also
touches on the tension between "serious" art and "mere" entertainment.

129 Powers has suggested narrative as "the elemental connection between literature, science,
cognition, and consciousness" ("Lakehouse" 457).

6. Neural Narrative    263

is treated as a symptom in its own right. True to the Jamesonian roots of such a project, the editors ask in their introduction whether the "syndrome syndrome" might not be "a symptom of something else in the political unconscious," such as a new biologism.[130] The phenomenon, they contend, may well be the "manifestation of crisis, a belated bid for relevance on the part of an increasingly marginalized body of intellectuals whose subjects—consciousness, identity, the self—have been taken over by scientists" (Lustig and Peacock 4). Viewed this way, a body of work such as Powers's, which draws on newly ascendant disciplines like cognitive science, neuroscience and evolutionary psychology and advances the view that literature is not only able to incorporate these disciplines' findings but actually on a par with science as a mode of epistemological inquiry, could surely be regarded as a helpful ally in claiming continued relevance for the academic study of literature.[131]

Thus we can see Powers not only as an actor in the field of literary production, but also as an agent that enables mutually beneficial follow-up communications between the artistic field of literature and Bourdieu's larger "intellectual field," which includes academia. This, in any case, is the conclusion with which I would like to end this chapter, since it directs our attention to an interesting phenomenon worthy of further study: against our initial intuitions, engagement with materialist models of mind might not necessarily result in a zero-sum game in which humanistic interpretations and meanings lose out to neo-naturalist facts. In the case of Powers, we can see how posthumanist or new materialist ideas can in fact serve to underwrite claims for the continual relevance of humanistic and literary practices, even though the methods used to arrive at these conclusions remain controversial and open to question and critique.

---

130  This amounts to a leading question, since a few pages later, the authors provide their answer: "Twenty years ago, the notion of social or cultural determination tended to take precedence. However, students in the early twenty-first century are much more likely to say that 'nature' (in the somewhat limiting formula) is at least as important as 'nurture,'" and that "[w]e live in, or think we live in, a world ruled by science, and if not by science then by nature-that which science tries to understand" (9).

131  This appears particularly pertinent once we conceive of the fields of literary and academic production as "arenas of struggle for legitimation," as Bourdieu does (Swartz 123; original emphasis).

# Conclusion

> We are at all moments in History and in matter; at one and the same time historical beings and "natural" ones, living in the meaning-endowment of the historical project as well as in the meaninglessness of organic life. No synthesis—either conceptual or experiential, let alone symbolic—is conceivable between these two disjoined realms.
>
> *Fredric Jameson, "Baudelaire as Modernist and Postmodernist"*

> To be a character is to have a textual existence and, momentarily, to appear to exist beyond it. To be a person is to inhabit a physical and fantasmatic body, to wear the mask which is truly your face, to speak with the voices of others—to be defined at your very heart by the non-personal; and, at any moment, to appear to have a life that exists beyond it.
>
> *John Frow, Character and Person*

## Summary and Findings

After an introduction to the concept of "materialist minds" in relation to recent U.S. literature and a discussion of key terms and concepts, the present study began with a chapter on the burgeoning genre of the "neuro-memoir," i.e., autobiographical writing that examines the connection between subjectivity and the nervous system in a biomedical context. This chapter demonstrated that a new materialism of the mind entails revisions of subjecthood. Neuro-memoirs, I argued, attempt to integrate the third-person perspectives of science and medicine with the first-person view of subjective experience, and thereby to account for cerebral subjectivity as well as narrative identity. Illustrating how new discourses of mental (dys)function give rise to new registers of self-understanding, the texts give voice to those who are personally affected by these epistemic transformations. Prefacing my subsequent discussions of fictional texts with an examination of autobiographical accounts composed by authors who, in the eyes of sociologists, qualify as "cerebral subjects" or "neurochemical selves" has gone some way, I hope, toward preventing their reduction to conceptual abstractions.

Having thus introduced the philosophical as well as the practical stakes of my topic, the next chapter shifted the focus from the memoir to the novel and focused on Don DeLillo, whose work I invoked as an "early and influential example" of literary fiction's engagement with the motif of materialist minds. Through four of the author's novels, I traced how DeLillo presents the new materialism of the mind alternatively as a concomitant effect of (post)modernity or as a force in its own right (albeit one that nonetheless produces effects resonant with postmodern art and philosophy). In these texts, the "decentering of the subject" is presented as an effect not only of medialization but of medicalization, a point previously neglected in DeLillo scholarship. Yet for all his critical commentary on the quantitative measurement and material manipulation of the mind as a questionable outgrowth of modern science and technology, DeLillo also proves genuinely curious about the biological basis of subjectivity and interested in the clues that fields like neuroscience and evolutionary biology may provide. Their findings, however, are never simply restated; in fact, DeLillo consistently presents the "cerebral subject" as an anthropological figure that is always mediated through cultural discourse and human concern, so that the new materialism of the mind is itself cast as a construct of consciousness, and as such, fit for literary design and metaphoric production.

David Foster Wallace, whose magnum opus *Infinite Jest* provided the subject of the subsequent chapter, was an ardent admirer of the older author's work, and we see DeLillo's influence not only in Wallace's use of neuroscientific research but also in his interest in the reciprocal relations between mind and body. *Infinite Jest* bears the stamp of the shift toward the biomedical paradigm that was taking place in the late eighties and early nineties, and it zeroes in on processes of conditioning, compulsion, and habit to complicate a Cartesian understanding of subjectivity as primarily mental and cognitive. In my analysis of the inverse trajectories of the two main characters, I argued against the predominating interpretation of the book as a therapeutic intervention, emphasizing instead its obsessive circularity. The text's cyclic dynamics perpetuate ambiguity and paradox, and they do so with recourse to a looped, recursive conception of embodied subjectivity, which provides a model for the continuous generation of contradictory and polysemous effects. Its apparent critique of volition and self-consciousness can never be the last word; rather, the text encourages us to engage in cyclic, potentially "infinite" readings, in a process resembling nothing more than the Möbius strip or the Serpienski triangle, Wallace's avowed structural model for his novel.

The last chapter focused on two novels by Wallace's contemporary Richard Powers. Similarly influenced by DeLillo's method,[1] Powers produces "novels of ideas" that question humanistic conceptions of selfhood by presenting the evolved organ of the brain as the origin of a constructed consciousness whose seeming unity belies the fact of its fragmentation. With Powers, the motif informing my study reaches a somewhat contradictory culmination: on the one hand, his engagement with "materialist minds" is more comprehensive than that of his predecessors; on the other, his willingness to accept the assumptions of evolutionary and neuroscientific theories of the mind translates into a less experimental, more unidirectional literary aesthetics that draws on scientific discourses for its thematic and formal aspects but never questions the fundamental validity of its theoretical models. Throughout much of these texts, Powers steers a middle course between deconstructing and reconstructing the human subject's capacities, moving from cognitive science to neurology and evolutionary psychology as the discourses licensing these revisions. Yet conspicuously, both novels end in what I call the apotheosis of narrative, a discursive strategy Powers implements to argue for the undiminished agency of the self as well as the continual relevance of literary fiction, which assumes a modeling function akin to that of the brain.

## Motifs and Tropes

My analysis yields a historical sequence of motifs and tropes that suggests that the presence of "materialist minds" in recent U.S. literature depends as much on literary tradition and intertextuality as it does on scientific and cultural contexts. In the 1970s, Don DeLillo introduces the lateralization and localization of cognitive, emotional, and linguistic capacities into U.S. literary fiction. While concepts like cerebral hemisphericity or the Triune brain originate in neuroscientific and neurobiological research, DeLillo receives them from reports about brain research that appear in the *New York Times* and *The New Yorker* from the late 1960s onward as well as from popular science publications like Nigel Calder's 1971 book *The Mind of Man*.[2] Emerging ideas about the materiality of mental life thus enter "serious"

---

1  Powers has written a glowing introduction to the 25th anniversary edition of *White Noise* and identified DeLillo elsewhere as "an enormous influence" ("Geeks," n. pag.).

2  See Burn, who argues that newspaper and magazine articles served as "an important storehouse of technical terms and concepts" for DeLillo, who incorporated "small phrases" from such sources into his novels ("Neuroscience" 210). On Calder's book as a source for DeLillo, see Burn, "Mapping" 38.

or highbrow literary fiction at the same time that they reach a larger audience through science journalism and the mass media.

This pattern will remain in place throughout the following decades; one can observe a dynamic of literary response to new materialist ideas as they migrate "from the lab to the social world" (Rose and Abi-Rached 229). This migration occurs with the help of authors and journalists, but also through transformations in the sphere of public and mental health. Following the 1980 publication of the DSM-III, interest shifts to pharmacology, as the idea of psychotropic drugs that work selectively on specific brain regions, functions, or neurotransmitters simultaneously gains traction in medical practice and cultural representation. This trend toward "biomedicalization" (Clarke et al.) leaves its mark in books such as Jamison's *An Unquiet Mind*, DeLillo's *White Noise*, and Wallace's *Infinite Jest*. Though the pharmaceutical paradigm continues to shape present-day conceptions of psychic life and mental illness, it is joined in the 1990s and 2000s by an increased interest in the modularity of mind, owing mainly to the influence of cognitive science, as well as in the evolutionary origin of brain functions, a topic popularized by publications like Steven Pinker's *How the Mind Works* (1997) and *The Blank Slate* (2002) and palpably present in Shawn's and Powers's books in particular.

But the role of materialist minds in American literature cannot be reduced to the response to, or representation of, scientific and cultural contexts; my analysis has also indicated the importance of literary models. It is noteworthy that the three novelists I have discussed share certain motifs and concepts, suggesting that intertextual transmission matters just as much as the engagement with extraliterary source material. Given DeLillo's influence on Wallace, *Great Jones Street*'s aphasia-inducing "product" can certainly be understood as providing a template for *Infinite Jest*'s lethal "Entertainment," which produces similar, if decidedly more severe, disabling effects. By the same token, we can regard *End Zone*'s figuration of football players as "substandard industrial robots" and "retarded computers" as a model for *Infinite Jest*'s "robotic" athletes whose mindlessly repeated training routines become "wired" into "the hardware, the C.P.S." (117-18). DeLillo's influence also accounts for the transmission of his interest in Paul MacLean's model of the Triune brain: it is taken up by Wallace, who specifies that the Entertainment's victims are affected "on some deep reptile-brain level" (*IJ* 549), as well as by Powers, who seizes upon the tripartite differentiation into "reptilian," "old mammalian," and "new mammalian" brain parts to delineate the psychic life of his characters (*EM* 17-18).

There are then cultural as well as artistic reasons for writers' increasing use of the materialist minds motif. On the one hand, materialist models of mind are becoming increasingly ubiquitous, from psychological theory to psychiatric practice and the cultural sphere; on the other, the archive of texts discussing such models is growing steadily, providing foils for subsequent literary treatments.

Don DeLillo's early novels, which are published in the first stages of the "neuro-scientific revolution,"[3] still have little more than a few publications to go on, while Wallace's *Infinite Jest* appears in a cultural climate undeniably more accustomed to, and pervaded by, medical materialism. Powers, finally, can draw on an entire tradition of cognitive science and neurophilosophy, whose proponents have become newly vocal and influential in scientific and intellectual circles by the turn of the twentieth century.[4] Given this steady agglomeration of material, both in the literary and the cultural sphere, it is only natural that these new textual bodies also call forth new designations, from the "third culture" (Brockman) and "neo-naturalism" (Kelleter, "Tale") in the academic realm to the "neuronovel" (Roth) or the "syndrome novel" (Burn, "Mapping") in the field of literary writing. Here, two trends are observable.

First, neuro-materialist ideas are becoming increasingly "naturalized" to the effect that novels published in the past two decades reveal a tendency to integrate biological and neural explanations into the description of characters' feelings, thoughts, and behaviors. Whereas DeLillo and Wallace still regard the neurobiology of the brain as an esoteric research field, a concomitant of postmodernity, or, at any rate, a relatively novel cultural determinant, and tend to use it primarily in metaphoric capacities, it acquires the status of an accepted "fact" of psychic life in more recent novels. Thus authors have begun to describe the "spikes" in dopamine and endorphine production during amorous encounters (Powers, *EM* 428), to correlate the flow of "natural opiates" with improvements in their characters' mood (Eugenides 104), to cast compulsion as an irrevocable neurological disease resisting signification (Ferris)[5], or to imagine dystopian scenarios in which drug experiments on human beings reveal their experience, emotions, and cognitive abilities as almost completely dependent on their internal neurochemical milieu (Saunders).[6] In this newfound attention to the subcutaneous determinants of sub-

---

3  The phrase is Edelman's (*Bright* xiii).

4  See for instance Brockman's collections on the "third culture" and the "new humanists," movements that, as Brockman writes, consist of "those scientists and other thinkers in the empirical world who, through their work and expository writing, are taking the place of the traditional intellectual in rendering visible the deeper meanings of our lives, redefining who and what we are" ("Introduction" 17).

5  About to commit suicide, after "his mind told him to pull the trigger," the protagonist of Ferris's the *Unnamed* finds himself caught "in a struggle so primitive that it could not be named" and has to concede that his body speaks "a persuasive language of its own, singular, subterranean," an expression of what he later calls "an unassailable cellular will" that supersedes conscious volition (109, 269).

6  In Saunders's dystopian short story "Escape from Spiderhead," experimenters administer drugs that dramatically affect the main character's perception, his "language centers," and libido (45, 53).

jectivity, we see how the neuro-materialist imaginary is shaped by the different levels of observation and description that can be brought into focus in the portrayal of human behavior. Whereas characters have traditionally been described in psychological and physiological terms, under the influence of cognitive science and neuroscience, the description of cognition, emotion, and action now opens up onto the previously unexplored realms of the cellular and the molecular as well as their electro-chemical interactions.

Second, this historical shift is accompanied by a gradual modification of the characteristics that the texts ascribe to the materialist minds they depict. While DeLillo and Wallace make much of the analogies and potential interfaces between humans and machines and mainly imagine fixed predispositions, Powers presents the brain as part of a nervous system that is constantly adapting to, and changing in accordance with, embodied experience in a social world.[7] We move, then, from an image of the material mind as manipulable but "hardwired" to one that emphasizes its plastic, flexible, and networked nature, "every path sculpting all the others" in a "web of signals" (Powers, *EM* 450).[8] It is no coincidence that the biology of subjectivity I have been tracing here is a shifting, evolving construction that sees its momentary culmination in the notion of neuroplasticity, itself an avatar of constant reconfiguration. As I argue in the following, *renewal* and *revision* may be the most appropriate terms we can use to describe the functions of materialist models of mind in recent American literature. The remainder of the conclusion will therefore be dedicated to a discussion of how these terms modulate four different aspects, or functions, of "materialist minds" in the texts I have examined: the conception of subjectivity, the representation of consciousness and character, the formal design and metaphoricity of literature, as well as its social and aesthetic functions.

## Renewal and Revision I: Conceptions of Subjectivity

Motivated in part by pragmatic, biographical concerns, as in the neuro-memoir, and in part by philosophical or aesthetic interest, as in the novels by DeLillo, Wallace, and Powers, reconceptualizing subjectivity has been a central concern of all

---

7  Here we can contrast the discussion of electrodes in DeLillo (244) and Wallace (*IJ* 472), the idea of fear as a primal instinct, the "earliest wetland secretions of dread" that are lodged in "brain stem and midbrain" (DeLillo, *RS* 381), and the notion of "hardwired" proclivities for substance abuse (Wallace, *IJ* 393, 546) with Powers's description of consciousness as "Matter that mapped other matter" and the brain as a "set of changes for mirroring change" (EM 364, 382).

8  This is, admittedly, a somewhat simplified picture that neglects the central role Wallace affords processes of conditioning and habit in *Infinite Jest*, a book that is concerned with the constitutive role of what Catherine Malabou calls "this plasticity that makes us" (*Brain* 7).

the texts considered here. As I have shown, medical and scientific discourses are of central importance for these revisions, yet each text reconfigures subjecthood in its own way. Though the representation or reimagining of the human subject in material and biological terms is a singular affair in each case, some general patterns can be observed. These emerge most clearly when juxtaposed with the polarity between the "essential," autonomous self of the Cartesian tradition and the revisionary *Subjektkritik* of postmodern and poststructuralist philosophies.

Descriptions of a historically dominant model of the subject are often invoked as a starting point or baseline for critical revisions: Nikki Sullivan's reference to "the humanist notion of the subject as a unique, rational, autonomous individual whose relations with others are secondary, and whose desires and actions are transparent to him or herself" can serve as a typical example here (41). This "Cartesian" concept of the self as stable, unitary, reliable, and primarily mental, i.e., contained within the confines of one's own head, has been called a "consensual orthodoxy of the west" (Belsey ix) that has been in place since the Enlightenment (Mansfield 13-24), though its roots reach back to antiquity.[9] In the texts I have discussed, it undergoes significant revision.

Here, biological, bodily and neural subjectivity is presented as mutable, manipulable, and therefore inherently vulnerable.[10] Traumatic brain injury, as exemplified historically by the Phineas Gage case and depicted in literary form in Powers's *The Echo Maker*, can lead to "explosive plasticity," the radical transformation of externally observable personality and internally experienced subjectivity (Malabou, *Wounded* 20).[11] But the cerebral or somatic subject is as susceptible to biochemical manipulation as it is to injury. In their respective neuro-memoirs, Lewis and Clune put the modification of volition and behavior through legal and illegal substances front and center, as does Wallace, who presents a veritable compendium of chemical compulsion in *Infinite Jest*. Reconceptualized as a switchboard for physical interactions, so that "the addict's need for dope opens his mind-

9   See Richard Rorty's description of the "picture of the self common to Greek metaphysics, Christian theology, and Enlightenment rationalism," which he views as based on "the idea that the human self has a center (a divine spark, or a truth-tracking faculty called 'reason')" (*Objectivity* 175, 188).

10  When Steven Pinker speaks of the "overwhelming evidence" that we can reduce the self to the activity of the brain, this is what he has in mind: "The supposedly immaterial soul, we now know, can be bisected with a knife, altered by chemicals, started or stopped by electricity, and extinguished by a sharp blow or by insufficient oxygen" (64). The novelty of this "evidence," however, is disputable: "You don't need futuristic new technologies to expose the brute fact that there's nothing but meat inside our heads," Paul Broks writes. "We've known this down the ages" (49).

11  In *The New Wounded*, Malabou discusses cases of severe brain injury in which "the patient's personality is transformed to such a degree that it might never regain its lost form" (47). For the concept of explosive plasticity, see also Malabou, *Ontology* 5-6.

body system to the world" (Clune 173), the human subject also becomes amenable to manipulation, or conditioning, through embodied practices and rituals, which Clune and Wallace present as essential to recovery: "you nod robotically and keep coming, and you sweep floors and scrub out ashtrays and fill stained steel urns with hideous coffee, and you keep getting ritually down on your big knees every morning and night," as *Infinite Jest*'s narrator describes the arduous process, emphasizing its corporeal components (350).

What emerges in such passages is a picture of the "susceptible somatic individual" (N. Rose, "Anomalies" 411), for whom habit and regimes of bodily management and care matter as much, if not more, than the conscious capacities of the Cartesian cogito. This reevaluation of the merits of self-consciousness also links Wallace with Powers, whose novels *Galatea 2.2* and *The Echo Maker* subscribe to a notion of the self as fundamentally deluded about the degree of its own transparency. In a more general sense, all the authors I have discussed attempt to come to terms with a revised picture of subjective awareness as merely the tip of the iceberg, perched precariously on a scaffold of automatic and unconscious low-level process that both enable and delimit the subject's epistemic reach.

If subjectivity is "all a question of brain chemistry, signals going back and forth, electrical energy in the cortex," as Heinrich suspects in DeLillo's *White Noise* (45), the self is little more than a belated justification following on the heels of neural processes, a narrative construction or façade that smoothes over what Julian Murphet calls "the scandal of an innermost multiplicity" (192). Not only is the subject unreliable and opaque to him- or herself; more fundamentally, an emphasis on the modularity of brain and mind calls into question our "intuition" of being a unitary, self-identical entity that "occupies" a body (Broks 107). In DeLillo's novels, drugs target the "language sector" (*GJS*) or the "fear-of-death part of the brain" (*WN* 200). In *Infinite Jest*, Wallace negotiates anxieties over the implications of neural "pleasure terminals" that might override the subject's conscious decisions (471). And in *The Echo Maker*, confusion ensues when "the part of [the] brain that recognizes faces" is split off from "the part that processes emotional association" (61). Likewise, in the realm of the neuro-memoir Hustvedt discusses the "various emotional systems in the brains of all mammals" (88), Shawn describes the evolutionary stratification of cerebral architecture (62), Lewis delineates how every subjective experience emerges from "a particular brain system, neurochemical flow, or synaptic process" (3), and Clune localizes addiction as "a memory disease" (1). The cumulative effect of all these fragmentations, localizations, and structurations is to disrupt the sense of a unitary self and disperse it into a distributed set of autonomous or automatic processes, a plurality of agencies replacing a central executive.

If subjectivity has always been conceived as a site of division and conflict, this newly emerging plurality of parts and processes only adds to the confusion. Little wonder, then, that the ordering powers of narrative are cast as an indispensable mechanism of integration and synthesis. This is particularly true for the neuro-memoir, where, in Carolyn Barros's scheme, the *persona* of the first-person narration provides a retrospective assessment of the *figura* of the cerebral, somatic, or neurochemical self. That, strictly speaking, no privileged position of evaluation can exist in a paradigm that installs fiction at the center of cognition is not necessarily seen as obstructing such projects of meaning-making.[12] On the contrary: the inescapability of narrative self-understanding and the inaccessibility of the neural and neurochemical processes underlying subjectivity's "wordless storytelling" (Damasio, *Feeling* 186) turn the ongoing investment in the "surface effects" of the self into an activity without alternative, in the full knowledge that such investments can only ever be provisional. We see this dynamic in Clune's memoir, where disavowals of selfhood ultimately give way to the cumulative agglomeration of markers of narrative identity, as well as in *The Echo Maker*, whose characters, faced with overwhelming evidence that all variants of experience are "fictional," finally resign themselves to a poietic mode of existence they deem "[j]ust as good as the real thing" (447).

In the absence of access to "the real," ontological grounding for a narrative reconceptualizations of the self is often provided through intersubjectivity and the realm of embodied experience, whose subjective sensations remain barred to "objective" scientific description. As an inherently social medium, narrative links first-person perspectives to the shared world of social meanings, a notion in which Powers's novels in particular regularly take refuge. Thus at the end of *Galatea 2.2*, the components of fiction are described as "public inventions" (328), while *The Echo Maker* supplies the handy formula, "If all forged, then all free," which is based explicitly on an intersubjective situation: "You. Me. Here" (426, 447). Similarly, in *Ratner's Star*, DeLillo makes the linguistic expression of embodied subjective experience the guarantor of ontological validity: "I can't get there but I know it is there to get to. On the other side is where it's free," Billy insists (370). In this sequence at the close of the book, DeLillo privileges "the body's fundamental reality" (*RS* 37), experienced in the irreducible quality of the first person, over third-person scientific inquiry. Thus when Billy comes upon an underground river, he feels "no special need to see it, photograph it or take samples home to study. He had *tasted* it, after all" (373; original emphasis).

One would not be amiss in locating philosophical precedents for these ideas in the relation between postmodernist and phenomenological conceptions of the subject. On the one hand, the idea that the world is only a neural representation and the self no more than a "useful fiction" maps as neatly onto the notion that "there is nothing outside of the text" (Derrida 158) as it does onto the characteris-

---

12  "Story was the storm at the cortex's core," as Dr. Weber suggests in *The Echo Maker* (414).

tically postmodern sense of "ontological instability and indeterminacy, the *loss* of a world that could be accepted [...] as a given of experience" (McHale 26; original emphasis). In the same vein, the prioritization of local, situational contexts over universal statements and the emphasis on intersubjectivity resonate with post-modernism's refusal of the *grands récits* and its attention to the significance of the "other" for subject-formation.[13] On the other hand, the realization that subjective experience remains an undeniable datum even (or especially) if one brackets "reality" to deal exclusively with *phenomena*, and the notion that such experience is crucially distributed throughout the body and entwined with the world have clear antecedents in pragmatist and phenomenological philosophies, whose insistence on the validity of embodied experience may seem to stand at odds with postmodern avowals of uncertainty.[14]

The texts I have examined generally reveal an uneasy relationship with postmodernism: their focus on the materiality of the mind can be seen both as a reaction against, and a continuation of, postmodern conceptions of the subject. "The standard social science model of everything being culturally constructed in some ways has it backwards," Richard Powers has argued. "Something must, in fact, construct culture, and something other than 'culture' does give language its shape, even before language shapes our sense of self." Powers's suggestion that the humanities are paying too little attention to the "couple of billion years of evolution" he proposes as an important cultural determinant is indicative of a sensibility that suffuses the texts in my corpus, namely the suspicion that the social constructivist theories of subjectivity developed by psychoanalysis, poststructuralism, and postmodernism leave something to be desired ("Generalist" 102).

Wallace, for one, has voiced doubts about the psychoanalytic assumption "that etiology and diagnosis pointed toward cure, that a revelation of imprisonment led to freedom" ("Unibus" 67), and *Infinite Jest*, with its palpable disdain for psychotherapy and its obsessive registering of pharmacological effects and chemical compounds, bears the mark of a revised conception of psychic life. As I have argued, this is also a central concern of the neuro-memoir. Though they hold psychoanalysis in high regard, both Jamison and Saks emphasize the necessity of biomedical intervention and medication. Shawn, meanwhile, reminds the reader that "our bodies and minds are perpetuating behaviors refined over millions of

---

13  "Postmodern thinking, if it means anything at all, means a philosophy of 'alterity,' a relentless attentiveness and sensitivity to the 'other,'" John Caputo argues (453).

14  This is not to give short shrift to the foundational importance of phenomenological thought for postmodern philosophies: as Laura Doyle points out, "the phenomenological helped to make the postmodern thinkable" (xiii), and both discourses operate with epistemological doubt to take us "beyond (or behind?) the individual *cogito*, the autonomous, self-willed subject" (Godway 161).

years" (47), and Hustvedt points out the limitations inherent in the "recent fashion for social construction" (183).

But for all these avowals of the need to account for biology in discussions of subjectivity, there is a simultaneous sense of a continuity that connects past critiques of the subject with new materialist perspectives. The apparent commensurability of neuroscientific thought and postmodern *Subjektkritik* in particular has already drawn some critical attention. In their conception of self-consciousness as "a sociocultural construct, a fiction that produces effects that are necessary and explainable but also problematic and amenable to critique," many neuroscientists appear to partake in the critique of the philosophy of the subject that is widely considered as a mainstay of postmodernism (Krüger 68; my translation). Unsurprisingly, literary texts that operate with, or refer to, materialist models of mind inherit this predisposition, so that the modular, stratified, and functionally differentiated nature of the brain translates into a reconceptualization of the human subject as fragmented, distributed, and "decentered."

This tension runs through all the texts I have discussed: motivated in part by the perceived shortcomings of previous conceptions and critiques of the subject, a reassessment of subjecthood in the materialist terms developed by the third-person discourses of science and medicine ends up reinforcing the very decentering effects those critiques initiated. In contrast, an emphasis on lived, embodied, and socially shared first-person experience serves to reinstall the validity and ineluctability of subjectivity as an epistemological and ethical category. There is without a doubt an element of philosophical correction or intervention to these re-imaginings of subjectivity, but they are not an end in themselves. Therefore, one also has to examine how these revisions provide the conceptual basis for further acts of renewal, specifically in the realm of literary production.

## Renewal and Revision II:
## The Representation of Consciousness and Character

Alan Palmer notes that "fictional minds" tend to develop in tandem with "parallel discourses" that refer to "real minds" (29), and if literary history is any indication, we can indeed expect new models of mind to be accompanied by novel ways of representing consciousness and selfhood in literature.[15] Jamesian psychology famously influenced the stream-of-consciousness technique, while Freudian psychoanalysis created an awareness of the ego's unconscious substrates that informed modernist aesthetics; later, the import of post-WWII French philosophy

---

15 Palmer mentions "psycholinguistics, psychology, and the philosophy of mind" as examples of such parallel discourses (29).

significantly shaped postmodern texts that dissolved individual consciousness into linguistic and semantic networks. Does the increasing presence of "materialist minds" in U.S. writing occasion a comparable aesthetic transformation? Do the revisions of subjectivity outlined above also affect the textual production of human consciousness and fictional characters?

Without denying each text's singular quality, we can make some general observations concerning the delineation of character under the sign of medical materialism. First, the engagement with materialist models of mind can (but does not have to) produce a "flattening" of interiority. DeLillo's novels are notable, and influential, in their refusal to provide their main characters with the kind of "deep" affective subjectivity that readers of psychological realism had grown accustomed to. While DeLillo retains the formal framework of the realist novel, most importantly a stable and "recognizable" diegetic reality devoid of openly metafictional elements,[16] he seems loath, particularly in his early work, to conform to customary modes of presenting characters' motivations and "inner lives." Understanding DeLillo's characters as "expressions of—and responses to—specific historical processes" (Lentricchia 2) or as "melded with their material and media environment" (Laist 5) goes some way toward explaining this "new kind of superficiality" (Jameson 9). But it is also striking that this flatness (which pertains not to characterization itself but to psychodynamic notions of interiority[17]) often appears in conjunction with discourses emphasizing the materiality of mind, such as psychopharmacology and neuroscience.

A similar, yet more selective effect can be observed in *Infinite Jest*, where Wallace has the Jamesonian "waning of affect" (10) take center stage in the form of the character of Hal Incandenza, who suffers from "anhedonia" and a lack of interiority: "inside Hal there's pretty much nothing at all, he knows" (694). Hal's condition is explicitly cast as the result of a misguided ideology that treats the entirety

---

16  Writing on Walter Abish and Don DeLillo, Winfried Fluck asks why it is that these rather experimental-minded authors "still retain an illusionist mode of representation as the basis of their aesthetic effects," and goes on to suggest that one explanation "for this surprising reemergence of realistic representation even in experimental writing may be that, in keeping with the realist tradition, this mode makes it possible to reinsert the question of experience into the narrative" ("Surface" 79). Note that Fluck does not speak here of experience per se, but rather the *question* of experience, which goes beyond the rather simplistic claim that the postmodern movement can be understood as, or reduced to, a self-referential enterprise that has since been "supplanted by a mode of writing that enthusiastically embraces the idea of a world beyond text" to include operations that problematize the very possibility of experience and its interrelations with modes of mediation (Kucharzewski 227). See also Civello for an assessment of DeLillo as a writer in the naturalist tradition.

17  In other words, DeLillo refuses the depth psychology that Alex Woloch regards as a central "generic achievement" of the realist novel (19).

of the human person as a machine, but the text also performs the emptying out of what Charles Taylor calls "our deep nature" (*Sources* 376) through its relentless focus on processes of conditioning and habit, which unite the novel's large cast of characters and have caused critics to suspect Wallace of fashioning a new kind of distributed and material selfhood based in embodiment (Russell) or "anti-interiority" (Freudenthal).

Powers, in contrast, remains dedicated to the affective grammar of liberal humanism and the traditional realist novel, though his consistent focus on the neural and biological structures by which emotion, cognition, and behavior are produced, as well as his repeated treatment of the self as a "deception" (*GA* 88) or "illusion" (*EM* 327), threatens to counteract his designated project of integrating first-person experience with third-person scientific discourse. As I have argued, it is precisely their refusal to translate the potentially explosive implications of neurophilosophy into a commensurate aesthetics that makes Powers's novels both more predictable and less radical than DeLillo's and Wallace's texts.

A concomitant of this flattening of interiority is a reduced sense of personal agency. Convinced by his girlfriend to get high before a game, Gary Harkness, the narrator-protagonist of DeLillo's *End Zone*, only watches in mute fascination as the other players wreak havoc all around him; finally, he just wanders off the field. This passage is paradigmatic not only in its illustration of the interdependency of subjectivity and its underlying neurochemical organization, but also in its suggestion that under a new materialist framework, it may be less productive to place one's trust in the powers of the cogito than to "let the conditions determine how our bodies behaved" (*EZ* 194). In the same vein, Bucky Wunderlick, who "remains mostly a passive recipient" in *Great Jones Street* (Osteen, "Dedalian" 149) and Jack Gladney, the spectacularly incompetent protagonist of *White Noise*, whose half-hearted attempt to spring into action and "become a killer" is rendered as an extended farce (*WN* 293), suggest that established models of volition and agency may be irreconcilable with a new paradigm in which human action is reduced, per Jack's intuition, to "molecules active in my brain, moving along neural pathways" (306).

DeLillo's protagonists thus resemble the "hero of non-action, the catatonic hero" that Hal envisages in *Infinite Jest*, a figure that encapsulates Wallace's own doubts about the limits of agency and free will (142). Paradigmatically contained in the AA slogan "My Best Thinking Got Me Here" (1026 n.135), corruption of the cogito figures as a central theme of this novel, which presents solipsism and selfishness as "parasitic on the fact of human consciousness" (Bolger 37). Utterly helpless in the face of addictions and compulsions and thus willing to submit to *programs* that condition their embodied subjectivity through the management of routines and rituals, the book's characters cede agency and autonomy to networks of material practices.[18] Programs are also important for Powers, but in *Galatea 2.2* and *The Echo Maker*, they become internalized as neural subroutines and evolutionary scripts, which underlie behavior and the retrospective justifications of the conscious self. The latter, in this scheme, is per se deluded and delayed, "always the last to know," so that Powers's characters constantly labor under the illusion of possessing an agency that has in fact been transplanted to low-level processes taking place in body and brain (*EM* 423).

It is probably no coincidence that the flattening out of interiority and the diminution of agency occasioned by materialist models of mind resembles postmodern ideas about the discursive nature of literary characters: Mark McGurl suspects that twentieth-century skepticism about the reality of fictional characters may in retrospect appear as "a quaint preface to the deeper and more widespread intimation of 'posthumanity,'" an anthropological figure that connects postmodern ontological doubt to our current cultural moment, "when neuroscience is letting the air out of some assumptions that have propped up our species' self-image for as long as we can remember" ("Zombie," n. pag.). But McGurl's worries about the effects of new materialist ideas on the novel, which sound a lot like Marco Roth's,[19] neglect how the revised picture of the "cerebral subject" or "neurochemical self" might also entail a *return* of responsibility.

Whether in the memoir or the novel: when literary "characters and persons" (Frow) are presented as inherently susceptible and mutable, a new premium is placed on management and self-care. We see this in the neuro-memoir, where the burden of managing and making sense out of one's cerebral and neurochemical embodiment falls squarely at the feet of the writing subject.[20] But we also see it in *Infinite Jest*, where the communality of twelve-step programs may go some toward replacing personal volition, while the decision to submit to them as well as the willpower to stay sober "one day at a time" remain the recovering addict's personal responsibility. Likewise, the characters in Powers's *The Echo Maker* are presented as dependent on the modularity of the evolutionary brain, but they are also tasked

---

18  Both tennis training and twelve-step programs are presented as perceptive technologies of self that work by "offering a set of practical steps [...] that must be applied rather than a series of beliefs that must be adhered to" (Bolger 33).

19  McGurl asks: "What should the novel do once consciousness has been physically 'explained'? What happens to the tradition of novelistic realism stemming from Austen when the reality is that we are all a bunch of tottering skin-bags animated by neural subroutines?" ("Zombie," n. pag.).

20  One can make a connection here to the concept of "neurodiversity," according to which conditions and forms of embodiment previously designated as pathological are recast as variations within a continuum, and the responsibility of managing them is (partly) transferred from public health professionals to the individuals themselves: see Jurecic, Ortega, "Cerebral," as well as Silberman.

with owning up to, and accepting, what the novel calls "the truth of our scattering" (164).

Thus we are faced with a curious situation in which the subject is simultaneously fragmented and left to piece itself back together again. The "plastic brain" is both the site of contesting autonomous neural processes and "a site of choice, prudence, and responsibility for each individual" (Rose & Abi-Rached 52). Therefore, even though the self is theorized as a mere epiphenomenon of material processes, it still remains tasked with coordinating the implications of these processes, as Ian Hacking ("Cartesian Vision") and Nikolas Rose (*Politics*) point out. Rather than truly subsuming the mental and the volitional under the physical, replacing personhood with "brainhood" and characters with cerebral routines, the human subject remains intact—at least in its role as the responsible administrator of the brain's properties and susceptibilities.[21]

Moving from literary characters to the representation of consciousness, we see similarly complex effects. The novel may be "an aesthetic map to and experience of the nature of the mind-brain," as Kay Young argues, but it also stands in a complicated relation to the "mind-brain's" material and mental components (9). On the one hand, the literary representation of consciousness always already implies a conceptual dualism in that it assumes a realm of interiority distinct from corporeal existence and aims to provide a representation of inner or "mental life" (Cohn 38).[22] On the other hand, there is an "anti-Cartesian aspect" to the tradition of novelistic consciousness originating in the modernist novel, due to the "influence of Bergsonism, pragmatism, and phenomenology," discourses that cast subjectivity as inextricably tied to, and predicated on, embodiment (B. Miller 7).

While early psychology's insights about the embodied, i.e., temporal and perspectival nature of subjectivity were readily translatable to literary texts, the reconceptualization of the mind at the neuroanatomical and molecular level is harder to integrate into aesthetic procedures. Julian Murphet contends that the "multiple in our very midst" constitutes "a scandal that confronts the residually humanist novel in its innermost recesses" (190, 192). Literary texts, which are often characterized as spaces that make it possible to enter another person's mind, can function as phenomenological simulators, depicting and performing subjective experience simultaneously (Palmer 29-30). Since the material substrates of subjectivity are not accessible to consciousness, they would appear capable of entering literature only if posited from a third-person perspective. Consequently, the

---

21  For the concept of "brainhood," see Birge as well as Vidal.

22  As Brook Miller argues, the literary representation of consciousness entails "the emergence of a non-material self (or at least a belief in a self) who feels distinct from materiality," yet the perception of oneself as "distinct from materiality" has to be understood as a "perceptual illusion" (2-3).

difficulty of including them rewrites the "hard problem" of consciousness studies as a problem of literary representation.

In other words, viewing human subjects as material objects is a tenuous affair in life as well as in literature. "Persons are singled out from the rest of our environment as recipients of love, affection, anger, and forgiveness," Roger Scruton writes ("Brain" 35), and as a phenomenon shaped by human concern, literature adopts this idea of the person, which thereby enters the "moral economy" of literary texts (Frow 120). But the concept of the person "resists translation into the idiom of neuroscience" (Scruton, "Brain" 35), which is why novels so often package information about the materiality of the mind in discursive passages, most commonly in characters' speech. This also explains why texts that use third-person narration to negotiate related themes sometimes tend to switch to the first person in passages that negotiate the merits of subjective experience.[23] More than anything, the contrast between these perspectives illustrates the difficulty of integrating objective scientific descriptions with phenomenological descriptions of subjective qualia.[24]

As a consequence of this difficulty of achieving integration, the engagement with materialist models of mind has not led to notable formal innovations in the literary representation of consciousness. The fact that the texts I have examined here, as well as others I have mentioned in passing, continue to operate with and within the aesthetic procedures handed down through literary history suggests that the arrival of a "new fiction" that would offer more than "hermeneutic access to mind" may still be a little ways off, or never arrive at all (Waugh, "Thinking" 79). But perhaps in this particular case we might want to look back, not ahead: Waugh, for instance, has argued that the ideas gleaned from new materialist sources may be more compatible with modernist writing than with contemporary literary texts.[25] For signs of an innovative impact of "materialist minds" on literary aesthetics, we will have to shift focus, from the representation of characters and consciousness to more general aspects of formal design and metaphoric activity.

---

23  See the "I Am Not Just This" and the "I Take a Drink" sections in *Ratner's Star* as well as Hal's first-person narration at the beginning and the end of *Infinite Jest*.

24  See Baker, *Saving* and *Naturalism*.

25  Waugh contends that the account of mind emerging from the cognitive neurosciences "seems uncannily to bear out the literary performance of thinking—and thinking about thinking—that happens in much modernist fiction" ("Thinking" 76). For a similar argument, see Lehrer, who argues that literary authors (Walt Whitman, George Eliot, Marcel Proust, Virginia Woolf and Gertrude Stein) anticipated the insights of contemporary neuroscience.

## Renewal and Revision III: Formal Design and Metaphoricity

As has been amply demonstrated, materialist theories of mind draw in no small measure on analogical thinking and metaphoric substitutions for their operative ideas and concepts (Bennett and Hacker 256-57; Jacobson 27-29).[26] But as my study has shown, the process of metaphoric exchange works both ways: with the rise of new discourses of mental (dys)function, new registers of self-understanding become available, and the concepts and figures of thought developed in science and medicine are readily adopted by literary authors to fashion their texts' formal features. The conceptions informing the texts I have considered here generally conform either to the cybernetic or the evolutionary metaphor, respectively casting human beings as machines or animals. More specifically, recurrent concepts, dynamics, and motifs within these "fundamental metaphors" (Daugman 11) have included the modularity of mind, the localization of brain regions, the nervous system's phylogenetic history, the representational nature (and limits) of consciousness, neural plasticity, as well as cerebral hemisphericity and the lateralization of brain functions.

Contrary to what critics like Marco Roth have suggested, these are not simple appropriative acts that import the reductionist orientation of the natural sciences along with their ideas. Literary authors have significant leeway in how they integrate new materialist discourses into their work, which is perhaps best illustrated by the innovative ways in which they transform theories into tropes, and concepts into metaphors. We have seen a particularly sophisticated example of this in *Ratner's Star*, where DeLillo models the central conflict as well as the setting of the novel on theories of the interdependency of brain/body and mind. Likewise, Wallace makes use of behaviorist ideas about the identity of physical and mental states to portray the ideology of conditioning at *Infinite Jest*'s tennis academy, and develops a circular narrative dynamic that, as I have argued, is based in notions of embodied subjectivity one finds in sources like Gregory Bateson's biological cybernetics. Powers engages in such processes of modeling most enthusiastically and overtly, discussing in interviews how *Galatea 2.2* establishes analogies between neural networks, brains, and books, or how *The Echo Maker* attempts to incorporate Daniel Dennett's multiple-drafts model into the representation of characters and consciousness.

Here as elsewhere, form and content can ultimately not be separated: when DeLillo uses the structural motif of lateralized brain functions to arrange an

26 See also Daugman: "perhaps nowhere else in the history of ideas has there been a more striking pattern of reliance on metaphors than in the history of reflection about the brain and the causes of behavior, and about the enigmatic relationship among brain, mental life, and personhood" (10).

oppositional relation between analytical and intuitive modes of thought, or when Wallace translates the concept of the double bind into a sentence structure that keeps circling its own refutation while also negotiating a dilemma on the level of content, thematic and formal aspects feed off each other. Accordingly, they cannot be understood in isolation. This, I contend, is where theories of the materiality of mind most notably shape literary aesthetics in formal and structural terms: not necessarily in the representation of consciousness or the delineation of character but in the transformation of medical and scientific concepts into operative dynamics of the texts' own constructions. Given the inseparability of form and content, it should come as no surprise that their thematic engagement with "materialist minds" also provides occasion for authors to implicitly or explicitly argue for the continuous relevance of literary forms.

## Renewal and Revision IV:
## The Relevance and Social Function of Literature

The neuro-memoir, the subject of my opening chapter, clearly has strong therapeutic and ethical elements as a mode of writing that promises to be of use not only to the author, whose articulation of his or her condition is tied to a hope for increased insight and recognition, but also to the reader, who may or may not be similarly afflicted but is bound to gain an understanding of the pragmatic and philosophical stakes inherent in the mind-matter relation as it presents itself in a historically specific, biomedical framework.[27] A strong sense of due response to a changing cultural situation also pervades the fictional works in my corpus, which, without exception, address contemporary concerns surrounding materialist anthropologies. Simply put, the novels I have discussed rely on new materialist ideas to the degree that they could not have been written at an earlier historical moment, and their authors insist on an epistemic relation between cultural situation and literary production, casting their work as comment or corrective.[28]

This much, at least, can be inferred from the authors' own paratextual statements. Positing the "idiosyncratic self [...] free and undivided" as both the proper subject of the novel and the "only thing that can match the enormous dimensions

---

27  Hustvedt's memoir, which guides the reader through a plethora of historical and contemporary theories about embodied subjecthood and ends in the author's integrative, performative avowal, "I am the shaking woman," may serve as an apt example of this "dual purpose" of the neuromemoir, which combines projects of identity formation and affirmation with educational or informative aspects (199).

28  See DeLillo's remark that a function of literature consists in "correcting, clearing up" ("Outsider" 64).

of social reality," DeLillo implicitly claims political and psychological relevance for his work ("Power" 62). Buttressing the vigor of his statement with an expletive, Wallace contends that fiction is "about what it is to be a fucking human being," an oft-quoted expression giving voice to the firm belief that literature has a part to play in contemporary projects of human self-description (McCaffery interview 131). Characterizing the novel as "a supreme connection machine," Powers places it in the service of a descriptive anthropology: its task is to "understand a person," and it succeeds when it "takes into consideration all of the contexts that that person inhabits" ("Generalist" 104).

Such positions entail the "elevation" of literature as a discursive mode, a tactic traditionally linked to claims of fiction's inherent value or usefulness (McGurl, *Novel*). True to this tradition, DeLillo, Wallace, and Powers present their work as necessary interventions, something that "rescues history from its confusions" (DeLillo, "Outsider" 64). This contextualization rests in no small part on a conception of literature as a means of producing knowledge, or accurate descriptions, of the category of the human. As my study has shown, materialist models of mind tend to generate a sense of ontological destabilization, containing as they do potential redescriptions of the human as "essentially" an animal or a machine. Fending off this looming threat of transfiguration requires a labor of resignification that the authors I have discussed are eager to take upon themselves, as evidenced by DeLillo's characterization of the writer as a "champion of the self" (Passaro interview 84) and Wallace's suggestion that it is the proper work of fiction "to dramatize the fact that we still 'are' human beings, now. Or can be" (McCaffery interview 131).

Not coincidentally, the notion that this labor of resignification or reaffirmation should fall to literary authors simultaneously validates their social function and confirms the relevance of fiction in the contemporary cultural ecology: in Powers's words, it supplies "an apology for fiction in a postfictional age" (Neilson interview 22). Much has been made of the fact that a number of contemporary authors have put forward theories about the functions of literature in a climate that they regard as increasingly irresponsive to their productions,[29] and while I hesitate to ascribe ulterior motives to poetological programs, there is a clearly observable correlation between the pronouncements of such programs, their underlying assumptions, and the reconceptualization of human subjectivity in materialist terms.

In my chapter on Powers, I have cited Jonathan Franzen's avowed suspicion that "cultural susceptibility to the charms of materialism," i.e., the "increasing willingness to see psychology as chemical," may be directly linked to "the postmodern resurgence of the oral and the eclipse of the written" in an age of mass media ("Brain" 33). Clearly Franzen shares with DeLillo, Wallace, and Powers an

---

29 See especially Fitzpatrick, *Anxiety*.

ideal of literature as perhaps the last vestige of the deep and truly human rather than the merely technological, popular, or profitable, and his argument refutes Marco Roth's claim that writers who engage with new materialist ideas necessarily do so in an attempt to piggyback on the cultural prestige of the natural sciences (n. pag.).[30] Opposition to, or doubts about, the new materialism of the mind are just as likely to reaffirm the role of the writer as both a chronicler and a critic of the changing cultural attitudes toward the physical substrates of subjectivity. In other words, while an engagement with today's "materialist minds" may affirm literature's role as a key medium for those aspects of human life—first-person interiority and subjective, "felt" experience—that both the natural sciences and the mass media have a notoriously hard time getting a handle on, the forms that this engagement eventually takes can in no way be predicted from the sheer fact of its occurrence.

The present study began with the question whether the incorporation of new materialist ideas into poetic practice might beget a new kind of literary naturalism. If what we mean by this is a reductionist, deterministic kind of writing whose relation to scientific sources is characterized by a credulous receptivity, the question has to be answered in the negative. A new materialist imaginary may indeed descend to molecular and cellular levels of analysis, but it does not have to end there. The most interesting and intellectually scrupulous theorists and writers do not neglect to account for the interrelations between substance, subjectivity, and the external world, so that the brain is cast not as the solitary origin of consciousness but as a relational or "mediating" organ, "embedded in the meaningful interactions of a living being with its environment" (Fuchs 198). We encounter this idea everywhere from Gerald Edelman's theory of neuronal group selection, where the organism's interactions with the world shape its neural makeup, to Antonio Damasio's incremental model of self-formation, where internal and external sensitivity produces the subject of experience.

Such notions are also clearly discernible in the literary texts I have examined. What shapes the "cerebral subject" in the neuromemoir more lastingly than any chemical substance is social relationality, embodied experience, and, not least, the act of fashioning these aspects into a narrative structure. Likewise, the hope for a miracle pill turns out to be a pipe dream in DeLillo's *White Noise*, while in *Ratner's Star* the moments that most approach some degree of personal authenticity revolve around unmediated, and unmedicated, subjective experience, as evidenced in the

---

30  However, in light of Franzen's conflation of medical materialism and media change, Roth's proposition that the new "interest in neurological anomaly" may be "symptomatic of an anxiety about the role of novelists in this new medical-materialist world, which happens also to be a world of giant publishing conglomerates and falling reading rates" appears decidedly less far-fetched (n. pag.).

sections narrated in the first person by Billy toward the end of the novel. In *Infinite Jest*, David Foster Wallace makes the case against a one-sided fixation on the vicissitudes and vulnerabilities of "the Head," i.e., the purely cognitive and intellectual, and returns time and again to cyclical dynamics that encompass (mental) subject and (material) substance in one inescapable loop. Powers, finally, emphasizes the deficiencies of Helen's disembodied virtual brain in *Galatea 2.2*, a book suggests that computation and textuality, or "information," are never enough on their own but most be complemented through embodied, and thus finite, psychobiological experience in the lifeworld. In *The Echo Maker*, Powers similarly insists on the a priori significance of intersubjective relationality and paints a picture of cerebral subjectivity as always already situated in the social and natural world.

We may be subjects of substance, these theories and texts suggest, but as such, we are also always open onto the world. This openness, in turn, ensures that those core competencies of literature that address the "immaterial" aspects of existence, like experience, subjectivity, and sociality, remain of continued and crucial importance. In addition, literature's inherent ambiguity and its actualization in the mind of the reader, along with the apparent inclination of authors to treat new materialist ideas as formal and thematic sources rather than end-all explanations, counteract attempts to fix the coordinates of the self within the confines of the brain and arrest the flux of social, cultural, and psychological meanings in some conception of physical substance as the ultimate ground of ontology.[31] Thus writers like Franzen and critics like Roth, who assume that an interest in the material, biological components of the self necessarily has a reductionist bent, are underestimating, and underselling, the complexity of new materialist theories as well as the creative mechanisms with which literary authors approach and adopt these ideas.

This observation, which replaces the assumption of uniform and predictable effects with a more open-minded interest in the forms and functions of artistic activity, is a good note to end on. If my study has succeeded in demonstrating one thing, I hope it has been the plurality of effects that recent U.S. writing has been able to produce out of its engagement with the materiality of mind. While they may, in sum, not constitute an altogether novel form of writing, the texts explored here should most certainly be viewed as expanding, rather than constricting, the scope of literature.

31  On physics as the definite horizon of reductionist thought, see L. Baker, *Naturalism*.

# Works Cited

Aaron, Daniel. "How to Read Don DeLillo." *Introducing Don DeLillo*. Ed. Frank. Lentricchia. Durham, NC: Duke University Press, 1991: 67-81.

Abi-Rached, Joelle M., and Nikolas Rose. "The Birth of the Neuromolecular Gaze." *History of the Human Sciences* 23.1 (2010): 11-36.

Adams, Jon. "The Sufficiency of Code: *Galatea 2.2* and the Necessity of Embodiment." *Intersections: Essays on Richard Powers*. Eds. Stephen Burn and Peter Dempsey. Champaign, IL: Dalkey Archive Press, 2008: 137-50.

Akins, Kathleen. "Lost the Plot? Reconstructing Dennett's Multiple Drafts Theory of Consciousness." *Mind & Language* 71.1 (1996): 1-43.

Allen, Amy. *The Politics of Our Selves: Power, Autonomy, and Gender in Contemporary Critical Theory*. New York, NY: Columbia University Press, 2008.

American Psychological Association. *Diagnostic and Statistical Manual of Mental Disorders*. 4th ed. Washington, D.C.: American Psychological Association, 1994.

---. *Diagnostic and Statistical Manual of Mental Disorders*. 5th ed. Washington, D.C.: American Psychological Association, 2013.

Ameriks, Karl. "From Kant to Frank: The Ineliminable Subject." *The Modern Subject: Conceptions of the Self in Classical German Philosophy*. Eds. Karl Ameriks and Dieter Sturma. Albany, NY: SUNY Press, 1995: 217-231.

Anderson, Linda. *Autobiography*. 2nd ed. London: Routledge, 2011.

Angell, Marcia. "The Epidemic of Mental Illness: Why?" *New York Review of Books* 58.11 (2011): 20-22.

---. "The Illusions of Psychiatry." *New York Review of Books* 58.12 (2011): 20-22.

Anger, Suzy. "Thomas Huxley, 'On the Hypothesis that Animals are Automata' (1874)." *Victorian Review* 35.1 (2009): 50-52.

Alanen, Lilli. *Descartes's Concept of Mind*. Cambridge, MA: Harvard University Press, 2003.

Aristotle. *Politics*. Trans. Benjamin Jowett. 1885. New York, NY: Dover, 2000.

Aronowitz, Stanley, ed. *Technoscience and Cyberculture*. New York, NY: Routledge, 1996.

Aubry, Timothy. *Reading as Therapy: What Contemporary Fiction Does for Middle-Class Americans*. Iowa City, IA: University of Iowa Press, 2011.

---. "Selfless Cravings: Addiction and Recovery in David Foster Wallace's *Infinite Jest*." *American Fiction of the 1990s: Reflections of History and Culture*. Ed. Jay Prosser. London: Routledge, 2008: 206-19.

Auster, Paul. *Winter Journal*. New York, NY: Henry Holt, 2012.

Babaee, Ruzbeh. "Sketch of Discourse and Power in Don DeLillo's *White Noise*." *International Journal of Comparative Literature & Translation Studies* 2.1 (2014): 30-33.

Badmington, Neil. "Introduction: Approaching Posthumanism." *Posthumanism*. Ed. Neil Badmington. Basingstoke: Palgrave MacMillan, 2000: 1-10.

Bailey, Andrew. *First Philosophy: Fundamental Problems and Readings in Philosophy*. 2nd ed. Peterborough, ON: Broadview Press, 2011.

Baker, Lynne Rudder. *Naturalism and the First-Person Perspective*. Oxford: Oxford University Press, 2013.

---. *Saving Belief: A Critique of Physicalism*. Princeton, NJ: Princeton University Press, 1988.

Baker, Gordon, and Katherine J. Morris. *Descartes' Dualism*. London: Routledge, 1996.

Bakhtin, Mikhail. *The Dialogic Imagination: Four Essays*. Trans. Caryl Emerson and Michael Holquist. 1981. Austin, TX: University of Texas Press, 2004.

---. *Problems of Dostoevsky's Poetics*. Trans. Caryl Emerson. 1984. Minneapolis, MN: University of Minnesota Press, 1999.

Barkow, Jerome H., Leda Cosmides, and John Tooby. "Introduction: Evolutionary Psychology and Conceptual Integration." *The Adapted Mind: Evolutionary Psychology and the Generation of Culture*. Eds. Jerome H Barkow, Leda Cosmides, and John Tooby. Oxford: Oxford University Press, 1992: 3-18.

Barrish, Phillip J. *The Cambridge Introduction to American Literary Realism*. Cambridge: Cambridge University Press, 2011.

Barros, Carolyn A. *Autobiography: Narrative of Transformation*. Ann Arbor, MI: University of Michigan Press, 1998.

Barthes, Roland. "The Death of the Author." 1967. *Image, Music, Text*. Trans. Stephen Heath. New York, NY: Hill and Wang, 1977: 142-7.

---. "An Introduction to the Structural Analysis of Narrative." 1966. *New Literary History* 6.2 (1975): 237-272.

Baskin, Jon. "Death is Not the End: David Foster Wallace: His Legacy and his Critics." *The Point* 1 (2009): n. pag. www.thepointmag.com/archive/death-is-not-the-end

Bateson, Gregory. "The Cybernetics of the 'Self': A Theory of Alcoholism." *Steps to an Ecology of Mind*. 1972. Northvale, NJ: Jason Aronson, 1987: 315-44.

Beckermann, Ansgar. *Gehirn, Ich, Freiheit: Neurowissenschaften und Menschenbild*. Paderborn: mentis, 2008.

Bell, Susan E., and Anne E. Figert, eds. *Reimagining (Bio)Medicalization, Pharmaceuticals and Genetics: Old Critiques and New Engagements*. London: Routledge, 2015.

Belsey, Catherine. *The Subject of Tragedy: Identity and Difference in Renaissance Drama*. London: Methuen, 1985.

Bennett, Maxwell R., and Peter M. S. Hacker. *History of Cognitive Neuroscience*. Sussex: Wiley-Blackwell, 2008.

---. *Philosophical Foundations of Neuroscience*. London: Blackwell, 2003.

Bentley, Nancy. "Neurological Modernity and American Social Thought." *Frantic Panoramas: American Literature and Mass Culture, 1870-1920*. Philadelphia, PA: University of Pennsylvania Press, 2009: 247.87.

Benveniste, Emile. *Problems in General Linguistics*. 1966. Coral Gables, FL: University of Miami Press, 1971.

Berger, James. "Testing Literature: Helen Keller and Richard Powers' [sic] Implementation H[elen]." *Arizona Quarterly* 58.3 (2002): 109-37.

Bertens, Hans. *The Idea of the Postmodern: A History*. London: Routledge, 1995.

Best, Stephen, and Sharon Marcus. "Surface Reading: An Introduction." *Representations* 108.1 (2009): 1-21.

Bezerra, Benilton. "Looking for Experience in the Brain: Psychoanalysis and the Project of Naturalizing Mind." *Neurocultures: Glimpses Into an Expanding Universe*. Eds. Francisco Ortega and Fernando Vidal. Frankfurt am Main: Peter Lang, 2011: 249-70.

Bieger, Laura. "'I Am No One': Self-Narration Between Continuity and Disorder in Richard Powers' [sic] *The Echo Maker*." *Ideas of Order: Narrative Patterns in the Novels of Richard Powers*. Eds. Antje Kley and Jan D. Kucharzewski. Heidelberg: Winter, 2012: 195-216.

Birge, Sarah. "Brainhood, Selfhood, or 'Meat with a Point of View': The Value of Fiction for Neuroscientific Research and Neurological Medicine." *The Neuroscientific Turn: Transdisciplinarity in the Age of the Brain*. Eds. Melissa M. Littlefield and Jenell M. Johnson. Ann Arbor, MI: University of Michigan Pres, 2012: 89-104.

Birkerts, Sven. *The Gutenberg Elegies: The Fate of Reading in an Electronic Age*. New York, NY: Farrar, Straus and Giroux, 1994.

Best, Stephen, and Sharon Marcus. "Surface Reading: An Introduction." *Representations* 108.1 (2009): 1-21.

Blair, Elaine. "A New Brilliant Start." Review of *Every Love Story is a Ghost Story: A Life of David Foster Wallace* by D.T. Max. *The New York Review of Books* 59.19 (2012): 12-16.

Blackmore, Susan. *Consciousness: A Very Short Introduction*. New York, NY: Oxford University Press, 2005.

---. Introduction. *Conversations on Consciousness: What the Best Minds Think about the Brain, Free Will, and What It Means to Be Human.* Ed. Susan Blackmore. Oxford: Oxford University Press, 2006: 1-10.

Boden, Margaret. *Mind as Machine: A History of Cognitive Science, Volume 1&2.* Oxford: Clarendon Press, 2006.

Bolger, Robert K. "A Less 'Bullshitty' Way to Live:" The Pragmatic Spirituality of David Foster Wallace." *Gesturing Toward Reality: David Foster Wallace and Philosophy.* Eds. Robert K. Bolger and Scott Korb. New York, NY: Bloomsbury, 2014: 31-52.

Boltanski, Luc, and Eve Chiapello. *The New Spirit of Capitalism.* 2004. Trans. Gregory Elliott. London: Verso, 2005.

Boswell, Marshall. *Understanding David Foster Wallace.* Columbia, SC: University of South Carolina Press, 2003.

Bould, Mark, and Sherryl Vint. "Of Neural Nets and Brains in Vats: Model Subjects in *Galatea 2.2* and *Plus.*" *Biography* 30.1 (2007): 84-105.

Bourdieu, Pierre. "The Field of Cultural Production, or: The Economic World Reversed." 1983. Trans. Richard Nice. *The Field of Cultural Production: Essays on Art and Literature.* Ed. Randal Johnson. New York, NY: Columbia University Press, 1993: 29-73.

---. "Field of Power, Literary Field and Habitus." 1986. Trans. Claud DuVerlie. *The Field of Cultural Production: Essays on Art and Literature.* Ed. Randal Johnson. New York, NY: Columbia University Press, 1993: 161-75.

---. "The Historical Genesis of a Pure Aesthetic." *The Field of Cultural Production: Essays on Art and Literature.* Ed. Randal Johnson. New York, NY: Columbia University Press, 1993: 254-66.

---. "The Intellectual Field: A World Apart." 1987. *In Other Words: Essays Towards a Reflexive Sociology.* Stanford, CA: Stanford University Press, 1990: 140-149.

---. *The Logic of Practice.* Stanford, CA: Stanford University Press, 1990.

Bourdieu, Pierre, and Loïc J. D. Wacquant. "The Logic of Fields." *An Invitation to Reflexive Sociology.* Eds. Pierre Bourdieu and Loïc J. D. Wacquant. Chicago, IL: The University of Chicago Press, 1997: 94-114.

Bourke, Joanna. *What it Means to be Human: Reflections from 1791 to the Present.* Berkeley, CA: Counterpoint Press, 2011.

Boxall, Peter. *Don DeLillo: The Possibility of Fiction.* London: Routledge, 2006.

Braidotti, Rosi. *The Posthuman.* New York, NY: Wiley & Sons, 2013.

Brandt, Stephan. *The Culture of Corporeality: Aesthetic Experience and the Embodiment of America 1945-1960.* Heidelberg: Winter, 2007.

Brennan, Stephen C. "Naturalism and Psychology." *The Oxford Handbook of American Literary Naturalism.* Ed. Keith Newlin. New York, NY: Oxford University Press, 2011: 182-202.

Brindley, Nicola. "'The truth of our scattering': (Post)Human Complexity in Richard Powers' [sic] *The Echo Maker*." *49th Parallel* 28 (2012): n. pag. www.49thparallel.bham.ac.uk/back/issue28/Brindley.pdf

Brockman, John. "Introduction: The Emerging Third Culture." *The Third Culture: Beyond the Scientific Revolution*. Ed. John Brockman. New York, NY: Touchstone, 1995: 17-37.

---., ed. *The New Humanists: Science at the Edge*. New York, NY: Sterling, 2003.

Brockmeier, Jens. "Identity." *Encyclopedia of Life Writing: Autobiographical and Biographical Forms*. Ed. Margaretta Jolly. London: Routledge, 2001: 455-56.

Brockmeier, Jens, and Donald A. Carbaugh. Introduction. *Narrative and Identity: Studies in Autobiography, Self and Culture*. Eds. Jens Brockmeier and Donald A. Carbaugh. Amsterdam: John Benjamins, 2001: 1-24.

Broks, Paul. *Into the Silent Land: Travels in Neuropsychology*. New York, NY: Grove Press, 2003.

Brown, Bill. "Materiality." *Critical Terms for Media Studies*. Eds. W. J. T. Mitchell and Mark B. N. Hansen. Chicago, IL: The University of Chicago Press, 2010: 49-63.

Brown, Ian. "The Question Isn't Why Some People Become Addicts, But Why We All Don't." Review of *Memoirs of an Addicted Brain* by Marc Lewis. *The Globe and Mail* 30 Sep. 2011: n. pag. www.theglobeandmail.com/life/health-and-fitness/the-question-isnt-why-some-people-become-addicts-but-why-we-all-dont/article556464/

Bruner, Jerome S. *Acts of Meaning*. Cambridge, MA: Harvard University Press, 1990.

---. *Actual Minds, Possible Worlds*. Cambridge, MA: Harvard University Press, 1986.

---. "The Autobiographical Process." *Current Sociology*. 43.2 (1995): 161-177.

---. "Life as Narrative." *Social Research* 71.3 (2004): 691-710.

---. "The Narrative Construction of Reality." *Critical Inquiry* 18.1 (1991): 1-21.

Bruner, Jerome, and Susan Weisser. "The Invention of Self: Autobiography and its Forms." *Literacy and Orality*. Eds. David R. Olson and Nancy Torrance. Cambridge: Cambridge University Press, 1991: 129-48.

Bruni, Frank. "The Grunge American Novel." *New York Times Magazine* 24 Mar. 1996: 38-41.

Bryson, Norman. "City of Dis: The Fiction of Don DeLillo." *Granta* 2 (1980): n. pag. granta.com/City-of-Dis-The-Fiction-of-Don-DeLillo/

Buckley, Jerome Hamilton. *The Turning Key: Autobiography and the Subjective Impulse since 1800*. Cambridge, MA: Harvard University Press, 1984.

Buell, Lawrence. *The Dream of the Great American Novel*. Cambridge, MA: Harvard University Press, 2014.

Burke, Kenneth. "Literature as Equipment for Living." *The Philosophy of Literary Form: Studies in Symbolic Action*. Louisiana State University Press, 1941: 293-304.

Burn, Stephen. *David Foster Wallace's* Infinite Jest: *A Reader's Guide*. 2nd ed. New York, NY: Continuum, 2012.

---. "Don DeLillo's *Great Jones Street* and the Science of Mind." *Modern Fiction Studies* 55.2 (2009): 349-368.

---. "The End of Postmodernism: American Fiction at the End of the Millennium." *American Fiction of the 1990s: Reflections of History and Culture*. Ed. Jay Prosser. London: Routledge, 2008: 220-34.

---. Introduction. *Intersections: Essays on Richard Powers*. Eds. Stephen Burn and Peter Dempsey. Champaign, IL: Dalkey Archive Press, 2008: xvii-xxxix.

---. *Jonathan Franzen at the End of Postmodernism*. London: Continuum, 2008.

---. "The Machine-Language of the Muscles: Reading, Sport, and the Self in *Infinite Jest*." *Upon Further Review: Sports in American Literature*. Eds. Michael Cocchiarale and Scott Emmert. Westport, CT: Praeger, 2004: 41-49.

---. "Mapping the Syndrome Novel." *Diseases and Disorders in Contemporary Fiction: The Syndrome Syndrome*. Eds. T. J. Lustig and James Peacock. London: Routledge, 2013: 35-52.

---. "Neuroscience and Modern Fiction." *Modern Fiction Studies* 61.2 (2015): 209-25.

---. "'Putting the Mind Back into Nature': The American Novel and the Science of Mind. *Romantic Presences in the Twentieth-Century*. Ed. Mark Sandy. Farnham: Ashgate, 2012: 191-207.

---. Review of *Consider David Foster Wallace*, ed. David Hering. *Modernism/modernity* 18.2 (2011): 465-68.

---. "'Webs of Nerves Pulsing and Firing': *Infinite Jest* and the Science of the Mind." *A Companion to David Foster Wallace Studies*. Eds. Marshall Boswell and Stephen J. Burn. New York, NY: Palgrave Macmillan, 2013: 59-86.

Burn, Stephen, and Peter Dempsey, eds. *Intersections: Essays on Richard Powers*. Champaign, IL: Dalkey Archive Press, 2008.

Burt, Stephen. "Surprising Powers: Richard Powers' [sic] Scientific Humanism." *Slate* 11 October 2006: n. pag. www.slate.com/articles/news_and_politics/book_blitz/2006/10/surprising_powers.html

Burton, Robert. *A Skeptic's Guide to the Mind: What Neuroscience Can and Cannot Tell Us About Ourselves*. New York, NY: St. Martin's Press, 2013.

Bustillos, Maria. "Philosophy, Self-Help, and the Death of David Wallace." *Gesturing Toward Reality: David Foster Wallace and Philosophy*. Eds. Robert K. Bolger and Scott Korb. New York, NY: Bloomsbury, 2014: 121-40.

Butler, Judith. *Giving an Account of Oneself*. New York, NY: Fordham University Press, 2005.

---. *The Psychic Life of Power: Theories in Subjection*. Stanford, CA: Stanford University Press, 1997.

---. "Violence, Mourning, Politics." *Precarious Life: The Powers of Mourning and Violence.* London: Verso, 2004: 19-49.

Byers, Thomas B. "The Crumbling Two-Story Architecture of Richard Powers' [sic] Fiction." *Transatlantica* 2 (2009): n. pag. transatlantica.revues.org/4510

Camerer, Colin, et al. "Neuroeconomics: How Neuroscience Can Inform Economics." *Journal of Economic Literature* 43.1 (2005): 9–64.

Calvino, Italo. "Quickness." *Six Memos for the Next Millennium.* 1988. London: Penguin, 2002: 31-54.

Campbell, Miranda. "Probing the Posthuman: Richard Powers' [sic] *Galatea 2.2* and the Mind-Body Problem." *Reconstruction* 4.3 (2004): n. pag. www.reconstruction.ws/043/Campbell.html

Carlisle, Greg. *Elegant Complexity: A Study Of David Foster Wallace's* Infinite Jest. Austin, TX: Sideshow Media Group, 2007.

Caputo, John. "Derrida and Theology: The Good News About Alterity." *Faith and Philosophy* 10 (1993): 453-470.

Caro, Mark. "The Next Big Thing: Can a Downstate Author Withstand the Sensation over His 1,079-Page Novel?" *Conversations with David Foster Wallace.* Ed. Stephen Burn. Jackson, MI: University Press of Mississippi, 2012: 53-57.

Carroll, Lewis. *Alice's Adventures in Wonderland* and *Through the Looking-Glass.* 1962. London: Puffin Books, 1997.

Cascardi, Anthony J. *The Subject of Modernity.* Cambridge: Cambridge University Press, 1992.

Cassirer, Ernst. *The Individual and the Cosmos in Renaissance Philosophy.* 1963. Trans. Mario Domandi. Chicago: The University of Chicago Press, 2010.

Cavarero, Adriana. *Relating Narratives: Storytelling and Selfhood.* 1997. Trans. Paul A. Kottman. London: Routledge, 2000.

Chalmers, David J. *The Conscious Mind: In Search of a Fundamental Theory.* Oxford: Oxford University Press, 1996.

---. "The Puzzle of Conscious Experience." *Scientific American* 273.6 (1995): 80-86.

Changeux, Jean-Pierre. *Neuronal Man: The Biology of Mind.* Trans. Laurence Garey. New York, NY: Oxford University Press, 1985.

Changeux, Jean-Pierre, and Paul Ricoeur. *What Makes Us Think: A Neuroscientist and a Philosopher Argue about Ethics, Human Nature, and the Brain.* Trans. M. B. DeBevoise. Princeton, NJ: Princeton University Press, 2000.

Chapman, Wes. "The Cognitive Literary Theory of Richard Powers's *Galatea 2.2.*" *Modern Fiction Studies* 61.2 (2015): 226-250.

Chodat, Robert. "Naturalism and Narrative, or, What Computers and Human Beings Can't Do." *New Literary History* 37.4 (2006): 685-706.

---. *Worldly Acts and Sentient Things: The Persistence of Agency from Stein to DeLillo.* Ithaca, NY: Cornell University Press, 2008.

Choudhury, Suparna, and Jan Slaby. "Introduction: Critical Neuroscience— Between Lifeworld and Laboratory." *Critical Neuroscience: A Handbook of the Social and Cultural Contexts of Neuroscience*. Eds. Suparna Choudhury and Jan Slaby. Oxford: Blackwell, 2012: 1-26.

Cioffi, Frank Louis. "'An Anguish Become Thing': Narrative as Performance in David Foster Wallace's Infinite Jest." *Narrative* 8.2 (2000): 161-81.

Civello, Paul. *American Literary Naturalism and Its Twentieth-Century Transformations: Frank Norris, Ernest Hemingway, Don Delillo*. Athens, GA: University of Georgia Press, 1994.

Clark, Andy. *Supersizing the Mind: Embodiment, Action, and Cognitive Extension*. Oxford: Oxford University Press, 2008.

Clark, Bruce, and Mark B. N. Hansen. "Introduction: Neocybernetic Emergence." *Emergence and Embodiment: New Essays on Second-Order Systems Theory*. Eds. Bruce Clarke and Mark B. N. Hansen. Durham, NC: Duke University Press, 2009: 1-25.

Clarke, Adele E., et al. *Biomedicalization: Technoscience, Health, and Illness in the U.S.* Durham, NC: Duke University Press, 2010.

Clark, Hilary A. "Encyclopedic Discourse." *SubStance* 21.1 (1992): 95-110.

Clune, Michael W. *White Out: The Secret Life of Heroin*. Center City, MN: Hazelden, 2013.

---. *Writing Against Time*. Stanford, CA: Stanford University Press, 2013.

Cohen, Samuel. "To Wish to Try to Sing to the Next Generation: *Infinite Jest's* History." *The Legacy of David Foster Wallace*. Eds. Samuel Cohen and Lee Konstantinou. Iowa City, IO: University of Iowa Press, 2012: 59-.

Cohn, Dorrit. *Transparent Minds: Narrative Modes for Presenting Consciousness in Fiction*. Princeton, NJ: Princeton University Press, 1983.

Colebrook, Claire. *Deleuze and the Meaning of Life*. London: Continuum, 2010.

---. "Vitalism and Theoria." *Mindful Aesthetics: Literature and the Science of Mind*. Eds. Chris Danta and Helen Groth. New York, NY: Bloomsbury, 2014: 29-46.

Connolly, William E. "Experience & Experiment." *Daedalus* 135 (2006): 67-75.

Conrad, Peter. *The Medicalization of Society: On the Transformation of Human Conditions into Treatable Disorders*. Baltimore, MA: Johns Hopkins University Press, 2007.

Conroy, Mark. "From Tombstone to Tabloid: Authority Figured in *White Noise*." *Critique* 35.2 (1994): 97-110.

Coole, Diana, and Samantha Frost. "Introducing the New Materialisms." *New Materialisms: Ontology, Agency, and Politics*. Ed. Diana Coole and Samantha Frost. Durham, NC: Duke University Press, 2010: 1-43.

Copeland, B. Jack. "The Turing Test." *Minds and Machines* 10.4 (2000): 519–39.

Cornwell, John. "Keeping Media in Mind." Review of *In Search of Memory: The Emergence of a New Science of Mind* by Eric Kandel. *Brain* 131 (2008): 304-307.

Cottingham, John. "The Mind-Body Relation." *The Blackwell Guide to Descartes' Meditations*. Ed. Stephen Gaukroger. Malden, MA: Blackstreet, 2006: 160- 78.

Cowart, David. "The DeLillo Era: Literary Generations in the Postmodern Period." *Terrorism, Media, and the Ethics of Fiction: Transatlantic Perspectives on Don DeLillo*. Eds. Peter Schneck and Philipp Schweighauser. London: Continuum, 2010: 223-42.

---. *Don DeLillo: The Physics of Language*. 2002. Rev. ed. Athens, GA: University of Georgia Press, 2003.

Crick, Francis. *The Astonishing Hypothesis: The Scientific Search for the Soul*. New York, NY: Touchstone, 1994.

Cromby, John, Tim Newton, and Simon J Williams. "Neuroscience and Subjectivity." *Subjectvity* 3.4 (2010): 215-26.

Cummins, Robert, and Martin Roth. "Meaning and Content in Cognitive Science." *The World in the Head*. Robert Cummins. London: Oxford University Press, 2010: 174-193.

Cunningham, Suzanne. *What is a Mind?: An Integrative Introduction to the Philosophy of Mind*. Indianapolis, IN: Hackett, 2000.

Damasio, Antonio R. *Descartes' Error: Emotion, Reason, and the Human Brain*. New York, NY: G. P. Putnam's Sons, 1994.

---. *The Feeling of What Happens: Body, Emotion, and the Making of Consciousness*. 1999. London: Vintage, 2000.

---. "How the Brain Creates the Mind." *The Hidden Mind*. Spec. issue of *Scientific American* 12.1 (2002): 4-9.

---. *Looking For Spinoza: Joy, Sorrow, and the Feeling Brain*. Orlando, FL: Harcourt, 2003.

---. *Self Comes to Mind: Constructing the Conscious Brain*. 2010. London: Vintage, 2012.

Danto, Arthur C. "Naturalism." *The Encyclopedia of Philosophy*. Ed. Paul Edwords. New York, NY: Macmillan, 1967: 448–450.

Daugman, John G. "Brain Metaphor and Brain Theory." *Computational Neuroscience*. Ed. Eric L. Schwartz. Cambridge, MA: MIT Press, 1990: 9-18.

Davidson, Donald. "The Material Mind." 1973. *Actions and Events*. Oxford: Oxford University Press, 2001: 245-60.

---. "Mental Events." 1970. *Actions and Events*. Oxford: Oxford University Press, 2001: 207-25.

---. "Psychology as Philosophy." 1974. *Actions and Events*. Oxford: Oxford University Press, 2011: 229-39.

Dawkins, Richard. *The Selfish Gene*. 1976. 2nd ed. Oxford: Oxford University Press, 1989.

de la Durantaye, Leland. "The Subsurface Unity of All Things, or David Foster Wallace's Free Will." *Gesturing Toward Reality: David Foster Wallace and Philosophy.* Eds. Robert K. Bolger and Scott Korb. New York, NY: Bloomsbury, 2014: 19-29.

de La Mettrie, Julien Offray. *Man a Machine.* Chicago, IL: Open Court, 1912.

de Man, Paul. "Autobiography as De-facement." *Modern Language Notes* 94.5 (1979): 919-30.

Deacon, Terrence. "The trouble with memes (and what to do about it)." *The Semiotic Review of Books* 10.3 (1999): 1-3.

DeCurtis, Anthony. "The Product: Bucky Wunderlick, Rock 'n Roll, and Don DeLillo's *Great Jones Street.*" *Introducing Don DeLillo.* Ed. Frank Lentricchia. Durham, NC: Duke UP, 1991: 131-41.

Deleuze, Gilles and Felix Guattari. *Anti-Oedipus: Capitalism and Schizophrenia.* 1972. Trans. Robert Hurley, et al. Minneapolis, MN: University of Minnesota Press, 1983.

DeLillo, Don. "'An Outsider in this Society': An Interview with Don DeLillo." Interview with Anthony DeCurtis. *Conversations with Don DeLillo.* Ed. Thomas DePietro. Jackson, MI: University of Mississippi Press, 2005: 52-74.

---. *End Zone.* 1972. London: Picador, 2004.

---. *Great Jones Street.* 1973. London: Penguin, 1994.

---. "Informal Remarks From the David Foster Wallace Memorial Service in New York on October 23, 2008." *The Legacy of David Foster Wallace.* Eds. Samuel Cohen and Lee Konstantinou. Iowa City, IO: University of Iowa Press, 2012: 23-24.

---. Interview with Thomas LeClair. *Conversations with Don DeLillo.* Ed. Thomas DePietro. Jackson, MI: University of Mississippi Press, 2005: 3-15.

---. *The Names.* 1982. New York, NY: Vintage, 1989.

---. "The Power of History." *New York Times Magazine* 7 Sept. 1997: 60-63.

---. *Ratner's Star.* 1976. New York, NY: Vintage, 1989.

---. *Underworld.* 1997. London: Picador, 1999.

---. *White Noise.* 1984. London: Picador, 1999.

den Dulk, Allard. "Good Faith and Sincerity: Sartrean Virtues of Self-Becoming in David Foster Wallace." *Gesturing Toward Reality: David Foster Wallace and Philosophy.* Eds. Robert K. Bolger and Scott Korb. New York, NY: Bloomsbury, 2014: 199-220.

Dennett, Daniel. "Astride the Two Cultures: A Letter to Richard Powers, Updated." *Intersections: Essays on Richard Powers.* Eds. Stephen Burn and Peter Dempsey. Champaign, IL: Dalkey Archive Press, 2008: 151-161.

---. *Consciousness Explained.* New York, NY: Back Bay Books, 1991.

---. "Heterophenomenology Reconsidered." *Phenomenology and the Cognitive Sciences* 6.1-2 (2007): 247-270.

---. "The Self as the Center of Narrative Gravity." *Self and Consciousness: Multiple Perspectives*. Eds. Frank S. Kessel et al. Hillsdale, NJ: Lawrence Erlbaum Associates, 1992: 103-15.

---. "The Self as a Responding—and Responsible—Artifact." *Annals of the New York Academy of Sciences* 1001 (2003): 39-50.

---. "Who's On First? Heterophenomenology Explained" Spec. Issue of *Journal of Consciousness Studies* 10.9-10 (2003): 19–30.

---. "Why Everyone Is a Novelist." *The Times Literary Supplement* 16-22 Sept. (1988): 466-474.

Dennett, Daniel, and Marcel Kinsbourne. "Time and the Observer: The Where and When of Consciousness in the Brain." *The Nature of Consciousness: Philosophical Debates*. Eds. Ned J. Block et al. Cambridge, MA: MIT Press, 1997: 141-74.

Derrida, Jacques. *Of Grammatology*. Trans. Gayatri Spivak. Baltimore, MA: Johns Hopkins University Press, 1976.

Descartes, René. *Discourse on Method* and *Meditations on First Philosophy*. Trans. Donald A. Cress. 4th ed. Indianapolis, IA: Hackett Publishing, 1998.

Dewey, Joseph. "Don DeLillo." *The Oxford Encyclopedia of American Literature*. Vol. 1. Ed. Jay Parini. New York, NY: Oxford University Press, 2004: 350-358.

---. *Understanding Richard Powers*. Columbia, SC: University of South Carolina Press, 2002.

DeWitt, Anne. *Moral Authority, Men of Science, and the Victorian Novel*. Cambridge: Cambridge University Press, 2013.

Didion, Joan. "On Keeping a Notebook." *Slouching Towards Bethlehem*. New York, NY: Delta, 1968: 131-41.

doCarmo, Stephen N. "Subjects. Objects, and the Postmodern Differend in Don DeLillo's *White Noise*." *LIT: Literature Interpretation Theory* 11.1 (2000): 1-33.

Dolphijn, Rick, and Iris van der Tuin, eds. *New Materialism: Interviews & Cartographies*. Ann Arbor, MI: Open Humanities Press, 2012.

Doyle, Laura. "Introduction: The Resistant Material." *Bodies of Resistance: New Phenomenologies of Politics, Agency, and Culture*. Ed. Laura Doyle. Evanston, Ill.: Northwestern University Press, 2001.

Draaisma, Douwe. "Echoes, Doubles, and Delusions: Capgras Syndrome in Science and Literature." *Style* 43.3 (2009): 429-41.

Dreyfus, Hubert. *What Computers Still Can't Do: A Critique of Artificial Reason*. Cambridge, MA: MIT Press, 1992.

Duménil, Gérard, and Dominique Lévy. *The Crisis of Neoliberalism*. Cambridge, MA: Harvard University Press, 2011.

Dumit, Joseph. *Picturing Personhood: Brain Scans and Biomedical Identity*. Princeton, NJ: Princeton University Press, 2004.

Dunning, David. "'Virtually Unlimited': The Elusiveness of Reality in *Infinite Jest*." *2010-2011 Penn Humanities Forum on Virtuality*. University of Pennsylvania Scholarly Commons, 2011: 1-29.

Eagleman, David M. *Incognito: The Secret Lives of the Brain*. New York, NY: Random House, 2011.

---. "The Brain on Trial." *Atlantic Monthly* 308:1 (2011): 112-123.

Eakin, Paul John. *Fictions in Autobiography: Studies in the Art of Self-Invention*. Princeton, NJ: Princeton University Press, 1985.

---. *How Our Lives Become Stories: Making Selves*. Ithaca, NY: Cornell University Press, 1999.

---. "Introduction: Mapping the Ethics of Life Writing." *The Ethics of Life Writing*. Ed. Paul John Eakin. Ithaca, NY: Cornell University Press, 2004: 1-16.

---. *Living Autobiographically: How We Create Identity in Narrative*. Ithaca, NY: Cornell University Press, 2008.

---. *Touching the World: Reference in Autobiography*. Princeton, NJ: Princeton University Press, 1992.

Eco, Umberto. "Postscript to *The Name of the Rose*." Trans. William Weaver. New York, NY: Harcourt Brace, 1984.

---. *A Theory of Semiotics*. Bloomington, IN: Indiana University Press, 1976.

Edelman, Gerald. *Bright Air, Brilliant Fire: On the Matter of the Mind*. New York, NY: Basic Books, 1992.

---. *Wider Than the Sky: The Phenomenal Gift of Consciousness*. New Haven, CT: Yale University Press, 2004.

Eckstein, Lars, and Christoph Reinfandt. "The Parody of 'Parody as Cultural Memory in Richard Powers's *Galatea 2.2*': A Response to Anca Rosu." *Connotations* 13.1-2 (2003/2004): 93-102.

Edelman, Gerald M. *Bright Air, Brilliant Fire: On the Matter of the Mind*. New York, NY: Basic Books, 1992.

---. *Neural Darwinism: The Theory of Neuronal Group Selection*. New York, NY: Basic Books, 1987.

---. *The Remembered Present: A Biological Theory of Consciousness*. New York, NY: Basic Books, 1989.

Edmundson, Mark. "Not Flat, Not Round, Not There Don DeLillo's Novel Characters." *Yale Review* 83.2 (1995): 107-24.

Ehrenberg, Alain. *Weariness of the Self: Diagnosing the History of Depression in the Contemporary Age*. Quebec City: McGill-Queen's University Press, 2009.

---. "Le sujet cérébral." *Esprit* 309 (2004): 130-55.

---. "Se définir par son cerveau." *Esprit* 411 (2015): 68-81.

---. "The 'Social Brain': An Epistemological Chimera and a Sociological Truth." *Neurocultures: Glimpses Into an Expanding Universe*. Eds. Francisco Ortega and Fernando Vidal. Frankfurt am Main: Peter Lang, 2011: 117-40.

Ellenberger, Henri. *The Discovery of the Unconscious: The History and Evolution of Dynamic Psychotherapy*. New York, NY: Basic Books, 1980.

Ellmann, Maud. *The Nets of Modernism: Henry James, Virginia Woolf, James Joyce, and Sigmund Freud*. Cambridge: Cambridge University Press, 2010.

Engles, Tim. "'Who Are You, Literally?': Fantasies of the White Self in White Noise." *Modern Fiction Studies* 45.3 (1999) 755-787.

Ercolino, Stefano. *The Maximalist Novel: From Thomas Pynchon's Gravity's Rainbow to Roberto Bolaño's 2666*. London: Bloomsbury, 2014.

Esposito, Roberto. *Bios: Biopolitics and Philosophy*. Trans. Timothy Campbell. Minneapolis, MN: University of Minnesota Press, 2008.

Eugenides, Jeffrey. *The Marriage Plot*. New York, NY: Farrar, Straus and Giroux, 2011.

Feinberg, Todd E. *Altered Egos: How the Brain Creates the Self*. Oxford, Oxford University Press, 2001.

---. "Some Interesting Perturbations of the Self in Neurology." *Seminars in Neurology* 17.2 (1997): 129-35.

Felski, Rita. "After Suspicion." *Profession* 8 (2009): 28-35.

---. "Suspicious Minds." *Poetics Today* 32.2 (2011): 215-34.

Ferris, Joshua. *The Unnamed*. 2010. London: Penguin, 2011.

Fest, Bradley J. "The Inverted Nuke in the Garden: Archival Emergence and Anti-Eschatology in David Foster Wallace's Infinite Jest." *boundary 2* 39.3 (2012): 125-49.

---. Review of *Consider David Foster Wallace*, ed. David Hering. *Critical Quarterly* 53.2 (2011): 102-06.

Ffytche, Matt. *The Foundation of the Unconscious: Schelling, Freud and the Birth of the Modern Psyche*. Cambridge: Cambridge University Press, 2011.

Fitz, Nick, and Derek Gumm. "Anomalous Monism." *Aporia* 20.2 (2010): 35-53.

Fitzpatrick, Kathleen. *The Anxiety of Obsolescence: The American Novel in the Age of Television*. Nashville, TN: Vanderbilt University Press, 2006.

---. "The Exhaustion of Literature: Novels, Computers, and the Threat of Obsolescence." *Contemporary Literature* 43.3 (2002): 518-59.

Fleissner, Jennifer. "Obsessional Modernity: The 'Institutionalization of Doubt.'" *Critical Inquiry* 34.1 (2007): 106-34.

---. "Symptomatology and the Novel." *Novel* 42.3 (2009): 387-92.

Fluck, Winfried. "Surface Knowledge and Deep Knowledge: The New Realism in American Fiction." *Neo-Realism in Contemporary American Fiction*. Ed. Kristiaan Versluys. Amsterdam: Rodopi, 1992: 65-85.

Fluck, Winfried, and Fabian Lindner. "Economics and Narrative." *American Economies*. Eds. Eva Boesenberg et al. Heidelberg: Winter, 2012: 83-101.

Fludernik, Monika. *Towards a 'Natural' Narratology*. London: Routledge, 1996.

Fodor, Jerry A. *The Modularity of Mind: An Essay on Faculty Psychology.* Cambridge, MA: MIT Press, 1983.

---. "You Can Fool Some of the People All of the Time, Everything Else Being Equal: Hedged Laws and Psychological Explanations." *Mind, New Series* 100 (1991): 19–34.

Foster, Hal. *The Return of the Real: The Avant-garde at the End of the Century.* Cambridge, MA: MIT Press, 1996.

Foucault, Michel. *The Hermeneutics of the Subject: Lectures at the Collège de France, 1981-82.* 2001. Ed. Fréderic Gros. Trans. Graham Burchell. New York, NY: Palgrave Macmillan, 2005.

---. *The History of Sexuality: An Introduction.* 1978. New York, NY: Vintage, 1990.

---. *The Order of Things: An Archaeology of the Human Sciences.* 1966. New York, NY: Vintage Books, 1994.

---. "Self Writing." *Ethics: Subjectivity and Truth.* Ed. Paul Rabinow. Trans. Robert Hurley et al. New York, NY: The New Press, 1997: 207-23.

---. "The Subject and Power." *Critical Inquiry* 8.4 (1982): 777-95.

---. "Technologies of the Self." *Technologies of the Self: A Seminar with Michel Foucault.* Eds. Luther H. Martin, et al. Amherst, MA: University of Massachusetts Press, 1988: 16-49.

Frank, Manfred. "Der Mensch bleibt sich ein Rätsel." Interview with Ulrich Schnabel and Thomas Assheuer. *Die Zeit* 27 Aug. 2009: 52-53.

---. "Is Subjectivity a Non-Thing, an Absurdity [Unding]?" *The Modern Subject: Conceptions of the Self in Classical German Philosophy.* Eds. Karl Ameriks and Dieter Sturma. Albany, NY: State University of New York Press, 1995: 177-98.

Franks, David D. "Mutual Interests, Different Lenses: Current Neuroscience and Symbolic Interaction." *Symbolic Interaction* 26.4 (2003): 613-30.

---. *Neurosociology: The Nexus Between Neuroscience and Social Psychology.* New York, NY: Springer, 2010.

Franzen, Jonathan. "Farther Away: 'Robinson Crusoe', David Foster Wallace, and the Island of Solitude." *Farther Away.* New York, NY: Farrar, Straus and Giroux, 2012: 15-52.

---. "Having Difficulty with Difficulty." Interview with Ben Greenman. *The New Yorker Online* 23 September 2002: n. pag. academic.evergreen.edu/curricular/fictionlab/documents/FranzenGreenmand.pdf

---. "My Father's Brain." *How to Be Alone: Essays.* New York, NY: Picador, 2003: 7-38.

---. "Perchance to Dream: In the Age of Images, a Reason to Write Novels." *Harper's* April 1996: 35-54.

Freud, Sigmund. "A Difficulty in the Path of Psychoanalysis." 1917. In *The Standard Edition of the Complete Psychological Works of Sigmund Freud.* Vol. 17. Ed. and trans. James Strachey and Anna Freud. London: Hogarth, 1955: 135–44.

---. *The Ego and the Id*. 1923. In *The Standard Edition of the Complete Psychological Works of Sigmund Freud*. Vol. 19. Ed. and trans. James Strachey and Anna Freud. 1960.

---. *Introductory Lectures on Psycho-analysis*. 1916. In *The Standard Edition of the Complete Psychological Works of Sigmund Freud*. Vol. 16. Ed. and trans. James Strachey and Anna Freud. London: Hogarth, 1963.

---. "On Narcissism: An Introduction." 1914, In *The Standard Edition of the Complete Psychological Works of Sigmund Freud*. Vol. 14. Ed. and trans. James Strachey and Anna Freud. London: Hogarth, 1957: 67–102.

---. *New Introductory Lectures on Psycho-Analysis*. Trans. W. J. H. Sprott. New York, NY: Norton, 1933.

---. *Project for a Scientific Psychology*. In *The Standard Edition of the Complete Psychological Works of Sigmund Freud*. Vol. 1. Ed. and trans. James Strachey and Anna Freud. London: Hogarth, 1966: 295-387.

Freudenthal, Elizabeth. "Anti-Interiority: Objectification and Identity in *Infinite Jest*." *New Literary History* 41.1 (2010): 191-211.

Frith, Chris. *Making Up the Mind: How the Brain Creates Our Mental World*. Malden; MA: Blackwell, 2007.

Frosh, Stephen. "Psychoanalysis in Britain: 'The rituals of destruction.'" *A Concise Companion to Modernism*. Ed. David Bradshaw. Malden, MA: Blackwell, 2003: 116-37.

Frost, Laura Catherine. *The Problem with Pleasure: Modernism and Its Discontents*. New York, NY: Columbia University Press, 2013.

Frow, John. *Character and Person*. Oxford: Oxford University Press, 2014.

Frye, Northrop. *The Anatomy of Criticism: Four Essays*. 1957. Princeton, NJ: Princeton University Press, 2000.

Fuchs, Thomas. "The Brain—A Mediating Organ." *Journal of Consciousness Studies* 18.7–8 (2011): 196–221.

Gagnier, Regenia. *Subjectivities: A History of Self-Representation in Britain, 1832-1920*. Oxford: Oxford University Press, 1991.

Gallagher, Shaun S. *How the Body Shapes the Mind*. New York, NY: Oxford University Press, 2005.

---. "Philosophical Conceptions of the Self: Implications for Cognitive Science." *Trends in Cognitive Sciences* 4.1 (2000): 14-21.

Gass, William H. "The Anatomy of Mind." *The World Within the Word: Essays*. New York, NY: Knopf, 1978: 208-52.

Gazzaniga, Michael. "Cerebral Specialization and Interhemispheric Communication: Does the Corpus Callosum Enable the Human Condition?" *Brain* 123 (2000): 1293-1326.

---. *The Ethical Brain*. New York, NY: Dana Press, 2005.

---. *The Social Brain: Discovering the Networks of Mind*. New York, NY: Basic Books, 1985.

---. "The Split Brain in Man." *Scientific American* 217.2 (1967): 24-29.

---. "The Split Brain Revisited." *Scientific American* Special Edition 12.1 (2002): 27-31.

---. *Who's in Charge? Free Will and the Science of the Brain*. New York, NY: Harper Collins, 2011.

Geertz, Clifford. "From the Native's Point of View: On the Nature of Anthropological Understanding." *Bulletin of the American Academy of Arts and Sciences* 28.1 (1974): 26-45.

Genette, Gerard. *Paratexts: Threshold of Interpretation*. 1987. Cambridge: Cambridge University Press, 1997.

Gergen, Kenneth J. *Invitation to Social Construction*. London: Sage, 1999.

Gergen, Kenneth J., and Mary M. Gergen. "Narratives of the Self." *Studies in Social Identity*. Eds. Theodore R. Sarbin and Karl E. Scheibe. New York, NY: Praeger, 1983: 254-73.

---. "Scanning the Landscape of Narrative Inquiry." *Social and Personality Psychology Compass* 4.9 (2010): 728–35.

Giddens, Anthony. The Constitution of Society, Cambridge: Polity Press, 1984.

Giles, Paul. "Afterword: Turn and Turn About." *Mindful Aesthetics: Literature and the Science of Mind*. Eds. Chris Danta and Helen Groth. New York, NY: Bloomsbury, 2014: 207-11.

---. "All Swallowed Up: David Foster Wallace and American Literature." *The Legacy of David Foster Wallace*. Eds. Samuel Cohen and Lee Konstantinou. Iowa City, IO: University of Iowa Press, 2012: 3-22.

---. "Sentimental Posthumanism: David Foster Wallace." *Twentieth Century Literature* 53.3 (2007): 327-44.

Gilmore, Leigh. *Autobiographics: A Feminist Theory of Women's Self-representation*. Ithaca, NY: Cornell University Press, 1994.

Girard, René. *Mimesis and Theory: Essays on Literature and Criticism, 1953-2005*. Ed. Robert Doran. Stanford, Ca: Stanford University Press, 2008.

Godway, Eleanor. "Toward a Phenomenology of Politics: Expression and Praxis." *Merleau-Ponty: Hermeneutics, and Postmodernism*. Eds. Thomas W. Busch and Shaun Gallagher. Albany, NY: State University of New York Press, 1992: 161-70.

Goodheart, Eugene. "Some Speculations on Don DeLillo and the Cinematic Real." *Introducing Don DeLillo*. Ed. Frank Lentricchia. Durham, NC: Duke UP, 1991: 117-30.

Gotman, Kélina. "The Neural Metaphor." *The Neuroscientific Turn: Transdisciplinarity in the Age of the Brain*. Eds. Melissa M. Littlefield and Jenell M. Johnson. Ann Arbor; MI: University of Michigan Press, 2012: 71-86.

Gould, Elizabeth, et al. "Neurogenesis in the Neocortex of Adult Primates." *Science* 15 October 1999: 548-52.

Graham, Elaine L. *Representations of the Post/human: Monsters, Aliens and Others in Popular Culture*. Manchester: Manchester University Press, 2002.

Grawe, Klaus, Ruth Donati, and Friederike Bernauer. *Psychotherapie im Wandel: Von der Konfession zur Profession*. 4th ed. Göttingen: Hogrefe, 1995.

Greenfeld, Liah. "An Invitation to a Dialogue: A Comment on Neuroscience and Culture." *Nationalism and the Mind: Essays on Modern Culture*. Oxford: Oneworld Publications, 2006: 162-74.

Gross, Charles G. *A Hole in the Head: More Tales in the History of Neuroscience*. Cambridge, MA: The MIT Press, 2009.

Grosz, Elizabeth. *Becoming Undone: Darwinian Reflections on Life, Politics, and Art*. Durham, NC: Duke University 2011.

---. *Volatile Bodies: Toward a Corporeal Feminism*. Bloomington, IL: Indiana University Press, 1994.

Groves, Christopher Robert. "Road-maps and Revelations: On the Somatic Ethics of Genetic Susceptibility. *New Genetics and Society* 32.3 (2013): 264-284.

Hacking, Ian. "The Cartesian Vision Fulfilled: Analogue Bodies and Digital Minds." *Interdisciplinary Science Review* 30 (2005): 153-166.

---. "Kinds of People: Moving Targets." *Proceedings of the British Academy* 151: 285-318.

---. "Making Up People." *Reconstructing Individualism: Autonomy, Individuality and the Self in Western Thought*. Eds. T. C. Heller et al. Stanford, CA: Stanford University Press, 1986: 222–236.

---. "Our Neo-Cartesian Bodies in Parts." *Critical Inquiry* 34.1 (2007): 78-105.

---. *Rewriting the Soul: Multiple Personality and the Sciences of Memory*. Princeton, NJ: Princeton University Press, 1995.

Hale, Dorothy J. "General Introduction" *The Novel: An Anthology of Criticism and Theory 1900-2000*. Ed. Dorothy J. Hale. Malden, MA: Blackwell, 2006: 1-16.

Hale, Nathan G. *Freud and the Americans: The Origin and Foundation of the Psychoanalytic Movement in America, 1876 - 1917*. New York, NY: Oxford University Press, 1971.

Hansen, Mark B. N. *Bodies in Code: Interfaces with Digital Media*. New York, NY: Routledge, 2006.

Harris, Charles B. "The Story and the Self: *The Echo Maker* and Neurological Realism." *Intersections: Essays on Richard Powers*. Eds. Stephen Burn and Peter Dempsey. Champaign, IL: Dalkey Archive Press, 2008: 230-59.

Harris, Sam. *Free Will*. New York, NY: Free Press, 2012.

Harvey, David. "The Body as Accumulation Strategy." *Environment and Planning D: Society and Space* 16.4 (1998): 401-421.

---. *A Brief History of Neoliberalism*. Oxford: Oxford University Press, 2005.

Haselstein, Ulla, Andrew S. Gross, and MaryAnn Snyder-Körber. "Introduction: Returns of the Real." *The Pathos of Authenticity: American Passions of the Real.* Heidelberg: Winter, 2010: 9-31.

Hassin, Ran R. et al. *The New Unconscious.* Oxford: Oxford University Press, 2005.

Hatavari et al. *The Traveling Concepts of Narrative.* Amsterdam: John Benjamins, 2013.

Hayles, N. Katherine. *How We Became Posthuman: Virtual Bodies in Cybernetics, Literature, and Informatics.* Chicago, IL: The University of Chicago Press, 1999.

---. "The Illusion of Autonomy and the Fact of Recursivity: Virtual Ecologies, Entertainment, and *Infinite Jest*." *New Literary History* 30.3 (1999): 675-97.

Hebb, Donald O. *The Organization of Behavior: A Neuropsychological Theory.* New York, NY: Wiley, 1949.

Heehs, Peter. *Writing the Self: Diaries, Memoirs, and the History of the Self.* New York, NY: Bloomsbury, 2013.

Hegel, Georg W. F. *The Phenomenology of Mind.* Trans. J. B. Baillie. London: George Allen & Unwin, 1966.

Herbrechter, Stefan. *Posthumanism: A Critical Analysis.* 2009. London: Bloomsbury, 2013.

Hering, David. "*Infinite Jest*: Triangles, Cycles, Choices & Chases." *Consider David Foster Wallace: Critical Essays.* Ed. David Hering. Los Angeles, CA: Sideshow Media, 2010: kindle file; n. pag.

Herman, David. "Autobiography, Allegory, and the Construction of Self." *British Journal of Aesthetics* 35.4 (1995): 351-61.

Hess, Ewa, and Hennric Jokeit. "Neurocapitalism." *Eurozine* 24 Nov. 2009: n. pag. www.eurozine.com/articles/2009-11-24-jokeit-en.html

Hirstein, William. *Confabulation: Views from Neuroscience, Psychiatry, Psychology and Philosophy.* Oxford: Oxford University Press, 2009.

Hirt, Stefan. *The Iron Bars of Freedom: David Foster Wallace and the Postmodern Self.* New York, NY: Columbia University Press, 2008.

Hoberek, Andrew. "Introduction: After Postmodernism." *Twentieth Century Literature* 53.3 (2007): 233-36.

Hoffmann, Gerhard. *From Modernism to Postmodernism: Concepts and Strategies of Postmodern American Fiction.* Amsterdam: Rodopi, 2005.

Hogan, Patrick Colm. *Cognitive Science, Literature, and the Arts: A Guide for Humanists.* New York, NY: Routledge, 2003.

Holland, Mary K. *Succeeding Postmodernism: Language and Humanism in Contemporary American Literature.* New York, NY: Bloomsbury, 2013.

Hood, Bruce. *The Self Illusion: How the Social Brain Creates Identity.* Oxford: Oxford University Press, 2012.

Horgan, John. *The Undiscovered Mind: How the Human Brain Defies Replication, Medication, and Explanation.* New York, NY: Touchstone, 1999.

Horn, Patrick. "Does Language Fail Us? Wallace's Struggle with Solipsism." *Gesturing Toward Reality: David Foster Wallace and Philosophy.* Eds. Robert K. Bolger and Scott Korb. New York, NY: Bloomsbury, 2014: 245-70.

Horwitz, Alan V., and Jerome C. Wakefield. *The Loss of Sadness: How Psychiatry Transformed Normal Sorrow into Depressive Disorder.* New York, NY: Oxford University Press, 2007.

Houser, Heather. "Wondrous Strange: Eco-Sickness, Emotion, and *The Echo Maker.*" *American Literature* 84.2 (2012): 381-408.

Howard, Jennifer. "The Afterlife of David Foster Wallace."*Chronicle of Higher Education* 06 January 2011: n. pag.
chronicle.com/article/The-Afterlife-of-David-Foster/125823/

Hume, David. *A Treatise of Human Nature.* Eds. David Fate Norton and Mary J. Norton. Oxford: Oxford University Press, 2001.

Humphrey, Nicholas. *A History of the Mind: Evolution and the Birth of Consciousness.* New York, NY: Copernicus, 1992.

Hurt, James. "Narrative Powers: Richard Powers as Storyteller." *The Review of Contemporary Fiction* 18.3 (1998): 24-41.

Hustvedt, Siri. *The Shaking Woman, Or A History of My Nerves.* 2010. London: Sceptre, 2011.

Huxley, Thomas H. "On the Hypothesis that Animals are Automata." *Fortnightly Review* 16.95 (1874): 555-80.

Ickstadt, Heinz. "'Asynchronous Messaging': The Multiple Functions of Richard Powers's Fictions." *Ideas of Order: Narrative Patterns in the Novels of Richard Powers.* Eds. Antje Kley and Jan D. Kucharzewski. Heidelberg: Winter, 2012: 23-44.

Ihde, Don, and Evan Selinger, eds. *Chasing Technoscience: Matrix for Materiality.* Bloomington, IN: Indiana University Press, 2003.

Illouz, Eva. *Saving the Modern Soul: Therapy, Emotions, and the Culture of Self-Help.* Berkeley, CA: University of California Press, 2008.

Jacobs, Timothy. "The Brothers Incandenza: Translating Ideology in Fyodor Dostoevsky's *The Brothers Karamazov* and David Foster Wallace's *Infinite Jest.*" *Texas Studies in Literature and Language* 49.3 (2007): 265-292.

Jacobson, Marcus. *Foundations of Neuroscience.* New York, NY: Plenum Press, 1983.

James, William. "Are We Automata?" *Mind* 4.13 (1879): 1-22.

---. *Essays in Radical Empiricism.* Cambridge, MA: Harvard University Press, 1976.

---. "Habit." 1890. *The Principles of Psychology. Volume 1.* New York, NY: Cosimo, 2007: 104-27.

---. "Religion and Neurology." *The Varieties of Religious Experience.* 1902. New York, NY: Barnes & Noble, 2004: 15-34.

Jameson, Fredric. *Postmodernism, or, The Cultural Logic of Late Capitalism.* Durham, NC: Duke University Press, 1991.

---. *Valences of the Dialectic.* London: Verso, 2009.

Jamison, Kay Redfield. *An Unquiet Mind: A Memoir of Moods and Madness*. New York, NY: Knopf, 1995.

Johnson, Gary. "Consciousness as Content: Neuronarratives and the Redemption of Fiction." Mosaic 41.1 (2008): 169–84.

Johnson, Mark. *The Meaning of the Body: Aesthetics of Human Understanding*. Chicago, IL: The University of Chicago Press, 2007.

Johnston, Adrian. *Prolegomena to Any Future Materialism: The Outcome of Contemporary French Philosophy*. Evanston, IL: Northwestern University Press, 2013.

Johnston, John. *The Allure of Machinic Life: Cybernetics, Artificial Life, and the New AI*. Cambridge, MA: MIT Press, 2008.

Jolly, Margaretta, ed. *Encyclopedia of Life Writing: Autobiographical and Biographical Forms*. Chicago, IL: Fitzroy Dearborn, 2001.

Jurecic, Ann. "Neurodiversity." *College English* 69.5 (2007): 421-42.

Kahneman, Daniel. *Thinking, Fast and Slow*. New York, NY: Farrar, Straus and Giroux, 2011.

Kandel, Eric. "Biology and the Future of Psychoanalysis: A New Intellectual Framework for Psychiatry Revisited." *American Journal of Psychiatry* 156 (1999): 505–524.

---. *In Search of Memory: The Emergence of a New Science of Mind*. New York, NY: Norton, 2006.

---. "A New Intellectual Framework for Psychiatry." *American Journal of Psychiatry* 155 (1998): 457–469.

Kauffmann, Oliver. "Brain Plasticity and Phenomenal Consciousness." *Neuroplasticity*. Special issue of *Journal of Consciousness Studies* 18.7-8 (2011): 46-70.

Kehily, Mary Jane. "Self-narration, Autobiography and Identity Construction." *Gender and Education* 7.1 (1995): 23-32.

Kelleter, Frank. "A Tale of Two Natures: Worried Reflections on the Study of Literature and Culture in an Age of Neuroscience and Neo-Darwinism." *Journal of Literary Theory* 1:1 (2007): 153–189.

---. *Serial Agencies: The Wire and Its Readers*. Winchester: Zero Books, 2014.

Keesey, Douglas. *Don DeLillo*. New York, NY: Twayne, 1993.

Kelly, Adam. "David Foster Wallace: the Death of the Author and the Birth of a Discipline." *Irish Journal of American Studies Online* 2 (2010): n. pag. www.ijasonline.com/Adam-Kelly.html

---. "Development Through Dialogue: David Foster Wallace and the Novel of Ideas." *Studies in the Novel* 44.3 (2012): 267-83.

Kelly, David R. "David Foster Wallace as American Hedgehog." *Freedom and the Self. Essays on the Philosophy of David Foster Wallace*. Eds. Steven M. Cahn and Maureen Eckert. New York, NY: Columbia University Press, 2015.

Kelly, Eugene. *The Basics of Western Philosophy*. Westport, CT: Greenwood Press, 2004.

Kelly, Daniel R. "David Foster Wallace as American Hedgehog." *Freedom and the Self: Essays on the Philosophy of David Foster Wallace.* Eds. Steven M. Cahn and Maureen Eckert. New York, NY: Columbia University Press, 2015: 109-32.

Kerby, Anthony Paul. *Narrative and the Self.* Bloomington, IN: Indiana University Press, 1991.

Kihlstrom, John F., and Stanley B. Klein. "Self-Knowledge and Self-Awareness." *Annals of the New York Academy of Sciences* 818.1 (1997): 5-17.

Kim, Jaegwon. "The Myth of Nonreductive Materialism." *Proceedings and Addresses of the American Philosophical Association* 63 (1989): 31–47.

Kimball, Roger. "'The Two Cultures' today: On the C. P. Snow-F. R. Leavis controversy." *The New Criterion* 12 February 1994: n. pag. www.newcriterion.com/articles.cfm/-The-Two-Cultures--today-4882

Kirsch, Adam. "The Importance of Being Earnest: David Foster Wallace." *Rocket and Lightship: Essays on Literature and Ideas.* New York, NY: Norton, 2015: 195-214.

Knight, Peter. "DeLillo, Postmodernism, Postmodernity." *The Cambridge Companion to Don DeLillo.* Ed. John N. Duvall. Cambridge: Cambridge University Press, 2008: 27-40.

Koch, Christoph. *The Quest for Consciousness: A Neurobiological Approach.* Englewood, CO: Roberts & Company, 2004.

Konstantinou, Lee. "No Bull: David Foster Wallace and Postironic Belief." *The Legacy of David Foster Wallace.* Eds. Samuel Cohen and Lee Konstantinou. Iowa City, IO: University of Iowa Press, 2012: 83-112.

Kramer, Peter. *Listening to Prozac.* New York, NY: Penguin, 1993.

Kringelbach, Morten L., and Kent C. Berridge. "The Functional Neuroanatomy of Pleasure and Happiness." *Discovery Medicine.* 9.49 (2010): 579–587.

Krüger, Hans-Peter, ed. *Hirn als Subjekt? Philosophische Grenzfragen der Neurobiologie.* Berlin: Akademie Verlag, 2007.

---. "Das Hirn im Kontext exzentrischer Positionierungen: Zur philosophischen Herausforderung der neurobiologischen Hirnforschung." *Hirn als Subjekt? Philosophische Grenzfragen der Neurobiologie.* Ed. Hans-Peter Krüger. Berlin: Akademie Verlag, 2007: 61-98.

Kucharzewski, Jan D. *Propositions about Life: Reengaging Literature and Science.* Heidelberg: Winter, 2011.

Kucich, John. "Postmodern Politics: Don DeLillo and the Plight of the White Male Writer." *Michigan Quarterly Review* 27.2 (1988): 328-41.

Lacan, Jacques. *The Language of the Self: The Function of Language in Psychoanalysis.* Trans. Anthony Wilden. Baltimore; MA: The Johns Hopkins Press, 1968.

Laist, Randy. *Technology and Postmodern Subjectivity in Don DeLillo's Novels.* New York, NY: Peter Lang, 2010.

Lakoff, George, and Mark Johnson. *Metaphors We Live By*. Chicago, IL: The University of Chicago Press, 1980.

---. *Philosophy In The Flesh: the Embodied Mind and its Challenge to Western Thought*. New York, NY: Basic Books, 1999.

Landgraf, Edgar. "Black Boxes and White Noise. Don DeLillo and the Reality of Literature." *Addressing Modernity: Social Systems Theory and U.S. Cultures*. Eds. Hannes Bergthaller and Carsten Schinko. Amsterdam: Rodopi, 2011: 85-112.

Latour, Bruno. "Agency at the Time of the Anthropocene." *New Literary History* 45.1 (2014): 1–18.

---. *Aramis, or the Love of Technology*. 1993. Trans. Catherine Porter. Boston, MA: Harvard University Press, 1996.

---. "A Collective of Humans and Nonhumans. Following Daedalus's Labyrinth." *Pandora's Hope: Essays on the Reality of Science Studies*. Cambridge, MA: Harvard University Press, 1999: 174-215.

---. "Do You Believe in Reality? News from the Trenches of the Science Wars." *Pandora's Hope: Essays on the Reality of Science Studies*. Cambridge, MA: Harvard University Press, 1999: 1-23.

---. "Powers of the Facsimile: A Turing Test on Science and Literature." *Intersections: Essays on Richard Powers*. Eds. Stephen Burn and Peter Dempsey. Champaign, IL: Dalkey Archive Press, 2008: 263-91.

---. *Reassembling the Social: An Introduction to Actor-Network-Theory*. Oxford: Oxford University Press, 2005.

Latour, Bruno, and Richard Powers. "A Dialog with Richard Powers in Honor of HAL." *Common Knowledge* 7.1 (1998): 177-191.

Leader, Darian. *Strictly Bipolar*. London: Penguin, 2013.

LeClair, Tom. *The Art of Excess: Mastery in Contemporary American Fiction*. Urbana, IL: University of Illinois Press, 1989.

---. *In the Loop: Don DeLillo and the Systems Novel*. Urbana, IL: University of Illinois Press, 1987.

---. "The Prodigious Fiction of Richard Powers, William Vollmann, and David Foster Wallace." *Critique* 38.1 (1996): 12-37.

LeDoux, Joseph. *The Emotional Brain*. New York, NY: Simon & Schuster, 1996.

---. *The Synaptic Self: How Our Brains Become Who We Are*. New York, NY: Viking, 2002.

Legrenzi, Paolo, and Carlo Umilta. *Neuromania: On the Limits of Brain Science*. Trans. Frances Anderson. Oxford: Oxford University Press, 2013.

Lehrer, Jonah. *Proust was a Neuroscientist*. Boston, MA: Houghton Mifflin, 2007.

---. "The Reinvention of the Self." *Seed Magazine* 22 February 2006: n. pag. seedmagazine.com/content/article/the_reinvention_of_the_self/

Lentricchia, Frank. Introduction. *New Essays on* White Noise. Ed. Frank Lentricchia. Cambridge: Cambridge University Press, 1991: 1-14.

Lejeune, Philippe. "The Autobiographical Pact." Trans. Katherine M. Leary. *On Autobiography*. Ed. Paul John Eakin. Minneapolis, MN: University of Minnesota Press, 1989: 3-30.

Lethem, Jonathan. Introduction. *The Vintage Book of Amnesia*. Ed. Jonathan Lethem. New York, NY: Vintage, xiii-xvii.

Levin, Martin. Review of *Americana* by Don DeLillo. *The New York Times* 30 May 1971: n. pag.
https://www.nytimes.com/books/97/03/16/lifetimes/del-r-americana.html

Levine, Joseph. "Materialism and Qualia: The Explanatory Gap." *Pacific Philosophical Quarterly* 64 (1983): 354-361.

Lewis, Marc. *Memoirs of an Addicted Brain: A Neuroscientist Examines His Former Life on Drugs*. 2011. New York, NY: Public Affairs, 2012.

Leys, Ruth. "The Turn to Affect: A Critique." *Critical Inquiry* 37 (2011): 434-72.

Libet, Benjamin. "Unconscious Cerebral Initiative and the Role of Conscious Will in Voluntary Action." *The Behavioral and Brain Sciences* 8 (1985): 529–566.

Lipsky, David. *Although of Course You End Up Becoming Yourself: A Road Trip With David Foster Wallace*. New York, NY: Broadway Books, 2010.

Littlefield, Melissa M., and Jenell M. Johnson. "Introduction: Theorizing the Neuroscientific Turn—Critical Perspectives on a Translational Discipline." *The Neuroscientific Turn: Transdisciplinarity in the Age of the Brain*. Eds. Melissa M. Littlefield and Jenell M. Johnson. Ann Arbor, MI: University of Michigan Pres, 2012: 1-25.

Liu, Jonathan. Review of *Memoirs of an Addicted Brain* by Marc Lewis. *The Boston Globe* 23 Mar. 2012: n. pag.
www.bostonglobe.com/arts/2012/03/22/memoirs-addicted-brain-neuroscientist-marc-lewis-discusses-his-drug-use-and-science-behind/

Lodge, David. "Consciousness and the Novel." *Consciousness and the Novel: Connected Essays*. 2002. London: Penguin, 2003: 1-91.

Luhmann, Niklas. *Aufsätze und Reden*. Ed. Oliver Jahraus. Stuttgart: Reclam, 2001.

---. *Social Systems*. Trans. John Bednarz, Jr., with Dirk Baecker. Stanford, CA: Stanford University Press, 1995.

---. "Die Tücke des Subjekts und die Frage nach dem Menschen." *Der Mensch – das Medium der Gesellschaft?* Eds. Peter Fuchs and Andreas Gö bel. Frankfurt am Main: Suhrkamp, 1994: 40–56.

---. "Why Does Society Describe Itself as Postmodern?" *Cultural Critique* 30 (1995): 171-86.

Luhrmann, Tanya Marie. *Of Two Minds: The Growing Disorder in American Psychiatry*. 2000. London: Picador, 2001.

---. "Subjectivity." *Anthropological Theory* 6.3 (2006): 345-61.

Lundberg, Chris. Review of *Giving an Account of Oneself* by Judith Butler. *Philosophy and Rhetoric* 40.3 (2007): 329-333.

Lustig, T. J. "'Two-way traffic'? Syndrome as Symbol in Richard Powers' [sic] *The Echo Maker*." *Diseases and Disorders in Contemporary Fiction: The Syndrome Syndrome*. Eds. T. J. Lustig and James Peacock. London: Routledge, 2013: 130-43.

Lustig, T. J., and James Peacock. Introduction. *Diseases and Disorders in Contemporary Fiction: The Syndrome Syndrome*. London: Routledge, 2013: 1-16.

Luria, Alexander. *The Autobiography of Alexander Luria: A Dialogue with The Making of Mind*. 1979. Eds. Michael Cole and Karl Levitin. Mahwah, NJ: Lawrence Erlbaum Associates, 2006.

Luther, Connie. "David Foster Wallace: Westward with Fredric Jameson." *Consider David Foster Wallace: Critical Essays*. Ed. David Hering. Los Angeles, LA: Sideshow Media Group Press, 2010: 49-61.

Lnych, Zack. *The Neuro Revolution: How Brain Science is Changing Our World*. New York, NY: St. Martin's Press, 2009.

Lyotard, Jean-François. *The Postmodern Condition: A Report on Knowledge*. Trans. Geoff Bennington and Brian Massumi. Manchester: Manchester University Press, 1984.

---. "A Postmodern Fable." 1993. *Postmodern Fables*. Trans. Georges Van Den Abbeele. Minneapolis, MN: University of Minnesota Press, 1997: 83-102.

MacIntyre, Alasdair. *After Virtue*. 1981. London: Bloomsbury, 2007.

MacLean, Paul D. "Paul D. MacLean." *The History of Neuroscience in Autobiography*. Vol. 2. Ed. Larry Squire. New York, NY: Academic Press, 1998: 246-75.

Macmillan, Malcolm. *An Odd Kind of Fame: Stories of Phineas Gage*. Cambridge, MA: MIT Press, 2000.

Malabou, Catherine. "Addiction and Grace: Preface to Félix Ravaisson's *Of Habit*." *Of Habit*. 1838. Trans. Clare Carlisle and Mark Sinclair. London: Continuum, 2008.

---. *The New Wounded: From Neurosis to Brain Damage*. Trans. Steven Miller. New York, NY: Fordham University Press, 2012.

---. *Ontology of the Accident: An Essay on Destructive Plasticity*. Trans. Carolyn Shread. Cambridge: Polity Press, 2012.

---. *Plasticity at the Dusk of Writing: Dialectic, Destruction, Deconstruction*. 2005. Trans. Carolyn Shread. New York, NY: Columbia University Press, 2010.

---. *What Should We Do with Our Brain?* Trans. Sebastian Rand. New York, NY: Fordham University Press, 2008.

Mansfield, Nick. *Subjectivity: Theories of Self from Freud to Haraway*. St Leonards: Allen & Unwin, 2000.

Marks-Tarlow, Terry, et al. "Varela and the Uroboros: The Psychological Significance of Reentry." *Cybernetics & Human Knowing* 9.2 (2002): 31-47.

Martensen, Robert L. *The Brain Takes Shape: An Early History*. Oxford: Oxford University Press, 2004.

Martin, Emily. *Bipolar Expeditions: Mania and Depression in American Culture.* Princeton, NJ: Princeton University Press, 2007.

---. "Self-making and the Brain." *Subjectivity* 3.4 (2010): 366-81.

Martin, Raymond, and John Barresi. *The Rise and Fall of Soul and Self: An Intellectual History of Personal Identity.* New York, NY: Columbia University Press, 2006.

Maté, Gabor. *In the Realm of Hungry Ghosts: Close Encounters with Addiction.* 2008. Berkeley, CA: North Atlantic Books, 2010.

Max, D.T. *Every Love Story Is a Ghost Story: A Life of David Foster Wallace.* New York, NY: Viking, 2012.

Mauss, Marcel. "A Category of the Human Mind: The Notion of Person; the Notion of Self." Trans. W. D. Halls. *The Category of the Person: Anthropology, Philosophy, History.* Eds. Michael Carrithers et al. Cambridge: Cambridge University Press, 1985: 1-25.

Mayes, Rick, and Allan V. Horwitz. "*DSM-III* and the Revolution in the Classification of Mental Illness." *Journal of the History of the Behavioral Sciences* 41 (2005): 249–267.

McAuley, Kyle. "The Specter Haunting the Contemporary Novel, Part I." *HASTAC* 31 December 2011: n. pag.
www.hastac.org/blogs/kylemcauley/2011/12/31/specter-haunting-contemporary-novel-part-i

McClure, John. "Postmodern Romance: Don DeLillo and the Age of Conspiracy." *Introducing Don DeLillo.* Ed. Frank. Lentricchia. Durham, NC: Duke University Press, 1991: 99-116.

McGilchrist, Iain. *The Master and His Emissary: The Divided Brain and the Making of the Western World.* New Haven, CT: Yale University Press, 2009.

McGinn, Colin. *The Mysterious Flame: Conscious Minds In A Material World.* New York, NY: Basic Books, 1999.

McGurl, Mark. *The Novel Art: Elevations of American Fiction after Henry James.* Princeton, NJ: Princeton University Press, 2001.

---. "The Institution of Nothing: David Foster Wallace in the Program." *boundary 2* 41.3 (2014): 27-54.

---. *The Program Era: Postwar Fiction and the Rise of Creative Writing.* Cambridge, MA: Harvard University Press, 2009.

---. "Zombie Renaissance." *n+1.* 9 (2010): n. pag.
https://nplusonemag.com/issue-9/reviews/the-zombie-renaissance/

McHale, Brian. *Postmodernist Fiction.* New York, NY: Methuen, 1987.

---. "What Was Postmodernism?" *electronic book review.* 20 December 2007: n. pag.
www.electronicbookreview.com/thread/fictionspresent/tense

McLaughlin, Brian P. "Epiphenomenalism." *The MIT Encyclopedia of the Cognitive Sciences.* Eds. Robert Andrew Wilson and Frank C. Keil. Cambridge, MA: MIT Press, 1999: 275-78.

Mead, George Herbert. "The Social Self." 1913. *Selected Writings*. Ed. Andrew J. Reck. Chicago, IL: The University of Chicago Press, 1964: 142-49.

Melley, Timothy. *Empire of Conspiracy: The Culture of Paranoia in Postwar America*. Ithaca, NY: Cornell University Press, 2000.

---. "Technology, Rationality, Modernity: An Approach to *White Noise*." *Approaches to Teaching DeLillo's* White Noise. Eds. Tim Engles and John N. Duvall. New York, NY: Modern Language Association of America, 2006: 73-83.

---. "A Terminal Case: William Burroughs and the Logic of Addiction." *High Anxieties: Cultural Studies in Addiction*. Eds. Janet Farrell Brodie and Marc Redfield. Berkeley, CA: University of California Press, 2002: 38-62.

Menand, Louis. "Head Case: Can Psychiatry Be a Science?" *The New Yorker* 01 Mar. 2010: n. pag.
www.newyorker.com/magazine/2010/03/01/head-case-2

Mendelson, Edward. "Encyclopedic Narrative: From Dante to Pynchon." *Modern Language Notes* 91.6 (1976): 1267-75.

---. "Gravity's Encyclopedia." *Mindful Pleasures: Essays on Thomas Pynchon*. Eds. George Levine and David Leverenz. Boston, MA: Little, Brown and Company, 1976: 161-195.

Miller, Brook. *Self-Consciousness in Modern British Fiction*. New York, NY: Palgrave Macmillan, 2013.

Miller, D. Quentin. "Deeper Blues, or the Posthuman Prometheus: Cybernetic Renewal and the Late-Twentieth-Century American Novel." *American Literature* 77.2 (2005): 379-407.

Merleau-Ponty, Maurice. *Phenomenology of Perception*. 1945. Trans Donald A. Landes. London: Routledge, 2012.

Mill, John Stuart. *On Liberty and Other Essays*. 1991. London: Penguin, 2008.

Mlodinow, Leonard. *Subliminal: The New Unconscious and What it Teaches Us*. London: Penguin, 2012.

Molesworth, Charles. "Don DeLillo's Perfect Starry Night." *Introducing Don DeLillo*. Ed. Frank Lentricchia. Durham, NC: Duke University Press: 143-56.

Moore, Lorrie. "Look for a Writer and Find a Terrorist." Review of *Mao II* by Don DeLillo. *The New York Times* 09 June 1991: n. pag.
https://www.nytimes.com/books/97/03/16/lifetimes/del-r-mao.html

Moore, Steven. "The First Draft of *Infinite Jest*." *The Howling Fantods* 28 May 2003: n. pag.
www.thehowlingfantods.com/ij_first.htm

Moretti, Franco. *Modern Epic: The World-system from Goethe to García Márquez*. 1994. Trans. Quintin Hoare. London: Verso, 1996.

Moses, Michael Valdez. "Lust Removed from Nature." *New Essays on* White Noise. Ed. Frank Lentricchia. Cambridge: Cambridge University Press, 1991: 63-86.

Mullins, Ryan David. "Theories of Everything and More: Infinite is not the End." *Gesturing Toward Reality: David Foster Wallace and Philosophy*. Eds. Robert K. Bolger and Scott Korb. New York, NY: Bloomsbury, 2014: 221-44.

Murison, Justine S. "'The Paradise of Non-Experts': The Neuroscientific Turn of the 1840s United States." *The Neuroscientific Turn: Transdisciplinarity in the Age of the Brain*. Eds. Melissa M. Littlefield and Jenell M. Johnson. Ann Arbor, MI: University of Michigan Pres, 2012: 29-48.

Murphet, Julian. "A Loose Democracy in the Skull: Characterology and Neuroscience." *Mindful Aesthetics: Literature and the Science of Mind*. Eds. Chris Danta and Helen Groth. New York, NY: Bloomsbury, 2014: 189-206.

Musgrave, David. *Grotesque Anatomies: Menippean Satire since the Renaissance*. Newcastle upon Tyne: Cambridge Scholars Publishing, 2014.

Nadeau, Robert. *Readings from the New Book on Nature: Physics and Metaphysics in the Modern Novel*. Cambridge, MA: University of Massachusetts Press, 1981.

Nagel, Thomas. "Freud's Anthropomorphism." *Freud: A Collection of Critical Essays*. Ed. Richard Wollheim. Garden City, NY: Anchor Books, 1974: 11-24.

---. *Mind and Cosmos: Why the Materialist Neo-Darwinian Conception of Nature Is Almost Certainly False*. Oxford: Oxford University Press, 2012.

---. "What Is It Like to Be a Bat?" *The Philosophical Review* 83.4 (1974): 435-450.

---. *The View from Nowhere*. Oxford: Oxford University Press, 1986.

Natalini, Roberto. "David Foster Wallace and the Mathematics of Infinity." *A Companion to David Foster Wallace Studies*. Eds. Marshall Boswell and Stephen J. Burn. New York, NY: Palgrave Macmillan, 2013: 43-58.

Neilson, Jim. "Dirtying Our Hands: An Introduction to the Fiction of Richard Powers." *Review of Contemporary Fiction* 18.3 (1998): 7-12.

Nicholls, Angus, and Martin Liebscher, eds. *Thinking the Unconscious: Nineteenth-Century German Thought*. Cambridge: Cambridge University Press, 2010.

Nida-Rümelin, Martine. "Human Agency and Neurophysiological Data." *Philosophie der Wissenschaft—Wissenschaft der Philosophie*. Eds. Gerhard Ernst and Karl-Georg Niebergall. Paderborn: Mentis, 2006: 205-32.

Nietzsche, Friedrich. "On the Death of God." *Main Currents of Western Thought: Readings in Western European Intellectual History from the Middle Ages to the Present*. Ed. Franklin Le Van Baumer. New Haven, CT: Yale University Press, 1978: 610-14.

North, Michael. *Machine-Age Comedy*. Oxford: Oxford University Press, 2009.

Northoff, Georg. *Neuropsychoanalysis in Practice: Brain, Self, and Objects*. Oxford: Oxford University Press, 2011.

---. *Philosophy of the Brain: The Brain Problem*. Amsterdam: John Benjamins, 2004.

Nünning, Ansgar. "Steps Towards a Metaphorology (and Narratology) of Crises: On the Functions of Metaphors as Figurative Knowledge and Mininarrations." *REAL* 25 (2009): 229-62.

Olds, James. "Pleasure Centers in the Brain." *Scientific American* Oct. 1956: 105-116.

Olster, Stacy. *Don DeLillo: Mao II, Underworld, Falling Man.* New York, NY: Continuum, 2011.

Ortega, Francisco. "The Cerebral Subject and the Challenge of Neurodiversity." *BioSocieties* 4 (2009): 425–45.

---. *Corporeality, Medical Technologies and Contemporary Culture.* Abingdon: Birkbeck Law Press, 2014.

---. "Toward a Genealogy of Neuroascesis." *Neurocultures: Glimpses into an Expanding Universe.* Eds. Francisco Ortega and Fernando Vidal. Frankfurt am Main: Peter Lang, 2011: 31-48.

Ortega, Francisco, and Fernando Vidal. "Approaching the Neurocultural Spectrum: An Introduction." *Neurocultures: Glimpses Into an Expanding Universe.* Eds. Francisco Ortega and Fernando Vidal. Frankfurt am Main: Peter Lang, 2011: 7-28.

---. "Brains in Literature/Literature in the Brain." *Poetics Today* 34.3 (2013): 327-60.

---. "Mapping the Cerebral Subject in Contemporary Culture." *RECIIS* 1.2 (2007): 255-59.

Ortner, Sherry B. "Subjectivity and Cultural Critique." *Anthropological Theory* 5.1 (2005): 31-52.

Osteen, Mark. "DeLillo's Dedalian Artists." *The Cambridge Companion to Don DeLillo.* Ed. John N. Duvall. Cambridge: Cambridge University Press, 2008: 137-50.

Palmer, Alan. "1945—: Ontologies of Consciousness." *Emergence of Mind: Representations of Consciousness In Narrative Discourse in English.* Ed. David Herman. Lincoln, NE: University of Nebraska Press, 2011: 273-98.

---. "The Construction of Fictional Minds." *Narrative* 10.1 (2002): 28-46.

Papineau, David. "Naturalism." *The Stanford Encyclopedia of Philosophy.* Ed. Edward N. Zalta. Spring 2009 Edition: n. pag.

plato.stanford.edu/archives/spr2009/entries/naturalism/

Pass, Phill. *The Language of Self: Strategies of Subjectivity in the Novels of Don DeLillo.* Oxford: Peter Lang, 2014.

Passaro, Vince. "Dangerous Don DeLillo." *New York Times Magazine* 19 May 1991: 34-36, 38, 76-77.

Paulson, William. "The Literary Canon in the Age of Its Technological Obsolescence." *Reading Matters: Narrative in the New Media Ecology.* Eds. Joseph Tabbi and Michael Wutz. Ithaca, NY: Cornell University Press, 1997: 227-49.

Pease, Donald. "New Americanists: Revisionist Interventions into the Canon." *Revisionary Interventions into the Americanist Canon.* Ed. Donald Pease. Durham, NC: Duke University Press, 1994: 1-37.

Pinker, Steven. *How the Mind Works.* New York, NY: Norton, 1997.

Pitts-Taylor, Victoria. "Social Brains, Embodiment, and Neuro-Interactionism." *The Routledge Handbook of Body Studies*. Ed. Bryan S. Turner. London: Routledge, 2012: 171-82.

---. "The Plastic Brain: Neoliberalism and the Neuronal Self." *Health* 14.6 (2010): 635-52.

---. "The Neurocultures Manifesto." *Social Text* online. April 06 2012. socialtext-journal.org/periscope_article/neurocultures-manifesto/

Porter, Roy. *Flesh in the Age of Reason: How the Enlightenment Transformed the Way We See Our Souls and Bodies*. 2003. London: Penguin, 2004.

---. *Madness: A Brief History*. Oxford: Oxford University Press, 2002.

Powers, Richard. "Being and Seeming: The Technology of Representation." *Context* 3 (2000a): n. pag.
www.dalkeyarchive.com/article/show/120

---. "Children of the Revolution." *American Book Review* 35.3 (2014): 8.

---. "A Conversation with Richard Powers." Interview with Jim Neilson. *Review of Contemporary Fiction* 18.3 (1998): 13-23.

---. "A Dialogue." Interview with Bradford Morrow. *Conjunctions* 34 (2000b): n. pag.
www.conjunctions.com/archives/c34-rp.htm

---. *The Echo Maker*. New York, NY: Picador, 2006.

---. *Galatea 2.2*. 1995. New York, NY: Picador, 2004.

---. "In the Lakehouse of Language: An Interview with Richard Powers." Interview with Jan Kucharzewski. *Propositions about Life: Reengaging Literature and Science*. Heidelberg: Winter, 2011: 455-62.

---. Interview with Stephen Burn. *Contemporary Literature* 49.2 (2008a): 163-179.

---. "The Last Generalist: An Interview with Richard Powers." Interview with Jeffrey J. Williams. *The Minnesota Review* 52-54 (2001): 95-114.

---. "Making the Rounds." *Intersections: Essays on Richard Powers*. Eds. Stephen Burn and Peter Dempsey. Champaign, IL: Dalkey Archive Press, 2008: 305-10.

---. "Richard Powers's Narrative Impulse." Interview with Jill Owens. *Powells.com* 10 Jan. 2007: n. pag.
www.powells.com/blog/interviews/richard-powerss-narrative-impulse-by-jill/

---. "Richard Powers, The Art of Fiction No. 175." Interview with Kevin Berger. *The Paris Review* 164 (2003): n. pag.
www.theparisreview.org/interviews/298/the-art-of-fiction-no-175-richard-powers

---. "Two Geeks on Their Way to Byzantium: A Conversation with Richard Powers." Interview with Harvey Blume. *The Atlantic online* 28 June 2000: n. pag.
https://www.theatlantic.com/past/docs/unbound/interviews/ba2000-06-28.htm

Protevi, John. *Political Affect: Connecting the Social and the Somatic.* Minneapolis, MN: University of Minnesota Press, 2009.

Pugh, Gilbert. "Cooperation or Incorporation: Psychoanalysis and Neuroscience." *Psychoanalysis and Neuroscience.* Ed. Mauro Mancia. Milan: Springer Italia, 2006: 33-62.

Ramachandran, V. S. "Consciousness and Body Image: Lessons from Phantom Limbs, Capgras Syndrome and Pain Asymbolia." *Philosophical Transactions of the Royal Society B: Biological Sciences* 353.1377 (1998): 1851–1859.

Reichel, André. "Snakes all the Way Down: Varela's Calculus for Self-Reference and the Praxis of Paradise." *Systems Research and Behavioral Science* 28.6 (2011): 646 – 662.

Relihan, Joel. "Late Arrivals: Julian and Boethius." *The Cambridge Companion to Roman Satire.* Ed. Kirk Freudenburg. Cambridge: Cambridge University Press, 2005: 109-22.

Renza, Louis A. Rev. of *Fictions in Autobiography: Studies in the Art of Self-Invention*, by Paul John Eakin. *Comparative Literature* 40.3 (1988): 269-74.

Revonsuo, Antti. *Consciousness: The Science of Subjectivity.* New York, NY: Psychology Press, 2010.

Richardson, Alan. "Brains, Minds, and Text." Review of *The Literary Mind* by Mark Turner. *Review* 20 (1998): 39-48

---. *British Romanticism and the Science of the Mind.* Cambridge, MA: Cambridge University Press, 2004.

Ricoeur, Paul. "Life in Quest of Narrative." *On Paul Ricoeur: Narrative and Interpretation.* Ed. David Wood. London: Routledge, 1991: 20-33.

---. "Narrative Identity." *Philosophy Today* 35.1 (1991): 73-81.

---. "On Interpretation." *From Text to Action: Essays in Hermeneutics II.* 1986. Trans. Kathleen Blamey and John B. Thompson. Evanston, IL: Northwestern University Press, 1991.

---. *Time and Narrative, Volume 3.* 1985. Trans Kathleen Blamey and David Pellauer. Chicago, IL: The University of Chicago Press, 1988.

Rieff, Philipp. 1966. *The Triumph of the Therapeutic: Uses of Faith after Freud.* Chicago, IL: The University of Chicago Press, 1987.

Robbe-Grillet, Alain. "A Future for the Novel." *For a New Novel: Essays on Fiction.* Evanston, IL: Northwestern University Press, 1989: 15-24.

Robinson, Marilynne. *Absence of Mind: The Dispelling of Inwardness from the Modern Myth of the Self.* New Haven, CT: Yale University Press, 2010.

---. Introduction. *The Death of Adam: Essays on Modern Thought.* New York, NY: Houghton Mifflin, 1998: 1-27.

Rorty, Amélie Oksenberg. "The Vanishing Subject: The Many Faces of Subjectivity." *Subjectivity: Ethnographic Investigations.* Eds. João Biehl et al. Berkeley, CA: University of California Press, 2007: 34-51.

Rorty, Richard. *Objectivity, Relativism, and Truth: Philosophical Papers, Volume I.* New York, NY: Cambridge University Press, 1991.

---. *Philosophy and the Mirror of Nature.* 1979. Princeton, NJ: Princeton University Press, 2009.

Rose, Hilary, and Steven Rose. *Genes, Cells and Brains: The Promethean Promises of the New Biology.* London: Verso, 2012.

Rose, Nikolas. "Becoming Neurochemical Selves." *Biotechnology, Commerce and Civil Society.* Ed. Nico Stehr. New Brunswick, NJ: Transaction, 2004: 89-128.

---. "The Neurochemical Self and its Anomalies." *Risk and Morality.* Eds. Richard Ericson and Aaron Doyle. Toronto: University of Toronto Press, 2003: 407- 437.

---. "Neurochemical Selves." *Society* 41.1 (2003): 46-59.

---. *The Politics of Life Itself: Biomedicine, Power, and Subjectivity in the Twenty-First Century.* Princeton, NJ: Princeton University Press, 2006.

Rose, Nikolas, and Joelle M. Abi-Rached. *Neuro: The New Brain Sciences and the Management of the Mind.* Princeton, NJ: Princeton University Press, 2013.

Rosen, Jeffrey. "The Brain on the Stand." *New York Times Magazine* 11 Mar 2007: n. pag.
www.nytimes.com/2007/03/11/magazine/11Neurolaw.t.html

Roth, Marco. "Rise of the Neuronovel." *n+1* 8 (2009): n. pag.
https://nplusonemag.com/issue-8/essays/the-rise-of-the-neuronovel/

Rowlands, Mark. "The New Science of the Mind: From Extended Mind to Embodied Phenomenology." Cambridge, MA: The MIT Press, 2010.

Rumelhart, David E., James L. McClelland, and the PDP Research Group. *Parallel Distributed Processing: Explorations in the Microstructure of Cognition.* 2 vols. Cambridge, MA: MIT Press, 1986.

Russell, Bertrand. *The Analysis of Mind.* 1921. New York, NY: Cosimo, 2004.

Russell, Emily. "Some Assembly Required: The Embodied Politics of *Infinite Jest*." *Arizona Quarterly* 66.3 (2010): 147-169.

Ryle, Gilbert. *The Concept of Mind.* 1949. London: Routledge, 2009.

Sacks, Oliver. *A Leg to Stand On.* 1984. New York, NY: Touchstone, 1998.

---. *The Man Who Mistook His Wife for a Hat and Other Clinical Tales.* 1970. New York, NY: Touchstone, 1998.

---. "Luria and 'Romantic Science.'" *The Cambridge Handbook of Cultural-Historical Psychology.* Eds. Anton Yasnitsky et al. Cambridge: Cambridge University Press, 2014: 517-28.

---. "Neurology and the Soul." *The New York Review of Books* 37.18 (1990): 44-50.

Saks, Elyn R. *The Center Cannot Hold: My Journey through Madness.* New York, NY: Hyperion, 2007.

Saltzman, Arthur. *This Mad "Instead": Governing Metaphors in Contemporary American Fiction.* Columbia, SC: University of South Carolina Press, 2000.

Sass, Louis A. "'Negative Symptoms', Common Sense, and Cultural Disembedding in the Modern Age." *Schizophrenia, Culture, and Subjectivity: The Edge of Experience*. Eds. Janis Hunter Jenkins and Robert John Barrett. Cambridge: Cambridge University Press, 2003:

Satel, Sally, and Scott O. Lilienfeld. *Brainwashed: The Seductive Appeal of Mindless Neuroscience*. New York, NY: Basic Books, 2013.

Saunders, George. "Escape from Spiderhead." *Tenth of December*. 2013. London: Bloomsbury, 2014: 45-82.

Sawyer, Robert Keith. *Explaining Creativity: The Science of Human Innovation*. 2nd ed. Oxford: Oxford University Press, 2012.

Schacter, Daniel L., and Donna Rose Addis. "The Cognitive Neuroscience of Constructive Memory: Remembering the Past and Imagining the Future. *Philosophical Transactions of the Royal Society* B 362 (2007): 773–786.

Schechtman, Marya. *The Constitution of Selves*. Ithaca, NY: Cornell University Press, 2007.

Schrag, Calvin O. *The Self after Postmodernity*. New Haven, CT: Yale University Press, 1997.

Schweiker, William. "Paul Ricoeur and the Prospects of a New Humanism." *Reading Ricoeur*. Ed. David M. Kaplan. Albany, NY: State University of New York Press, 2008: 89-108.

Scott, A.O. "The Panic of Influence." *New York Review of Books* 47.2 (2000): 39-43.

Scruton, Roger. "My Brain and I." *The New Atlantis* 42 (2014): 35-49.

----. "Neurononsense and the Soul." *In Search of Self: Interdisciplinary Perspectives on Personhood*. Ed. Jacobus Wentzel Van Huyssteen, et al. Grand Rapids, MI: Wm. B. Eerdmans Publishing, 2011: 338-356.

Searle, John R. *Consciousness and Language*. Cambridge: Cambridge University Press, 2002.

---. *The Rediscovery of the Mind*. Cambridge, MA: The MIT Press, 1992.

Sedgwick, Eve Kosofsky. "Epidemics of the Will." *Tendencies*. Durham, NC: Duke University Press, 1993: 130-42

Seigel, Jerrold. *The Idea of the Self: Thought and Experience in Western Europe since the Seventeenth Century*. Cambridge: Cambridge University Press, 2005.

---. "Problematizing the Self." *Beyond the Cultural Turn: New Directions in the Study of Society and Culture*. Eds. Lynn Hunt and Victoria Bonnell. Berkeley, CA: University of California Press, 1999: 281-314.

Shaw, Christopher Ariel, and Jill C. McEachern, eds. *Toward a Theory of Neuroplasticity*. Philadelphia, PA: Psychology Press, 2001.

Shawn, Allen. *Wish I Could Be There: Notes from a Phobic Life*. 2007. New York, NY: Penguin, 2008.

Sheehan, James J., and Morton Sosna, eds. *The Boundaries of Humanity: Humans, Animals, Machines*. Berkeley, CA: University of California Press, 1991.

Sherrington, Charles S. *Man on his Nature.* 1940. Cambridge: Cambridge University Press, 1948.

Shieber, Stuart M. Introduction. *The Turing Test: Verbal Behavior as the Hallmark of Intelligence.* Ed. Stuart M. Shieber. Cambridge, MA: The MIT Press, 2004: 1-14.

Shiller, Robert J. *Animal Spirits: How Human Psychology Drives the Economy, and Why It Matters for Global Capitalism.* Princeton, NJ: Princeton University Press, 2009.

---. "When a Stock Market Theory Is Contagious." *The New York Times* Oct. 18, 2004: n. pag.
www.nytimes.com/2014/10/19/business/economy/when-a-stock-market-theory-is-contagious.html

Shklovsky, Viktor. "Art as Technique." 1917. *Russian Formalist Criticism: Four Essays.* Eds. Lee T. Lemon and Marion J. Reis. Lincoln, NE: University of Nebraska Press, 1965: 3-24.

Sielke, Sabine. "The Subject of Literature, or: (Re-)Cognition in Richard Powers' [sic] (Science) Fiction." *Ideas of Order: Narrative Patterns in the Novels of Richard Powers.* Eds. Antje Kley and Jan D. Kucharzewski. Heidelberg: Winter, 2012: 239-61.

Silberman, Steve. *NeuroTribes: The Legacy of Autism and the Future of Neurodiversity.* New York, NY: Avery, 2015.

Singer, Wolf. "Selbsterfahrung und neurobiologische Fremdbeschreibung: Zwei konfliktträchtige Erkenntnisquellen." *Deutsche Zeitschrift für Philosophie* 52.2 (2004): 235–55.

---. "Verschaltungen legen uns fest. Wir sollten aufhören, von Freiheit zu sprechen." *Hirnforschung und Willensfreiheit: Zur Deutung der neuesten Experimente.* Ed. Christian Geyer. Frankfurt: Suhrkamp, 2004: 30-65.

Silva, Matt. "The 'Powers' to 'Kraft' Humanist Endings to Posthumanist Novels: *Galatea 2.2* as a Rewriting of *Operation Wandering Soul*." *Critique* 50.2 (2009): 208-24.

Slaby, Jan. "The Brain Is What We Do with It." Review of *What Should We Do with Our Brain?* By Catherine Malabou. *Journal of Consciousness Studies* 17 (2010): 235-240.

Slaby, Jan, and Fabian Bernhardt. "Der verblassende Glanz des Cogito. Ricœurs frühes Subjektdenken revisited." Thimo Breyer and Daniel Creutz, eds. *Phänomenologie des praktischen Sinns—Die Willensphilosophie Paul Ricœurs im Kontext.* München: Fink, 2014. Draft Manuscript: 1-31.
janslaby.com/downloads/slabybernhardt_ricoeur_web052013.pdf

Smith, Laurence D. *Behaviorism and Logical Positivism: A Reassessment of the Alliance.* Stanford, CA: Stanford University Press, 1986.

Smith, Paul. *Discerning the Subject.* Minneapolis, MN: University of Minnesota Press, 1988.

Smith, Roger. *Inhibition: History and Meaning in the Sciences of Mind and Brain.* Berkeley, CA: University of California Press, 1992.

Smith, Sidonie A. "Material Selves: Bodies, Memory, and Autobiographical Narrating." *Narrative and Consciousness: Literature, Psychology, and the Brain.* Eds. Gary D. Fireman et al. Oxford: Oxford University Press, 2003: 86-114.

Smith, Zadie. "Brief Interviews with Hideous Men: The Difficult Gifts of David Foster Wallace." *Changing My Mind: Occasional Essays.* London: Hamish Hamilton, 2009: 257-300.

Smythies, John Raymond. *The Dynamic Neuron: A Comprehensive Survey of the Neurochemical Basis of Synaptic Plasticity.* Cambridge, MA: MIT Press, 2002.

Snow, C. P. *The Two Cultures and the Scientific Revolution.* Cambridge: Cambridge University Press, 1959.

---. "The Two Cultures: A Second Look." *The Two Cultures: and A Second Look.* Cambridge: Cambridge University Press, 1963.

Snyder, Sharon. "The Gender of Genius: Scientific Experts and Literary Amateurs in the Fiction of Richard Powers." *Review of Contemporary Fiction* 18.3 (1998): 84-96.

Solms, Mark, and Oliver Turnbull. *The Brain and the Inner World: An Introduction to the Neuroscience of Subjective Experience.* New York, NY: Other Press, 2010.

Solomon, Robert C. *Continental Philosophy since 1750: The Rise and Fall of the Self.* Oxford: Oxford University Press, 1988.

---. "Freud's Neurological Theory of Mind." *Freud: A Collection of Critical Essays.* Ed. Richard Wollheim. Garden City, NY: Anchor Books, 1974: 25-52.

Somers, Margaret R. "The Narrative Constitution of Identity: A Relational and Network Approach." *Theory and Society* 23.5 (1994): 605-649.

---. "Narrativity, Narrative Identity, and Social Action: Rethinking English Working-Class Formation." *Social Science History* 16.1 (1992): 591-630.

Sparrow, Tom, and Adam Hutchinson, eds. *A History of Habit: From Aristotle to Bourdieu.* Lanham, MA: Lexington, 2013.

---. Introduction. *A History of Habit: From Aristotle to Bourdieu.* Eds. Tom Sparrow and Adam Hutchinson. Lanham, MA: Lexington, 2013: 1-16.

Spence, Donald. *Narrative Truth and Historical Truth: Meaning and Interpretation in Psychoanalysis.* New York, NY: Norton, 1984.

Sperry, Roger W. "In Search of Psyche." *The Neurosciences: Paths of Discovery.* Eds. Frederic G. Worden et al. Cambridge, MA: The MIT Press, 1975: 425-34.

Spinoza, Benedict de. *Ethics.* 1677. Trans. Edwin Curley. London: Penguin, 1996.

Sprinker, Michael. "Fictions of the Self: The End of Autobiography." *Autobiography: Essays Theoretical and Critical.* Ed. James Olney. Princeton, NJ: Princeton University Press, 1981: 321-42.

Spolsky, Ellen. *Gaps in Nature: Literary Interpretation and the Modular Mind.* Albany, NY: State University of New York Press, 1993.

Squire, Larry R., and Eric R. Kandel. *Memory: From Mind to Molecules*. New York, NY: Scientific American Library, 1999.

Staes, Toon. "Rewriting the Author: A Narrative Approach to Empathy in Infinite Jest and The Pale King." *Studies in the Novel* 44.4 (2012): 409-427.

Stedman, Gesa. "Brain Plots: Neuroscience and the Contemporary Novel." *The Literary Mind* [REAL 24]. Eds. Jürgen Schlaeger and Gesa Stedman. Tübingen: Narr, 2008: 113-24.

Stent, Gunther S. *Paradoxes of Free Will*. Philadelphia, PA: American Philosophical Society, 2002.

Stiegler, Bernard. *Technics and Time 1: The Fault of Epimetheus*. 1994. Trans. Richard Beardsworth and George Collins. Stanford, CA: Stanford University Press, 1998.

---. *Technics and Time 2: Disorientation*. 1996. Trans. Stephen Barker. Stanford: Stanford University Press, 2009.

Strawson, Galen. "Against Narrativity." *Ratio* 17.4 (2004): 428-52.

---. "Real Naturalism." *London Review of Books* 35.18 (2013): n. pag. www.lrb.co.uk/v35/n18/galen-strawson/real-naturalism

---. "The Phenomenology and Ontology of the Self." *Exploring the Self*. Ed. Dan Zahavi. Amsterdam: John Benjamins, 2000: 39-54.

---. "Tales of the Unexpected." Review of *Making Stories: Law, Literature, Life*, by Jerome S. Bruner. *The Guardian* 10 January 2004: n. pag. www.theguardian.com/books/2004/jan/10/society.philosophy

Strawson, Peter Frederick. "Freedom and Resentment." *Proceedings of the British Academy* 48 (1962): 1–25.

Strecker, Trey. "Ecologies of Knowledge: The Encyclopedic Narratives of Richard Powers and his contemporaries." *Review of Contemporary Fiction* 18.3 (1998): 67-71.

Sullivan, Nikki. *A Critical Introduction to Queer Theory*. New York, NY: New York University Press, 2003

Swarts, Jonathan. *Constructing Neoliberalism: Economic Transformation in Anglo-American Democracies*. Toronto: University of Toronto Press, 2013.

Swartz, David. *Culture and Power: The Sociology of Pierre Bourdieu*. Chicago, IL: The University of Chicago Press, 1997.

Szasz, Thomas. *The Medicalization of Everyday Life: Selected Essays*. Syracuse, NY: Syracuse University Press, 2007.

Tabbi, Joseph. "Afterthoughts on *The Echo Maker*." *Intersections: Essays on Richard Powers*. Eds. Stephen Burn and Peter Dempsey. Champaign, IL: Dalkey Archive Press, 2008: 219-229.

---. *Cognitive Fictions*. Minneapolis, MN: University of Minnesota Press, 2002.

---. *Postmodern Sublime: Technology and American Writing from Mailer to Cyberpunk*. Ithaca, NY: Cornell University Press, 1995.

Tabbi, Joseph, and Michael Wutz. Introduction. *Reading Matters: Narrative in the New Media Ecology*. Ithaca, NY: Cornell University Press, 1997: 1-28.

Tallis, Frank. *Hidden Minds: A History of the Unconscious*. London: Profile Books, 2002.

Tallis, Raymond. *Aping Mankind: Neuromania, Darwinitis and the Misrepresentation of Humanity*. Durham: Acumen, 2011.

---. "Saving the Self." *Philosophy Now* 63 (2007): n. pag. philosophynow.org/issues/63/Saving_the_Self

Talvitie, Vesa. *Freudian Unconscious and Cognitive Neuroscience: From Unconscious Fantasies to Neural Algorithms*. London: Karnac Books, 2009.

Tanner, Tony. "Afterthoughts on DeLillo's *Underworld*." *Raritan* 17.4 (1998): 48-71.

Taylor, Charles. *Human Agency and Language: Philosophical Papers 1*. Cambridge: Cambridge University Press, 1985.

---. "Inwardness and the Culture of Modernity." *Philosophical Interventions in the Unfinished Project of Enlightenment*. Eds. Axel Honneth, et al. Cambridge, MA: The MIT Press: 88-110.

---. *Sources of the Self: The Making of the Modern Identity*. Cambridge, MA: Harvard University Press, 1989.

Thompson, Evan. *Mind in Life: Biology, Phenomenology, and the Sciences of Mind*. Cambridge, MA: Harvard University Press, 2007

Thorne, Christian. *The Dialectic of Counter-Enlightenment*. Cambridge, MA: Harvard University Press, 2009.

Thornton, Davi Johnson. *Brain Culture: Neuroscience and Popular Media*. Piscataway, NJ: Rutgers University Press, 2011.

Thrailkill, Jane F. "Ian McEwan's Neurological Novel." *Poetics Today* 32:1 (2011): 171-201.

Thrift, Nigel. "I Just Don't Know What Got into Me: Where is the Subject?" *Subjectivity* 22.1 (2008): 82-89.

Timmer, Nicoline. *Do You Feel it Too? The Post-postmodern Syndrome in American Fiction at the Turn of the Millennium*. Amsterdam: Rodopi, 2010.

Toal, Catherine. "Corrections: Contemporary American Melancholy." *Journal of European Studies* 33.3-4 (2003): 305-22.

Tompkins, Jane. *Sensational Designs: The Cultural Work of American Fiction 1790-1860*. New York, NY: Oxford University Press, 1985.

Tougaw, Jason. "Brain Memoirs, Neuroscience, and the Self: A Review Article." *Literature and Medicine* 30.1 (2012): 171-92.

---. "Touching Brains." *Modern Fiction Studies* 61.2 (2015): 335-58.

Touraine, Alain. *Return of the Actor: Social Theory in Postindustrial Society*. 1984. Trans. Myrna Godzich. Minneapolis, MN: University of Minnesota Press, 1988.

Trefil, James S. *The Nature of Science: An A-Z Guide to the Laws and Principles Governing Our Universe* Boston, MA: Houghton Mifflin, 2003.

Trilling, Lionel. "The Meaning of a Literary Idea." *The Liberal Imagination: Essays on Literature and Society*. New York, NY: Viking, 1950: 281-303.

Turing, Alan. "Computing Machinery and Intelligence." *Mind* 59.236 (1950): 433-60.

Turk, David J., et al. "Out of Contact, Out of Mind: The Distributed Nature of the Self." *Annals of the New York Academy of Sciences* 1001 (2003): 65-78.

Turner, Mark. *The Literary Mind: The Origins of Thought and Language*. Oxford: Oxford University Press, 1996.

---. *Reading Minds: The Study of English in the Age of Cognitive Science*. Princeton, NJ: Princeton University Press, 1991.

Uttal, William R. *The New Phrenology: The Limits of Localizing Cognitive Processes in the Brain*. Cambridge, MA: The MIT Press, 2003.

Valverde, Mariana. *Diseases of the Will: Alcohol and the Dilemmas of Freedom*. Cambridge: Cambridge University Press, 1998.

Varela, Francisco J. "The Ages of Heinz von Foerster." Introduction to *Observing Systems* by Heinz von Foerster. Seaside, CA: Intersystems Publications, 1981: xiii-xviii.

---. "A Calculus for Self-reference." *International Journal of General Systems* 2.1 (1975): 5–24.

Varela, Francisco J., Evan Thompson, and Eleanor Rosch. *The Embodied Mind: Cognitive Science and Human Experience*. 1991. Cambridge, MA: MIT Press, 1993.

Veggian, Henry. *Understanding Don DeLillo*. Columbia, SC: University of South Carolina Press, 2015.

Vermeule, Blakey. "The Terrible Master: David Foster Wallace and the Suffering of Consciousness (with guest Arthur Schopenhauer)." *Gesturing Toward Reality: David Foster Wallace and Philosophy*. Eds. Robert K. Bolger and Scott Korb. New York, NY: Bloomsbury, 2014: 103-20.

Vidal, Fernando. "Brainhood, Anthropological Figure of Modernity." *History of the Human Sciences* 22.1 (2009): 5-36.

Vitzthum, Richard C. *Materialism: An Affirmative History and Definition*. Amherst, NY: Prometheus, 1995.

Wacker, Norman. "Mass Society/Mass Novel: the Politics of Representation in Don DeLillo's Libra." *Works and Days* 8.1 (1990): 67-88.

Wald, Carol Ann. "Reflexivity, reproduction, and evolution: from von Neumann to Powers." *Mosaic* 39.2 (2006): n. pag.

Wall, Stephanie. "Neurogenesis in the Human Brain: Fact or Fiction?" *Serendip Studio* 14 January 2008: n. pag. serendip.brynmawr.edu/exchange/node/1827

Wallace, David Foster. "Back in New Fire." *Both Flesh and Not: Essays*. London: Penguin, 2012: 167-76.

---. "Deciderization 2007: A Special Report." *Both Flesh and Not: Essays*. London: Penguin, 2012: 299-317.

---. "E Unibus Pluram: Television and U.S. Fiction." *A Supposedly Fun Thing I'll Never Do Again: Essays and Arguments*. 1997. London: Abacus, 1998: 21- 82.

---. *Fate, Time, and Language: An Essay on Free Will*. New York, NY: Columbia University Press, 2011.

---. *Infinite Jest*. 1996. New York, NY: Back Bay Books, 2006.

---. Interview with Dave Eggers. *The Believer* 1.8 (2003): n. pag. www.believermag.com/issues/200311/

---. Interview with Larry McCaffery. *Review of Contemporary Fiction* 13.2 (1993): 127-50.

---. Interview with Michael Silverblatt. *Bookworm*. National Public Radio. KCRW, Santa Monica, 3 Aug. 2000. www.kcrw.com/news-culture/shows/bookworm/david-foster-wallace-3

---. "Looking for a Garde of Which to be Avant: An Interview with David Foster Wallace." Interview with Hugh Kennedy and Geoffrey Polk. *Conversations with David Foster Wallace*. Ed. Stephen Burn. Jackson, MI: University Press of Mississippi, 2012: 11-21.

---. *The Pale King*. New York, NY: Little, Brown and Company, 2011.

---. "The *Salon* Interview: David Foster Wallace." Interview with Laura Miller. *Conversations with David Foster Wallace*. Ed. Stephen Burn. Jackson, MI: University Press of Mississippi, 2012: 58-65.

---. *This is Water: Some Thoughts, Delivered on a Significant Occasion, about Living a Compassionate Life*. New York, NY: Little, Brown and Company, 2009.

---. "Westward the Course of Empire Takes Its Way." *Girl with Curious Hair*. 1989. London: Abacus Books, 2012: 231–373.

Watt, Ian. *The Rise of the Novel: Studies in Defoe, Richardson, and Fielding*. 1957. London: Pimlico, 2000.

Waugh, Patricia. "The Naturalistic Turn, the Syndrome, and the Rise of the Neo-Phenomenological Novel." *Diseases and Disorders in Contemporary Fiction: The Syndrome Syndrome*. Eds. T. J. Lustig and James Peacock. London: Routledge, 2013: 17-34.

---. "Thinking in Literature: Modernism and Contemporary Neuroscience." *The Legacies of Modernism: Historicising Postwar and Contemporary Fiction*. Ed. David James. Cambridge: Cambridge University Press, 2014: 75-95.

Wegner, Daniel. *The Illusion of Conscious Will*. Cambridge, MA: The MIT Press, 2002.

Weinstein, Arnold. *Nobody's Home: Speech, Self, and Place in American Fiction from Hawthorne to DeLillo*. New York, NY: Oxford University Press, 1993.

White, Hayden. *The Content of the Form: Narrative Discourse and Historical Representation*. Baltimore, MA: The Johns Hopkins University Press, 1987.

---. *Metahistory: The Historical Imagination in Nineteenth-Century Europe*. Baltimore, MA: The Johns Hopkins University Press, 1973.

---. "The Value of Narrativity in the Representation of Reality." *Critical Inquiry* 7.1 (1980): 5-27.

Wilcox, Leonard. "Baudrillard, DeLillo's *White Noise*, and the End of Heroic Narrative. *Contemporary Literature* 32.3 (1991): 346-365.

Williams, David. *The Trickster Brain: Neuroscience, Evolution, and Narrative*. Lanham, MD: Lexington Books, 2012.

Williams, Raymond. *The Long Revolution*. 1961. London: Penguin, 1965.

Wills, David. *Dorsality: Thinking Back through Technology and Politics*. Minneapolis, MN: University of Minnesota Press, 2008.

---. *Prosthesis*. Stanford, CA: Stanford University Press, 1995.

Wilson, Elizabeth A. *Neural Geographies: Feminism and the Microstructure of Cognition*. New York, NY: Routledge, 1998.

---. *Psychosomatic: Feminism and the Neurological Body*. Durham, NC: Duke University Press, 2004.

Wilson, Timothy D. *Strangers to Ourselves: Discovering the Adaptive Unconscious*. Cambridge, MA: Belknap Press, 2002.

Winslow, Donald J. *Life-Writing: A Glossary of Terms in Biography, Autobiography, and Related Forms*. 2nd ed. Honolulu; HI: University of Hawaii, 1995.

Wolfe, Cary. *Animal Rites: American Culture, the Discourse of Species, and Posthumanist Theory*. Chicago, IL: The University of Chicago Press, 2003.

---. *What Is Posthumanism?* Minneapolis, MN: University of Minnesota Press, 2010.

Woloch, Alex. *The One vs. the Many: Minor Characters and the Space of the Protagonist in the Novel*. Princeton, NJ: Princeton University Press, 2003.

Wood, James. "Brain Drain: The Scientific Fiction of Richard Powers." *The New Yorker* October 05, 2009: n. pag. www.newyorker.com/magazine/2009/10/05/brain-drain

---. "The Digressionist." Rev. of *Oblivion* by David Foster Wallace. *The New Republic* 26 Aug. 2004: 26-31.

Wood, Mary Elene. *Life Writing and Schizophrenia: Encounters at the Edge of Meaning*. Amsterdam: Rodopi, 2013.

Wood, Michael. "Post-Paranoid." Review of *Underworld* by Don DeLillo. *London Review of Books* 20.3 (1998): n. pag. www.lrb.co.uk/v20/n03/michael-wood/post-paranoid

Woods, Angela. *The Sublime Object of Psychiatry: Schizophrenia in Clinical and Cultural Theory*. Oxford: Oxford University Press, 2011.

Worthington, Marjorie. "The Texts of Tech: Technology and Authorial Control in *Geek Love* and *Galatea 2.2*." *Journal of Narrative Theory* 39.1 (2009): 109-133.

Wright, J. Lenore. *The Philosopher's "I": Autobiography and the Search for the Self*. Albany, NY: SUNY Press, 2006.

Yehnert, Curtis A. "'Like Some Endless Sky Waking Inside': Subjectivity in Don DeLillo." *Critique* 42.4 (2001): 357-366.

Young, Kay. *Imagining Minds: The Neuro-Aesthetics of Austen, Eliot, and Hardy.* Columbus, OH: Ohio State University Press, 2010.

Young, Kay, and Jeffrey L. Saver. "The Neurology of Narrative." *SubStance* 30 (2001): 72-84.

Zahavi, Dan. "Self and Other: The Limits of Narrative Understanding." *Narrative and Understanding Persons.* Daniel D. Hutto. Cambridge: Cambridge University Press, 2007: 179-201.

Zahavi, Dan, and Josef Parnas. "Phenomenal Consciousness and Self-Awareness: A Phenomenological Critique of Representational Theory." *Journal of Consciousness Studies* 5.5–6 (1998): 687-705.

Zimmer, Carl. *Soul Made Flesh: How The Secrets of the Brain were Uncovered in Seventeenth-century England.* 2004. London: Arrow Books, 2005.

Žižek, Slavoj. "Cultural Studies versus the 'Third Culture.'" *The South Atlantic Quarterly* 101.1 (2002): 19-32.

Zola, Émile. *The Experimental Novel and Other Essays.* Trans. Belle M. Sherman. New York, NY: Haskell House, 1964.

Zwilgmeyer, Franz. *Stufen des Ich: Bewusstseinsentwicklung der Menschheit in Gesellschaft und Kultur.* Fellbach: Bonz, 1981.

# Social and Cultural Studies

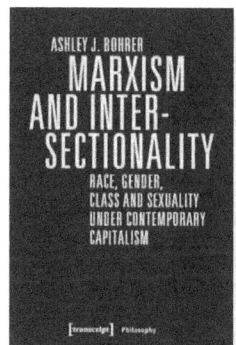

Ashley J. Bohrer
**Marxism and Intersectionality**
Race, Gender, Class and Sexuality
under Contemporary Capitalism

2019, 280 p., pb.
29,99 € (DE), 978-3-8376-4160-8
E-Book: 26,99 € (DE), ISBN 978-3-8394-4160-2

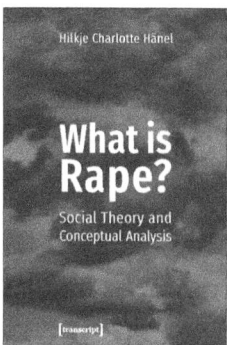

Hilkje Charlotte Hänel
**What is Rape?**
Social Theory and Conceptual Analysis

2018, 282 p., hardcover
99,99 € (DE), 978-3-8376-4434-0
E-Book: 99,99 € (DE), ISBN 978-3-8394-4434-4

Jasper van Buuren
**Body and Reality**
An Examination of the Relationships
between the Body Proper, Physical Reality,
and the Phenomenal World Starting from Plessner
and Merleau-Ponty

2018, 312 p., pb., ill.
39,99 € (DE), 978-3-8376-4163-9
E-Book: 39,99 € (DE), ISBN 978-3-8394 4163-3

# Social and Cultural Studies

Sabine Klotz, Heiner Bielefeldt,
Martina Schmidhuber, Andreas Frewer (eds.)
**Healthcare as a Human Rights Issue**
Normative Profile, Conflicts and Implementation

2017, 426 p., pb., ill.
39,99 € (DE), 978-3-8376-4054-0
E-Book: available as free open access publication
E-Book: ISBN 978-3-8394-4054-4

Michael Bray
**Powers of the Mind**
Mental and Manual Labor
in the Contemporary Political Crisis

2019, 208 p., hardcover
99,99 € (DE), 978-3-8376-4147-9
E-Book: 99,99 € (DE), ISBN 978-3-8394-4147-3

Iain MacKenzie
**Resistance and the Politics of Truth**
Foucault, Deleuze, Badiou

2018, 148 p., pb.
29,99 € (DE), 978-3-8376-3907-0
E-Book: 26,99 € (DE), ISBN 978-3-8394-3907-4
EPUB: 26,99 € (DE), ISBN 978-3-7328-3907-0

**All print, e-book and open access versions of the titles in our list
are available in our online shop  www.transcript-verlag.de/en!**

CPSIA information can be obtained
at www.ICGtesting.com
Printed in the USA
JSHW021529201120
9729JS00004B/35